The Haze Problem in Southeast Asia

Despite the efforts of Southeast Asian governments and of ASEAN, transboundary haze continues to be a major environmental problem in Southeast Asia. This book demonstrates that the issue is complex, and explains why efforts to solve the problem in purely political terms are ineffective, and likely to continue to be ineffective. The book shows how state-led, state-incentivized agribusiness development lies at the heart of the problem, leading to a large rise in palm oil production, with extensive clearing of forests, leading to deliberate or accidental fires and the resulting haze. Moreover, although the forest clearing is occurring in Indonesia, many of the companies involved are Malaysian and Singaporean; and, further, many of these companies have close relationships with the politicians and officials responsible for addressing the problem and who thereby have a conflict of interest. The author concludes by discussing the huge difficulties involved in overturning this system of 'patronage politics'.

Helena Varkkey is a senior lecturer in the Department of International and Strategic Studies at the University of Malaya in Kuala Lumpur, Malaysia.

Routledge Malaysian Studies Series

Published in association with Malaysian Social Science Association (MSSA)

The Routledge Malaysian Studies Series publishes high quality scholarship that provides important new contributions to knowledge on Malaysia. It also signals research that spans comparative studies, involving the Malaysian experience with that of other nations.

This series, initiated by the Malaysian Social Science Association (MSSA) to promote study of contemporary and historical issues in Malaysia, and designed to respond to the growing need to publish important research, also serves as a forum for debate on key issues in Malaysian society. As an academic series, it will be used to generate new theoretical debates in the social sciences and on processes of change in this society.

The Routledge Malaysian Studies Series will cover a broad range of subjects including history, politics, economics, sociology, international relations, geography, business, education, religion, literature, culture and ethnicity. The series will encourage work adopting an interdisciplinary approach.

1 **The State of Malaysia**
Ethnicity, equity and reform
Edited by Edmund Terence Gomez

2 **Feminism and the Women's Movement in Malaysia**
An unsung (r)evolution
Cecilia Ng, Maznah Mohamad and tan beng hui

3 **Governments and Markets in East Asia**
The politics of economic crises
Jungug Choi

4 **Health Care in Malaysia**
The dynamics of provision, financing and access
Edited by Chee Heng Leng and Simon Barraclough

5 **Politics in Malaysia**
The Malay dimension
Edited by Edmund Terence Gomez

6 **Privatization in Malaysia**
Regulation, rent-seeking and policy failure
Jeff Tan

7 **The State, Development and Identity in Multi-Ethnic Societies**
Ethnicity, equity and the nation
Edited by Nicholas Tarling and Edmund Terence Gomez

8 **Race and Multiculturalism in Malaysia and Singapore**
Edited by Daniel P.S. Goh, Matilda Gabrielpillai, Philip Holden and Gaik Cheng Khoo

9 **Media, Culture and Society in Malaysia**
Edited by Yeoh Seng Guan

10 **Islam and Politics in Southeast Asia**
Edited by Johan Saravanamuttu

11 **Malaysia's Development Challenges**
Graduating from the middle
Edited by Hal Hill, Tham Siew Yean and Ragayah Haji Mat Zin

12 **Ethnicization and Identity Construction in Malaysia**
Frederik Holst

13 **Malaysia and the Developing World**
The Asian Tiger on the Cinnamon Road
Jan Stark

14 **Affirmative Action, Ethnicity and Conflict**
Edited by Edmund Terence Gomez and Ralph Premdas

15 **The Other Kuala Lumpur**
Living in the shadows of a globalising Southeast Asian city
Edited by Yeoh Seng Guan

16 **Government-Linked Companies and Sustainable, Equitable Development**
Edited by Edmund Terence Gomez, François Bafoil and Cheong Kee Cheok

17 **The Haze Problem in Southeast Asia**
Palm oil and patronage
Helena Varkkey

The Haze Problem in Southeast Asia

Palm oil and patronage

Helena Varkkey

LONDON AND NEW YORK

First published 2016
by Routledge
2 Park Square, Milton Park, Abingdon, Oxon OX14 4RN

and by Routledge
711 Third Avenue, New York, NY 10017

First issued in paperback 2017

Routledge is an imprint of the Taylor & Francis Group, an informa business

British Library Cataloguing in Publication Data
A catalogue record for this book is available from the British Library

Library of Congress Cataloging in Publication Data
Varkkey, Helena, author.
The haze problem in Southeast Asia : palm oil and patronage /
Helena Varkkey.
pages cm — (Routledge Malaysian studies series ; 17)
Includes bibliographical references and index.
1. Air—Pollution—Political aspects—Southeast Asia. 2. Haze—
Environmental aspects—Southeast Asia. 3. Environmental
protection—Political aspects—Southeast Asia. I. Title. II. Series:
Routledge Malaysian studies series ; 17.
RA576.7.A85V37 2015
363.739'20959—dc23
2015002876

ISBN 13: 978-0-8153-5511-3 (pbk)
ISBN 13: 978-1-138-85864-0 (hbk)

Typeset in Times New Roman
by FiSH Books Ltd, Enfield

For Evan

Contents

List of figures and table xi
List of acronyms and abbreviations xii
Acknowledgements xiv
Preface xvi

1 Introduction 1
Background 2
Research rationale and literature review 12
Research parameters and methods 20
Book structure and outline 24
Notes 26
References 27

2 The Indonesian oil palm sector and haze 35
Global demand for palm oil 35
Southeast Asia's 'green gold' 38
Oil palm plantations and fires in Indonesia 48
Conclusion 58
Notes 58
References 59

3 The state as facilitator of regionalization 68
Economic regionalization 68
The regionalization of the Southeast Asian oil palm sector 72
Dealing with backlash as a result of haze 90
Conclusion 98
Notes 99
References 103

4 Regionalization and patronage politics 112
Patronage politics 112
Local patronage networks 119
Patronage networks and land licensing 125
Patronage networks and haze-producing fires 136
Conclusion 148
Notes 150
References 151

5 The regionalism of haze mitigation at the ASEAN level 160
Political regionalism 161
The ASEAN Way in ASEAN-level haze-mitigation initiatives 169
Adopt-A-District: whither commercial plantations? 193
Conclusion 202
Notes 203
References 204

6 Conclusion 214

Index 220

List of figures and table

Figures

1.1 Framework of this book 11
2.1 Market share of vegetable oils, 2013 36
2.2 World production of palm oil, 1995–2014 38
2.3 CPO production by country, 2012/2013 40
2.4 Area harvested of oil palm fruit in Indonesia, 1961–2012 44
2.5 Ownership of oil palm plantation land in Indonesia, 2011 45
2.6 Breakdown of Indonesia's 2011 GDP by sector 46
2.7 Parties responsible for fire in Indonesia, 1997 50
3.1 Country of origin of investors in the oil palm sector in Indonesia, 2004 75
5.1 Organizational structure of ASEAN environmental and haze cooperation 173
5.2 ASEAN initiatives relating directly to haze 176

Table

2.1 Peat and palm oil in Indonesia, 2008 55

List of acronyms and abbreviation

ADB	Asian Development Bank
AFC	Asian financial crisis
AMDAL	*analisis mengenai dampak lingkungan* or environmental impact assessment
API	Air Pollution Index
APIMI	Association of Plantation Investors of Malaysia in Indonesia
APMI	ASEAN Peatland Management Initiative
ASEAN	Association of Southeast Asian Nations
ASMA	Alam Sekitar Malaysia
ASMC	ASEAN Specialized Meteorological Centre
ATHP	ASEAN Agreement on Transboundary Haze Pollution
BSP	Bakrie Sumatra Plantations
CAFE	Clean Air for Europe
CEO	chief executive officer
CLRTAP	Convention on Long-Range Transboundary Air Pollution
CPO	crude palm oil
DPRD	Dewan Perwakilan Rakyat Daerah or Regional House of Representatives
EDB	Economic Development Board
EMA	Environmental Management Act
EPF	Employees Provident Fund
EU	European Union
FDI	foreign direct investment
FIL	Law Number 1/1967 on Foreign Investment
GAPKI	Gabungan Pengusaha Kelapa Sawit Indonesia or Indonesian Palm Oil Association
GAR	Golden-Agri Resources
GDP	gross domestic product
GEC	Global Environment Centre
GLC	government-linked company
HGU	*Hak Guna Usaha* or Right to Cultivation
HMS	ASEAN Sub-Regional Haze Monitoring System
HPK	*hutan produksi konversi* or convertible production forest

HTTF	ASEAN Haze Technical Task Force
IMF	International Monetary Fund
IOI	IOI Corporation Berhad
IUP	*izin usaha perkebunan* or plantation business permit
KLK	Kuala Lumpur Kepong Berhad
MATRADE	Malaysian External Trade Development Corporation
MIDA	Malaysian Industrial Development Authority
MOU	memorandum of understanding
MP	member of parliament
MPOC	Malaysian Palm Oil Council
MSC	Ministerial Steering Committee
MSTE	Ministry of Science, Technology and Environment
NCR	native customary rights
NFP	national focal points
NGO	non-governmental organization
PCD	Pollution Control Department
PKO	palm kernel oil
PMD	Prime Minister's Department
PNB	*Permodalan Nasional Berhad*
POA	Plan of Action
POE	Panel of Experts
PSI	Pollutant Standards Index
PT	*perseroan terbatas* or limited liability company
PT API	PT Adei Plantation and Industry
PT SMART	PT Sinar Mas Agro Resources and Technology
RAN	Rainforest Action Network
REDD	United Nations Collaborative Programme on Reducing Emissions from Deforestation and Forest Degradation in Developing Countries
RHAP	ASEAN Regional Haze Action Plan
RSPO	Roundtable for Sustainable Palm Oil
SEP	Strategic Economic Plan
SLDB	Sarawak Land Development Board
SRFA	ASEAN Sub-Regional Fire-Fighting Arrangement
THP	Tabung Haji Plantations
TNC	transnational corporation
UN	United Nations
UNEP	United Nations Environment Programme
UNIPEX	Uniform International Pollutant Index
ZOPFAN	Zone of Peace, Freedom and Neutrality

Acknowledgements

This book would not have been possible without the scholars, government and ASEAN officials, journalists, NGO representatives and other individuals in Indonesia, Malaysia and Singapore who kindly shared their experiences and thoughts with me during my fieldwork. My research was also greatly aided by the good people at University of Malaya, the Ministry of Higher Education Malaysia and the University of Sydney, who were most generous in providing funding in the form of scholarships, travel grants and employment opportunities.

I am deeply indebted to Dr Susan Park, my supervisor, for guiding and encouraging me along this academic journey. Without her, I may still be floundering to this day. Special thanks also to Dr Lily Rahim, Dr Charlotte Epstein and Dr Ariadne Vromen at the University of Sydney, as well as Dr Helen Nesadurai at Monash Malaysia, Dr Mark Beeson at Murdoch University, Dr Peter Dauvergne at the University of British Columbia, Dr Natasha Hamilton-Hart at the University of Auckland and Dr Terence Gomez at the University of Malaya, who offered invaluable advice and insightful comments on the many drafts of this book.

I was also blessed with the unwavering support of my friends and family throughout this project. My husband, Ezuan, and my parents, Varkkey and Julia were my constant motivators, first readers and sounding boards throughout this process, albeit mostly from afar. I am especially grateful to my father, for his patience and dedication in proofreading this book again and again throughout the publication process.

I am also grateful to Peter Sowden and his team at Routledge for their guidance and advice during the publishing process. Finally, I must acknowledge here that I have previously published certain sections of this book in the form of journal articles. Full publication details of these articles are as follows:

Muhamad Varkkey, H. 2011. Plantation Land Management, Fires, and Haze in Southeast Asia. *Malaysian Journal of Environmental Management* 12, 33–41.

Muhamad Varkkey, H. 2012. The Asean Way and Haze Mitigation Efforts. *Journal of International Studies* 85, 77–97.

Quah, E. and Varkkey, H. 2013. The Political Economy of Transboundary Pollution: Mitigation Forest Fires and Haze in Southeast Asia. *In:* SEI, H. H. (ed.) *The Asian Community: Its Concepts and Prospects.* Tokyo: Soso Sha, 323–358.

Varkkey, H. 2011. ASEAN as a 'Thin' Community: The Case Against Adopting the EU Acid Rain Framework for Transboundary Haze Management in Southeast Asia. *Jebat: Malaysian Journal of History, Politics and Strategic Studies* 38, 1–26.

Varkkey, H. 2012. Patronage Politics as a Driver of Economic Regionalisation: The Indonesian Oil Palm Sector and Transboundary Haze. *Asia Pacific Viewpoint* 53, 314–329.

Varkkey, H. 2012. The Growth and Prospects of the Oil Palm Plantation Industry in Indonesia. *Oil Palm Industry Economic Journal* 12, 1–13.

Varkkey, H. 2013. Malaysian Investors in the Indonesian Oil Palm Plantation Sector: Home State Facilitation and Transboundary Haze. *Asia Pacific Business Review* 19, 381–401.

Varkkey, H. 2013. Oil Palm Plantations and Transboundary Haze: Patronage Networks and Land Licensing in Indonesia's Peatlands. *Wetlands* 33, 679–690.

Varkkey, H. 2013. Patronage Politics, Plantation Fires and Transboundary Haze. *Environmental Hazards* 12, 200–217.

Varkkey, H. 2013. Regional Cooperation, Patronage, and the ASEAN Agreement on Transboundary Haze Pollution. *International Environmental Agreements: Politics, Law and Economics* 14, 65–81.

Preface

Transboundary haze pollution is an almost annual occurrence in Southeast Asia. Haze originates from peat and forest fires, mostly in Indonesia. Most of these fires are man-made, and are linked to land-clearing activities of local and foreign commercial oil palm plantations. This book employs the concepts of regionalization and regionalism to offer a political economy explanation of the persistence of haze. The regionalization of the oil palm sector has resulted in a concentration of Malaysian and Singaporean plantation companies in Indonesia, alongside local companies. State facilitation and similar patronage cultures have been the two major drivers of this regionalization, and this has resulted in transboundary haze. First, state-facilitated regionalization has ensured that Malaysian and Singaporean plantation companies enjoyed home state protection while operating in Indonesia. Second, similar patronage cultures in Indonesia, Malaysia and Singapore have allowed Malaysian and Singaporean companies to easily adapt to the Indonesian business landscape. This has resulted in environmental policy paralysis caused by reduced state capacity to make and carry out effective policies. State capacity is reduced because political and administrative patrons (in both home and host states) are inclined to act in the interests of clients, and not that of the society at large. This has allowed local and foreign companies to develop attractive but fire-prone peatlands, and to use fire as a cost-effective way to clear land, with little fear of prosecution. Confronted with negative backlash from civil society, Southeast Asian nations have attempted haze mitigation solutions at the ASEAN level. However, the ASEAN model of regionalism has allowed members to shape ASEAN initiatives in the spirit of the ASEAN Way, also resulting in policy paralysis caused by reduced organizational capacity to make and enforce effective initiatives and agreements. These outcomes thus have done little to curb haze, but instead have largely continued to favour national and elite commercial interests. Therefore, economic regionalization of the Southeast Asian oil palm sector is a major driver of transboundary haze, and (both home and host) state vested interests within the sector are the main cause of the continued failure of ASEAN haze-mitigation efforts.

1 Introduction

Transboundary haze is the Southeast Asian region's first and most publicly identifiable regional environmental crisis (Elliott, 2003). This haze has been an annual recurring problem in Southeast Asia since the 1980s (Mayer, 2006: 202–203), and is still a serious problem in the region today.

Haze originates from peat and forest fires, mostly in Indonesia. Research has shown that most of these fires are manmade. While previous scholars have identified poverty and developmental issues as driving haze (arguing that slash-and-burn agriculture by lesser-educated swidden farmers is a major cause of these uncontrolled fires), more recent research has established a clear link between haze-producing fires and commercial oil palm plantations in Indonesia. These commercial plantations have been found to contribute up to 80 per cent of the haze in the region (Caroko *et al.*, 2011: 21; Casson, 2002: 234–239; Colfer, 2002: 316; Fairhurst and McLaughlin, 2009: 7–34; Tan *et al.*, 2009: 422). As a result, haze continues to plague Southeast Asia on an almost annual basis, with Indonesia, Malaysia and Singapore suffering the worst of its effects, both in terms of socioeconomic well-being and public health. Haze mitigation activities in turn largely originate at the Association of Southeast Asian Nations (ASEAN) level, however these initiatives continuously fail to effectively mitigate haze (Chang and Rajan, 2001: 666; Nguitragool, 2011: 357; Tan, 2005: 3–4; Tay, 2002: 74; Yahaya, 2000: 49).

This is the puzzle that this book will engage with: why have the governments of Indonesia, Malaysia and Singapore thus far failed to effectively address the regional haze problem despite clear evidence of the culpability of the oil palm plantation sector in Indonesia?

Research such as this is timely and important. This research deals with a real-world problem that is continuing to bring severe socioeconomic harm to a significant number of the Southeast Asian people. While there seems to be much visible activity at the ASEAN level to address the issue, the proof of the futility of these efforts is visible every year when haze returns to blanket the region during the dry season. New academic insight is needed to explain the persistence of this issue despite these mitigation efforts, especially in the light of recent increased evidence of the link between haze-producing fires and commercial oil palm plantations (Sawit Watch, 2007: 1; WALHI *et al.*, 2009). This has brought new issues to the surface, especially those of linkages between business and political elites at the local, national and regional levels.

Background

The term 'haze' normally denotes a naturally occurring climatic condition in which visibility is affected, for example 'heat haze' (McLellan, 2001: 254). However the term has been used in the Southeast Asian region to refer to 'sufficient smoke, dust, moisture, and vapour suspended in air to impair visibility' (ASEAN Secretariat, 2008). Haze pollution is transboundary when 'its density and extent is so great at the source that it remains at measurable levels after crossing into another country's airspace' (ASEAN Secretariat, 2008). Since 1982, this 'haze' pollution developed into an almost annual occurrence in the region, with the worst episodes being in the period of 1997 to 1998, 2006 to 2007 (ASEAN Secretariat, 2008; Suwarsono *et al.*, 2007: 1) and most recently in mid-2013. The negative effects of haze pollution can be observed at the global level, with increased carbon emissions exacerbating climate change, and at the regional level, with serious socioeconomic effects in Indonesia and its neighbouring countries.

At the global level, these haze-causing fires contribute to climate change by releasing large amounts of carbon into the atmosphere. It was estimated that during the 1997–1998 fires, 2.5 million metric tonnes of carbon dioxide was released into the air (Koh, 2008: 225). Largely as a result of these annual fires, Indonesia in 2011 was ranked as the world's third largest emitter of carbon dioxide, after industrial giants like the United States and China (Greenpeace, 2007: 13; Hameiri and Jones, 2013: 468; Hunt, 2010: 187–190). Forests and land fires contribute up to 85 per cent of Indonesia's emissions (Hameiri and Jones, 2013: 468–469). Research has shown that the recapturing of this lost carbon would take 692 years (Danielsen *et al.*, 2008: 6). This is a serious concern for the region. An Asian Development Bank (ADB)-United Kingdom study found that the Southeast Asian region will be the worst effected region in the world as a result of climate change, as the region possesses unique natural ecosystems and resources such as fisheries and rainforests that feed the world and help sustain the global environment (*Antara Magazine*, 2009).

The more visible effects of haze pollution can be observed at the regional level. The haze affects the health of some 75 million people and the economies of six Southeast Asian nations: Indonesia, Malaysia, Singapore, Thailand, Brunei and the Philippines (Mayer, 2006: 202–203). The haze was also reported to have visibly affected areas as far off as the United States-administered Northern Mariana Islands and Guam in the Pacific Ocean. The 1997–1998 episode cost the region US$2.8 billion in forest and agricultural losses and $272 million in carbon releases. It reduced industrial production by $157 million, fisheries by $16 million and tourism revenue by $280 million (Severino, 1999). It also cost $941 million in short-term health damage and $25 million in fire-fighting efforts (Severino, 1999). While the haze can affect up to six Southeast Asian countries, the states that are the most severely affected in the region, due to their position as either a source or in close proximity to the fires, are Indonesia, Malaysia, and Singapore. These states are the focus of this book.

Densely forested Indonesia has been identified as the source of most of the haze-producing fires in the region, and has thus been one of the states suffering the worse effects of haze pollution. The fires and haze of 1997 was the worst in history for Indonesia. The Indonesian government declared the situation a 'natural calamity' that year when air pollution levels reached 1,890 micrograms per cubic meter (Djuweng and Petebang, 1997), many times above the tolerable level set by the World Health Organization and the Indonesian government, which is 130 and 150 micrograms per cubic meter respectively (*Jakarta Post*, 2004). The status of the fires and haze was elevated to a 'disaster' in 1999 (Dennis, 1999: 52), and a state of emergency was declared in the Sumatran province of Riau that year when the Pollutant Standards Index (PSI) there reached 978. A PSI of above 400 is considered extremely hazardous and life-threatening to the elderly and frail[1] (*Jakarta Post*, 1999b). In the following years, almost annual haze occurrences have become a routine for Indonesians living in fire-prone areas (*Jakarta Post*, 1999a), especially during the dry months of August to October (Suwarsono *et al.*, 2007).

Those closest to the source of the fires, mostly in the large island of Sumatra and the Indonesian side of the Borneo Island, Kalimantan, suffered the worst of the effects of the haze (Keraf [I35], 2010). At its most severe, the haze no longer looked like smoke but contained noticeable white particles (*Jakarta Post*, 1999b) and visibility was reduced to a mere 50 metres (Gunawan, 2002b). Schools in affected areas were closed down for extended periods (*Jakarta Post*, 2006a) or had their lessons shortened so that the students were not subjected to prolonged exposure to haze (*Jakarta Post*, 2004). Areas close to the flames experienced extraordinary heat (Hafild, 1997), while locations further away reported that the haze blocked out the warmth of the sun (*Jakarta Post*, 1999b). The locals complained that the smoke was hurting their eyes and also of increased respiratory problems (*Jakarta Post*, 1997a). It was estimated that in 1997, up to 20 million Indonesians sustained health troubles because of the haze (Hafild, 1997), while some hospitals reported that patient numbers exceeded the capacity levels (Djuweng and Petebang, 1997). At least 12 elderly people died in Jambi, reportedly of respiratory infections blamed on the thick haze (*Jakarta Post*, 1997c). The severe haze in 2006 saw 81 per cent of the days between September and November rated as 'unhealthy/very unhealthy/dangerous', with 30 days in October rated 'dangerous' (Harrison *et al.*, 2009: 159). Major cities such as Jambi, Pekanbaru, Surabaya, Medan and Bandung experienced only on average 22 to 62 days of good air quality that year (Widianarko, 2009: 5).

The fires and haze also took a toll on local infrastructure and economies. Bad visibility due to smoke hampered land, sea and air transportation (*Jakarta Post*, 1997a). Thick smoke prevented flights from landing in provincial airports for weeks (*Jakarta Post*, 1987). The haze also delayed air operations to relieve drought-stricken villages (*Jakarta Post*, 1997b). The 1997 haze was blamed for the fatal crash of a Garuda Indonesia airplane (Djuweng and Petebang, 1997), and the 1999 haze was blamed for a fatal tanker accident in Siak River, Sumatra (Saharjo, 1999: 142). A bus crash in Medan in 2002, killing five passengers, was also blamed on low visibility due to haze (Gunawan, 2002a). As a result, airlines, travel agencies and bus companies saw their revenues and profits predictably plummet during each haze season (Djuweng and Petebang, 1997). Transportation disruptions also caused price hikes of daily needs and food scarcity in some areas (*Jakarta Post*, 1997a). The 1997 fires and haze cost Indonesia between $9 and $10 billion according to ADB estimates (Jones, 2006: 436), equivalent to 4.5 per cent of Indonesia's gross domestic product (GDP) for the year (Ruitenbeek, 1999: 110–111). Out of this, short-term damage during the three-month haze period amounted to $1 billion in lost revenue and healthcare expenditure. The rest was attributed to lost tourist revenue, cancelled flights and airport closures (*Jakarta Post*, 1997d), which was estimated to be $111 million (Applegate *et al.*, 2002: 296–297).

Much of this haze travelled across national boundaries to Indonesia's closest neighbours, Malaysia and Singapore. Malaysia suffered 'the most serious haze occurrence in Malaysian history' in September 1997 (Law [M29], 2010). On 19 September 1997, the Malaysian government declared a state of emergency for the state of Sarawak when the Malaysia Air Quality Index[2] reached 600. The emergency lasted for ten days, closing schools and offices. At one point, the index of Sarawak's capital city, Kuching, went beyond 800, upon which the government even considered evacuation (Dauvergne, 1998: 13–14). Sarawak reported economic losses amounting to RM1 billion ($325 million) during the ten-day shutdown (Tawie, 1997). The August 2005 haze episode saw yet another state of emergency in several areas in the Peninsula (*Bernama*, 2005), and severe haze conditions continued into 2006.

Damage to local Malaysian sectors as a result of the 1997 haze cost a total of $321 million. This amounted to a damage of some $15 per capita for Malaysia (Othman, 2003: 244–245). According to these estimates, the most seriously affected local economic sectors were tourism (40 per cent of total national damage or losses due to haze) and fisheries (5 per cent) (Mohd Shahwahid and Othman, 1999). The months following the 1997 haze saw tourism arrivals fall by 13 per cent compared to the year before (BBC, 1999) as the haze kept tourists away (Dauvergne, 1998: 13–14). General productivity (49 per cent), along with public health (3 per cent), was significantly affected as well (Mohd Shahwahid and Othman, 1999). This drop was linked to missed production opportunities due to number of workdays lost, and reduced productivity due to the diminished health of the remaining workforce (Mohd Shahwahid and Othman, 1999). The health of around 18 million Malaysians, or 82 per cent of the general population, was put at risk by the 1997 haze (Mohd Shahwahid and Othman, 1999). The Health Ministry reported a 10 per cent rise in haze-linked medical cases such as asthma, respiratory diseases and conjunctivitis (Foong, 1991). There was also a significant increase in the number of people seeking treatment at clinics and hospitals, as well as of buying medicine for self-treatment during the haze periods (Mohd Shahwahid and Othman, 1999).

Singapore suffered on equally severe terms. For Singapore, the haze usually occurs during National Day season (9 August), and 'it often casts a dark cloud over the feeling of that special day' (Interviewee S21, 2010). As a small island state, 'Singapore is especially vulnerable to atmospheric pollution that can blanket the whole country at once' (Interviewee S14 and Interviewee S15, 2010). Indeed, as a result of the haze, Singapore has suffered a significant negative impact on the economy, especially on business, tourism and citizen health (Fernandez, 1997). Researchers estimated a loss of at least $69 million during the 1997 episode (Hon, 1999: 79). More than 36,000 working days were lost. The tourism industry in Singapore suffered the heaviest financial losses out of all the sectors in 1997, with 84 per cent of the total estimated losses of the year as a result of the haze and an additional 10 per cent from airline losses (Hon, 1999: 79). The number of tourists fell by 10 per cent and hotel occupancy rates dropped to 67 per cent (*Straits Times*, 1998). A follow-up study during the return of severe haze in 2006 put estimated losses at $79 million within just the first hazy month of the year (*Today*, 2006), largely due to the forced closure of Singapore's main Changi airport (Ghani [S6], 2010). The haze in 2009 also caused a measurable 20 per cent increase in the number of patients with haze-related health problems (*Singapore Government News*, 2010).

Latest regional haze episodes in the region include July 2009 (Then, 2009), October 2010, throughout 2011 and in mid-2013. The haze episode in 2010 (Simamora and Adamrah, 2010) triggered drastic drops in air quality in areas in Indonesia, Malaysia and Singapore (Lee and Chan, 2009; Then *et al.*, 2009). In February 2011, forest fires razed large sections of forests (including peatlands) in North Sumatra, Jambi and Riau over three days, which produced thick haze that reached Malaysia and Singapore. Later during the dry season in July to September 2011, fires destroyed hundreds of hectares of protected forest on the slopes of Mount Sipiso-Piso in Sumatra, with the resulting haze descending over the Lake Toba resort area in North Sumatra and spreading overseas (Feng, 2011; *Jakarta Post*, 2011). June 2013 saw the predictable return of haze to the region again, with fires detected in various places in Sumatra, most intensely in the Riau province. The smoke haze spread as usual to Malaysia and Singapore, with Singapore experiencing its worst ever PSI ratings, reaching higher than 400 that year (Woo, 2013). The haze continued well into 2014 as the start of the annual fire season in Indonesia in June saw a huge jump in the number of detectable forest fires in Riau. While areas in Singapore saw moderate PSI levels in June and July 2014, areas in Malaysia during the same period reported unhealthy air quality levels (Channel NewsAsia, 2014; Winifred and Ng, 2014).

This section has shown that the haze is an extremely serious environmental and socioeconomic problem at the global as well as the regional level, with Indonesia, Malaysia and Singapore suffering the brunt of its effects. The following section focuses on the research question and argument proposed in this book.

Research question

Haze can result from both natural causes and human activities. Natural spontaneous fires can occur due to extremely dry conditions, for instance from a spark as a result of two branches rubbing together (Colfer, 2002: 310). Human activities include accidental and deliberate forest burnings, open rubbish burnings and emissions from factories or motor vehicles (Othman, 2003: 244–245). The Southeast Asian haze is commonly understood to be caused by smoke from grass, forest and more seriously, peat fires (Cotton, 1999: 331–332), mainly in Indonesia and to a lesser extent in Malaysia.

The occurrence of haze has increased in intensity and frequency since the 1990s (Suwarsono *et al.*, 2007: 1), alongside the burgeoning development of large-scale agribusiness plantations in Southeast Asia. Due to dwindling primary forests in the region, the 1990s saw a shift of economic focus from logging to plantation crops, especially oil palm plantations (Sawit Watch, 2007: 1; WALHI *et al.*, 2009). As detailed in Chapter 2, Indonesia is currently the largest palm oil producer in the world, and Malaysian and Singaporean firms are among the largest investors in Indonesia's oil palm plantation sector. Indonesia produces over 33.5 million tonnes of palm oil annually (indexMundi, 2014), which amounts to 52 per cent of world production (Agriculture Corner, 2012). Indonesian palm oil output is growing at around 14 per cent per year (Van Gelder, 2004: 12). This large and increasing output is supported by continued land clearing for plantation expansion (Cooke, 2006: 9).

Researchers have identified rapid commercial land clearing using fire, especially for oil palm plantations, to be the major source of haze (Sawit Watch, 2007: 1; WALHI *et al.*, 2009). Commercial open burning is preferred because this is the cheapest method to clear land in preparation for planting (Interviewee I49, 2011). However, despite this evidence, the states most affected by the haze have not chosen to engage with plantation companies directly on this matter. ASEAN-level initiatives have also failed to engage with these actors. As a result, commercial open burning in Indonesia has largely continued unchecked, and haze continues to make its return to the region during the annual dry season. Drawing on an analysis of foreign investment trends and business practises in the oil palm sector, this book aims to contribute to the larger understanding of why these commercial plantations in Indonesia have been able to carry out these illegal burning activities with such impunity. Such an understanding is pertinent for finding solutions to mitigate the recurring problem of transboundary haze in the region.

Considering the significance of the oil palm sector to the Indonesian and regional economy (Butler *et al.*, 2009: 68; Koh and Wilcove, 2007: 993; Stone, 2007: 1491; Tan *et al.*, 2009: 421–424), this study asks the following question: why have the governments of Indonesia, Malaysia and Singapore thus far failed to effectively address the regional haze problem despite clear evidence of the culpability of the oil palm plantation sector in Indonesia? This book proposes that the economic regionalization of the Southeast Asian oil palm sector is a major driver of transboundary haze. It also argues that state vested interests within the sector are the main cause of the continued failure of regional-level ASEAN haze mitigation efforts.

On the surface, the answer to why the haze persists is clear. The haze persists because Indonesia, Malaysia and Singapore have not been engaging with the correct actors to address this problem in a manner that would have a lasting impact on regional levels of air pollution, as will be shown in Chapter 5. While the actors largely responsible for haze have been identified as local and foreign (mostly Malaysian and Indonesian) commercial plantation companies operating in the outer islands of Indonesia, the states involved have largely only engaged with community actors: forest-dwelling communities that practice small-scale slash and burn agriculture. However, community agriculture is only a minor contributor of the smoke that results in haze (Tan [S7], 2010).

With Malaysian- and Singaporean-owned plantations implicated in causing fires alongside local Indonesian plantations, the involvement of Malaysian and Singaporean firms in this sector, especially since their home countries suffer the worse effects of their practises, becomes of great concern. Therefore, on a deeper level of analysis, the flaw in actor engagement has its roots in the nature of regional integration in Southeast Asia. The process of regional integration attempts to achieve mutual gains from regional-level cooperation (Yoshimatsu, 2006: 115), either through regional economic cooperation or regional political cooperation. Hurrell (1995), Katzenstein (1997) and Breslin and Higgott (2003) have identified two major varieties of regional integration: regionalization and regionalism. Historically, regional economic integration in Southeast Asia has taken the path of (informal) regionalization, while regional political integration has taken the path of (formal) regionalism (Katzenstein, 1997: 31).

Regionalization refers to often undirected 'processes of integration that arise from markets, private trade and investment flows, and the policies and decisions of companies' (Breslin and Higgott, 2003: 177). These private businesses will often time push ahead with the construction of a regional economy (Katzenstein, 1997: 34). Therefore, regionalization is the outcome of natural economic forces (Wyatt-Walter, 1995: 77); a bottom-up process (Pempel, 2005: 19–20) primarily driven by the private sector (Beeson, 2007: 5). It involves 'autonomous economic processes which lead to higher levels of economic interdependence within a given geographical area' (Hurrell, 1995: 334), alongside further integrative developments (Katzenstein, 1997: 34). According to Hurrell (1995: 334), this includes the 'growth of intra-firm trade, the increasing numbers of international mergers and acquisitions, and the emergence of increasingly dense networks of strategic alliances between firms'. Therefore, it is a process that deepens the integration of particular regional spaces through the redefining and reconfiguration of social and economic relations occurring over a regional terrain, often resulting in the emergence of common forms of market organization and economic strategy (Payne, 2004: 18–19).

In the Southeast Asian context, Sim (2006: 490–491) has noted two distinct drivers of regionalization: the role of the state as facilitator, and similar patronage cultures. Accordingly, state facilitation and patronage politics has played a key role in the regionalization of the Southeast Asian oil palm plantation sector and has also been a major driver of transboundary haze. Regionalization in Southeast Asia, while largely informal and market-driven, is notably also state-facilitated. Southeast Asian governments have frequently taken official actions designed to stimulate or support such behaviour by private sector actors (Pempel, 2005: 19–20). Regionalization in Southeast Asia often involves governments sanctioning the relaxation of barriers to trade and investment (such as the mutual exchange of goods, services, capital and people), and facilitating the provision of incentives to investment (Breslin and Higgott, 2003: 178–179).

Malaysian and Singaporean plantation firms facing scarcity of land in their home states have therefore invested heavily in the Indonesian oil palm plantation sector (Mathew [M8], 2010), facilitated by home governments and encouraged by the relaxation of barriers to foreign investment for the sector in Indonesia in the 1990s (Interviewee M24 and Interviewee M25, 2010; Interviewee M28, 2010). These companies were often either government-linked companies (GLCs) or well-established plantation companies in their home state, often with government elites having vested interests in them, as explained in Chapter 3. These vested interests further encouraged government facilitation of these firms in Indonesia beyond the mere brokering of entry. This government involvement continues well after the establishment of these firms in Indonesia, with states using their influence and resources to defend their firms operating there when faced with accusations of open-burning misconduct.

The second driver of regionalization is the role of cultural familiarity (Sim, 2006: 499–500), particularly the culture of patronage that has become such a dominant identity among many countries in Southeast Asia. Sim (2006: 490) argues that the regionalization of Southeast Asian firms to neighbouring countries is often related to 'psychic distance'. Psychic distance is the extent of similarities that countries share in terms of language, education, business practises, culture and industrial development. These firms thus would more willingly consider initial entry to a foreign market that is relatively close to their home country in terms of psychic distance (Sim, 2006: 490). Familiarity with cultures within the same region also lowers transaction costs associated with doing business. Similar cultural heritage and attitudes further encourage cooperation and trust between investors and locals in the host country (Terjesen and Elam, 2009: 1105–1106).

Likewise, patronage ties have also largely driven outcomes in the region's oil palm plantation sector. The similarities of the patronage culture between Indonesia, Malaysia and Singapore have enabled even deeper regional integration of the sector, where Malaysian and Singaporean companies were able to effectively insert themselves into local patronage networks (Interviewee I49, 2011), compared to other foreign firms like Dutch or American ones. As a result of this, Malaysian and Singaporean firms have been able to easily dominate the industry compared to these foreign firms, and today control around half of all Indonesia's oil palm plantation area (Adnan, 2013; Down to Earth, 2007; Maruli, 2011; PalmOilHQ, 2009).

Because of these patronage networks, environmental policies, especially those related to land use and fire, usually suffer from weakened state capacity resulting in policy paralysis. State capacity is the ability of the government machinery to create and implement coherent official goals and policy programmes, '*especially over the actual or potential opposition of powerful social groups*' (Knutsen, 2013: 2 (emphasis added); see also Skocpol, 1985). It determines whether these regulations are enforced, revenues collected, benefits distributed and programmes completed. It is therefore an important determinant of the success or failure of policies, and the bureaucracies that implement said policies (Ting, 2011: 245). Policy paralysis thus is a situation where the government is unable to do these things (Amy, 1983: 345; Tambulasi, 2010: 335), in other words, the state's ability to utilize their autonomy effectively is reduced (Glassman and Samatar, 1997: 179). In this case, state capacity is reduced when powerful patrons in the government and administration have little interest in making and carrying out policies that are restrictive to the practises of their clients. These patrons are instead usually more interested in securing alliances and undermining social opposition to their actions (Glassman and Samatar, 1997: 179).

Maintaining current practises in the region's oil palm plantation sector is indeed an area of crucial economic interest for the states concerned, both due to its contribution to GDP and as a source of patronage for the ruling elite, as will be detailed in Chapter 4. Hence, with the protection of these networks, plantation companies (as 'clients' of these patrons within the government) have been able to conduct themselves on the ground in Indonesia with impunity, including conducting open burning that produces haze, in the interests of cost-efficiency. As a whole, it is unsurprising that plantation companies have not viewed the transnational effects of haze and its mitigation as a priority, as economic regionalization does not presuppose any specific impact on relations between states within the region (Hurrell, 1995: 335).

Regionalism on the other hand refers to top-down (Pempel, 2005: 19), state-led projects of cooperation that emerge as a result of intergovernmental treaties and dialogues (Breslin and Higgott, 2003: 177). It is a conscious policy of states to coordinate activities and arrangements in a greater region (Wyatt-Walter, 1995: 77) and implies a degree of intentionality as states engage in an essentially political process of collaboration (Beeson, 2007: 5). In other words, this process can help solve coordination problems (Doner, 1997: 202).[3] Hurrell (1995: 336–337) explains that this type of political regionalism focuses on regional inter-state cooperation, involving the negotiation and construction of inter-state agreements or regimes. According to him, regionalism 'may involve the creation of formal institutions, but it can often be based on a much looser structure, involving patterns of regular meetings with some rules attached, together with mechanisms for preparation and follow up' (Hurrell, 1995: 336). Such innovative arrangements can serve many purposes: to respond to external challenges; to coordinate regional positions in international negotiation forums; to secure welfare gains; to promote common values; or to solve common problems arising from intensified regional interdependence (Hurrell, 1995: 336–337). Furthermore, they can also provide incentives to encourage parties to redefine their national interests in support of these agreements, and also provide sufficient information to these parties to ensure the smooth implementation of said agreements (Doner, 1997: 199–202).

High levels of regionalism however cannot guarantee the effectiveness of solving common problems (Hurrell, 1995: 336–337). This *model* of regionalism is an important determinant of whether the regionalism process is effective in solving regional problems or not. The main criteria of the ASEAN model of regionalism is the maintenance of national sovereignty (Kim, 2011: 422; Murray, 2010: 311–313). In the words of Kiichi Fujiwara, 'state sovereignty and regional cooperation expanded in unison' in ASEAN (in Katzenstein, 1997: 35). This model of regionalism therefore enables member states to control the scope, depth and speed of regionalism in ASEAN, which best suit their national interests (Kim, 2011: 416). Hence, ASEAN has displayed only weak formal institutionalization of regionalism, with only scattered signs of institutional deepening and minimal accretion of centralized powers (Katzenstein, 1997: 33–34). Thus, Katzenstein (1997: 33–34) describes ASEAN as a 'remarkably modest ... decentralized intergovernmental ... congress'.

When faced with the haze, a common problem that arose from increased levels of regional economic interdependence but with potentially political consequences, states of the region elected to address the issue at the ASEAN level (Letchumanan [A6], 2010). However, policies related to haze at the regional level also suffered from policy paralysis. The ASEAN model of regionalism that emphasizes national sovereignty and self-determination (Interviewee A7, 2010; Narine, 1998: 555; Smith, 2004: 418; Zainal Abidin [M38], 2010) has allowed member states to shape collective mitigation initiatives at the ASEAN level in accordance with the interests of their political and economic elites. This has weakened ASEAN's capacity to create and enforce haze mitigation efforts that serve collective regional interests. Instead, the cooperative agreements that were produced were (as predicted by the literature above) designed to protect national economic interests and preserve state sovereignty, and to deflect responsibility on the haze issue (Tan [S7], 2010; Yahaya [M13], 2010). For example, as explained in Chapter 5, the ASEAN Agreement on Transboundary Haze Pollution (ATHP) was a highly watered-down document that enshrined national economic interests and state sovereignty, while deflecting responsibility on haze (Tan [S7], 2010; Yahaya [M13], 2010).

Furthermore, as an organization focused on promoting economic cooperation and development among its members (Smith, 2004: 418), states at the ASEAN level were reluctant to engage with big business interests on the haze issue. For example, the Adopt-A-District programmes that were implemented under the ATHP framework were focused mainly on educating smallholders, and did not significantly involve larger plantations (Udiansyah [I15], 2010). This reluctance can be explained by the vested interests of home and host governments in this sector, as discussed extensively in Chapter 3 on state facilitation and Chapter 4 on patronage politics. A crackdown on commercial open burning among big businesses would result in a significant increase of land clearing costs, and by extension reduced profitability in the sector. Once again, it becomes visible that patronage ties drive outcomes. The regionalism of haze mitigation through ASEAN initiatives have failed to curb haze because of the undue influence of patronage networks in the oil palm plantation sector.

This study therefore uses these varieties of regional integration as a lens through which the failure of ASEAN and regional governments to effectively mitigate haze can be analysed. While the *source* of the haze has its roots in intense economic regionalization in the oil palm sector, ASEAN states have elected for *solutions* that were rooted in political regionalism. Importantly, patronage ties have driven outcomes at both the national and regional level. First, home and host governments with vested interests in these companies are encouraging and assisting the regionalization and 'opening up' of the sector, to the point that local, Malaysian and Singaporean companies can conduct themselves on the ground in Indonesia with impunity, including conducting open burning that produces haze. Second and at the same time, regional governments at the ASEAN level have used the ASEAN model of regionalism to their advantage by ensuring that ASEAN haze initiatives were shaped in a way that preserved the status quo in the sector instead of effectively mitigating haze. Simply put, states involved have chosen to adhere to the ASEAN Way when dealing with the haze to preserve crucial economic interests. This situation of intense economic regionalization in Southeast Asia's oil palm plantation sector and the high levels of political regionalism at the ASEAN level have resulted in outcomes that protect the interests of big businesses. A visualization of the argument is depicted in Figure 1.1, where protection and patronage is clearly shown to drive outcomes at both the national and regional levels, resulting in reduced state and organizational capacity alongside policy paralysis, further ensuring the continuity of the haze problem year after year.

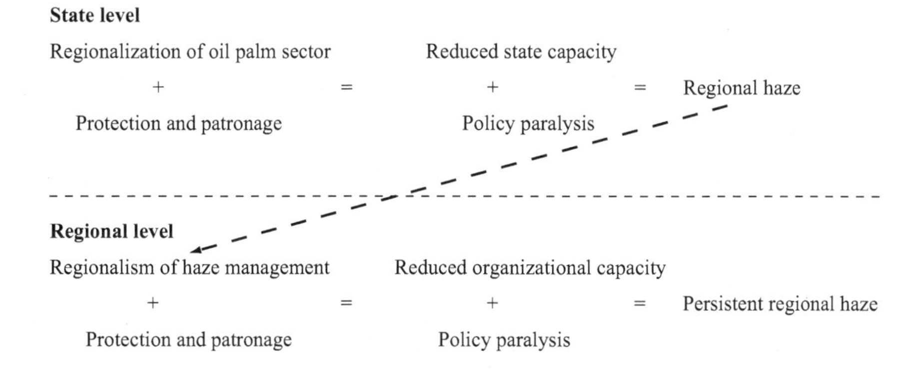

Figure 1.1 Framework of this book

Therefore, with ASEAN-level initiatives that continue to be aimed at the wrong actors, the haze in the region continues to persist. Hence, high levels of political regionalism cannot guarantee the effectiveness of solving such common problems (Hurrell, 1995: 336), and the high levels of cooperation at the ASEAN level over haze have not, and indeed will not, guarantee effective outcomes. This study therefore focuses on how the economic regionalization in the sector (driven by home state protection and host-state patronage) continues to produce haze and ensure the failure of regional-level ASEAN haze mitigation efforts. Hence, this book offers an alternative explanation to the persistence of haze in the region, at once addressing the limitations of earlier explanations by other scholars, as explained below.

Research rationale and literature review

Dauvergne (1994: 497–499) proposed that one of the reasons environmental problems in Southeast Asia continued unchecked was because of the inadequacy of conventional explanations. While acknowledging that most explanations include an assortment of contributing factors, the literature can be broadly categorized according to which factors were viewed as the most important causes of open burning and the resultant transboundary haze. This review classifies the literature into four major categories arising roughly in chronological order: with the early group of scholars focusing on developmental issues, the second on economic motivations, the third focusing on flawed public policy, and more recent scholars focusing on arguments of weak regional governance. In contrast, this study argues that the persistence of the haze can be explained by a combination of intense regionalization in Southeast Asia's oil palm plantation sector and the failure of environmental regionalism at the ASEAN level, with vested interests and patronage politics playing important roles in both instances. The following paragraphs briefly identify these groups of scholars together with their major arguments, and then show how this study addresses the limitations of these arguments and offers an alternative and more comprehensive explanation for the persistence of the haze.

Earlier academic works on the subject of haze was generally influenced by government-sanctioned reports on sources of haze that identified swidden agriculture as a main source of fires (*Jakarta Post*, 2006b: 55). For example, Colfer (2002), Quah and Johnston (2001) and Varma (2003) identified poverty and developmental issues as the major reason for the persistence of haze. They pointed out that haze persists because of certain development-related underlying causes that lead to unsustainable traditional practices. These include poverty, rapid population growth and ignorance; as 'it is the poor and the hungry that destroy their immediate environment to survive' (Dauvergne, 1994: 500). Colfer (2002: 313–316) pointed out poverty and unfulfilled subsistence needs meant that people would use fire more often to encourage the regrowth of certain plants, for example plants that attract deer that can be caught as food or for sale. Poverty also meant that fires were one of the only tools available to these communities when they felt the need to defend their rights, and ignorance meant that they could not comprehend the larger effects of these fires, resulting in many fires going out of control. These unaddressed developmental issues were identified to be the major reason for the persistence of the haze-producing fires.

However, as the link between fires and commercial oil palm plantations became clearer (Sawit Watch, 2007: 1; WALHI *et al.*, 2009) scholars moved away from developmental arguments. A second strand of scholars began to consider economic motivations for the persistence of the haze. Foreign debt is generally considered one of the most important economic forces driving this (Dauvergne, 1994: 501–502). The argument is that in order to service their debts, tropical countries have been forced to plunder their natural resources (Bramble, 1987: 193). For example, Gellert (1998: 77–81) argued that since the 1980s, the World Bank gave specific assistance to the Indonesian government to make direct investments in oil palm in the country (Samsul *et al.*, 2007: 6), on the premise that this would be ecologically more sustainable than shifting cultivation, provide foreign exchange to Indonesia and alleviate poverty for millions of smallholder families. However, the Bank failed to consider the cost of mechanical land clearing, forcing estates to resort to the cheaper method of clearing land with fire. Gellert (1998: 81) and Marinova (1999: 72) also pointed out that International Monetary Fund (IMF) reforms that were part of a loan package given to Indonesia in the aftermath of the Asian financial crisis (AFC) in 1997 essentially drove forest degradation and fires. For example, Indonesia was required to open its economy further to foreign direct investment (FDI). Given that Indonesia's competitive advantages were in natural resources, FDI, especially from neighbouring Malaysia and Singapore, flowed into extractive and resource-intensive sectors, like oil palm plantations (Marinova, 1999: 77). IMF instructions to Indonesia to lift the ban on CPO exports, initially put into place due to concern of cooking oil shortages during the AFC, further encouraged investments into oil palm and the unscrupulous practices like commercial open burning that came along with it (Gellert, 1998: 81).

The third strand of scholars identified flawed public policy as the major explanation for haze. Scholars such as Eaton and Radojevic (2001: 248), Aiken (2004: 74) and Thompson (2001: 17) argued that Indonesia's general policy mix was not able to avoid the prevalence of harmful land-clearing techniques and gross inefficiencies in exploiting its tropical forest resources. They emphasized the destructive impact of tropical government policies developed by various bureaucratic departments, due to the low status of environmental issues in the bureaucratic structure (Dauvergne, 1994: 502–503). Specifically, agro-conversion policies such as concession[4] licensing have encouraged unsustainable and destructive forest development. Aiken (2004: 74) has argued that the government's policies of providing incentives and subsidies for the conversion of degraded forests to oil palm plantations have encouraged rapid land conversion, usually using fire. Also, the relatively short periods of concessions (20 years) granted to private companies did not favour careful, long-term forest management (Eaton and Radojevic, 2001: 248; Thompson, 2001: 14). Mayer (2006: 213) also argued that the government's decentralization policies 'failed to anticipate effects of regional autonomy reforms, which limit the central government's ability to organize fire management on the ground'.

As ASEAN haze mitigation efforts increased and became more visible, scholars began to focus on regional governance to explain the persistence of haze. This fourth strand of scholars argued that the type of governance that has developed in Southeast Asia over haze issues have been ineffective, inefficient and illegitimate (Koh and Robinson, 2002: 1–2). Scholars such as Tan (2005: 3–4), Tay (2002: 74), Yahaya (2000: 49), Nguitragool (2011: 357), Elliott (2003), Aggarwal and Chow (2010: 282–286) and Chang and Rajan (2001: 666) have argued that while regional environmental governance can be instrumental in finding solutions to collective action problems like the haze, the ASEAN approach to regional cooperation, the so-called 'ASEAN Way', does not work when dealing with environmental challenges such as fires. The ASEAN Way is a set of behavioural norms enshrined in the Treaty of Amity and Cooperation 1976, and also informal procedural norms, which prescribe how regional interactions should be carried out. This includes the search for consensus, the principles of sensitivity and politeness, a non-confrontational negotiation process, behind-the-scenes discussions, an emphasis on informal and non-legalistic procedures, non-interference and flexibility (Kivimaki, 2001: 16). Scholars have argued that due to strict adherence to this ASEAN Way, environmental problems in ASEAN are still approached through the state sovereignty system. The notion of sovereignty, which forms the basis of the non-interference principle, impedes collective problem-solving methods when dealing with natural resources, as other states are not allowed to pressure members into acting in accordance with collective interest (Tan, 2005: 3–4). Therefore, ASEAN has emphasized policy pronouncements and rhetoric over actual implementation of effective haze mitigation efforts (Chang and Rajan, 2001: 666). Declarations and agreements adopted at the ASEAN level usually articulate mere 'principles' for regional environmental cooperation but rarely include guidelines for national environmental practices that could be construed as 'intervention' (Elliott, 2003: 29). Due to this, ASEAN member states struggle to find a balance between respecting each others' sovereignty and cooperatively managing environmental issues that affect the whole region (Tan, 2005: 3–4).

These previous studies attempted to explain the persistence of the haze from a singular perspective, either discussing the source or the solution individually. The persistence of the haze was caused either by underdevelopment (Varma, 2003), debt pressure (Marinova, 1999) or flawed public policy (Aiken, 2004), and weakness in the ASEAN Way was identified as the reason why ASEAN solutions failed (Tan, 2005). These explanations isolated different agents and underlying factors that result in transboundary haze, but do not provide a broader context in which to understand the persistence of the problem (Dauvergne, 1994: 497–499). As discussed above, this book at once engages with the source and the (failing) solution. Furthermore, by adopting the method of political economic analysis, it draws out moral debates while maintaining a critical engagement with the economic argument (Anderson, 2004: 144–137). By doing this, the study emphasizes different factors that extend and update the literature on the underlying reasons for the persistence of haze.

Previous literature has correctly identified that the major actors responsible for on-the-ground burning are commercial oil palm companies (Casson, 2002: 234–239; Caroko *et al.*, 2011: 21; Colfer, 2002: 316; Fairhurst and McLaughlin, 2009: 7–34; Tan *et al.*, 2009: 422), and yet other literature has correctly pointed out that mitigation efforts have largely been focused at the ASEAN level (ASEAN Secretariat, 1995: 1–5; Letchumanan [A6], 2010; Severino, 2006: 112–114; Yahaya, 2000: 45). Taken together, as this research does, it becomes clear that the persistence of the haze can be explained by a combination of intense regionalization in Southeast Asia's oil palm plantation sector (the source) and the failure of environmental regionalism at the ASEAN level (the solution), with vested interests and patronage politics playing important roles in both instances.

To update the arguments of the first strand of scholars, an extension of the developmental explanation of haze is provided by pointing out that while swidden agriculture may contribute marginally to fires and haze, the more serious cause of haze-producing fires have their roots in rapid commercial land change, especially for the opening up of oil palm plantations. Based on satellite data, it is estimated that 80 per cent of the fires were started by plantation companies or their sub-contractors for land clearing purposes (Richardson, 2010: 22), while the remaining 20 per cent could be traced to slash-and-burn farmers (Casson, 2002: 221–242). Therefore, the developmental argument can be further updated by including an analysis of an additional actor: corporate plantations. Hence, this book focuses on the oil palm plantation industry as latest data show that the biggest fires were either directly or indirectly related to large-scale companies' land clearing activities (Colfer, 2002: 316). While swidden agriculture may have been a serious case for concern before the oil palm boom in Indonesia in the 1990s, the developmental explanation has to be updated for present times, where the source of fires have been identified as commercial rather than swidden.

The writings of the second and third strand of scholars on the connection of the oil palm plantation sector to haze have been indirect, and can be further updated and extended by including discussion on different factors. For example, national-level governance factors such as external debt pressure and flawed public policies have been blamed for the increased focus on oil palm as a plantation crop in Indonesia. This book emphasizes different factors, arguing instead that regional-level corporate economic motivations have driven the pooling of plantation investments in Indonesia, which in turn has encouraged commercial open burning there. Recognizing the wealth of land available in Indonesia, local, Malaysian and Singaporean companies flocked to invest there, often with the encouragement and assistance of governments. Strategic planning, state facilitation and the effective use of patronage networks by both local and foreign companies meant that commercial plantation lands were often in secluded areas (Rukmantara [I45], 2011), and included forbidden peatlands that release a lot of smoke haze when burned, as explained in Chapter 2. This seclusion and networks of protection also ensured that plantation companies regularly escaped monitoring and prosecution for illegal open burning, despite government policies and regulations.[5] The following paragraphs break down this analysis further, by detailing first how the arguments of the second strand of scholars that link foreign debt pressures to haze can be extended, and then discussing how the arguments of the third strand of scholars who point to flawed public policies as the major driver of haze can also be updated for present times.

The second strand of scholars as discussed above point to foreign debt pressures as the major driver of haze. Indeed, the IMF conditionalities did open doors for foreign investments. However, this only partially explains why the foreign investors that did enter the sector (mostly Malaysian and Singaporean ones) were able to conduct themselves with impunity in the face of open burning allegations. The IMF conditionalities merely facilitated the entry of these firms; their behaviour on the ground is largely unrelated to the IMF. Even with rapid entry of foreign investments into the sector in Indonesia, and rapid opening up of land, this does not 'guarantee' fires and haze. As Chapters 2 and 4 explain, haze is caused by land being opened in a particularly unsustainable manner. Local and foreign companies were allowed to carry out their activities in this manner because of home state protection and patronage networks. These two elements, which are explained in Chapters 3 and 4 respectively, have allowed these companies to carry out their activities with impunity, including clearing land by burning which is a direct cause of haze.

The third strand of scholars identifies flawed public policy as the major explanation of haze. Mayer's (2006: 213–214) argument, that Indonesia's flawed decentralization policies in the late 1990s have driven haze-causing fires, was found to be a useful extension to this approach. As mentioned above, she argued that the government's decentralization policies did not adequately take into account the effects of regional autonomy reforms, which hindered the ability of the central government to carry out effective fire management on the ground. While regional authorities now found themselves overwhelmed with new responsibilities and revenues, this was not matched by the required technical and administrative capacity to properly manage them. Newly empowered regional authorities granted various new and additional types of land and plantation licenses to cooperatives, individuals and companies. Decentralization had also caused serious confusion about who actually has the rightful authority to grant approvals for land use redesignation, land clearing and plantation development at the local level, and the exact process of how these activities should be legally carried out (Mayer, 2006: 213–214).

This study supports Mayer's analysis of flawed decentralization policies as a factor in explaining the persistence of haze, but extends her thesis further by arguing that it is exacerbated by patronage networks. It applies McCarthy's (2002: 77) theorization that, with decentralization, the governance of local national resources should now be understood in terms of particular socio-political structures found in remote forested areas, i.e. modern, decentralized patronage networks. As elites at the district level obtain more administrative power, they would also exert increased control over access to the most valuable resources in the area (McCarthy, 2002: 80). As explained above, patronage networks further encourage policy paralysis, when governments are limited in their capacity to create good public policy, as Mayer has argued previously, but also to implement any good policies that happen to exist (Amy, 1983: 345; Tambulasi, 2010: 335). Hence, an analysis is provided of how these networks have enabled well-connected plantation companies to better exploit the post-decentralization administrative confusion, further driving fires and haze. The underlying motivator for pro-agribusiness policies in the Indonesian oil palm sector has actually been such patronage politics, a link that has only been alluded to previously in works by Eaton and Radojevic (2001), Aiken (2004) and Thompson (2001) in relation to the haze.

Indeed, the role of patronage is an important element that drives the argument of economic regionalization. This element and its connection to environmental degradation and haze have been touched on previously by scholars. For example, previous works by Dauvergne (1995, 1997) and Cotton (1999) inform the patronage argument in this book. Dauvergne's works address the issue of natural resource exploitation and deforestation in Southeast Asia in the 1990s. As succinctly summarized by Beeson (2007: 242), Dauvergne argued that 'Japanese multi-national corporations dominate the trade in tropical timber in Southeast Asia, utilizing their overwhelming economic leverage ruthlessly to exploit the region's natural resources'. Dauvergne (1995: 75) refers to this as 'Japan's ecological shadow'. He argued that these Japanese multinationals' capacity to manipulate indigenous economic and political actors across the region has enabled them to effectively exploit the region's resources to satisfy such demand (Beeson, 2007: 242: Dauvergne, 1995: 75). Particularly, Dauvergne argued that, spurred on by the demand of the Japanese markets, indigenous political and economic actors developed strategies of 'modern patron-client relations' within the timber industry that helped ensure a steady supply of raw materials for Japan (Dauvergne, 1995: 75).

Dauvergne argued that as compared to the traditional patronage relationships of the pre-colonial era (explained extensively in Chapter 3), relationships between the patron and client during this time became based less on blind or reflexive loyalty, obligation and honour. Instead, encouraged by Japanese demand, these bonds became more monetized, calculations more explicit, and concern more centered on the rate of return from the relationship than on its durability (Dauvergne, 1997: 46). With regional governments eager to cash in on Japanese demand, and patron-client relations easily formed on the basis of monetary gains, wealthy elites were able to secure licenses and concessions to clear primary forests for timber with impunity. This enabled the rise of 'crony capitalism' in Indonesia and other Southeast Asian countries, which led to the politicization of natural resources. These reciprocal patronage relationships spurred the development of policies that favour powerful economic and political interests (Dauvergne, 1994: 503) and the development of governance systems that lacked political willingness and institutional capacity to enforce their own environmental regulations (Pasong and Lebel, 2000: 415). This further encouraged deforestation and environmental degradation in Southeast Asia. In separate works, Dauvergne (1994, 1998) also linked these deforestation activities to the fires and haze plaguing the region at that time.

Along similar lines, patronage politics and its link to haze was also discussed by Cotton in 1999. He also applied the patronage argument in the context of large-scale logging concessionaires during the turn of the century. Like Dauvergne, he argued that patronage politics has resulted in weak state capacity and policy paralysis within the logging sector. In this way, he argued that 'the specific use by the elite of the bureaucratic instruments that came into their hands as a result of the pursuit of modernization compromised and undermined the rational-legal capacity of the state to deal with the problem' (Cotton, 1999: 341–342). This was complemented by the regime's development priorities, which required a free hand to be given to the business activities of the chosen clients.

This book extends the above analysis in three original ways. First, the book notes that the connection between patronage politics and haze has not been given much academic attention since Dauvergne's and Cotton's works. Indeed, there have been different causes of haze at different times throughout Indonesia's history, reflecting its agricultural and economic development trends. Dauvergne's and Cotton's works correctly focused on deforestation by logging concessionaires, which were a major contributor to haze at the time of their writing. This study extends and updates the analysis for the present time, where logging has largely given way to oil palm plantations in the region, while haze has continued to persist.

Second, this book adopts and extends Dauvergne's concept of modern patronage relations in the context of Malaysian and Singaporean firms in Indonesia. It proposes that the modernization and monetization of patronage relations in Indonesia has allowed foreign plantation companies, particularly Malaysian and Singaporean ones, to operate with impunity within Indonesia by inserting themselves into local patronage networks. Since patronage relations were no longer based on long-term loyalty, these 'newcomer' firms from Malaysia and Singapore were able to also easily establish their own patronage relations with Indonesian elites. Therefore, patronage politics in the Indonesian oil palm plantation sector, which took over from logging as the major agricultural sector (and the then major producer of haze) in the post-Suharto era, is the current driver for haze.

Third, this book differs from Dauvergne's works in terms of its understanding of the driver of patronage networks. Dauvergne argued that through foreign aid and overseas developmental assistance, Japan (which is *external* to the Southeast Asian region) was able to encourage the development of patron-client networks in order to feed Japan's insatiable appetite for timber resources (Dauvergne, 1997: 12–13). This study instead identifies *internal* drivers within the region of patronage networks; in particular the process of regionalization of the oil palm sector, which saw an influx of investments from Malaysia and Singapore further driving the conversion of land into plantations in Indonesia. It notes that the similar patronage cultures shared between major players in Indonesia, Malaysia and

Singapore further entrenched patronage politics as a way of business in Indonesia's oil palm sector, resulting in weak state capacity and policy paralysis that has allowed haze to persist to present times. This element of patronage analysis is useful in drawing attention to the distributional implications of social and productive relationships, and the ways in which particular group interests (in this case, the elite groups) are facilitated by social development and policy changes, which is an important criterion of political economic analysis (Anderson, 2004: 144–137).

The fourth and final strand of scholars that this book engages with is the scholars who argue that weak regional governance is the major cause of the persistence of the haze. These scholars argued that haze persists because of the limitations posed by the ASEAN Way of regional engagement on haze mitigation initiatives. These scholars have argued that because the ASEAN Way is too deeply engrained in the process of regional governance in ASEAN, member states cannot imagine ASEAN functioning any other way (Kamaruddin [M26], 2010; Lew [M6] and Interviewee M7, 2010; Nagulendran [M34] and Interviewee M35, 2010; Syarif [I2], 2010). Therefore, Aggarwal and Chow (2010: 282–286) insist that ASEAN states 'undoubtedly desire the elimination of the haze problem', but were unable to balance this with their stronger desire to comply with the broader ASEAN Way norms, especially those of non-interference and decision making based on consensus. This book updates this analysis by proposing that states do not blindly follow the ASEAN Way principles in ASEAN due to some deeply ingrained 'habit'. Instead, states *choose* to adhere to the ASEAN Way norms if it is in their interests to do so. This ASEAN model of regionalism therefore enables member states to control the scope, depth and speed of regionalism in ASEAN, which best suit their national interests (Kim, 2011: 416). Hence, states are free to decide whether or not to adhere to the ASEAN Way, depending on whether it is in their best interests. In this case, the protection of these elite interests, and a country's power of veto over effective policy creation, innovation and implementation, is more important than responding to regional cooperation through ASEAN (Cotton, 1999: 341–342). Therefore, instead of being a limiting effect on state behavior, the ASEAN Way can be better explained as tools for political action that states can selectively use in line with their interests (Khoo, 2004: 42).

Overall, the persistence of the haze issue is not purely a political problem that can be dealt with regionalism, but instead has its roots in economic regionalization. Regionalism and regionalization in Southeast Asia exist in two distinct spheres. When these spheres overlap, it is usually to facilitate even more economic interdependence and integration through ASEAN. However, effective regional-level haze mitigation would involve significant interference into the integration process and practices of the region's oil palm sector, something that is very unlikely due to powerful vested interests and patronage networks. Therefore, the notion of resolving haze issues at the ASEAN level cannot possibly be effective because it is unable to engage effectively with the economic sources of the problem. In all these ways, by using the concept of the varieties of regional integration, specifically ideas of economic regionalization and political regionalism as a framework by which to view and analyze the question of the persistence of haze, this book offers an original and comprehensive way of understanding the regional haze problem. The following section covers the scope of this study and the various methods that were used to uncover information for analysis.

Research parameters and methods

As noted above, this research is qualitative in nature, rooted in political economy, which understands that economic factors and political decisions are closely connected. The study parameters were first determined by the scope of effects of the regional haze. As discussed above, the haze affects up to six Southeast Asian countries with varying levels of severity. With an overwhelming amount of fires originating in Indonesia, the country is commonly regarded as the main culprit of the haze. Its closest neighbours, Singapore and Malaysia, are the most severely affected (Mayer, 2006: 204). Furthermore, these three states have also been the most active participants in ASEAN-level haze mitigation initiatives. For example, for the Adopt-A-District programmes, the only active participants were Indonesia, Malaysia and Singapore (Interviewee M32, 2010; Interviewee S4 and Interviewee S5, 2010; Nagulendran [M34] and Interviewee M35, 2010). This shows that these three states are the major players involved in engagement over haze issues in the region, which is why this book limits its analysis to these three states.

The second determinant of scope was the Indonesian oil palm plantation sector itself. Preliminary analysis showed that the major business interests in the sector can be traced back to either local, Malaysian or Singaporean companies. In fact, Malaysia is the largest foreign investor in this sector, and Singaporean firms, while not one of the largest groups of investors, are significantly spearheaded by Chinese-Indonesian investors that have channeled their operations offshore to Singapore (WALHI and Sawit Watch, 2009). It must also be noted here that while there is mounting evidence that commercial open burning in this sector is the major cause of haze (Casson, 2002; Tan [S7], 2010: 234–239,), it cannot be denied that there are other smaller sources of haze. As mentioned above, this includes slash-and-burn agriculture, fires arising from community conflict, natural fires and industrial pollution (Othman, 2003: 244–245). However, to determine the answer to the persistence of haze, this book analyzes the (overwhelmingly) primary source of haze only (Tan [S7], 2010). Hence, collection of data for this study on haze was done primarily in Indonesia, Malaysia and Singapore, and mainly in the context of local and foreign oil palm plantation companies (largely Malaysian and Singaporean) operating in Indonesia.

Finally, the discussions and analysis in this book are limited to events occurring up to just before the Indonesian ratification of the Agreement on Transboundary Haze Pollution on 16 September 2014 (*Jakarta Post*, 2014). Fieldwork and on the ground research for this book was carried out before the said agreement was ratified, and thus this book will not attempt to provide analysis on the significance of this new turn of events. Furthermore, the effects of this very recent development would require prolonged observation, which will no doubt pique the interest of many future researchers. It is hoped that this book will serve as a helpful resource to inform future research on the subject.

Studying the process of regional integration 'on the ground' in a particular industry is extremely important, as opposed to a 'bird's eye view perspective'. This can be achieved by using the triangulation of multiple methods to analyze various sources of data (Louis, 1982: 7). Triangulation involves data collected at different places, sources, times, levels of analysis or perspectives (King *et al.*, 2004: 192). Methods commonly involved in triangulation include hands-on field research and systematic interviews among relevant individuals (Gill *et al.*, 2008: 291), supplemented by a search of historical literature (Lande, 1983: 438–450). It is the use of these methods in a way that complement each other, drawing from the strengths and minimizing the weaknesses of either type of method by using data from one set to supplement the other (Johnson and Onwuegbuzie, 2004: 14–15). It illuminates different aspects of phenomena, enabling richer descriptions (Giddings and Grant, 2007: 53–59). Accordingly, the methods for data collection for this book include semi-structured interviews, media and archival research. It triangulates qualitative information obtained from interviews, government and organizational reports and documents, as well as magazine and newspaper articles written around the time of the event as primary sources, complementing these with secondary sources from books, scholarly articles and media commentary, as is discussed in the following subsections. However, owing to the difficulty of doing empirical research on such a sensitive topic, there are certain points that unavoidably have to be reliant on interview data alone.

Semi-structured interviews

Interviews in the field are useful for showing variations of individual behaviour between people of different social strata, locations and over time (Gill *et al.*, 2008: 291). After approval was obtained from the Human Research Ethics Committee of the University of Sydney,[6] semi-structured interviews with 138 people were conducted over a period of six months in the year 2010, three months in 2011 and another three months in 2012. Convenience sampling was used to select interviewees; this was based on whether these individuals were willing to be interviewed when approached. On top of that, the 'snowball' method was also used, where interviewees were asked to suggest someone else who might be willing or appropriate for the study (Sommer, 2006). In the end, individuals who were interviewed ranged from government officials, journalists, non-governmental organizations (NGOs) and academics in Indonesia, Malaysia and Singapore, as well as present and former staff of the ASEAN Secretariat.

Semi-structured interviews 'consist of several key questions that help to define the areas to be explored, but also allows the interviewer or interviewee to diverge in order to pursue an idea or response in more detail' (Gill *et al.*, 2008: 291). These interviews are not directed towards establishing 'objective facts' (Crouch and McKenzie, 2009: 485) but are helpful in reconstructing negotiations, understanding the purpose of actions and to elicit the response of staff and officials towards them (Gusterson, 2008: 103). This helps provide deeper understanding of the individuals' views, experiences, beliefs and motivations.

Particularly, this research displays the usefulness of hands-on methods such as semi-structured interviews for exploring particularly sensitive topics (Gill *et al.*, 2008: 292; Pezalla, 2012: 165–170), as it allows for easier expression of non-conformity (Stokes and Bergin, 2006: 28). This was particularly useful for this research topic that deals with informal institutions and personal relationships that might be considered sensitive, such as issues of patronage. By conversing with relevant persons on the ground, the author was able to obtain insights that may not otherwise be found in written sources.

Even though there was a core set of questions prepared for the interviews, common strategies such as 'branching' (tailoring interviews to individual interests and identities) and 'building' (interviews that build upon earlier interviews) were employed (Gusterson, 2008: 104). Enhanced validity can be ensured by facilitating a close association with the respondents in a more natural, conversational setting (Crouch and McKenzie, 2009: 483). Accordingly, effort was made to facilitate these interviews in the suggested conversational setting. To ensure this, most of the interviews were conducted face-to-face. However, a small set of follow-up phone interviews were also conducted during the second and third fieldwork periods in 2011 and 2012.

Some interviewees allowed the author to use their real names for this research and some preferred to remain anonymous. Therefore, the author devised a system to maintain uniformity in the classification of interview sources for this book. To indicate the country or institution where the interview was conducted, the letters 'I' for Indonesia, 'M' for Malaysia, 'S' for Singapore and 'A' for ASEAN are used, along with a number to indicate the order in which the interviews were conducted. For example, an interviewee who allowed himself or herself to be named, and was the tenth to be interviewed in Singapore, would appear referenced as, 'Ali [S10]'. An anonymous interviewee in Malaysia would be referenced as 'Interviewee M5'.

The author was not able to interview any Singaporean plantation company representatives, as Singaporean companies were uncooperative when contacted. Most denied having any plantation investments in Indonesia, despite other sources, including Indonesian government representatives confirming this (Interviewee I7 and Interviewee I8, 2010). Sometimes the author was asked to contact other departments, but was given phone numbers or email addresses that were not working. In fact, information on Singaporean plantation companies in general was hard to obtain. This business secrecy is somewhat of a norm in Singapore, especially in terms of environmental reporting and investments abroad. Surveys conducted by Perry and Teng (1999: 310) reveal a low commitment to environmental disclosure among Singaporean organizations. More recent surveys show that only 20 per cent of the listed companies on the Singapore Stock Exchange make environmental disclosures in their annual reports (Batra, 2013). Other researchers have experienced similar difficulties. For example, Hiratsuka (2006) also cited lack of available data on FDI outflows from Singapore. This weakness was compensated for by using extra resources, such as company annual reports and secondary information from other interviewees. Another notable issue with interviewees was the author's efforts in speaking to those listed on the ASEAN Panel of Experts (POE) on haze. Many of the 'experts' that were contacted declined to be interviewed on the pretext that they were not actually 'experts' on the issue at all. This could be significant in showing that ASEAN's procedures of selection of these experts were flawed (perhaps deliberately so), but further analysis of this lies beyond the scope of this research.

Media and archival research

Media and archival research was also conducted and analyzed together with the interviews at all stages of this research. Triangulation of interview, media and archival research data was essential in better understanding the circumstances surrounding particular pieces of information, and also to verify the accuracy of the information obtained. Media (mainly newspaper) research was a very important primary resource for this study, as the publicity from haze events meant that there was extensive coverage of the matter in the media. Therefore, there was a substantial amount of newspaper articles written around the time of haze events that were useful as primary sources for this research. Research was limited to the highest circulated English newspaper in each country. This included *The Jakarta Post* and *The Jakarta Globe* for Indonesia, *The Star* and *The New Straits Times* for Malaysia and *The Straits Times* for Singapore. With these parameters, selected keywords were run through the Dow Jones Factiva programme to obtain newspaper coverage on this topic. However other relevant sources from other newspapers (including *Bahasa Malaysia* and *Bahasa Indonesia* papers), radio and television were also included as necessary. Media research was also assisted by archives at the *New Straits Times* in Malaysia and in the Singapore National Library.

Archival research proved important for obtaining official Indonesian, Malaysian and Singaporean government documents, ASEAN documents and documents published by relevant organizations. Especially useful also were non-governmental publications and company annual reports. Several archives that are part of the ASEAN-Institute of Strategic and International Studies network in Malaysia, Singapore and Indonesia were helpful as starting points for archival research into this topic, namely the Centre for Strategic and International Studies in Indonesia, the Institute of Strategic and International Studies in Malaysia and the Singapore Institute of International Affairs. Other archives that proved useful were the ASEAN Secretariat Library in Indonesia, the Department of Environment Library in Malaysia and the Institute for South East Asian Studies in Singapore. The concern of 'preferred memory' where archivists exert strong influence over the material selection (Houck, 2006: 134–135) was taken into account for this research. For example, the Department of Environment Library in Malaysia mainly contained governmental publications, and extra care was taken to corroborate evidence found here with other sources. With triangulation, interviews and other media again helped to fill in the gaps and minimize weaknesses of this method (Johnson and Onwuegbuzie, 2004: 15).

Book structure and outline

In order to present the argument in a systematic manner, this book is laid out in six chapters. The following chapter, Chapter 2, lays the foundations for linking the regional oil palm industry to transboundary haze. The first section provides a general introduction to oil palm, noting its efficiency as a crop, palm oil's versatility as a source of food, biofuel and for industrial uses, and the ever-increasing demand for palm oil worldwide. The second section focuses on Southeast Asia as the major producing region for palm oil in the world. It discusses the regional trend of state-led development that relies on agribusiness as a major sector, and how oil palm developed into an important crop for the region. The section then focuses on how economic regionalism of the oil palm sector brought many Malaysian and Singaporean plantation companies into Indonesia, making Indonesia the world's largest producer of palm oil today, with ambitions for continued dominance in the sector. The final section of this chapter then establishes the link between commercial oil palm plantations in Indonesia and the region's transboundary haze. It argues that the continued expansion of commercial plantations into degraded lands and peatlands in Indonesia, mainly using fire, is a major cause of the smoke that travels across national boundaries as haze. Overall, this chapter shows that economic motivations have been a major driver of transboundary haze. In the interest of cost efficiency, Indonesian, Malaysian and Singaporean companies have used, and continue to use, fire as a cheap way to open up new plantation land to meet worldwide demand for palm oil. This chapter raises an important point on the state-led nature of agribusiness development in the region and signals the trend of vested interests existing between the state and agribusiness sectors.

A better understanding of investment trends and motivations within the Indonesian oil palm plantations sector is pertinent in the face of recent increased evidence of the link between illegal peat and forest fires and commercial oil palm plantations (Sawit Watch, 2007: 1; WALHI *et al.*, 2009). Hence, Chapters 3 and 4 respectively address two drivers of economic regionalization in the Southeast Asian context, and show that each of them has also been a driver of transboundary haze. The third chapter focuses on the first driver: the role of the state as a facilitator of economic regionalization of the oil palm sector in the region. The first section of the chapter introduces the concept of economic regionalization as used in the literature, noting that while economic regionalization in the Southeast Asian context has indeed been market driven, the state has played an important role as facilitator of the process. The subsequent section addresses the regionalization process from the Indonesian, Malaysian and Singaporean perspectives respectively, focusing on government facilitation of the process that resulted in many Malaysian and Singaporean GLCs and well-connected plantation firms establishing plantations in Indonesia. This section highlights how many

Malaysian and Singaporean government elites have vested interests in these firms. Section three of this chapter notes that vested interests of home governments in these firms further encourage home state involvement and facilitation to ensure the well-being of these plantation firms in the regionalization process. This explains why Malaysian and Singaporean governments have been observed using their influence and resources to defend their firms in Indonesia when faced with accusations of open-burning misconduct that threatened the continued profitability of their firms in Indonesia.

Chapter 4 addresses the second driver of economic regionalization: the role of cultural familiarity, particularly the culture of patronage that is common among many countries in Southeast Asia. The similarities of the patronage culture between Indonesia, Malaysia and Singapore have enabled even deeper regional integration of the sector, where Malaysian and Singaporean companies were able to effectively insert themselves into local patronage networks (Interviewee I49, 2011), compared to other foreign firms operating in Indonesia. It further argues that with the protection of these networks, plantation companies (as 'clients' of these patrons within the government) have been able to conduct themselves on the ground in Indonesia with impunity. The first section of this chapter offers a brief review of the patronage literature. The second section explores patronage linkages that exist between local, Malaysian and Singaporean plantation companies and Indonesian government elites. The third and fourth sections discuss how the atmosphere of patronage has encouraged policy paralysis in terms of land use and fire management in Indonesia, where the influence of patrons have rendered related policies either weak, unenforced or both. This has been instrumental in enabling companies to develop fire-prone peatlands, and to use fire as a cost-effective way to clear land, with little fear of prosecution. This cost-cutting has enabled extraordinarily high profits in the sector year after year, with plantations delivering an average of 47 per cent earnings growth in 2011 (Di, 2011: 1). This chapter points out that patronage politics has not only been instrumental in driving the regionalization of the sector, but also has been an important driver of transboundary haze.

Chapter 5 argues that the regionalism of haze mitigation through ASEAN initiatives have failed to curb haze because of the undue influence of patronage networks in the oil palm plantation sector. The ASEAN model of regionalism that emphasizes national sovereignty and self-determination (Interviewee A7, 2010; Narine, 1998: 555; Smith, 2004: 418; Zainal Abidin [M38], 2010) has allowed member states to shape collective mitigation initiatives at the ASEAN level in accordance with the interests of political and economic elites. This chapter therefore proposes that the states involved have chosen to adhere to the ASEAN Way when dealing with the haze to preserve crucial economic interests. Hence, the organization's capacity to create and carry out effective policies is reduced, which has resulted in haze initiatives that protect elite corporate interests, preserve state sovereignty and deflect responsibility on the haze issue (Tan [S7], 2010; Yahaya [M13], 2010). The first section introduces the concept of political regionalism. It notes that while regionalism has been viewed in the literature as an important strategy for resolving common environmental problems (as proven by the European experience with acid rain), the ASEAN model of regionalism, with its selective use of the ASEAN Way principles by member states, has not been conducive to this. The second section reviews the ASEAN haze initiatives, arguing that states chose to adhere to the ASEAN Way principles while shaping these initiatives. As a result, these initiatives have largely been ineffective in curbing haze but effective in protecting the interests of the business elites. Special focus is given here on the influence of patronage politics on Indonesia's decision not to ratify the ATHP for more than a decade, and how Indonesia's non-ratification has seriously limited the effectiveness of this treaty during this time. The third section then focuses on the Malaysian and Singaporean Adopt-A-District programmes in Indonesia, as part of the ASEAN initiatives. These programmes show again the influence of patronage politics; initiatives on the ground rarely involve commercial plantations and do not scrutinize their activities. As a whole, this chapter shows that ASEAN is not the appropriate forum to effectively carry out haze mitigation because the ASEAN style of regionalism allows for undue influence into the shaping and implementation of policies from the region's political and economic elites.

The final chapter provides a conclusion and summary of the arguments of this book. In short, the persistence of haze can be explained by a combination of intense economic regionalization in Southeast Asia's oil palm plantation sector (the source) and the failure of environmental regionalism at the ASEAN level (the solution), with vested interests and patronage politics playing important roles in both instances. The intense economic regionalization of the Southeast Asian oil palm plantation sector and the state-driven and market-led political regionalism at the ASEAN level have resulted in outcomes that protect the interests of big businesses, while allowing transboundary haze to persist. This explains why the governments of Indonesia, Malaysia and Singapore have thus far failed to effectively address the regional haze problem despite clear evidence of the culpability of the Indonesian oil palm plantation sector. In a classic manifestation of the free-rider problem, the importance of the oil palm industry to the Indonesian, Malaysian and Singaporean economies, coupled with the vested interests that have been cultivated among elites in the sector, takes priority over the well-being of Indonesian, Malaysian and Singaporean societies, which continue to suffer annually as a result of haze.

Notes

1 A reading below 100 is moderate; a reading of 100–200 is unhealthy; 200–300 is considered very unhealthy. At 300–400, this is considered hazardous and the population is advised to stop all outdoor activities.

2 The Malaysia Air Quality Index is a simulated version of the Uniform International Pollutant Index (UNIPEX) and a linearized version of the United States PSI. It was developed in 1994 to keep the public informed of daily air quality during the haze. An index of 0–50 is good, 51–100 moderate, 101–199 unhealthy and 200–299 very unhealthy (ASEAN Secretariat, 1995). An index of above 300 in considered

hazardous to human health and other living things (Jabatan Alam Sekitar, 1994). The index was later replaced with the Air Pollutant Index. An emergency would be declared when the Air Pollutant Index hits 500. Schools would be closed when the Air Pollutant Index registers 400.

3 See Doner (1997) for an interesting case study of how Japan, through a range of its institutions, helped to solve coordination problems among East Asian states that arose with rampant economic regionalization in the region during the mid-1980s.

4 'Concessions' are areas allocated by a government for industrial-scale plantations (ArcGIS, 2014). This does not include smallholder landholdings.

5 Industry 'regulations' also exist, in the form of the Roundtable for Sustainable Palm Oil (RSPO). The RSPO website describes the RSPO as an internationally recognized and most trusted eco-labelling system for the palm oil industry, which certifies that the palm oil used in a particular product is produced in a sustainable manner (RSPO, 2009). RSPO certification criteria do include zero-burning requirements. This thesis however does not include the RSPO in its discussions as RSPO is a voluntary labeling system without universal membership, in contrast with the laws and policies discussed in this book that are applicable to all oil palm companies operating in Indonesia.

6 Approval obtained on 3 February 2010, with Ref. No. 12-2009/12389.

References

Adnan, H. 2013. Helping to clear the haze Eight Malaysian-owned firms under Indonesian probe. *The Star*, 25 June 2013.

Aggarwal, V.K. and Chow, J.T. 2010. The perils of consensus: How ASEAN's meta-regime undermines economic and environmental cooperation. *Review of International Political Economy,* 17, 262–290.

Agriculture Corner 2012. *Top Ten Palm Oil Producers 2012.* Available: www.agricorner.com/top-ten-palm-oil-producers-2012/ [accessed 1 August 2014].

Aiken, S.R. 2004. Runaway fires, smoke-haze pollution, and unnnatural disasters in Indonesia. *Geographical Review,* 94, 55.

Amy, D.J. 1983. Environmental Mediation: An Alternative Approach to Policy Stalemates. *Policy Sciences,* 15, 345–365.

Anderson, T. 2004. Some thoughts on method in political economy. *Journal on Australian Political Economy,* 54, 135–145.

Antara Magazine 2009. ASEAN Secretariat holds workshop on climate change. *Antara.* Jakarta: Financial Times Information Limited.

Applegate, G., Smith, R., Fox, J.J., Mitchell, A., Packham, D., Tapper, N. and Baines, G. 2002. Forest fires in Indonesia: Impacts and Solutions. *In:* Colfer, C. J. and Resosudarmo, I.A.P. (eds) *Which Way Forward? People, forests and policymaking in Indonesia.* Singapore: Institute of Southeast Asian Studies.

Arcgis 2014. *GFW Oil Palm Concessions.* Available: www.arcgis.com/home/item.html?id=b367054157894fac86d136284bb72f9b [accessed 5 August 2014].

Asean Secretariat 1995. *ASEAN Meeting on the Management of Transboundary Pollution.* Kuala Lumpur.

Asean Secretariat 2008. Information on Fire and Haze. *In:* DIVISION, E. (ed.) *HazeOnline.* Jakarta: ASEAN Secretariat.

Batra, G.S. 2013. Environment Management and Environmental Disclosures: A Comparison of Corporate Practices Across Malaysia, Singapore and India. *South Asian Journal of Management,* 20, 62–96.

BBC 1999. World: Asia-Pacific Row over Malaysian haze. BBC News, 6 August 1999.

Beeson, M. 2007. *Regionalism and Globalization in East Asia: Politics, Security and Economic Development,* New York, Palgrave.

Bernama. 2005. Haze worsens, two areas declared emergency. *Bernama Daily Malaysian News,* 11 August 2005.

Bramble, B.J. 1987. The Debt Crisis: The Opportunities. *Ecologist,* 17: 193.

Breslin, S. and Higgott, R. 2003. Nre regionalism(s) in the global political economy. Conceptual understanding in historical perspective. *Asia Europe Journal,* 1, 167–182.

Butler, R.A., Lian, P.K. and Ghazoul, J. 2009. REDD in the red: Palm oil could undermine carbon payment scheme. *Conservations Letters,* 2, 67–73.

Caroko, W., Komarudin, H., Obidzinski, K. and Gunarso, P. 2011. Policy and institutional frameworks for the development of palm oil-based biodiesel in Indonesia. Working Paper, 2011 Jakarta. Center for International Forestry Research.

Casson, A. 2002. The political economy of Indonesia's oil palm sector. *In:* Colfer, C.J. and Resosudarmo, I.A.P. (eds) *Which Way Forward? People, forests and policymaking in Indonesia.* Singapore: Institute of South East Asian Studies.

Chang, L.L. and Rajan, R.S. 2001. Regional Versus Multilateral Solutions to Transboundary Environmental Problems: Insights from the Southeast Asian Haze. *Transboundary Environmental Problems in Asia*, 655–670.

Channel Newsasia 2014. Indonesia fires spark Singapore, Malaysia haze warning. Channel NewsAsia, 25 June 2014.

Colfer, C.J.P. 2002. Ten propositions to explain Kalimantan's fires. *In:* Colfer, C.J. and Resosudarmo, I.A.P. (eds) *Which Way Forward? People, forests and policymaking in Indonesia.* Singapore: Institute of Southeast Asian Studies.

Cooke, F.M. 2006. Recent developments and conservation interventions in Borneo. *In:* Cooke, F.M. (ed.) *State, Communities and Forests in Contemporary Borneo.* Canberra: The Australian National University E Press.

Cotton, J. 1999. The 'haze' over Southeast Asia: Challenging the ASEAN mode of regional engagement. *Pacific Affairs,* 72, 331–351.

Crouch, M. and Mckenzie, H. 2009. The Logic of Small Samples in Interview-Based Qualitative Research. *Social Science Information,* 45.

Danielsen, F., Beukema, H., Burgess, N.D., Parish, F., Bruhl, C., Donald, P.F., Murdiyarso, D., Phalan, B., Reijnders, L., Struebig, M. and Fitzherbert, E.B. 2008. Biofuel Plantations on Forested Lands: Double Jeopardy for Biodiversity and Climate. *Conservation Biology*, 1–19.

Dauvergne, P. 1994. The politics of deforestation in Indonesia. *Pacific Affairs,* 66, 497–518.

Dauvergne, P. 1997. *Shadows in the Forest: Japan and the politics of timber in Southeast Asia,* Cambridge, The MIT Press.

Dauvergne, P. 1998. The political economy of Indonesia's 1997 forest fires. *Australian Journal of International Affairs,* 52, 13–17.

Dauvergne, P.J.M. 1995. Shadows in the forest: Japan and the politics of timber in Southeast Asia. Doctor of Philosophy thesis, University of British Columbia.

Dennis, R. 1999. *A review of fire projects in Indonesia.* Bogor: Center for International Forestry Research.

Di, S. 2011. Tread Cautiously. *Indo Plantations Sector Outlook.* Jakarta: CLSA Asia Pacific Markets.

Djuweng, S. and Petebang, E. 1997. Choking haze shows nature can still teach us lessons. *Jakarta Post*, 28 September 1997.

Doner, R.F. 1997. Japan in East Asia: Institutions and Regional Leadership. *In:* Katzenstein, P.J. and Shiraishi, T. (eds) *Network Power: Japan and Asia.* Ithaca: Cornell University Press.

Down to Earth 2007. Oil Palm Plantation Expansion in Indonesia. Down to Earth: International Campaign for Ecological Justice in Indonesia.

Eaton, P. and Radojevic, R. 2001. *Forest Fires and Regional Haze in Southeast Asia,* New York, Nova Science Publishers, Inc.

Elliott, L. 2003. ASEAN and environmental cooperation: norms, interests and identity. *The Pacific Review,* 16, 29–52.

Fairhurst, T. and Mclaughlin, D. 2009. Sustainable oil palm development in degraded land in Kalimantan. Kent: World Wildlife Fund.

Feng, Z. 2011. Haze returns: NEA says it could last through weekend. *The Straits Times,* 30 September 2011.

Fernandez, W. 1997. S'pore playing active role in fighting haze. *The Straits Times,* 29 September 1997.

Foong, P.Y. 1991. 10pc rise in haze-linked health woes. *The Star,* 12 October 1991.

Gellert, P.K. 1998. A brief history and analysis of Indonesia's forest fire crisis. *Indonesia,* 65.

Ghani [S6], A. 17 May 2010. *RE: former Straits Times Press Reporter.*

Giddings, L.S. and Grant, B.M. 2007. A Trojan Horse for Positivism? A critique of Moxed Methods Research. *Advances in Nursing Science,* 30.

Gill, P., Stewart, K., Treasure, E. and Chadwick, B. 2008. Methods of data collection in qualitative research: Interviews and focus groups. *British Dental Journal,* 204.

Glassman, J. and Samatar, A.I. 1997. Development grography and the third-world state. *Progress in Human Geography,* 21, 164–198.

Greenpeace 2007. *How the Palm Oil Industry is Cooking the Climate.* Jakarta: Greenpeace.

Gunawan, A. 2002a. Haze blamed for five deaths in horror crash. *Jakarta Post,* 21 March 2002.

Gunawan, A. 2002b. Haze forces airlines to cancel flights to N. Sumatra. *Jakarta Post,* 16 March 2002.

Gusterson, H. 2008. Ethnographic Research. *In:* Klotz, A. and Prakash, D. (eds) *Qualitative Methods in International Relations.* New York: Palgrave Macmillan.

Hafild, E. 1997. Late response to forest fires. *Jakarta Post,* 7 October 1997.

Hameiri, S. and Jones, L. 2013. The politics and governance of non-traditional security. *International Studies Quarterly,* 57, 462–473.

Harrison, M.E., Page, S.E. and Limin, S.H. 2009. The global impact of Indonesian forest fires. *Biologist,* 56.

Hiratsuka, D. 2006. *Outward FDI from an Intraregional FDI in ASEAN: Trands and Drivers.* Dicsussion Paper. Institute of Developing Economies, 1–16.

Hon, P.M.L. 1999. Singapore. *In:* Glover, D. and Jessup, T. (eds) *Indonesia's Fires and Haze: The Cost of Catastrophe.* Singapore: Institute of Southeast Asian Studies.

Houck, D.W. 2006. On or About June 1988. *Rhetoric and Public Affairs,* 9.

Hunt, C. 2010. The costs of reducing deforestation in Indonesia. *Bulletin of Indonesian Economic Studies,* 46, 187–192.

Hurrell, A. 1995. Explaining the resurgence of regionalism in world politics. *Review of International Studies,* 21, 331–358.

Indexmundi 2014. *Indonesia Palm Oil Production by Year.* IndexMundi.

Interviewee A7. 1 July 2010. *RE: formerly of ASEAN Environment Division.*

Interviewee I7 and Interviewee I8. 28 June 2010. *RE: Ministry of Environment*
Interviewee I49. 1 December 2011. *RE: Leuser Foundation.*
Interviewee M24 and Interviewee M25. 12 April 2010. *RE: a major Malaysian plantation corporation.*
Interviewee M28. 14 April 2010. *RE: TH Plantations.*
Interviewee M32. 19 April 2010. *RE: formerly of Department of Environment.*
Interviewee S4 and Interviewee S5. 14 May 2010. *RE: National Environment Agency.*
Interviewee S14 and Interviewee S15. 19 May 2010. *RE: Ministry of Environment and Water Resources.*
Interviewee S21. 26 May 2010. *RE: former Environmental Reporter, Straits Times Press.*
Jabatan Alam Sekitar 1994. *Facts and Figures of Haze Episode in Malaysia*. Kuala Lumpur: Kementerian Sains, Teknologi dan Alam Sekitar.
Jakarta Post 1987. Indonesia's environment. *Jakarta Post*, 24 September 1987.
Jakarta Post 1997a. Indonesia reiterates thick haze apology. *Jakarta Post*, 6 October 1997.
Jakarta Post 1997b. Soeharto apologises to ASEAN members for haze. *Jakarta Post*, 17 September 1997.
Jakarta Post 1997c. Twelve die of haze-related infections. *Jakarta Post*, 7 November 1997.
Jakarta Post 1997d. WWF puts costs of 1997 haze for RI at $1 billion. *Jakarta Post*, 26 February 1998.
Jakarta Post 1999a. Haze covers the country's blue skies again. *Jakarta Post*, 24 August 1999.
Jakarta Post 1999b. Haze puts Riau in state of emergency. *Jakarta Post*, 5 August 1999.
Jakarta Post 2004. Haze thickens in Sumatra and Kalimantan, affects Malaysia. *Jakarta Post*, 16 October 2004.
Jakarta Post 2006a. Choking haze continues billowing across region. *Jakarta Post*, 6 October 2006.
Jakarta Post 2006b. Smothering Kalimantan waits for rains. *Jakarta Post*, 2 November 2006.
Jakarta Post 2011. Govt predicts fewer forest fires this year, critics not convinced. *Jakarta Post*, 5 August 2011.
Jakarta Post 2014. RI ratifies haze treaty. *Jakarta Post*, 17 September 2014.
Johnson, R.B. and Onwuegbuzie, A.J. 2004. Mixed methods research: A research paradigm whose time has come. *Educational Researcher*, 33.
Jones, D.S. 2006. ASEAN and transboundary haze pollution in Southeast Asia. *Asia Europa Journal*, 4.
Kamaruddin [M26], H. 13 April 2010. *RE: Lecturer, Faculty of Law, UKM.*
Katzenstein, P.J. 1997. Introduction: Asian regionalism in comparative perspective. *In:* Katzenstein, P.J. and Shiraishi, T. (eds) *Network Power: Japan and Asia.* Ithaca: Cornell University Press.
Keraf [I35], S. 28 July 2010. *RE: former Minister of the Environment and Vice Chairman of Commission 7 (Environment, Energy and Research and Development), Parliament of Indonesia.*
Khoo, N. 2004. Deconstructing the ASEAN security community: a review essay. *International Relations of the Asia Pacific*, 4, 35.
Kim, M. 2011. Theorizing ASEAN Integration. *Asian Perspectives*, 35, 407–435.
Kivimaki, T. 2001. The long peace of ASEAN. *Journal of Peace Studies*, 38.
King, G., Koeohane, R.O. and Verba, S. 2004. The importance of research design. *In:* Brady, H.E. and Collier, D. (eds) *Rethinking Social Inquiry: Diverse Tools, Shared Standards.* Oxford: Rowman & Littlefield Publishers, Inc.

Knutsen, C.H. 2013. Democracy, State Capacity, and Economic Growth. *World Development,* 43, 1–18.

Koh, K.L. 2008. A breakthrough in solving the Indonesian haze? *In:* Hart, S. (ed.) *Shared Resources: Issues of Governance.* Gland, Switzerland: International Union for the Conservation of Nature and Natural Resources.

Koh, K.L. and Robinson, N.A. 2002. Regional environmental governance: Examining the Association of South East Asian Nations (ASEAN) model. *In:* Esty, D.C. and Ivanova, M.H. (eds) *Global Environmental Governance: Options and Opportunities.* Yale: Yale Center for Environmental Law and Policy.

Koh, L.P. and Wilcove, D.S. 2007. Cashing in palm oil for conservation. *Nature,* 448, 993–994.

Lande, C.H. 1983. Political clientelism in political studies: Retrospect and prospects. *International Political Science Review,* 4, 435–454.

Law [M29], H.D. 15 April 2010. *RE: former Minister, Ministry of Natural Resources and Environment.*

Lee, Y.P. and Chan, L.L. 2009. The haze is back. *The Star*, 30 May 2009.

Letchumanan [A6], R. 25 June 2010 2010. *RE: Head, ASEAN Environment Division.*

Lew [M6], S. and Interviewee M7. 18 March 2010. *RE: Peatland Programme, Global Environment Center.*

Louis, K.S. 1982. Multisite/multimethod studies: An introduction. *The American Behavioral Scientist,* 26.

Marinova, N. 1999. Indonesia's fiery crises. *Journal of Environment and Development,* 8, 70–81.

Maruli, A. 2011. Half of RI's oil palm plantations foreign-owned. *Antara Magazine.* Jakarta: Financial Times Information Limited.

Mathew [M8], K. G. 20 March 2010. *RE: former Plantation Manager, Sime Darby Plantation.*

Mayer, J. 2006. Transboundary perspectives on managing Indonesia's fires. *The Journal of Environment and Development,* 15, 202–233.

McCarthy, J.F. 2002. Power and interest on Sumatra's rainforest frontier: Clientelist coalitions, illegal logging and conservation in the Alas Valley. *Journal of Southeast Asian Studies,* 33, 77–106.

McLellan, J. 2001. From denial to debate. And back again! Malaysian press coverage of the air pollution and 'haze' episodes, July 1997–July 1999. *In:* Eaton, P.A.R. M. (ed.) *Forest Fires and Haze in Southeast Asia.* New York: Nova Science Publishers.

Mohd Shahwahid, H.O. and Othman, J. 1999. Malaysia. *In:* Glover, D. and Jessup, T. (eds) *Indonesia's Fires and Haze: The Cost of Catastrophe.* Singapore: Institue of Southeast Asian Studies.

Murray, P. 2010. The European Union as an integration entrepreneur in East Asia: Yardstick or cautionary tale? Australian Political Studies Association Conference, 27–29 September. Melbourne.

Nagulendran [M34], K. and Interviewee M35. 20 April 2010. *RE: Deputy Under Secretary, Ministry of Natural Resources and Environment and officer.*

Narine, S. 1998. ASEAN and the management of regional security. *Pacific Affairs,* 71, 195.

Nguitragool, P. 2011. Negotiating the Haze Treaty. *Asian Survey,* 51, 356–378.

Othman, J. 2003. Linking agricultural trade, land demand and environmental externalities: Case of oil palm in South East Asia. *ASEAN Economic Bulletin,* 20, 244–55.

Palmoilhq. 2009. *Indonesia still on the radar for Malaysian palm oil planters.* Cairns.

Available: www.palmoilhq.com/PalmOilNews/indonesia-still-on-the-radar-for-malaysian-palm-oil-planters/ [accessed 10 October 2014].

Pasong, S. and Lebel, L. 2000. Political transformation and the environment in southeast Asia. *Environment,* 42, 8.

Payne, A. 2004. Rethinking development inside international political economy. *In:* Payne, A. (ed.) *The New Regional Politics of Development.* Hampshire: Palgrave Macmillan.

Pempel, T. J. 2005. Introduction: Emerging webs of regional connectedness. *In:* Pempel, T.J. (ed.) *Remapping East Asia: The construction of a region.* Ithaca: Cornell University Press.

Perry, M. and Teng, T.S. 1999. An overview of trends related to environmental reporting in Singapore. *Environmental Management and Health,* 10, 310–320.

Pezalla, A.E. 2012. Researching the researcher-as-instrument: an exercise in interviewer self-reflexivity. *Qualitative Research,* 12, 165–185.

Quah, E. and Johnston, D. 2001. Forest fires and environmental haze in Southeast Asia: Using the 'stakeholder' approach to assign costs and responsibilities. *Journal of Environmental Management,* 63, 181–191.

Richardson, C.L. 2010. *Deforestation due to palm oil plantations in Indonesia. Towards the Sustainable Production of Palm Oil,* 2010 Australia.

RSPO 2009. *About RSPO.* Zurich. Available: www.rspo.org [accessed 17 August 2014].

Ruitenbeek, J. 1999. Indonesia. *In:* Glover, D. and Jessup, T. (eds) *Indonesia's Fires and Haze: The Cost of Catastrophe.* Singapore: Institute of Southeast Asian Studies.

Rukmantara [I45], A. 14 November 2011 2011. *RE: Former environmental journalist, Jakarta Post.*

Saharjo, B. H. 1999. The role of human activities in Indonesian forest fire problems. *In:* Suhartoyo, H. and Toma, T. (eds) *Impacts of Fire and Human Activities on Forest Ecosystems in the Tropics.* Samarinda, Indonesia. Tropical Forest Research Center, Mulawarman University.

Samsul, Firman, Muhib, Syarwani, Helmi, Nurdin and Zakaria 2007. The Golden Crop? Palm oil in post-tsunami Aceh. Aceh: Eye on Aceh.

Sawit Watch 2007. Palm oil for biofuels increases social conflicts and undermines land reform in Indonesia. *Open letter to the European Parliament, the European Commission, the goverments and citizens of the European Union.* Bogor: Sawit Watch.

Severino, R.C. 2006. *Southeast Asia in Search of an ASEAN Community: Insights from the former ASEAN Secretary-General,* Singapore, ISEAS.

Severino, R.F. 1999. Fighting the Haze: A Regional and Global Responsibility. *Final Regional Workshop of the Regional Technical Assistance Project on Strengthening ASEAN's Capacity to Prevent and Mitigate Transboundary Atmospheric Pollution.* Jakarta: ASEAN Secretariat.

Sim, A.B. 2006. Internationalization strategies of emerging Asian MNEs: Case study evidence on Singaporean and Malaysian firms. *Asia Pacific Business Review,* 12, 487–505.

Simamora, A.P. and Adamrah, M. 2010. Govt says haze from RI, blames traditional farmers. *Jakarta Post,* 23 October 2010.

Singapore Government News 2010. Number of haze affected patients on the rise in Singapore. *Singapore Government News,* 22 October 2010.

Skocpol, T. 1985. Bringing the state back in. *In:* Evans, P.B., Rueschemayer, D. and Skocpol, T. (eds) *Bringing the state back in.* Cambridge: Cambridge University Press.

Smith, A.L. 2004. ASEAN's Ninth Summit: Solidifying Regional Cohesion, Advancing External Linkages. *Contemporary Southeast Asia,* 26, 416.

Sommer, B. 2006. *Types of Samples*. California: UC Davis. Available: http://psychology.ucdavis.edu/sommerb/sommerdemo/sampling/types.htm [accessed 9 July 2014].
Stokes, D. and Bergin, S. 2006. Methodology or 'methodolatry'? An evaluation of focus group and depth interviews. *Qualitative Market Research,* 9.
Stone, R. 2007. Can palm oil plantations come clean? *Science,* 317, 1491.
Straits Times 1998. President unhappy with Singapore, says AWSJ. *The Straits Times*, 5 August.
Suwarsono, Roswiniarti, O., Noviar, H., Albar, I., Phonekeo, C.J.S.B.V. and Song, Y. 2007. *Influence of climate variation and vegetation greenness on fire occurence: A case study in Central Kalimantan province.* Jakarta: Indonesian National Institute of Aeronautics and Space and Geoinformatics Center, Asian Institute of Technology.
Syarif [I2], L.M. 24 June 2010 2010. *RE: Chief, Cluster of Security and Justice Governance, Kemitraan Partnership.*
Tambulasi, R.I.C. 2010. Local Government Without Governance: A New Institutional Perspective of Local Governance Policy Paralysis in Malawi. *Public Policy and Administration,* 26, 333–352.
Tan [S7], A.K. J. 17 May 2010. *RE: Vice Dean, Faculty of Law, NUS.*
Tan, B. 2005. The Norms that Weren't: ASEAN's Shortcomings in Dealing with Transboundary Air Pollution. *International Environmental Politics,* Spring 2005.
Tan, K.T., Lee, K.T., Mohamed, A.R. and Bhatia, S. 2009. Palm oil: Addressing issues and towards sustainable development. *Renewable and Sustainable Energy Reviews,* 13, 420–427.
Tawie, S. 1997. Sarawak lost RM1 billion during 10-day emergency. *New Straits Times*, 6 October 1997.
Tay, S.S.C. 2002. Fires and Haze in Southeast Asia. *In:* Noda, P.J. (ed.) *Cross-Sectoral Partnerships in Enhancing Human Security.* Tokyo: Japan Center for International Exchange.
Terjesen, S. and Elam, A. 2009. Transnational entrepreneurs' venture internationalization strategies: A practice theory approach. *Entrepreneurship Theory and Practice,* 1093–1116.
Then, S. 2009. Asean braces for the haze … yet again. *The Star*, 29 April 2009.
Then, S., Wong, J. and Chiew, H. 2009. Thick haze in many parts of Sarawak. *The Star*, 7 August 2009.
Thompson, H. 2001. Crisis in Indonesia: Forests, fires and finances. *Electronic Green Journal,* 1, 1–19.
Ting, M.M. 2011. Organizational Capacity. *The Journal of Law, Economics and Organization,* 27, 245–271.
Today 2006. $79m up in smoke for S'pore; Economists estimate losses in tourism, productivity, health costs since start of haze. *Today*, 13 October 2006.
Udiansyah [I15]. 28 July 2010. *RE: Faculty of Forestry, Lambung Mangkurat University.*
Van Gelder, J.W. 2004. *Greasy palms: European buyers of Indonesian palm oil.* Castricum: Friends of the Earth.
Varma, A. 2003. The economics of slash and burn: A case study of the 1997–1998 Indonesian forest fires. *Ecological Economics,* 46, 159–171.
WALHI and Sawit Watch 2009. Memorandum: Issues Surrounding Malaysia Palm Oil Investments and Plantation Operations in Indonesian Palm Oil Industry. WALHI and Sawit Watch.

WALHI, Sawit Watch and CELCOR 2009. Malaysian Palm Oil and Logging Investments and Operations. *Factsheet.* WALHI, Sawit Watch and CELCOR.
Widianarko, B. 2009. *Democratization, Decentralisation and Environmental Conservation in Indonesia.* Asia-pacific NGO Environmental Conference, 2009 Kyoto.
Winifred, A. and N.G.B. 2014. Haze sends air quality to unhealthy levels. *Malay Mail,* 25 June 2014.
Woo, S.B. 2013. Haze meeting: Govts agree to share concession maps. *Today,* 18 July 2013.
Wyatt-Walter, A. 1995. Regionalism, globalization, and world economic order. *In:* Fawcett, L. and Hurrell, A. (eds) *Regionalism in World Politics: Regional Organization and International Oder.* Oxford: Oxford University Press.
Yahaya [M13], N. 26 March 2010. *RE: former Deputy Secretary General, Ministry of Natural Resources and Environment.*
Yahaya, N. 2000. Transboundary Air Pollution: Haze Pollution in Southeast Asia and its Significance. *Journal of Diplomacy and Foreign Relations,* 2, 41–50.
Yoshimatsu, H. 2006. Collective Action Problems and Regional Integration in ASEAN. *Contemporary Southeast Asia,* 28, 115.
Zainal Abidin [M38], A. 29 April 2010. *RE: Deputy Director, Pusat Tenaga Malaysia.*

2 The Indonesian oil palm sector and haze[1]

This chapter lays the foundations for linking the regional oil palm industry to transboundary haze. It is divided into three sections. The first section provides a general introduction to oil palm, noting its efficiency as a crop, its versatility as a source of food, biofuel and its industrial uses, and the ever-increasing demand for palm oil worldwide. The second section focuses on Southeast Asia as the major producing region for palm oil in the world. It discusses the regional trend of state-led development that relies on agribusiness as a major sector, and how oil palm came to be such an important crop for the region. The section then focuses on how economic regionalism of the oil palm sector brought many Malaysian and Singaporean plantation companies into Indonesia, making Indonesia the world's largest producer of palm oil today, with ambitions for continued dominance in the sector. The final section of this chapter then establishes the link between commercial oil palm plantations in Indonesia and the region's transboundary haze. It points out that the continued expansion of commercial plantations into degraded lands and peatlands in Indonesia, mainly using fire, is a major cause of the smoke that travels across national boundaries as haze.

Overall, this chapter notes that economic motivations have been a major driver of transboundary haze. In the interests of cost efficiency, Indonesian, Malaysian and Singaporean companies have used, and continue to use, fire as a cheap way to open up new plantation land to meet worldwide demand for palm oil. This chapter raises an important point on the state-led nature of agribusiness development in the region, and signals the trend of vested interests existing between the state and agribusiness sectors. The role of the state discussed here lays the foundation for the arguments presented in following chapters of this book, which note that state-facilitated economic regionalization, motivated by patronage politics, is an important driver of haze (presented in Chapters 3 and 4), while state-driven political regionalism has caused the continued failure of ASEAN haze mitigation initiatives (Chapter 5).

Global demand for palm oil

Palm oil is an important global source of food and biofuel, and also has various industrial uses. Palm oil consumption and use has a recorded history of 5,000 years (Malaysian Palm Oil Council, 2006: 5). From its West African origins, the oil palm tree (*Elaeis guineensis*) has flourished throughout the tropics and is now grown in at least 16 countries around the world (Wahid *et al.*, 2004: 1–8). Of 13 major vegetable oils produced in the world, palm oil holds the largest single share of the market, accounting for around 35 per cent of world production (see Figure 2.1) (Di, 2011b: 3; GreenPalm, 2014; Richardson, 2010: 8).

The oil palm is a highly efficient crop, which is a factor in its attractiveness (Fairhurst and McLaughlin, 2009: 3–4; Richardson, 2010: 8). Among the major vegetable oils, palm oil has the lowest production cost (Fairhurst and McLaughlin, 2009: 3–4; Samsul *et al.*, 2007: 5). The oil palm needs a smaller land area to produce a target quantity of oil. For example, oil palm occupies only 9.2 million hectares of agricultural land to produce its share of global oils and fats output (Stone, 2007: 1491). For a similar output, soybean production would require almost ten times the production area (Stone, 2007: 1491).

Once harvested, the fleshy part of the fruit is processed into crude palm oil (CPO), while the oil contained in the nut is processed into palm kernel oil (PKO). The processing of the CPO produces palm stearin and palm olein (Samsul *et al.*, 2007: 5). The stearin, which is solid at room temperature, is used mainly for industrial purposes (cosmetics, soaps, detergents, candles, lubricating oils etc.). The liquid olein is used exclusively in foodstuffs (cooking oil, margarines, creams and in cakes and pastries) (Koh and Wilcove, 2007: 993; Samsul *et al.*, 2007: 5). Palm oil today is an important food source and a major source of lipids for a large amount of the world's population (Wahid *et al.*, 2004: 1–8).

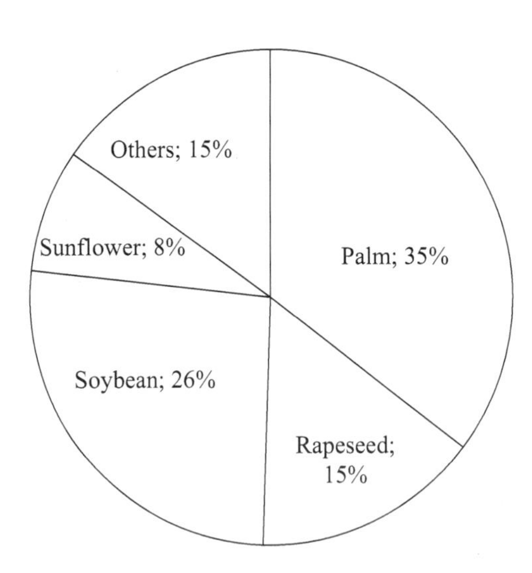

Figure 2.1 Market share of vegetable oils, 2013

Source: Adapted from Oil World Database, 2014 and cited in GreenPalm, 2014

Palm oil's industrial and edible versatility has ensured increasing demand for palm oil-derived products worldwide, particularly in emerging economies such as China, India, Pakistan and the Middle East (Butler *et al.*, 2009: 68). Today, palm oil is the most traded oil in the global oils and fats market (Malaysian Palm Oil Council, 2006: 7). China imports around 20 million tonnes yearly, while India imports 16.5 million tonnes and Pakistan 2.5 million tonnes (Butler *et al.*, 2009: 68). The increase in demand has been traced back to the rise in spending power in these countries and general global population growth (UOB Kay Hian, 2011b: 10).

With the world's population expected to display continued exponential growth (UOB Kay Hian, 2011b: 10), palm oil has the potential to be an even more important source of fats and vegetable oil to feed people around the globe (Fairhurst and McLaughlin, 2009: 3–4; Tan *et al.*, 2009: 421–424). Palm oil's significant price discount to soy oil (at an average of US$260 cheaper per tonne, and peaking at $495 cheaper) (Yeoh *et al.*, 2011a: 16) has further boosted its popularity, especially during the recent global financial crisis, as markets shifted to less expensive edible oils (Tan and Oetomo, 2011: 1; Yeoh *et al.*, 2011b: 1). Furthermore, there has been a steady decline in global soy bean and rapeseed production due to lower crop yields in the United States and China (Tan, 2011: 1; Yeoh *et al.*, 2011c: 7). As a result, there was a steady 10 per cent increase in demand for CPO in 2008 and 8 per cent in 2009 (Yeoh *et al.*, 2011b: 4).

A recent additional market for palm oil is biofuels (Koh and Wilcove, 2007: 993). The high petroleum prices in 2005 and 2006, and a heightened worldwide awareness on climate change, led many countries to consider biofuels as a form of renewable energy (Basiron, 2007: 291–294). Europe (especially countries such as Italy, Spain and the Netherlands) (UOB Kay Hian, 2011a: 6), Latin America (Argentina and Brazil) and the United States have particularly strong ambitions for bioenergy (Raman *et al.*, 2008: 3; Yeoh *et al.*, 2011b: 1). For example, the European Union (EU) has adopted policies that encourage the import and use of biofuels as an alternative to fossil fuels (Sawit Watch, 2007: 1). The comparatively cheaper CPO has made it an attractive biofuel for biodiesel blends and direct burning for the energy sector (UOB Kay Hian, 2011b: 4). For example, in 2011 alone, 3–4 million tonnes of palm-oil based biodiesel was channeled into alternative energy use (UOB Kay Hian, 2011b: 11), which is about 6–8 per cent of global supply (UOB Kay Hian, 2011a: 6). This trend is expected to sustain the high worldwide demand for this crop over the coming years (Koh and Wilcove, 2007: 993).

Oil palm cultivation has experienced tremendous expansion in recent years due to this overwhelming demand (Wahid *et al.*, 2004: 1–8), earning it the nickname 'green gold' (Othman, 2003: 245–255). Figure 2.2 shows that global palm oil production in 2014 reached almost 63 million metric tonnes (USDA, 2014). CPO prices have almost tripled since 2006, from $478 per tonne to a peak of $1,230 in 2011 (Tan and Oetomo, 2011: 20), despite the sharp global economic downturn in 2008. Prices continue to remain strong and stable in current years, hovering around $755 (Adnan, 2014). Analysts' projections have estimated future

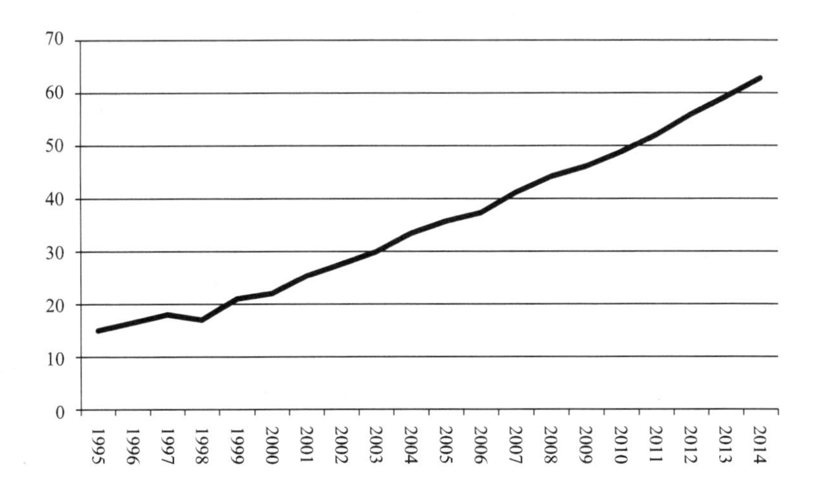

Figure 2.2 World production of palm oil, 1995–2014 (million metric tonnes)
Source: Adapted from Wilmar, 2010 and cited in USDA, 2014

CPO prices to go up to $820 by the end of the year (Adnan, 2014). The demand for CPO is forecasted to double in the next 20 to 30 years (Sandker *et al.*, 2007: 37), and world production of palm oil is expected to increase by 32 per cent to meet this demand (World Growth, 2011: 4–8). It has been estimated that an increase in the planted area of up to 12 million hectares is needed worldwide over the next 40 years to match this (Fairhurst and McLaughlin, 2009: 3–4). The next section discusses Southeast Asia as the heart of the world's oil palm industry.

Southeast Asia's 'green gold'

Throughout the decades, Southeast Asian states have viewed their abundant and fertile land as a rightful source of wealth to be exploited. In the mid-1900s, newly independent Southeast Asian states used the forestry and agricultural knowledge inherited from their colonial masters in their pursuit of nation building and economic development (Gellert, 2005: 1346). States formally recognized the forestry and agricultural sectors' role as engines for overall economic growth. For example, Southeast Asian states developed policies towards forestry and agriculture that moved beyond micro level and sector-specific concerns and took steps to ensure that the overall macro policy environment was conducive to the growth of the agricultural sector (Than, 1998: 8). With the abundance of pristine forests in the region, logging was a major growth sector during the 1960s and 1970s (Roberti, 1989: 54–56). However, the steady reduction of pristine forest areas in the region due to unsustainable clearing of these forests for timber eventually stagnated the industry (Sumiani *et al.*, 2007: 896–898), and the economic focus of Southeast Asian states began to shift to agribusiness in the 1980s (Roberti, 1989: 54–56).

By the early 1990s, agribusiness was hailed as Southeast Asia's 'next economic miracle' (Roberti, 1989: 54–56), with annual agricultural output of the region increasing an average of 3.8 per cent yearly (Roberti, 1989: 54–56). The term 'agribusiness' came into popular use since the mid-1950s and implies the shift from 'farming as a way of life' to 'farming as a business' (Sutton, 2001: 90–94). It reflects the recent major increase in corporate investment in agriculture. Today, the term is widely used to describe 'an integrated farming system which links farm operations with both upstream and downstream manufacturing and distribution' (Sutton, 2001: 90). The plantation approach within agribusiness is defined as the large-scale production of tropical crops by a uniform system of cultivation under central management (Sutton, 2001: 90–94), either through corporations working the land directly or through the setting up of a contract farming system between the core plantation management and surrounding land-owning locals for added efficiency. Consequently, an increasing amount of logged land was converted into plantation and cropland for agribusiness. As output increased in the 1990s, Southeast Asia's resource wealth and relatively cheap labour sustained production enclaves for the export of primary agricultural products (Jomo, 2003: 16), and economic strategies in the region converged around export-oriented resource exploitation (Hirsch and Warren, 1998: 6). Countries in Southeast Asia have since emerged as important producers and suppliers in the international market for agro-food (Sutton, 2001: 90–94).

As part of this agribusiness boom in the region, the oil palm, grown either on freshly cleared forests or on old croplands, has developed into one of the most economically important plantation crops in the region (Koh and Wilcove, 2007: 993). Currently, Southeast Asia is the dominant palm oil production region in the world (Wahid *et al.*, 2004: 1–8) due to the widespread suitability of the land and tropical weather for this crop (Butler *et al.*, 2009: 68). Palm oil is a major agro-industrial commodity for the economies of Indonesia and Malaysia (Othman, 2003: 245–255), which are the two largest producers of the oil in the world, contributing a combined total of more than 87 per cent of world production (see Figure 2.3) (Ong and Chai, 2011: 4). Singapore in turn is developing into a major plantation and palm oil refining investor for the region, an important trading hub for both palm oil and biodiesel, as well as a 'capital intensive, high technology, research and development based service' for the region's oil palm sector (World Growth, 2011: 4–8; Pichler, 2011: 1). In this way, Indonesia, Malaysia and Singapore are of central importance to the world's oil palm sector (Pichler, 2011: 10).

The Indonesian, Malaysian and Singaporean governments have been instrumental in the development of this sector. The rise of the oil palm plantation sector in Southeast Asia has followed similar patterns of the previous natural resource booms in these countries, like timber and rubber. First, under the legislative regimes inherited from the colonial period, land that belonged to forest-dwelling peoples and shifting farmers (known as native customary rights or NCR land) was

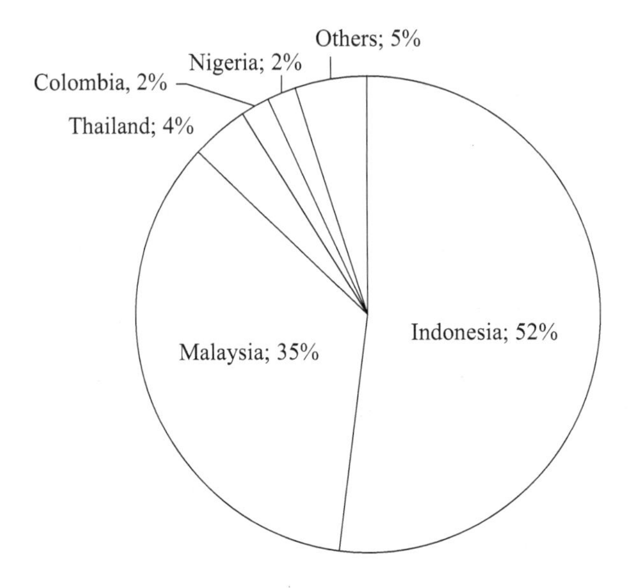

Figure 2.3 CPO production by country, 2012/2013
Source: Adapted from Agriculture Corner, 2012

not formally recognized by the governments and was thus insecure. This helped facilitate the transformation of NCR land into oil palm plantations, especially in Indonesia and Malaysia (McCarthy and Cramb, 2009: 112–114).

Second, the attitudes of the decision-making elite in countries such as Malaysia and Indonesia, that viewed natural resource exploitation as a tool to aid development, were also visible in policy narratives related to these plantations. Pristine forests or degraded land were identified as 'wasteland' or 'idle' land if it was not exploited to its full potential (McCarthy and Cramb, 2009: 112–114). Scholars note that:

> by counterpoising smallholder marginality and underdevelopment to the modernity of contemporary estate agriculture, these decision-makers provided a rationale for transforming the frontier in accordance with the agendas of politico-bureaucratic and corporate actors that favoured plantation development for personalistic economic and political purposes.
>
> (McCarthy and Cramb, 2009: 112–114)

Therefore, this political will to develop through exploitation encouraged conversion, and resulted in policies that attempt to 'rehabilitate' lands to make productive use of them (Colfer, 2002: 319–320). Thus, these government officials worked closely with plantation companies and central and local elites in the development of oil palm plantations, forming a complex web of elite patronage linkages that further drove land conversion (Masripatin *et al.*, 2009: 6; McCarthy and Cramb, 2009: 112–114; Pichler, 2011: 13), as is explored in Chapter 4 on patronage networks.

In 2008, Indonesia overtook Malaysia to become the world's biggest producer of palm oil (Bernama, 2010; Jarvis *et al.*, 2010: 2–12; McCarthy, 2010: 822–844; Reuters, 2011; World Growth, 2011: 4–13). By then, Indonesia was producing over 20 million tonnes of palm oil annually (indexMundi, 2014) and contributing to more than 50 per cent of world production (Agriculture Corner, 2012) (see Figure 2.3 for more recent data). The following subsection details the importance of the oil palm sector to Indonesia, as well as its future projections for rapid growth.

The oil palm plantation sector in Indonesia

With a total land area of 1,890,754 hectares, Indonesia extends 5,110 kilometres east to west and 1,888 kilometres north to south. Indonesia is made up of 18,110 islands that enjoy a year-round tropical climate and consistently high rainfall. Due to these geographical conditions, Indonesia is considered a highly biologically affluent country, with huge agricultural potential (Widianarko, 2009: 2). Therefore, Indonesia pinned great hopes on agribusiness to help solve a number of its developmental problems such as poverty, overpopulation and unemployment (Barber, 1998: 4–35). Development thus became the justification for natural resource exploitation, with the systematic exploitation of these natural resources providing the much needed capital for said development (Barber, 1998: 4–35). Therefore, shortly after independence, in what was called 'one of the largest land grabs in history', the Indonesian government appropriated 90 per cent of all forest land, thereby almost completely centralizing government control over forest resources and negating NCR claims (Duncan, 2007: 711–724).

The Indonesian government foresaw that by taking control of the land and developing commercial cash crops in the provinces there would be a lifting of rural incomes, which in turn should reduce the incidence of poverty and labour migration to the cities (Schwarz, 1990: 58–60). Indeed, agriculture remains the most important sector in Indonesia in terms of employment, providing jobs for more than 50 per cent of the Indonesian workforce. Outside Java, where most of the industry is concentrated, two-thirds of the population still work the land (Than, 1998: 5). Furthermore, for the Indonesian government, agribusiness was 'a substantial source of state revenue, a resource for political patronage, a safety valve for scarcities of land and resources in densely populated Java, and a vehicle … to spread … ideological, political, security, and economic objectives into the hinterlands' (Barber, 1998: 4–35).

The export of natural resources played a central role in economic growth and quickly became the largest source of foreign currency for Indonesia (Nomura, 2009: 622–627). In the mid-1960s, Indonesia was one of the world's poorest countries, with a per capita income of just $50 (Barber, 1998: 4–35). However, with this natural resource and agricultural focus, the economy displayed an average annual growth rate of 6.5 per cent from the year 1967. There was a fall of -13.6 per cent in gross domestic product (GDP) in 1998 during the Asian financial crisis (AFC), but agricultural growth remained fairly constant during this time, with only the finance, manufacturing and construction sectors experiencing serious contractions that year (Brown, 2006: 995–991). Indonesia's economic development was praised by the World Bank in 1994 as 'one of the best in the developing world' (Barber, 1998: 4–35). Currently Indonesia is a major producer of estate crops such as rubber, cocoa, coconut, coffee, tea and most importantly oil palm (Schwarz, 1990: 58–60).

There has been three distinct stages in the process of Indonesia's forest exploitation: first, the creation of a large timber and plywood industry in the 1970s and 1980s; second, the campaign to become the world's largest pulp and paper producer during the 1990s; and the third and current stage, the drastic expansion of oil palm plantations starting from the late 1990s (Gellert, 1998: 65). Large-scale oil palm plantations can be considered a relatively new industry to Indonesia, with serious expansion beginning in the late 1990s (Law [M29], 2010).

Indonesia was the entry point of the oil palm tree into the Southeast Asian region during the colonial era, when the Dutch brought over four African palms in 1848 to be planted in Buitenzorg Botanical Garden (now Bogor) in Indonesia. These palms formed the foundation for the oil palm industries in both Malaysia and Indonesia (Wahid *et al.*, 2004: 3). Indonesia's oil palm frontier initially expanded from the Dutch core commercial plantation belt in North Sumatra, beginning in 1911 (McCarthy and Cramb, 2009: 114–117; Sawit Watch, 2007: 1–2). Following a slow start, the oil palm plantations gradually extended into surrounding areas in the 1970s, especially those conveniently close to existing plantation facilities, like Riau in South Sumatra (McCarthy and Cramb, 2009: 114–117).

During the 1980s, the world price of palm oil surpassed the price of rubber (McCarthy and Zen, 2010: 155–156). The lucrative economic returns from palm oil in neighbouring Malaysia (which was an early mover for palm oil) attracted Indonesia to expand its oil palm cultivation (Basiron, 2007: 291). Consequently in Indonesia, smallholders and to a greater extent, large plantations began to shift from logging and pulp and paper production to oil palm production (McCarthy and Zen, 2010: 155–156). The outer islands of Indonesia was the target for the establishment of these new plantations, with continued expansion in Sumatra (holding around 73 per cent of plantation area), then spreading to Kalimantan, Sulawesi and West Papua (McCarthy and Cramb, 2009: 114–117).

CPO was considered to be a strategic commodity for Indonesia (Menteri Pertanian Republik Indonesia, 2003: 1–2) not only for trade, but also because it is the main raw ingredient of locally consumed cooking oil. Furthermore, the CPO production process in Indonesia was very efficient due to the high yield from trees that could be harvested all year round (3,511 kilolitres per hectare) (Suharto, 2011: 19), low price of labour, ideal climate and rich soil conditions (Samsul *et al.*, 2007: 1). An industry study commissioned by PT[2] Purimas Sasmita (an Indonesian oil palm plantation firm) found Indonesia to be the most efficient producer of CPO in the world, with the cost of production 14.3 per cent lower than the world average and 8.3 per cent lower than Malaysia (Chalil, 2008: 15). As a result, palm oil in Indonesia could be produced at lower cost compared to other edible oils (Casson, 2002: 221–242). Further, being about six times bigger that Malaysia in terms of land area, the Indonesian oil palm industry was able to grow swiftly (Basiron, 2007: 291; Nature, 2007: 3).

Indonesia started rapidly opening up oil palm plantations in Sumatra and Kalimantan in the 1980s (Indonesian Government, 1998). This was fuelled by a specific policy goal that was formulated by the Indonesian government in the 1980s to surpass Malaysia as the world's largest palm oil producer (Van Gelder, 2004: 19). Expansion was pursued largely through the privatization of previously state-run estates, particularly through the Estate Transmigration Programme and the Plantation Revitalization Programme. This marked the starting point of serious patronage politics in this sector, as these programmes granted extensive new concessions to well-connected large-scale conglomerate firms typically led by Sino-Indonesians with close connections to the regime's apex (Casson, 2002: 221–242; McCarthy, 2010: 822–844; McCarthy and Cramb, 2009: 114–117). The significance of these patronage connections are discussed extensively in Chapter 4 on patronage networks in the sector.

After local Indonesian investors had established themselves in the oil palm sector during the 1980s, the government of Indonesia briefly opened up the oil palm industry to foreign investors in the early 1990s to further boost the sector (McCarthy and Cramb, 2009: 114–117). As detailed in Chapter 3, this marked the beginning of the regionalization of Southeast Asia's oil palm sector, as investments tended to come mainly from the neighbouring Malaysia and Singapore. As a result, area harvested with oil palm in Indonesia increased from around 70,000 hectares in the 1960s to 1.6 million hectares by 1997 (see Figure 2.4). Correspondingly, production increased from 167,669 metric tonnes in 1967 to 5.4 million metric tonnes in 1997, amounting to an increase of around 12 per cent per annum (Casson, 2002: 221–242). By 1997, Indonesia was already producing 30 per cent of global palm oil (Samsul *et al.*, 2007: 6). Expansion during this time period coincided with the first serious haze events in the region (ASEAN, 1992) due to the drastic rate of land conversion for oil palm plantations using fire, as explained further in this chapter.

During the AFC period of 1997 to 1999, Indonesia experienced drastic political change and serious economic crisis. In connection with this, from early 1998 through to mid-1999, the palm oil boom subsided and oil palm area expansion slowed significantly (Casson, 2002: 221–242), with many plantation companies suffering financial difficulties (Interviewee M41, 2010). To overcome this, the Indonesian government once again opened up forest concessions to foreign companies (Mathew [M8], 2010) while offering attractive foreign investment opportunities (Rifin, 2010: 174). Therefore, Malaysian and Singaporean business interests facing scarcity of land in their home states (Rajenthran, 2002: 1) once again entered Indonesia after the AFC on the invitation of the Indonesian govern-

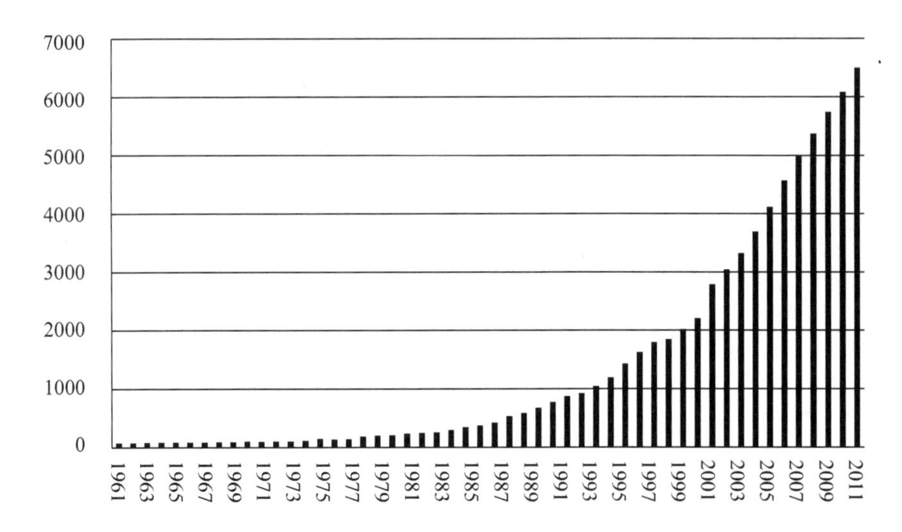

Figure 2.4 Area harvested of oil palm fruit in Indonesia, 1961–2012 ('000 hectares)
Source: Adapted from: FAOSTAT, 2012

ment to help take over failed Indonesian plantation companies (Interviewee M28, 2010). This further deepened the regionalization of this sector, as elaborated in the next chapter.

By the year 2000, there was already a high level of economic regionalization and interdependence between local, Malaysian and Singaporean interests in the sector. With the help of these foreign investments, the industry recovered and production of CPO grew exponentially (Nature, 2007: 3). There is now an increasing amount of modern, highly efficient oil palm plantation companies (both local and foreign) operating in Indonesia, further increasing efficiency and output (Butler *et al.*, 2009: 68). Currently private plantation companies dominate oil palm plantations in the country. In 2011, plantations owned by private companies made up 51 per cent of all oil palm plantation land, smallholder plantations made up 42 per cent, and state plantations made up the remaining 7 per cent, as shown in Figure 2.5 (Boer *et al.*, 2012: 67; Ministry of Agriculture, 2013). Out of the 42 per cent of land owned by smallholders, an estimated quarter of these are part of 'nucleus-plasma'[3] schemes where private plantations are required to prepare plantation areas for surrounding communities that would in turn run these plantations under formal partnership with these companies (Ministry of Agriculture, 2013). Hence, in addition to the 51 per cent directly controlled by private companies, these private plantations indirectly also control an additional estimated 11 per cent of smallholder landholdings through these nucleus-plasma arrangements, bringing a total of around 62 per cent of all oil palm plantation land in Indonesia being under the purview of private companies.

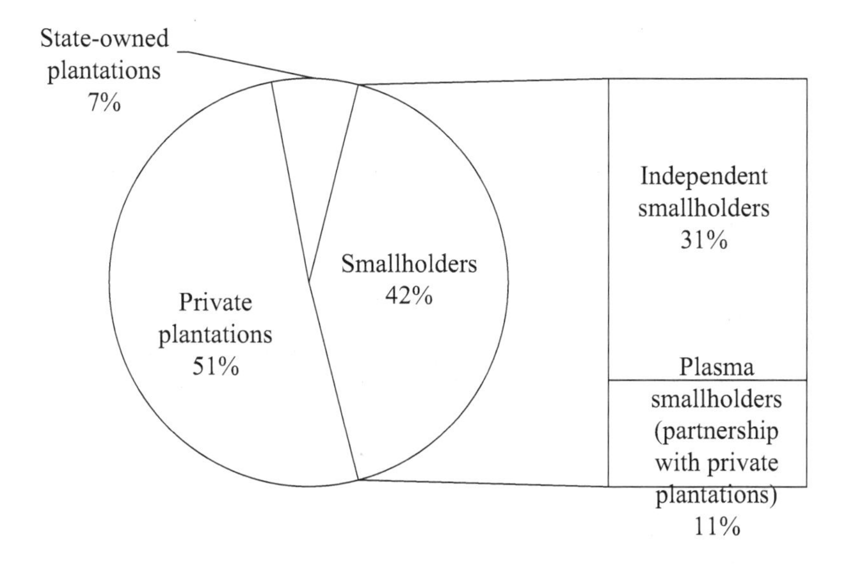

Figure 2.5 Ownership of oil palm plantation land in Indonesia, 2011
Source: Adapted from Ministry of Agriculture, 2013; Boer *et al.*, 2012: 67

With the post-crisis collapse of many other key Indonesian industries in 1998, the plantation sector was hailed as the saviour of the country's economy. That year, the total land area of oil palm increased to about 2.01 million hectares, before increasing to 5.74 million hectares in 2010, almost tripling within that time (see Figure 2.4) (FAOSTAT, 2012; Wicke *et al.*, 2011: 194–200,). Accordingly, Indonesia's palm oil output maintained a steady growth rate of around 14 per cent per year (Van Gelder, 2004: 12). By 2011, almost 11 million hectares of land had been officially allocated for oil palm plantations (Slette and Wiyono, 2011). That year, oil palm plantations represented more than 10 per cent of agricultural land in Indonesia (World Growth, 2011: 4–13).

The prolific growth of the oil palm sector has conferred important economic benefits to Indonesia. This sector has become a vital source of revenue, foreign exchange and employment (Ministry of Forestry, 2009: 30; Sandker *et al.*, 2007: 37–40) to the government, public and private sectors of Indonesia. First, in terms of revenue, the flourishing palm oil industry contributes around 7 per cent of Indonesia's GDP annually, as shown in Figure 2.6 (Albanese, 2012; Bank Indonesia, 2014; Das, 2014: 5). It also contributes substantially to government revenue, with a progressive export tax scheme where the government captures an increasing portion of gains as CPO prices climb (Di, 2011a: 4). Planting oil palm can yield estimated net present values of between $3,835 and $9,630 per hectare per year (Lee, 2011: 1), compared to the average of between $1,283 and $1,416 per hectare per year for other crops in Indonesia (Prasetyo *et al.*, 2009: 416–426).

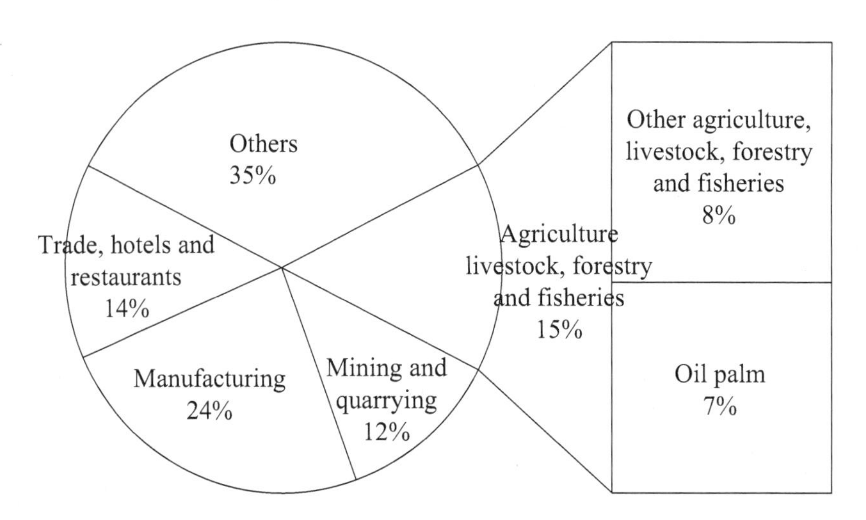

Figure 2.6 Breakdown of Indonesia's 2011 GDP by sector
Source: Adapted from: Albanese, 2012; Bank Indonesia, 2014; Das, 2014

Second, palm oil has become a vital source of foreign exchange. Indonesia exports over 77 per cent of its palm oil production (Jarvis *et al.*, 2010: 2–12) due to the fact that international market prices have been consistently higher than domestic ones (Chalil, 2008: 29). The CPO industry recorded the highest growth in export revenues among all major sectors in Indonesia (Chalil, 2008: 10–11). By 2009 the export value of palm oil was $15 billion, representing almost 9 per cent of total export revenue (Ewing, 2011: 7; World Growth, 2011: 4–13). The main destinations of Indonesian CPO are to other Asian countries, with over 42 per cent going to India and China (Bangun, 2014). There is also a significant amount of export to Malaysia and Singapore for downstream processing, further reflecting the level of economic regionalization in the sector (Rifin, 2010: 180).

Third, the Indonesian government also regards palm oil as an important contributor to its poverty alleviation strategy (Hameiri and Jones, 2013: 471). It is viewed as a vehicle for social and economic development in rural areas (Samsul *et al.*, 2007: 6), especially in terms of employment. The industry employs roughly 20 million people (Simamora, 2011); 4.5 million people through direct employment on plantations (900,000 people) and downstream processing (3.6 million people), and the rest through related service industries and remittances (World Growth, 2011: 4–13). The director general of Estate Crops reported that because of palm oil, farmers' incomes have increased to $1,607 per household per hectare per year in 2011, from $920 in 2005, which works out to an average increase of 12.24 per cent annually (Caroko *et al.*, 2011: 18). In order to maintain these lucrative returns, the Indonesian government has projected and planned for a continued expansion of the sector, as is detailed next.

Future projections for the Indonesian oil palm sector

The oil palm sector is a very important sector for the future of the Indonesian economy. Indonesia plans to achieve annual economic growth rates of 7.5 per cent over the period of 2011 to 2015, and expansion of oil palm plantations is among the 22 major economic activities identified by the government to reach this goal (Wibisino *et al.*, 2011: 15). With world commodity prices for palm oil expected to stay above the 1980–2005 average at least until the end of this decade (Butler *et al.*, 2009: 68), and the new and growing demand for biofuels locally and around the world, the Indonesian government has continued to target the oil palm plantation sector for rapid expansion.

In 2004, the directorate general of Plantation Production and Development Indonesia determined that there were approximately 32 million hectares of land suitable for oil palm plantation development in the country (USDA, 2009). Approximately 50 per cent of all agricultural expansion in Indonesia now involves expansion in oil palm production (Wicke *et al.*, 2011: 194–200), with a planting rate of 400,000 hectares annually (Sawit Watch, 2007: 1–2). The government has announced plans to bring another 7 million hectares of land under oil palm cultivation, effectively doubling the crop's planted area in the near future (McCarthy and Zen, 2010: 155–156). Existing regional development plans have already allotted 20 million hectares for new plantations, mostly in Sumatra, Kalimantan, Sulawesi and West Papua (Colchester *et al.*, 2006: 12). Government authorities are processing permits for about 1.5 million hectares more, and an additional 2.1 million hectares are at the proposal stage (Caroko *et al.*, 2011: 3). The government's goal is to eventually increase its oil palm plantation area to at least 30 million hectares (World Rainforest Movement, 1998), with an aim of almost doubling its CPO output from 2011 to 2020, to reach 40 million tonnes per year by 2020 (Boer *et al.*, 2012: 4; Hameiri and Jones, 2013: 471; Taylor and Supriatna, 2014).

Indonesia has devised plans and policies to address the demand for biofuels in particular as well, in the light of local and global (especially European) demand (Sawit Watch, 2007: 1–2). Locally, Indonesia's National Energy Policy 2006 (Caroko *et al.*, 2011: 1) has targeted that biodiesel derived from palm oil will replace 20 per cent of the diesel consumed in the country in the near future (Zhou and Thomson, 2009: 11). This was stated in Presidential Directive No. 1 of 2007 on the Accelerated Development on Oil Palm Plantations for Bio-Diesel (Munadar *et al.*, 2010) and the Presidential Instruction (No. 1/2006) on the Supply and use of Biofuel as a Source of Alternative Energy (Samsul *et al.*, 2007). To achieve this goal, a taskforce was established to coordinate biofuels development in the country, called the Timnas Bahan Bakar Nabati (National Biofuel Development Team) (Caroko *et al.*, 2011: 1). Hence, Indonesia has introduced new plans to allocate 6 million tonnes of palm oil to the biofuel industry each year (World Growth, 2011: 4–8). This policy also aims to increase palm oil-based biodiesel production capacity from 600 million liters to 3 billion litres by 2017. To achieve this, the Indonesian government has allocated $1.1 billion to establish up to 11 more palm oil-based biodiesel production plants (Rist *et al.*, 2010: 1010–1011). To supply these plants, the Ministry of Forestry had identified around 22.8 million hectares of convertible forest that have the potential to be used for the production of biofuels (Caroko *et al.*, 2011: 4). In line with this, the government developed further plans in 2006 allocating 4 million additional hectares of land by 2015 to investors interested in planting new crops to specifically boost biofuels production (Greenpeace, 2007: 13).

These projections and plans reflect the Indonesian government's continued commitment to reap the benefits of this lucrative sector, seemingly at any cost (Interviewee I49, 2011). With only 53 million hectares left of 'frontier forest' (Fatah and Udiansyah, 2009), Indonesia's goal to increase oil palm hectarage to 30 million from the current 7 million would mean that upon completion of this expansion, only 30 million hectares of frontier forests would remain. According to many environmental groups and scholars, this rate of conversion is unsustainable, not least in terms of haze production (Fatah and Udiansyah, 2009; Harrison *et al.*, 2009: 161; Hunt, 2010: 187–190,). As argued above, these attitudes towards continued expansion and exploitation can be traced back to the natural resource exploitation trend espoused since the early days of independence in Indonesia (Barber, 1998: 4–35), which as Chapter 4 will show, is bolstered by powerful patronage politics that further encourage exploitative policies for the elites' own advantage (McCarthy and Cramb, 2009: 112–114; Samsul *et al.*, 2007: 7). The unsustainable nature of the Indonesian oil palm plantation sector is further elaborated below, focusing on how continued expansion in the sector has caused, and will continue to cause, regional haze in Southeast Asia.

Oil palm plantations and fires in Indonesia

Natural resource exploitation of the type prevalent in the Southeast Asian region, especially Indonesia, often leads to an unbalanced development strategy that sacrifices the environment for the sake of economic gains at all costs (Koh and Wilcove, 2007: 994). As one scholar puts it, 'the root causes of environmental degradation are in social structures reinforced by the development paradigm. The paradigm is the villain' (Mittelman, 1998: 854). As a result, states such as Indonesia often relegate the environment low on their lists of priorities (Koh and Wilcove, 2007: 994). Environmental degradation was viewed as unavoidable, short-term costs of 'development', or 'externalities' of growth that could (and should) be dealt with later (Gellert, 2005: 1346–1358). It was widely accepted that the uses and abuses of the natural environment by elite entrepreneurs were vital to produce the developmental 'miracle' (Chang and Rajan, 2001: 665) in Indonesia, and this understanding provided justification for the development of patronage networks that supported the environmentally degrading operations of these elite entrepreneurs in the name of development. This included rapid conversion and opening of forestlands by the commercial elite for mining, timber and cash crops, especially oil palm (Sumiani *et al.*, 2007: 896–898).

The environmental consequences of such a path of exploitation are found in widespread deforestation, pollution of waterways, degradation of agricultural land, poor air quality and declining populations of fish and wildlife (Raman, 2006: 38–40). This has led to the loss of biodiversity, loss of habitat for endangered species such as the orangutan, greenhouse gas emissions from carbon stock changes in soil and biomass (WALHI and Sawit Watch, 2009: 1–5; Wicke *et al.*, 2011: 193) and most visibly, the frequent occurrence of environmental disasters such as the widespread regional haze as a result of increased forest fires, as this region 'pays the price' for rushing its growth (Ngai, 1998: 14).

Forest fires in Southeast Asia have been extensively recorded since the nineteenth century (Eaton and Radojevic, 2001: 2), particularly in Indonesia and to a lesser extent, other heavily forested countries such as Malaysia and Thailand. Indonesia has experienced severe conflagrations, especially in the provinces of Kalimantan and Sumatra, since 1982, when 3.6 million hectares of tropical forests were destroyed. At the time, these fires were described as the worst fires the world had ever seen, and was dubbed the 'Great Fire of Borneo' (Dennis, 1999). However, more than a decade later in 1997–1998 the extent of the fires was the worst Indonesia had seen in 50 years (*Jakarta Post*, 1998). These fires resulted in an estimated 10 million hectares burned around Indonesia (*Jakarta Post*, 2009), destroying bushland and forests, including national parks and other high-conservation value areas (Dauvergne, 1998: 13–17). Forest fires have severe impact on the surrounding environment, affecting biodiversity, the natural hydrological cycle, the microclimate and of course air quality due to smoke haze (UNCTAD, 2009: 100).

Significantly, it was found that the percentage of forested area affected by fire was highest in areas that have been moderately or highly disturbed by human activity, especially commercial plantation activity (Gellert, 1998: 66). In these highly disturbed landscapes, there has been evidence that 'the incidence of fire in Indonesian forests is being decoupled from El Niño-driven draughts and that there is a positive feedback between fire, deforestation and drainage, which has greatly increased the risk of fire, even during non-El Niño dry seasons' (Page *et al.*, 2009: 893). Indeed, a comparison of fire hotspot maps from the period of 2001 to 2004 and the period of 2004 to 2008 published by Friends of the Earth Malaysia shows that more and larger fires have been progressively occurring on commercial oil palm plantation land (Ramakrishna [M20], 2010). A World Wildlife Fund for Nature study showed that 65 per cent to 80 per cent of forested area burned in East Kalimantan was in forest concessions and estate crops (Saharjo, 1999: 143). Statistics from the Indonesian Secretariat for Forest Protection (Sekretariat Kerjasama Kelestarian Hutan Indonesia), an NGO, showed that 60 per cent of the fires in 1994 were on plantation areas while 37 per cent more were on transmigration and timber concession areas. Only 2 per cent were in conserved forest areas, where nomadic tribes reside and conduct small-scale agriculture (*Jakarta Post*, 1994). Conservative World Bank estimates of the 1997 fires placed plantation fires at a lower percentage (35 per cent), but this still accounted for the highest single source of fires that year (see Figure 2.7) (Jones, 2006: 434).

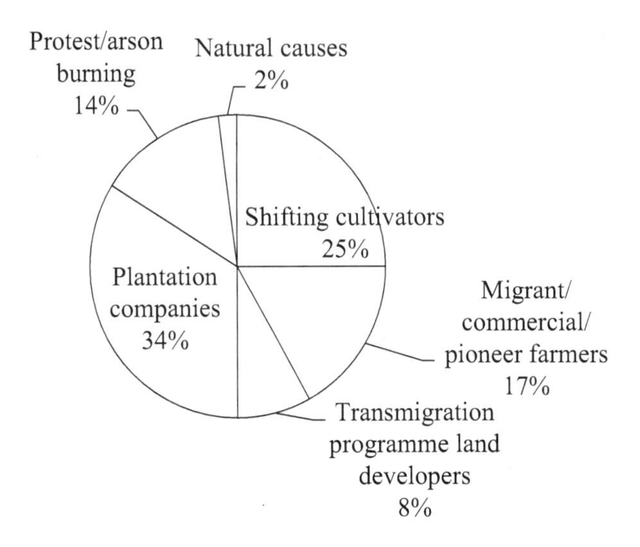

Figure 2.7 Parties responsible for fire in Indonesia, 1997

Source: Adapted from Jones, 2006: 434

It has been shown that these fires do not merely tend to occur in highly disturbed areas but are also largely deliberately started by humans. Interviewees explained that while the cyclical El Niño phenomenon, which causes a prolonged drought across the country every three to seven years, creates conditions ripe for hotspots (Suwarsono [I3], 2010), 'it cannot be denied that most of these fires are man-made' (Surya [I9] and Akbar [I10], 2010). From the 1970s, the haze made a minor appearance every five years or so, coinciding with the five-year schedule of forest burning by slash-and-burn farmers and the El Niño dry weather pattern. However, following the shift of focus from logging to oil palm cultivation in Indonesia in the 1990s, there was an almost annual and more intense occurrence of haze, coinciding with the schedule of annual open burning during the dry season to clear land on plantations (Gan, 1972: 3). Therefore, it was widely accepted that the 1997 haze around the Southeast Asian region, and the other haze events following that, were caused by smoke coming from deliberate large-scale commercial burning for land clearance and conversion into oil palm plantations (Caroko *et al.*, 2011: 21; Casson, 2002: 234–239; Colfer, 2002: 316; Fairhurst and McLaughlin, 2009: 7–34; Tan *et al.*, 2009: 422).

Satellite images from the Centre for Remote Imaging, Sensing and Processing in Singapore in 2004 have provided strong evidence linking fires to the deliberate actions of oil palm plantation companies (Lee [S20], 2010; Moore [I5], 2010; Surya [I9] and Akbar [I10], 2010; Syaf [I27], 2010; Syarif [I2], 2010; Tan [S7], 2010). Hotspot[4] maps superimposed over concession maps suggest that many plantation companies were systematically setting fire to both peatlands and other areas for land clearing (Arif [I41], 2011; Ramakrishna [M20], 2010). For example, a recent study by the World Resources Institute identified that in Sumatra during the peak fire month of June 2013, the density of fire alerts is three to four times higher within commercial concession boundaries compared to outside these boundaries. The study found 1.3 fire alerts per hectare of land within concession areas, compared to only 0.4 fire alerts per hectare outside concession areas (World Resources Institute, 2013). The biggest fires were found to be either directly or indirectly related to companies' land-clearing activities (Colfer, 2002: 316). Evidence of previous systematic burning has also been found on plantation land through charcoal fragments (Fairhurst and McLaughlin, 2009: 7–34). Based on satellite data, it is estimated that 80 per cent of the fires were set by plantation companies or their subcontractors for land-clearing purposes (Richardson, 2010: 22), while the remaining 20 per cent were set by slash-and-burn farmers (Casson, 2002: 221–242).

This highlights the inadequacy of the developmental explanation of haze adopted by the Indonesian government and scholars such as Colfer (2002), Varma (2003), Quah and Johnston (2001), as previously detailed in Chapter 1. They argued that swidden and smallholder agriculture and related developmental issues like poverty, rapid population growth and ignorance were major drivers of haze (Colfer, 2002: 313–316; *Jakarta Post*, 2006: 55). However, while swidden agriculture may contribute marginally to fires and haze as stated above, this book shows that the more serious cause of haze-producing fires have their roots in rapid commercial land change, especially for the opening up of oil palm plantations.

One explanation for the push for rapid oil palm expansion in Indonesia is that yield per hectare there is not increasing, but may instead be declining because of the degradation of soil quality (Cooke, 2006: 9). Hence, in order to make maximum profit, continued expansion of hectarage is necessary (Suharto, 2011: 20). Therefore, plantation companies have to continue to convert new land into plantations to keep up with demand. The following sections discuss two types of land use change often employed in Indonesia for conversion into oil palm plantations and how they are linked with increase in fires: first, of degraded logged-over forests and old cropland, and second, the more serious issue of the conversion of pristine peatlands.

Conversion of degraded lands

Land degradation is described as 'a long term loss of ecosystem function and services, caused by disturbances from which the system cannot recover unaided' (Fairhurst and McLaughlin, 2009: 8). Decades of uncontrolled logging in Indonesia[5] have left wide, clear-cut areas degraded and ready for conversion into crops such as oil palm (Dauvergne, 1998: 13–17). Some land conversion also occurs on old croplands as well, where land for oil palm is obtained by converting other agricultural crops that have lower market values such as cocoa, rubber and coconut (Tan *et al.*, 2009: 423; Wicke *et al.*, 2011: 201–203).

The unsustainable exploitation of forest land was further driven by specific agro-conversion policies in Indonesia that encouraged natural resource exploitation by large-scale conglomerates (Dauvergne, 1994: 502). For example, as discussed above, the Indonesian government viewed these degraded land as 'wasteland' or 'idle' land going to waste if not exploited to its full potential (McCarthy and Cramb, 2009: 112–114). Therefore, the Indonesian government has encouraged firms to clear these otherwise 'idle' logged forests and croplands for the establishment of the more lucrative oil palm plantations (Colfer, 2002: 311). With the government's encouragement, it is expected that the conversion of logged tropical forests for oil palm plantations will continue throughout the decade (Butler *et al.*, 2009: 68).

These logged areas and former croplands are much more fire-prone than old-growth forest areas because they are generally drier than virgin forests, more open and often times contain a floor of dead wood and kindling that provide the 'fuel' for fires (Dauvergne, 1998: 13–17; Hurst, 1987: 173). For example, dry branches can sometimes rub against each other and provide the spark for a fire (*Jakarta Post*, 1994). Besides accidental fires, companies also often deliberately set fire to these areas. Fire is the fastest and cheapest way to clear logged-over forests and croplands[6] (Caroko *et al.*, 2011: 21), as it is useful in clearing vegetation left over from logging and old crops (Dauvergne, 1998: 13–17). Burning is also a practical way of disposing unwanted by-products such as straw and husks that have no immediate value or use (Applegate *et al.*, 2002: 294). The ash produced is also believed to give a shot of fertilizer to the soil. In contrast, the method of mechanically 'windrowing' remaining timber, by raking them up into large long piles and letting them rot over time, is expensive and slow, and also could harbour pests and vermin (Rowland [I39], 2011). Clearing degraded land with machines and chemicals can cost up to $200 per hectare (Dauvergne, 1998: 13–17), while clearing land using fire can cost as little as $5 (Salim, 2007). Sometimes plantations companies also purposely light fires to reclassify forestland and NCR land as degraded land so that they can be legally converted into plantations (Casson, 2002: 234–239; Colfer, 2002: 318).

These deliberate fires can get out of control and spread to a wider area than intended, often spreading outside plantation areas and destroying pristine forests. While the burning of these degraded lands does not create the smouldering, persistent fires and thick, sooty smoke like those on peatlands (discussed in the next section), the substantial scale of these fires does significantly contribute to the problem of haze in the region. Therefore, the conversion of degraded lands as encouraged by the Indonesian government is a significant driver for haze in the region. Combined with the smoke produced from peatfires, the resulting haze becomes a serious concern.

Conversion of peatlands

Tropical lowland peatswamps are a major type of forestland commonly found in Southeast Asia. The region is estimated to have 27 million hectares of peatlands or

6 per cent of total peatlands in the world (Tan *et al.*, 2009: 423). Indonesia is the fourth largest in the world in terms of peatland area (Hilman, 2010), being home to about 83 per cent of the region's peatlands (Wetlands International, 2014), with a total of 26.5 million hectares or 12 per cent of its total land area (Tan *et al.*, 2009: 423). These lands are mostly located in large areas in between river basins in Borneo, Sumatra and Irian Jaya (Parish, 2011: 2). Most of Indonesia's peatlands are in a 'critical phase of degradation' (Satyawan [I20], 2010), with about 45 per cent currently deforested or drained (Page, 2011: 5; Suharto, 2010: 8).

Peat generally occurs along coasts and in terrestrial conditions on low-lying, poorly drained sites, and are identifiable for their waterlogged, fluctuating water table conditions that gives it a characteristic 'blackwater' appearance (Phillips, 1998: 651–660). Natural peatswamp forests are also important water catchment and control systems. As natural aquifers, they absorb and store water during the rainy season and slowly release it during dry periods. In this way, peatswamps help provide water during draughts and also reduce flood peaks during wet periods (Samsul *et al.*, 2007: 22). Coastal peatswamps also act as buffers between freshwater and marine systems, preventing excessive saline intrusion into coastal areas and protecting off-shore fisheries from on-shore pollution (Phillips, 1998: 654–660).

Peatswamps also play an important role in the global carbon balance (Phillips, 1998: 654–660). Tropical peatlands are important carbon sinks (Parish and Looi, 2011: 2), as carbon is stored in the peat that is formed from organic material like tree and vegetation litter, sediments and organic soil that have accumulated over the past thousands of years (Parish and Looi, 2011: 2–3), some since the last ice-age glacial retreat more than 8,000 years ago (Blain *et al.*, 2006: 8). The anaerobic conditions in these peatswamps and low availability of nutrients greatly constrains the decomposition of these organic materials, so that carbon stocks continue to grow (Parish and Looi, 2011: 2–3). Many peatlands also continue to sequester carbon from the atmosphere as peatland plants conduct photosynthesis, and many also act as carbon sediment traps from watershed resources (Parish and Looi, 2011: 2–3). The litter in these swamps accumulate to form a layer of peat of up to 20 metres thick in some parts (Parish, 2011: 2).

Large-scale development of Indonesian peatlands began during the 1960s due to land and population pressure. Traditionally, drained and reclaimed peatswamp land was only desirable for the development of highways, housing and industrial use (Phillips, 1998: 652–665), like industrial wastewater treatment and energy production (Blain *et al.*, 2006: 8). Agricultural development trends in the past had been to avoid peatswamps altogether (Phillips, 1998: 665). Deep peat is considered a 'problem soil' due to various constraints to agricultural development, including surface subsidence due to soil shrinkage and compacting, decomposition, leaching, loss of peat material during reclamation and the irreversible drying that makes this soil extremely fire-prone (Wibisino [I44], 2011). To convert and prepare peatswamps for planting, the swamp has to be cleared from vegetation, drained and dried so that the water table drops (Maitar [I12], 2010; Syaf [I27], 2010). This is done by constructing draining ditches that allow water to drain out of the area (Blain *et al.*, 2006: 8). Without adequate draining, plantation trees are unstable and readily subject to windthrow (trees uprooted by wind). However, if cleared and allowed to dry out, the peat shrinks (Maitar [I12], 2010; Syaf [I27], 2010), revealing soil that is acidic, low in oxygen and inorganic ions, high in carbon and has high concentrations of humic acid (Phillips, 1998: 651–660). These are very infertile conditions that are unsuitable for most crops (Maitar [I12], 2010; Syaf [I27], 2010). Because of these constraints, and because of the functional importance of peatswamps to the ecosystem as discussed above, it has been asserted that undisturbed peatswamps, especially those more than 2 metres deep, may be more valuable to humans, than if it is drained and developed for short-term profit production that results in unsustainable and irreversible damage to the peatswamp ecosystem (Phillips, 1998: 654).

However, the burgeoning need for land brought about by the oil palm boom in countries such as Indonesia has encouraged the conversion of peatlands to oil palm plantations (Maitar [I12], 2010; Syaf [I27], 2010). Despite its unsuitability for other crops, peatlands are quite suitable for the growth of oil palm when deeply drained (Tan *et al.*, 2009: 423). Research has shown that oil palm has a high tolerance for areas with fluctuating water tables (Liew, 2010: 88), and oil palm grown on reclaimed peatsoil has a particularly high fruit production (Ministry of Forestry, 2009: 30). By the 1980s, with most inland forests cleared, plantation companies began building dykes to dry peatswamps to increase their acreage (Nowak, 2008: 190), and the reclamation of peatlands increased drastically as most new oil palm plantation land was opened up on reclaimed peatswamps (Wicke *et al.*, 2011: 193–194). While the constraints discussed above make oil palm development on peat soil more expensive (Maitar [I12], 2010; Syaf [I27], 2010) (with set up costs on peatlands almost double as compared to set up costs on regular mineral soil) (Liew, 2010: 41), higher oil palm trading prices have made this economically viable (Maitar [I12], 2010; Syaf [I27], 2010).

Opening up peatlands for plantations is also attractive to concessionaires because of the valuable timber growing in these areas (Wibisino [I44], 2011). On regular timber production forests there are strict rules for timber extraction, with only a small percentage of logs allowed to be logged every year to maintain sustainability. However, with forested peatlands, concessionaires are allowed to log and cull all the trees in the area in the process of land clearing (Interviewee M44, 2012). Furthermore, while most peatswamp forests are 'megadiverse' in terms of both flora and fauna (Parish, 2011: 3), they usually have a single species or very few species of trees dominating the plant community. Commonly dominating Indonesia's peatland forests are the alan (*Shorea albida*), ramin (*Gonystylus bancanus*) and terentang (*Campnosperma spp*) trees, which are all highly valuable commercial timber (Phillips, 1998: 651–660; Wibisino [I44], 2011). Because of this, companies setting up plantations in peatland areas were often connected to established logging companies. These companies were able to use their expertise to profitably log the peatlands of all valuable timber before conversion (Casson, 2002: 221–242). The profit from the sale of this timber usually fueled further peatland expansion (Stone, 2007: 1491).

Another reason peatlands are highly attractive to concessionaires is because peatlands are usually free from claims of NCR and land-use rights. This is because, due to the wet nature of peatlands, communities rarely settle there. Therefore, acquiring peatlands is a good way to avoid highly publicized conflicts with increasingly vocal indigenous and local communities (Wibisino [I44], 2011), which usually involves high compensation costs. Even though development on peat does have its additional costs as explained above, compensation costs can run even higher, and by establishing plantations on 'empty' peatlands, companies do not have to share profits with the community (Interviewee M44, 2012). The usually secluded nature of peatlands (far away from towns and cities) also usually mean that plantation companies can conduct their practices far away from monitoring by environmental authorities (Casey [I46], 2011; Rukmantara [I45], 2011).

As a result, of the existing 7 million hectares of palm oil concessions in Indonesia, approximately 2 million hectares, or 27 per cent is located on peatlands (Silvius and Kaat, 2010: 13–23), and a further three million more have been licensed for conversion in the future (see Table 2.1) (Suharto, 2010: 8). Furthermore, over 50 per cent of new oil palm plantation areas are planned in peatland areas (Greenpeace, 2007: 33). This amounts to an annual expansion of 150,000 to 200,000 hectares per year (Silvius and Kaat, 2010: 23).

The sensitive nature and ecological importance of peatlands justified special legislation restricting development on peatlands. Both Presidential Decree No. 32/1990 and Indonesian Government Regulation No. 26/2008 state that peat of more than 3 metres deep should automatically be designated as protected areas (Ministry of Forestry, 2009: 11–54; PanEco Foundation, 2008: 1). Also, the Regulation of the Ministry of Agriculture No. 14/2009 stipulates that if there is a concession on peat with more than 30 per cent of its total concession having a peat thickness of more than 3 metres, then the entire concession should not be opened (Wibisino *et al.*, 2011: 28). Furthermore, there are Ministry of Agriculture spatial planning guidelines that identify areas of peat more than 76 centimetres deep as unsuitable for conversion to agriculture (BAPPENAS, 2009; Ministry of Forestry, 2009: 11–54). There is also a standing instruction through the Ministry of Agriculture's Instruction to the Governors of Indonesia No. 301/TU.210/M/12/2001 (13 December 2007) stating that the issuing of new plan-

Table 2.1 Peat and palm oil in Indonesia, 2008

Indonesia	*Hectares*
Land area	190,000,000
Area consisting of peat	26,500,000
Area of which is degrading	12,500,000
Area licensed for conversion	5,000,000
Area converted to palm oil	2,000,000
% of palm oil on peat	27

Source: Adapted from Silvius and Kaat, 2010: 16; Kaat and Silvius, 2011: 3; Suharto, 2010: 8

tation concessions on peatlands is temporarily forbidden, pending further instructions. Essentially, this means that issuing of plantation concessions on peatlands across Indonesia is wholly forbidden (PanEco Foundation, 2008: 1). Hence, Indonesia actually has very clear policies on the use of peatsoil that, if properly observed, should lead to the sustainable management of peatlands.

However, despite this, research has shown that, up to 25 per cent of concessionaires, including local and foreign companies alike, deviate from this rule and plant on deep peat anyway (Silvius and Kaat, 2010: 21). All these plantation lands and future plantations on peat are essentially 'illegal' because they contravene national laws and policies (Interviewee I49, 2011). However, these laws are rarely enforced and thus, with the protection that these companies receive as a result of home-state facilitation and host-state patronage, these companies are very rarely prosecuted. This is extensively discussed in Chapter 3 on state facilitation and Chapter 4 on patronage networks respectively.

In terms of haze, problems arise during draining and preparation operations (Basiron, 2007: 289–295). Once the valuable timber is removed to be sold (Wibisino [I44], 2011), the peat is usually burned to remove any remaining vegetation (Stone, 2007: 1491), either by the company directly or by using subcontractors (Colfer, 2002: 318). Much like the conversion of degraded lands discussed above, burning peatlands is a fast way to clear unwanted weeds and grass in preparation for planting (Interviewee I21, 2010; Maitar [I12], 2010; Moore [I5], 2010; Surya [I9] and Akbar [I10], 2010) and reduces the risk of pests.

Furthermore, using machinery is problematic and expensive on the soft peatlands, with the soggy soil hindering the use of bulldozers (Interviewee I21, 2010; Maitar [I12], 2010; Moore [I5], 2010; Surya [I9] and Akbar [I10], 2010). Clearing land mechanically on peatlands costs an average of around $200 per hectare (Salim, 2007); clearing land by excavator is $440 per hectare, using a bulldozer is $380 per hectare, and hiring local villagers to use axes and chainsaws to clear land would incur costs of $83 per hectare (Zakaria *et al.*, 2007: 25). As mentioned earlier, clearance by fire could cost a mere $5 (Salim, 2007). Burning (specifically the ash that it produces) also omits or reduces the need for expensive alkaline fertilizer; the prices of which has been steadily rising in the past years and is expected to continue to rise (Yeoh *et al.*, 2011a: 22), which is otherwise required to increase the acidity of peatlands to levels that are suited to oil palm growth (Zakaria *et al.*, 2007: 25).

Therefore, one way of keeping the costs down is to clear land using fire (Colfer, 2002: 318; Interviewee I21, 2010; Maitar [I12], 2010; Moore [I5], 2010; Surya [I9] and Akbar [I10], 2010). Maintaining these low production costs is key to a plantation's continued profitability, especially since the process of draining peatlands is already expensive (Interviewee I49, 2011). As explained above, although not all plantation firms clear land by way of burning, field observations coupled with satellite imagery strongly suggest that some of the larger plantation groups do conduct open burning on peatlands (Raman *et al.*, 2008: 3–5), as many interviewees attest (Interviewee I21, 2010; Maitar [I12], 2010; Moore [I5], 2010; Surya [I9] and Akbar [I10], 2010).

Even for the companies that do not deliberately use fire, disturbance to the naturally waterlogged condition in peatlands create extremely dry conditions and hotspots (*Jakarta Post*, 1994). Once the peatswamp water table drops from draining, it dries very quickly, making it naturally fire-prone (Albar [I17], 2010; Maitar [I12], 2010; Resosudarmo [I26], 2010; Swajaya [I37], 2010; Syaf [I27], 2010). Fires require dry fuel, oxygen and a spark to start (Colfer, 2002: 310), and these elements are easily found on drained peatlands. Accidental fires further contribute to the drastic rate of deforestation and air pollution in Indonesia (Rukmantara, 2006). Accordingly, research has proven that 90 per cent of transboundary haze in the southern portion of Southeast Asia is linked to such peatland fires (Global Environment Center, 2010: 3). Drastic land conversion like this further degrades and dries out the natural landscape in such a way that future hotspots and accidental fires are liable to occur again and are likely to be more severe (Colfer, 2002: 309; Greenpeace, 2007: 18; Raman *et al.*, 2008: 21).

Furthermore, fires on peatlands, especially deep peat, are extremely hard to put out. This is because the fires often extend underground and thus are not visible to the naked eye. Therefore, conventional methods of fire-fighting (Parliament of Singapore, 1998) and regular dousing is inadequate and often extensive flooding of vast areas of peat is needed. Peat fires have serious negative environmental ramifications in terms of climate change and of course haze, which is the focus of this book.

Peatlands have an important role to play in the climate change equation. As mentioned earlier, peatlands are good carbon sinks, thus when peat burns, carbon that was trapped in these sinks is released into the atmosphere, exacerbating global warming and climate change (Ministry of Forestry, 2009: 53). Because of the high use of peatlands for oil palm plantations, the carbon stock on oil palm plantations on average in Indonesia is about 40 tons per hectare[7] (Claudell *et al.*, 2011: 5). As a result, the carbon emissions due to peat fires there was estimated between 3,000 to 9,000 metric tonnes in 1997 (Yew *et al.*, 2010: 21). Emissions from degraded or destroyed peatlands are around 1.8 gigatonnes of carbon dioxide per year, which is equal to 4 per cent of total worldwide greenhouse gas emissions from less than 0.1 per cent of global land surface. Fires account for about 70 per cent of Indonesia's annual emissions from peatlands, and the remaining 30 per cent come from emissions as a result of peatland drainage (Silvius and Kaat, 2010: 7). Under a business-as-usual scenario, peat will be the main source of emissions for Indonesia by 2020, alongside energy sources (Suharto, 2010: 6). At the Copenhagen Climate Conference in 2009, Indonesia had committed to undertake voluntary mitigation actions to achieve 26 per cent emission reductions by 2020 (Suharto, 2010: 4); under this business-as-usual scenario, achieving this will be problematic.

Other than the release of carbon into the atmosphere, the more visible effects of burning peatlands is the release of smoke, which, when in sufficient amounts to travel across boundaries, results in what is known as transboundary haze pollution. The underground peatfires cover large areas and smoulder sometimes for weeks. The smoke that is released by these smouldering fires is usually thick and sooty, because of the organic material contained in the peat. This smoke is the main cause of the regional haze. It was found that more than 60,000 peatland fires occurred between 1997 to 2009 causing the haze problem in the region (Tan *et al.*, 2009: 423). It is estimated that 60 per cent of carbon dioxide and particulates in smoke and haze came from peatfires due to forest conversion burning, while others have estimated that about 80 per cent of the haze problem is caused by burning on peatsoil (Silvius and Kaat, 2010: 9).

Despite these serious environmental concerns, local, Malaysian and Singaporean plantation companies continue to convert peatlands and degraded forest lands in Indonesia, often using fire (Jiwan, 2011: 8). Therefore, what exists is a situation where 'everyone is burning and the whole system operates based on burning' (Moore [I5], 2010). The economic motivation for this is very strong; clearing land with fire is up to 40 times cheaper than using machinery or chemicals (Salim, 2007). Simply put, to not burn would be uncompetitive (Moore [I5], 2010). As a result, there has been no indication that the long-term average emissions from peat fires have changed substantially between 1990 and 2008 (Wibisino *et al.*, 2011: 13). As one interviewee stated, 'the mindset of the plantations is that it is fine if there is haze for around a week, because they are gaining so much' in terms of profit (Syarif [I2], 2010).

Conclusion

As this chapter has clearly shown, it has become apparent that haze-producing forest and peat fires are not merely the result of dry weather or poor methods of community-based shifting cultivation, but the actions of business conglomerates engaged in premeditated burning for commercial gain with total disregard for the environment. The next chapter discusses how, due to the process of economic regionalization that has focused Malaysian and Singaporean plantation interests in Indonesia, this practice is not limited to local plantation firms, but is often carried out by foreign firms as well. Haze mitigation is a limiting factor to this sector; by limiting the opening of fire-prone land, growth in the sector would slow and profits would drop. By practising zero burning, plantations have to 'waste' money on more expensive mechanical land clearing procedures. With such potential for profit, coupled with continued facilitation by home governments and patronage support within Indonesia as discussed in the next chapters, unsustainable commercial land clearing for oil palm plantations is likely to continue into the foreseeable future.

Notes

1 Parts of this chapter have appeared in Muhamad Varkkey (2011) and Varkkey (2012).
2 'PT' stands for *Perseroan Terbatas*, which means limited liability company.
3 Under the Ministry of Agriculture Regulation Number 26/Permentaan/OT.140//2/ 2007 Guidance on Plantation Business License, a licensed plantation company has the duty to develop a minimum of 20 per cent of its total area for surrounding smallholders. The formal partnership between private plantations and smallholders has to be

endorsed by the regent or mayor, and would involve cooperation for transportation of fresh fruit bunches, procurement of goods (harvest tools, agrochemicals etc) processing, and marketing.

4 A 'hotspot' is an area where the temperature is high and thus fire-prone (Suwarsono [I3], 2010). There may also be 'false hotspots'; for instance at industrial areas, volcanoes and mines, which are not fire-prone. Fires resulting from hotspots are commonly known as 'forest fires', even though they may occur outside forest areas such as in large oil palm plantations and traditional farmlands (Susatya, 2008). Most of Indonesia's hotspots were located in Sumatra and Kalimantan, and if left unabated, can result in the fires that produce smoke and haze.

5 During the mid-1900s, Indonesia's forest cover was an estimated 133 million hectares, or around two-thirds of its land area (Barber, 1998: 4–35) (64 per cent of its total land area) (Suharto, 2011: 13), and Indonesia had some of the most extensive concentrations of tropical hardwoods in the world. However, these forests have now been over-logged by decades of 'no-holds barred exploitation' (Barber, 1998: 4–35). Indonesia is losing approximately 2.8 million hectares of forest every year (Fatah and Udiansyah, 2009).

6 The low cost of the fire method for clearing land also makes this method attractive to smallholders, both independent ones and those formally linked to plantation companies through 'nucleus-plasma' schemes. However, despite this, evidence detailed above has shown that most haze-causing fires can be traced back to commercial and not smallholder plantations. There are a few reasons for this. First, because of their comparatively limited land ownership, these smallholders do not open up new areas every year (unlike many commercial plantations), and usually stick to a five-year-once schedule of forest burning (Gan, 1972: 3). Second, these farmers are usually equipped with traditional local knowledge to better control these fires so that they do not get out of hand (Boer, 2002). And third, smallholders usually are not found in peatland areas due to their waterlogged nature (Wibisino [I44], 2011), and thus do not make use of these areas for farming, instead sticking to forests and degraded land. As explained in the following section, fires on peatlands produce the thick, sooty smoke that most seriously contribute to haze. While fires on pristine forests and degraded land also produce smoke, this is usually not as persistent and does not travel long distances as smoke from peatfires. And generally, only commercial plantations have the political clout and funds to gain access to these peatland areas for development.

7 This figure would be much lower if more plantations were established on degraded lands instead of the carbon-rich peat.

References

Adnan, H. 2014. CPO prices hit below RM2,400 level. *The Star*, 4 June 2014.

Agriculture Corner. 2012. *Top Ten Palm Oil Producers 2012*. Available: www.agricorner.com/top-ten-palm-oil-producers-2012/ [accessed 1 August 2014].

Albanese, M. 2012. *Is There Palm Oil in That?* [Online]. Rainforest Alliance. Available: http://thefrogblog.org/2012/08/21/is-there-palm-oil-in-that/ [accessed 4 August 2014].

Albar [I17], I. 13 July 2010. *RE: Head, Directorate of Forest Fire Control, Ministry of Forestry.*

Applegate, G., Smith, R., Fox, J. J., Mitchell, A., Packham, D., Tapper, N. and Baines, G. 2002. Forest fires in Indonesia: Impacts and solutions. *In:* Colfer, C. J. and Resosudarmo, I. A. P. (eds) *Which Way Forward? People, forests and policymaking in Indonesia.* Singapore: Institute of Southeast Asian Studies.

Arif [I41], J. 4 November 2011 2011. *RE: Forest Campaigner, Greenpeace Southeast Asia.*

Asean Secretariat 1992. *Report of Workshop on Transboundary Pollution of Haze in ASEAN Countries*. Balikpapan, Indonesia, pp. 4–6.

Bangun, D. 2014. Exploring demand-side incentives for sustainable palm oil in Asia. *UNORCID Roundtable.* PowerPoint Presentation: United Nations Office for REDD+ Coordination in Indonesia.

Bank Indonesia 2014. *National Accounts*. Jakarta. Available: www.bi.go.id/sdds/series/NA/index_NA.asp [accessed 4 August 2014].

BAPPENAS 2009. *Reducing Carbon Emissions from Indonesia's Peat Lands: Interim report of a multidisciplinary study.* Jakarta: BAPPENAS.

Barber, C. V. 1998. Forest resource scarcity and social conflict in Indonesia. *Environment*, 40, 4.

Basiron, Y. 2007. Palm oil production through sustainable plantations. *European Journal of Lipid Science and Technology*, 109, 289–295.

Bernama 2010. Palm oil sector to become larger contributor to GDP. *Bernama Daily Malaysian News*, 30 March.

Blain, D., Row, C., Alm, J., Byrne, K. and Parish, F. 2006. Wetlands. *2006 IPCC Guidelines for National Greenhouse Gas Inventories*. Kuala Lumpur.

Boer, C. 2002. Forest and fire suppression in East Kalimantan, Indonesia. *In:* Moore, P., Ganz, D., Lay, C. T., Enters, T. and Durst, P. B. (eds) Communities in flames: proceedings of an international conference on community involvement in firemanagement. Bangkok. Food and Agriculture Organization of the United Nations, Regional Office for Asia and the Pacific.

Boer, R., Nurrochmat, D. R., Ardiansyah, M., Hariyadi, Purwawangsa, H. and Ginting, G. 2012. Indonesia: Analysis of implementation and financing gaps *Project Report.* Bogor: Center for Climate Risk and Opportunity Management, Bogor Agricultural University

Brown, R. A. 2006. Indonesian corporations, cronysim, and corruption. *Modern Asian Studies*, 40, 953–992.

Butler, R. A., Lian, P. K. and Ghazoul, J. 2009. REDD in the red: Palm oil could undermine carbon payment scheme. *Conservations Letters*, 2, 67–73.

Caroko, W., Komarudin, H., Obidzinski, K. and Gunarso, P. 2011. Policy and institutional frameworks for the development of palm oil-based biodiesel in Indonesia. Working Paper, Jakarta: Center for International Forestry Research.

Casey [I46], M. 22 November 2011. *RE: Writer, Associate Press.*

Casson, A. 2002. The political economy of Indonesia's oil palm sector. *In:* Colfer, C. J. and Resosudarmo, I. A. P. (eds) *Which Way Forward? People, forests and policymaking in Indonesia.* Singapore: Institute of South East Asian Studies.

Chalil, D. 2008. An Empirical Analysis of Assymetric Duopoly in the Indonesian Crude Palm Oil Industry. PhD thesis, University of Sydney.

Chang, L. L. and Rajan, R. S. 2001. Regional versus multilateral solutions to transboundary environmental problems: Insights from the Southeast Asian haze. *World Economy*, 24, 655–670.

Claudell, S., Ruysschaert, D., Darsoyo, A., Zen, R., Gea, G. and Singleton, I. 2011. *Developing Palm-oil Production on Degraded Land: Technical, economic, biodiversity, climate, legal and policy implications*. Washington, DC: International Finance Corporation, World Bank Group.

Colchester, M., Jiwan, N., Andiko, Sirait, M., Firdaus, A. Y., Surambo, A. and Pane, H. 2006. *Promised Land: Palm Oil and Land Acquisition in Indonesia: Implications for Local Communities and Indegenous Peoples.* Bogor: Sawit Watch.

Colfer, C. J. P. 2002. Ten propositions to explain Kalimantan's fires. *In:* Colfer, C. J. and Resosudarmo, I. A. P. (eds) *Which Way Forward? People, forests and policymaking in Indonesia.* Singapore: Institute of Southeast Asian Studies.

Cooke, F. M. 2006. Recent developments and conservation interventions in Borneo. *In:* Cooke, F. M. (ed.) *State, Communities and Forests in Contemporary Borneo.* Canberra: The Australian National University E Press.

Das, N. 2014. *Creating Demand for Sustainable Palm Oil through Tariff Policies in India and Indonesia.* Oxford, UK: Global Canopy Programme.

Dauvergne, P. 1994. The politics of deforestation in Indonesia. *Pacific Affairs*, 66, 497–518.

Dauvergne, P. 1998. The political economy of Indonesia's 1997 forest fires. *Australian Journal of International Affairs*, 52, 13–17.

Dennis, R. 1999. A review of fire projects in Indonesia. Bogor: Center for International Forestry Research.

Di, S. 2011a. Export tax shield. *Indo Plantations Sector Outlook.* Jakarta: CLSA Asia Pacific Markets.

Di, S. 2011b. Tread Cautiously. *Indo Plantations Sector Outlook.* Jakarta: CLSA Asia Pacific Markets.

Duncan, C. R. 2007. Mixed outcomes: The impact of regional autonomy and decentralization on indegenous ethnic minorities in Indonesia. *Development and Change*, 438, 711–733.

Eaton, P. and Radojevic, R. 2001. *Forest Fires and Regional Haze in Southeast Asia*, New York, Nova Science Publishers, Inc.

Ewing, J. J. 2011. *Forests, Food and Fuel: REDD+ and Indonesia's land-use conundrum.* Asia Security Initiative Policy Series. Singapore: S. Rajaratnam School of International Studies.

Fairhurst, T. and Mclaughlin, D. 2009. Sustainable oil palm development in degraded land in Kalimantan. Kent: World Wildlife Fund.

Faostat 2012. *Area Harvested of Oil Palm Fruit in Indonesia – 1961–2012.* Geneva: Food and Agriculture Organization of the United Nations.

Fatah, L. and Udiansyah 2009. *An Assessment of Forest Management Options for Preventing Forest Fire in Indonesia.* South Kalimatan: Economy and Environment Program For South East Asia.

Gan, T. L. 1972. Smoke Haze over Singapore. *Meteorological Memoir.* Meteorological Service Singapore.

Gellert, P. K. 1998. A brief history and analysis of Indonesia's forest fire crisis. *Indonesia*, 65.

Gellert, P. K. 2005. The shifting natures of 'Development': Growth, crisis and recovery in Indonesia's forests. *World Development*, 33, 1345–1364.

Global Environment Center 2010. Technical Workshop on the Development of the ASEAN Peatland Fire Prediction and Warning System. Workshop Report. Kuala Lumpur: ASEAN Peatlands Forest project.

Greenpalm 2014. *Vegetable Oil Production 2013: Tonnes.* PowerPoint Presentation. Available: www.slideshare.net/GreenPalmOil/2013-global-vegtable-oil-production [accessed 1 August 2014].

Greenpeace 2007. *How the Palm Oil Industry is Cooking the Climate.* Jakarta: Greenpeace.

Hameiri, S. and Jones, L. 2013. The politics and governance of non-traditional security. *International Studies Quarterly*, 57, 462–473.

Harrison, M. E., Page, S. E. and Limin, S. H. 2009. The global impact of Indonesian forest fires. *Biologist*, 56.

Hilman, M. 2010. Policy on Peat and Climate Change in Indonesia. PowerPoint Presentation. Workshop on Options for Carbon FInancinf to Support Peatland Management: Ministry of Environment, Indonesia.

Hirsch, P. and Warren, C. 1998. Introduction: through the environmental looking glass. *In:* Hirsch, P. and Warren, C. (eds) *The Politics of Environment in Southeast Asia: Resources and Resistance.* New York: Routledge.

Hunt, C. 2010. The costs of reducing deforestation in Indonesia. *Bulletin of Indonesian Economic Studies*, 46, 187–192.

Hurst, P. 1987. Forest destruction in South East Asia. *Ecologist*, 17, 170–174.

Indexmundi 2014. *Indonesia Palm Oil Production by Year.* IndexMudi. Available: www.indexmundi.com/agriculture/?country=id&commodity=palm-oil&graph=production [accessed 8 August 2014].

Indonesian Government 1998. Bahan informasi dalam rangka pertemuan working group for Sub Regional Fire Fighting Arrangement (ARA) di Singapura pada tanggal 6 Mei 1998. Pekanbaru: Department Kehutanan dan Perkebunan Kantor Wilayah Propinsi Riau.

Interviewee I21. 16 July 2010. *RE: Telapak.*

Interviewee I49. 1 December 2011. *RE: Leuser Foundation.*

Interviewee M28. 14 April 2010. *RE: TH Plantations.*

Interviewee M41. 11 May 2010. *RE: Ministry of Plantation Industries and Commodities.*

Interviewee M44. 5 January 2012. *RE: Global Environment Center.*

Jakarta Post 1994. Kalimantan, SUmatra forest fires turn into blaming game. *Jakarta Post*, 3 October 1994.

Jakarta Post 1998. Haze from forest fires blankets areas in Riau. *Jakarta Post*, 16 February 1998.

Jakarta Post 2006. Smothering Kalimantan waits for rains. *Jakarta Post*, 2 November 2006.

Jakarta Post 2009. Curbing the haze. *Jakarta Post*, 19 June 2009.

Jarvis, D., Richmond, N., Phua, K. H., Pocock, N., Sovacool, B. K. and D'agostino, A. 2010. Palm oil in Southeast Asia. *Asian Trends Monitoring Bulletin*, 4, 9–14.

Jiwan, N. 2011. *What's Happening in the Indonesian Palm Oil Industry*. Bogor: Sawit Watch.

Jomo, K. S. 2003. Reforming East Asia for sustainable development. *Asian Business and Management*, 3, 7–38.

Jones, D. S. 2006. ASEAN and transboundary haze pollution in Southeast Asia. *Asia Europa Journal*, 4, 434–440.

Kaat, A. and Silvius, M. 2011. *Impacts of Biofuel Demands on Carbon Dioxide Emissions from Peatlands*. Jakarta: Wetlands International.

Koh, L. P. and Wilcove, D. S. 2007. Cashing in palm oil for conservation. *Nature*, 448, 993–994.

Law [M29], H. D. 15 April 2010. *RE: former Minister, Ministry of Natural Resources and Environment.*

Lee [S20], P. O. 26 May 2010. *RE: Fellow, Regional Economic Studies, Institute for South East Asian Studies.*

Lee, P. O. 2011. *Time to save ASEAN's forests. Viewpoints.* Singapore: Institute of South East Asian Studies.

Liew, S. F. 2010. *A Fine Balance: Stories from peatland communities in Malaysia*, Kuala Lumpur: Malaysian Palm Oil Council.

Maitar [I12], B. 2 July 2010. *RE: Forest Campaign Team Leader, Greenpeace-Southeast Asia.*

Malaysian Palm Oil Council 2006. *Oil Palm: Tree of life*, Kuala Lumpur, Malaysian Palm Oil Council.

Masripatin, N., Rufi'ie, Ginoga, K., Gintings, N., Siregar, C. A., Sugardiman, R., Wibowo, A., Darmawan, W. S., Rahman, S., Maryani, R., Pribadi, A., Nurfatriani, F., Puspasari, D., Imamnudin, R. and Pradjadinata, S. 2009. National Strategy: Reducing Emissions from Deforestation and Forest Degradation in Indonesia, Readiness Phase Draft – August 2009. Jakarta: Ministry of Forestry.

Mathew [M8], K. G. 20 March 2010. *RE: former Plantation Manager, Sime Darby Plantation.*

McCarthy, J. and Cramb, R. A. 2009. Policy narratives, landholder engagement, and oil palm expansion on the Malaysian and Indonesian frontiers. *The Geographical Journal*, 175, 112–123.

McCarthy, J. and Zen, Z. 2010. Regulating the oil palm boom: Asessing the effectiveness of environmental governance approaches to agro-industrial pollution in Indonesia. *Law and Policy*, 32, 153–179.

McCarthy, J. F. 2010. Process of inclusion and adverse incorporation: oil palm and agrarian change in Sumatra, Indonesia. *The Journal of Peasant Studies*, 37, 821–850.

Menteri Pertanian Republik Indonesia 2003. Keputusan Menteri Pertanian Nomor: 250/Kpts/KP.150/4/2003 Tentang Pembentukan Komisi Minyak Sawit Indonesia. Jakarta.

Ministry of Agriculture 2013. Corporate Social Responsibility (CSR) in Indonesian Plantation. Public–Private Dialogue on Investment 2013, Asia Pacific Economic Cooperation (APEC), 2013 Jakarta. PowerPoint Presentation.

Ministry of Forestry 2009. REDD Methodology and Strategies Summary for Policy Makers. *REDDI: Reducing Emissions from Deforestation and Forest Degradation in Indonesia.* Jakarta: Ministry of Forestry, Indonesia Forest Climate Alliance.

Mittelman, J. H. 1998. Globalisation and environmental resistance politics. *Third World Quarterly*, 19, 847–872.

Moore [I5], P. F. 27 June 2010. *RE: Project Manager, IUCN-WWF Project Firefight Southeast Asia.*

Muhamad Varkkey, H. 2011. Plantation land management, fires, and haze in Southeast Asia. *Malaysian Journal of Environmental Management*, 12, 33–41.

Munadar, A., Ruth, D. and Putra, A. 2010. Rejection REDD Plus program Australia–Indonesia in Jambi. Position Paper. Jambi: Regional Executive WALHI Jambi.

Nature 2007. Focus on surfectants. *Nature*, 3.

Ngai, W. C. 1998. Responding to landslide hazards in rapidly developing Malaysia: A case of economics versus environmental protection. *Disaster Prevention and Management*, 7, 14–27.

Nomura, K. 2009. A perspective on education for sustainable development: Historical development of environmental education in Indonesia. *International Journal of Educational Development*, 29, 621–627.

Nowak, B. S. 2008. Environmental degradation and its gendered impact on coastal livelihoods options among Btsisi' household of Peninsular Malaysia. *Development*, 51, 186–192.

Ong, C. T. and Chai, L. S. 2011. Plantation (Malaysia). *Sector Update.* Kuala Lumpur: Maybank.

Othman, J. 2003. Linking agricultural trade, land demand and environmental externalities: Case of oil palm in South East Asia. *ASEAN Economic Bulletin*, 20, 244–55.

Page, S. 2011. Tropical Peatland Research. Powerpoint Presentation. University of Leicester: Department of Geography.

Page, S., Hoscilo, A., Wosten, H., Jauhiainen, J., Silvius, M., Rieley, J., Ritzema, H., Tansey, K., Graham, L., Vassander, H. and Limin, S. 2009. Restoration ecology of lowland tropical peatlands in Southeast Asia: Current knowledge and future research directions. *Ecosystems*, 12, 888–905.

Paneco Foundation 2008. Vanishing Tripa: The continuous destruction of a unique ecosystem by palm oil plantations. Banda Aceh: PanEco Foundation.

Parish, F. 2011. *An Overview of Asian Wetlands.* Kuala Lumpur: Wetlands International.

Parish, F. and Looi, C. C. 2011. Options and needs for enhanced linkage between the Ramsar Convention on Wetlands Convention on Biological Diversity and UN Framework Convention on Climate Change. *Wetlands, Biodiversity and Cimate Change.* Kuala Lumpur: Global Environment Network.

Parliament Of Singapore 1998. ASEAN Environment Ministers' Meeting (Progress towards addressing problems of fires and haze pollution) (1998-04-02). Singapore: Parliament of Singapore.

Phillips, V. D. 1998. Peatswamp ecology and sustainable development in Borneo. *Biodiversity and Conservation*, 7, 651–671.

Pichler, M. 2011. Palm oil and agrofuels in Southeast Asia: A political ecology framework for studying human-nature interactions and the role of the state. International Conference on International Relations and Development, Thailand.

Prasetyo, F. A., Suwarno, A., Purwanto and Hakim, R. 2009. Making policies work for Payment for Environmental Services (PES): An evaluation of the experiences of formulating conservation policies in districts of Indonesia. *Journal of Sustainable Forestry*, 28, 415–433.

Quah, E. and Johnston, D. 2001. Forest fires and environmental haze in Southeast Asia: Using the 'stakeholder' approach to assign costs and responsibilities. *Journal of Environmental Management*, 63, 181–191.

Rajenthran, A. 2002. Indonesia: An overview of the legal framework of Foreign Direct Investment. ISEAS Working Papers: Economics and Finance. Singapore: Institute of Southeast Asian Studies.

Ramakrishna [M20], S. 7 April 2010. *RE: Coordinator, Malaysian Environmental NGOs.*

Raman, M. 2006. Environmental struggles in Malaysia. *Development*, 49, 38–42.

Raman, M., Van Schaik, A., Richter, K. and De Clerck, P. 2008. Malaysian palm oil – green gold or green wash? A comment on the sustainability claims of Malaysia's palm oil lobby, with a special focus on the state of Sarawak. Kuala Lumpur: Friends of the Earth.

Resosudarmo [I26], B. P. 22 July 2010. *RE: Associate Professor, Development and Environmental Economics.*

Reuters 2011. Update 1 – Wilmar to invest $900 mln in Indonesia palm oil product plants. Reuters, 7 February 2011.

Richardson, C. L. 2010. Deforestation due to palm oil plantations in Indonesia. Towards the Sustainable Production of Palm Oil, Australia. Nimbin, Australia: The Palm Oil Action Group.

Rifin, A. 2010. The effect of export tax on Indonesia's Crude palm Oil (CPO) export competitiveness. *ASEAN Economic Bulletin*, 27, 173–84.

Rist, L., Feintrenie, L. and Levang, P. 2010. The livelihood impacts of oil palm: Smallholders in Indonesia. *Biodiversity and Conservation*, 19, 1009–1024.

Roberti, M. 1989. Agribusiness: Asia's next economic miracle. *Asian Finance*, 15, 54–56.
Rowland [I39], I. 3 November 2011. *RE: Tropical Forest Conservation Manager, The Royal Society for the Protection of Birds.*
Rukmantara [I45], A. 14 November 2011. *RE: Former environmental journalist, Jakarta Post.*
Rukmantara, A. 2006. Forest fires bring shame to nation: SBY. *Jakarta Post*, 23 April 2006.
Saharjo, B. H. 1999. The role of human activities in Indonesian forest fire problems. *In:* Suhartoyo, H. and Toma, T. (eds) *Impacts of Fire and Human Activities on Forest Ecosystems in the Tropics*. Samarinda, Indonesia: Tropical Forest Research Center, Mulawarman University.
Salim, E. 2007. The haze: Economic and social ramifications. *ISEAS Regional Outlook Forum 2007*. Singapore: Institute of South East Asian Studies.
Samsul, Firman, Muhib, Syarwani, Helmi, Nurdin and Zakaria 2007. *The Golden Crop? Palm oil in post-tsunami Aceh*. Aceh: Eye on Aceh.
Sandker, M., Suwarno, A. and Campbell, B. M. 2007. Will forests remain in the face of oil palm expansion? Simulating change in Malimau, Indonesia. *Ecology and Society*, 12, 37–40.
Satyawan [I20], L. S. 16 July 2010. *RE: Lecturer, Forest Fire, Department of Silviculture, Institute Pertanian Bogor.*
Sawit Watch 2007. Palm oil for biofuels increases social conflicts and undermines land reform in Indonesia. *Open letter to the European Parliament, the European Commission, the goverments and citizens of the European Union*. Bogor: Sawit Watch.
Schwarz, A. 1990. No business like agribusiness. *Far Eastern Economic Review*, 148 (16), 19 April, 58.
Silvius, M. and Kaat, A. 2010. Peat Swamp Forests and Palm Oil. Powerpoint Presentation. Indonesia.
Simamora, A. P. 2011. SBY vows to protect palm oil interests. *Jakarta Post*, 26 March 2011.
Slette, J. P. and Wiyono, I. E. 2011. Oilseeds and products update 2011. USDA Foreign Agriculture Service.
Stone, R. 2007. Can palm oil plantations come clean? *Science*, 317, 1491.
Suharto, R. 2010. *Challenges Faced by Indonesian Palm Oil*. Yogyakarta: Indonesian Palm Oil Commission.
Suharto, R. 2011. *Sustainable Palm Oil Development in Indonesia*. Jakarta: Indonesia Palm Oil Commission.
Sumiani, Y., Haslinda, Y. and Lehman, G. 2007. Environmental reporting in a developing country: A case study on status and implementation in Malaysia. *Journal of Cleaner Production*, 15, 895–901.
Surya [I9], M. T. and Akbar [I10], A. 30 June 2010. *RE: Deputy Directors, Wahana Lingkungan Hidup Indonesia.*
Susatya, A. 2008. Hot spots: A burning issue for Indonesia. *Jakarta Post*, 26 August 2008.
Sutton, K. 2001. Agribusiness on a grand scale – Felda's sahabat complex in East Malaysia. *Singapore Journal of Tropical Geography*, 22, 90–105.
Suwarsono [I3]. 24 June 2010. *RE: Researcher, Remote Sensing Applications and Technology Development Center, Indonesian National Institute of Aeronautics and Space.*
Swajaya [I37], N. 30 July 2010. *RE: Country Permanent Representative to ASEAN, Ministry of Foreign Affairs.*

Syaf [I27], R. 24 July 2010. *RE: Director of Conservation Information, Wahana Informasi.*
Syarif [I2], L. M. 24 June 2010. *RE: Chief, Cluster of Security and Justice Governance, Kemitraan Partnership.*
Tan [S7], A. K. J. 17 May 2010. *RE: Vice Dean, Faculty of Law, NUS.*
Tan, C. W. 2011. Double beneficiaries. *Plantations Sector Outlook.* Kuala Lumpur: CLSA Asia Pacific Markets.
Tan, K. T., Lee, K. T., Mohamed, A. R. and Bhatia, S. 2009. Palm oil: Addressing issues and towards sustainable development. *Renewable and Sustainable Energy Reviews*, 13, 420–427.
Tan, T. M. and Oetomo, T. 2011. Back to Basics – Who, what and how? *Asia Palm Oil Sector.* Kuala Lumpur: Credit Suisse.
Taylor, M. and Supriatna, Y. 2014. Indonesia lawmakers draft bill to slash foreign ownership of plantations. Reuters, 15 August 2014.
Than, M. 1998. Introductory overview: Development strategies, agricultural policies and agricultural development in Southeast Asia. *ASEAN Ecnomic Bulletin*, 15, 1–12.
UNCTAD 2009. TNCs and Agricultural Production in Developing Countries. *World Investment Report 2009: Transnational Corporations, Agricultural Production and Development.* Geneva: UNCTAD.
Uob Kay Hian 2011a. Agricultural commodities gaining attention. *Plantation-regional.* Kuala Lumpur: UOB Kay Hian.
Uob Kay Hian 2011b. Plantation sector: Peak production growth is over; upgrade to market weight. Change of Recommendation. *Regional.* Kuala Lumpur: Regional Research Team, UOB Kay Hian.
USDA 2009. *INDONESIA: Palm Oil Production Growth To Continue.* USDA Foreign Agricultural Service. Available: www.pecad.fas.usda.gov/highlights/2009/03/Indonesia/ [accessed 8 August 2014].
USDA 2014. *Table 19: World: Palm Oil, Coconut Oil, and Fish Meal Supply and Distribution.* Foreign Agricultural Service, USDA
Van Gelder, J. W. 2004. *Greasy Palms: European buyers of Indonesian palm oil.* Castricum: Friends of the Earth.
Varkkey, H. 2012. The growth and prospects of the oil palm plantation industry in Indonesia. *Oil Palm Industry Economic Journal*, 12, 1–13.
Varma, A. 2003. The economics of slash and burn: A case studyof the 1997–1998 Indonesian forest fires. *Ecological Economics*, 46, 159–171.
Wahid, M. B., Abdullah, S. N. A. and Henson, I. E. *Oil palm – Achievements and potential. 'New directions for a diverse planet'.* Proceedings of the 4th International Crop Science Congress, 2004 Brisbane. Australian Agronomy Conference.
WALHI and Sawit Watch 2009. *Memorandum: Issues Surrounding Malaysia Palm Oil Investments and Plantation Operations in Indonesian Palm Oil Industry.* WALHI and Sawit Watch.
Wetlands International 2014. *Tropical Peat Swamp Forests.* Available: www.wetlands.org/Whatarewetlands/Peatlands/Tropicalpeatswampforests/tabid/2739/Default.aspx [accessed 8 August 2014].
Wibisino [I44], I. T. C. 10 November 2011. *RE: Wetlands International.*
Wibisino, I. T. C., Silber, T., Lubis, I. R., Rais, D. S., Suryadiputra, N., Silvius, M., Tol, S. and Joosten, H. 2011. *Peatlands in Indonesia's National REDD+ strategy.* Bogor: Wetlands International.
Wicke, B., Sikkema, R., Dornburg, V. and Faaij, A. 2011. Exploring land use changes and the role of palm oil production in Indonesia and Malaysia. *Land Use Policy*, 28, 193–206.

Widianarko, B. 2009. *Democratization, Decentralisation and Environmental Conservation in Indonesia.* Asia-pacific NGO Environmental Conference, Kyoto.

World Growth 2011. *The Economic Benefit of Palm Oil to Indonesia.* Virginia: World Growth.

World Rainforest Movement 1998. *Sawit Watch: An Indonesian network against oil palm plantations.* Available: www.wrm.org.uy/oldsite/bulletin/14/Indonesia2.html [accessed 8 August 2014].

World Resources Institute 2013. *Figure 1: Fire Alerts ber hectare in Sumatra, Indonesia.* Washington, DC Available: https://time2transcend.files.wordpress.com/2013/07/fire_density-wri.png [accessed 5 August 2014].

Yeoh, S., Chan, Y. J. and Srinath, A. 2011a. Supply side support in 2012; Top picks – Wilmar and Sime Darby. *ASEAN Plantations.* Kuala Lumpur: J. P. Morgan.

Yeoh, S., Srinath, A. and Chan, Y. J. 2011b. ASEAN Plantations: Downside risks and opportunities; a look at 2008/2009. *Asia Pacific Equity Research.* Kuala Lumpur: J. P. Morgan.

Yeoh, S., Srinath, A. and Chan, Y. J. 2011c. ASEAN Plantations: Upcoming data-points, upside and risk factors. *Asia Pacific Equity Research.* Kuala Lumpur: J. P. Morgan.

Yew, F. K., Sundram, K. and Basiron, Y. 2010. Estimation of GHG emissions from peat used for agriculture with special reference to palm oil. *Journal of Oil Palm and the Environment*, 1, 17–25.

Zakaria, A., Theile, C. and Khaimur, L. 2007. *Policy, Practice, Pride and Prejudice: Review of legal, environmental and social practises of oil palm plantation companies of the Wilmar Group in Sambas District, West Kalimantan (Indonesia).* Netherlands: Milieudefensie.

Zhou, A. and Thomson, E. 2009. The development of biofuels in Asia. *Applied Energy*, 86, 11–20.

3 The state as facilitator of regionalization[1]

As detailed below, interviewees stated that the practice of haze-producing land-clearing using fire is not limited to local plantation firms, but is often carried out by Malaysian and Singaporean firms operating in Indonesia as well (Rukmantara [I45], 2011; Tan [S7], 2010). These firms are often easily able to escape prosecution even when confronted with evidence of complicity in these fires. This book argues that the economic regionalization of the Southeast Asian oil palm plantation sector is a major driver of transboundary haze.

In the Southeast Asian context, Sim (2006: 490–491) has noted two distinct drivers of regionalization: the role of the state as facilitator and similar patronage cultures. This chapter focuses on the first driver, the role of the state as a facilitator of economic regionalization of the oil palm sector in the region. It is divided into three sections. The first section of the chapter introduces the concept of economic regionalization as used in the literature, noting that while economic regionalization in the Southeast Asian context has been market-driven, the state has played an especially important role as facilitator of the process. The subsequent section addresses the regionalization process from the Indonesian, Malaysian and Singaporean perspectives respectively, focusing on government facilitation of the process that resulted in many Malaysian and Singaporean government-linked companies (GLCs) and well-connected oil palm plantation firms establishing plantations in Indonesia. This section highlights how many Malaysian and Singaporean government elites have vested interests in plantation firms. Section three of this chapter notes that vested interests of home governments in these firms further encourage home state involvement and facilitation to ensure the well-being of these plantation firms in the regionalization process. This explains why Malaysian and Singaporean governments have been observed using their influence and resources to defend their firms in Indonesia when faced with accusations of open-burning misconduct that threatened the continued profitability of their firms in Indonesia.

Economic regionalization

Vernon Henderson (1994: 83) has argued that locational choices for the outward movement of firms are less 'accidental' or a function of history, but instead can be largely explained by measurable economic magnitudes, such as local wages, taxes, urban scale and the like. As outlined in the introductory chapter, there are two major varieties of regional integration: 'regionalization' and 'regionalism' (Breslin and Higgott, 2003; Hurrell, 1995; Katzenstein, 1997). Generally, regional economic integration in Southeast Asia has taken the path of 'regionalization'. Economic regionalization refers to often undirected 'processes of integration that arise from markets, private trade and investment flows, and the policies and decisions of companies' (Breslin and Higgott, 2003: 177). It involves 'autonomous economic processes which lead to higher levels of economic interdependence within a given geographical area' (Hurrell, 1995: 334). According to Hurrell (1995: 334), this includes the 'growth of intra-firm trade, the increasing numbers of international mergers and acquisitions, and the emergence of increasingly dense networks of strategic alliances between firms'.

Explanations of the regionalization of firms are generally based on theories derived from Western trends of internationalization and regionalization. This includes the investment development path theory; the Uppsala model (Sim, 2006: 490); and the product cycle theory (Haji Mat Zin, 1999: 471). The investment development path theory relates the net outward investment of a country to its stage of economic development (Sim, 2006: 489–490). Countries that are at a low level of economic development usually experience little inward or outward investment. As the country develops, there should be an increase in inward investment, especially for import substitution, and some outward investment, particularly in less-developed neighbouring countries. Further economic development would promote a decline in inward investment and an increase in outward investment (normally to overcome high labour costs and to seek markets or strategic assets). As a country achieves developed status, outward investment will continue to increase, with production becoming internationalized (Sim, 2006: 489–490).

The Uppsala model proposes incrementally higher commitments to regional business expansion based on knowledge acquisition about the regional market. The first step normally involves export to a country via an agent or independent representative, followed by the establishment of a sales subsidiary and eventually production there (Sim, 2006: 490). And the product cycle theory promotes regionalization to the less-developed economies to lower costs in the interest of price competitiveness. First, production will be located in the most advanced country where high income can support the new products. Local companies increasingly substitute labour with capital-intensive technology until the product matures and becomes standardized. This results in economies of scale that stimulates large-scale production and enables it to be exported. However, transport and production costs influence the firm's decision to relocate. When the product becomes standardized to undifferentiable levels and has to be competitively priced, the firms would be forced to move to the less-developed economies to lower costs (Haji Mat Zin, 1999: 471).

While informative in explaining regionalization in general, these Western theories on economic regionalization have often neglected the institutional or contextual perspectives that have been very important in the regionalization process of Southeast Asian firms. In the Southeast Asian context, Sim (2006: 490–491) has noted two distinct drivers of regionalization: the role of the state as facilitator and similar patronage cultures. Focusing here on the first driver, this section notes that state facilitation and assistance across borders has been important for economic regionalization in the region, especially in the oil palm sector. This is because of high levels of involvement from the state in the regionalization process (Beeson, 2004: 157), where Southeast Asian governments often have vested interests in firms that regionalize. Therefore, states often can be observed acting to uphold and defend the best interests of these firms (Scott, 1972: 92), which explains why states often can be seen to defend their firms operating in Indonesia when faced with accusations of causing haze-producing fires. Chapter 4 addresses the second driver, the importance of patronage politics in the regionalization of these firms, noting how Malaysian and Singaporean investments have been especially adept in integrating themselves into the Indonesian oil palm plantation industry, due to the similarities of patronage cultures between these countries (Interviewee I49, 2011), which is also useful in evading legal ramifications concerning haze-producing fires.

In the Southeast Asian context, economic regionalization, while still largely informal and market-driven, has been actively facilitated by both home (origin of firm) and host (destination of investment) states (Breslin and Higgott, 2003: 178–179; Pempel, 2005: 21). Over time, the benefits of regionalization became increasingly obvious to Southeast Asian policy makers, and this explains the changing attitudes towards it in the region during the early 1980s (Sim, 2005: 34–37). This shifted from an overwhelmingly negative view, reflected in policies designed to keep foreign firms out, to one where considerable resources are spent towards encouraging regionalization and attracting foreign (especially regional) firms inwards (Lipsey and Sjoholm, 2011: 56–57). Both home and host states recognized the potential of economic regionalization to enhance their international and domestic competitiveness, as best practices and technological knowledge can spill over through links with suppliers and competitive imitation among other industry players (Carney and Dieleman, 2011: 108). Indeed, Southeast Asian governments viewed economic regionalization as a 'strategic instrument external to the market that could potentially change market outcomes' (Goh *et al.*, 2001: 42) in favour of local and regional, instead of international players.

Many regional governments therefore introduced specific government policies to encourage economic regionalization (Goh *et al.*, 2001: 42), and also proactively coordinated regional investment outflows and inflows (Rasiah *et al.*, 2010: 333). For example, home governments often offered fiscal incentives to these companies by exempting taxes on their income derived from offshore investments (Rasiah *et al.*, 2010: 338–340). Furthermore, home governments have been known to coordinate their promotional strategies by compiling details of investors, listing out their capabilities, and promoting their interests on various platforms, including websites, embassies and trade ministries located in neighbouring countries. These platforms are also used by home governments to draw their firms' attention to potential business opportunities abroad (Rasiah *et al.*, 2010: 340). Furthermore, some host governments have sanctioned the relaxation of barriers to trade and investment (like the mutual exchange of goods, services, capital and people), especially for regional neighbours as a way to facilitate investment from within the region (Breslin and Higgott, 2003: 178–179). Host governments often have streamlined incentives and grant packages offered especially to regional firms (Rasiah *et al.*, 2010: 347–348).

Host governments also often coordinate with home governments to help investors by improving information flows, reducing risks and red tape (Rasiah *et al.*, 2010: 338–340), and facilitating access to business contacts and government officials in host countries (Goh *et al.*, 2001: 42). Neighbouring governments also often proactively engage in bilateral negotiations with each other to establish infrastructural links (Breslin and Higgott, 2003: 178–179) on behalf of investors. All these factors were instrumental in encouraging companies to establish their production bases in neighbouring countries in the region (Goh and Wong, 2011: 499–501). As a result, the regionalization of Southeast Asian firms grew in prominence in the early 1980s (Sim, 2005: 34–37). In short, unlike traditional Western concepts of regionalization that are primarily market-driven, economic regionalization in Southeast Asia has to be understood as being simultaneously market-driven and state-facilitated, and that the two processes are intrinsically linked (Pereira, 2005: 393).

Scholars have noted that there are several strategic drivers for the regionalization of firms to neighbouring countries: efficiency-seeking, asset-seeking and market-seeking factors (Carney and Dieleman, 2011: 107–108; Lipsey and Sjoholm, 2011: 42; Rasiah *et al.*, 2010: 338). Each strategy has the potential of improving the company's performance by lowering costs, improving competitiveness or producing additional revenues (Carney and Dieleman, 2011: 107–108). For Malaysian and Singaporean firms, the most important consideration driving regionalization has been efficiency-seeking factors (Carney and Dieleman, 2011: 107–108; Lipsey and Sjoholm, 2011: 42; Rasiah *et al.*, 2010: 341). Efficiency-seeking outward investment is generally targeted at gaining access to low-cost inputs such as cheap labour, land, natural resources and raw materials (Carney and Dieleman, 2011: 107–108; Lipsey and Sjoholm, 2011: 42; Rasiah *et al.*, 2010: 341). Therefore, the costs of production are especially important for the location of production networks in neighbouring countries, alongside other factors such as wages, productivity, infrastructure, tariffs and taxes (Lipsey and Sjoholm, 2011: 42).

These efficiency considerations of Malaysian and Singaporean firms were closely related to issues of dwindling land supply faced by both countries by the early 1980s. Due to land scarcity and degradation as a result of decades of 'no-holds barred exploitation' (Barber, 1998: 4–35), alongside rising farm wages (Hiratsuka, 2006: 6; Interviewee M41, 2010; *New Straits Times*, 2006: 221–242,), the governments of Singapore and Malaysia actively encouraged plantation investors to expand their operations to neighbouring states in Southeast Asia (Rasiah *et al.*, 2010: 341), especially to the abundant lands of neighbouring Indonesia. In Indonesia, the availability of vast, highly diversified natural resources, a huge potential domestic market, a competitive and productive labour force and a market-oriented economic policy have made it an attractive destination for regional investors (Rajenthran, 2002: 1). In turn, Indonesia required capital investment, expertise and technology for better uses of arable land, which was not available locally (UNCTAD, 2009: 99). Therefore, the Indonesian government also encouraged entry of regional firms, especially for the natural resource sector, according them an important role to help address investment scarcity in Indonesia (Rajenthran, 2002: 9).

With these inducements and encouragement from both host and home countries, Indonesia has become a major investment destination for Malaysian and Singaporean investments, especially in the oil palm sector (UNCTAD, 2009: 101–102), as it offered an attractive mix of political order, labour docility, land availability and lax regulation (Johnston, 2005: 177). Therefore, affluent companies in Malaysia and Singapore, with the assistance of their governments, began to carefully pursue strategies to relocate low value-added, land-intensive and labour-intensive operations to Indonesia, at once reducing local demand for land and unskilled foreign labour (Rasiah *et al.*, 2010: 340). As a result, investments from Malaysian and Singaporean companies in the Indonesian oil palm plantation sector have been particularly active due to attractive economies of scale in terms of land and labour costs (Hiratsuka, 2006: 6; Interviewee M41, 2010; *New Straits Times*, 2006: 221–242). Hence, the concentration of Malaysian and Singaporean plantation interests in neighbouring Indonesia is indicative of high levels of economic regionalization of the Southeast Asian oil palm plantation sector.

The regionalization of the Southeast Asian oil palm sector

As mentioned above, Southeast Asia gradually shifted from a negative view of foreign direct investment (FDI) and regionalization to a positive one (Lipsey and Sjoholm, 2011: 56–57). Improved economic performance in a resource based-industry such as oil palm in a resource abundant country such as Indonesia often requires internal shifts in the structures of interest and power, and the advent of external economic and political conditions that offer opportunities for growth (Rosser, 2007: 38). The following section details this internal shift in Indonesia first, to provide a better understanding of how Malaysian and Singaporean plantation firms eventually gained a solid foothold in the Indonesian oil palm sector. Indonesia's approach to foreign investment in general and in the oil palm plantation sector in particular was cautiously optimistic before settling into the current investment-friendly atmosphere, especially after the Asian financial crisis (AFC) when foreign investments in the natural resource sector were viewed as an important element of the country's economic recovery (Mathew [M8], 2010).

The regionalization of the Indonesian oil palm sector

The legal framework for foreign investment activities in Indonesia are based on Law Number 1/1967 on Foreign Investment (FIL) (amended by Law No.

11/1970) (Rajenthran, 2002: 1). It consists of 31 articles that detail Indonesia's legislative regulations towards FDI, which include policies on licensing, land use and closed or restricted sectors (Rajenthran, 2002: 9). As Indonesia required technology, investment and a better use of arable land (UNCTAD, 2009: 99), the FIL is designed to attract foreign capital, expertise and technology that can then be used to transform local potential economic resources into tangible economic strengths (Rajenthran, 2002: 1; UNCTAD, 2009: 99) and to promote partnerships with foreign entities (Caroko *et al.*, 2011: 8; Rasiah *et al.*, 2010: 338–340).

Indonesia has attempted to make its foreign investment rules more accommodating over the years, albeit with occasional back-tracking (Carney and Dieleman, 2011: 106). From the 1960s until 1983, the government of Indonesia's policy was to promote FDI by offering a variety of generous fiscal incentives, which included dividend tax exemptions and tax holidays, investment allowances and accelerated deprecation (Rajenthran, 2002: 29). However, in 1984 there was a dramatic policy reversal in Indonesia. All investor incentives were reversed through the Tax Law of 1984, in order to encourage local entrepreneurship that was lagging behind at the time. But in 1994, another dramatic policy shift materialized, where the fiscal incentives prior to 1984 were reintroduced after local involvement in entrepreneurship had improved. In particular, the Tax Law of 1984 was amended that year to offer incentives in priority sectors and locations (especially remote areas) through accelerated deprecation and amortization, the ability to carry forward losses for up to ten consecutive years and to reduce income tax, as detailed in Article 26 of Law No. 7/1983 and Law No. 10/1994 (Rajenthran, 2002: 9).

All of these enhancements however did not have any significant effect on investments in the oil palm plantation sector until the early 1990s, when there was a revision of the 'negative list' of sectors that were blocked from FDI, which included oil palm (Rajenthran, 2002: 9). After local Indonesian investors had established themselves in the oil palm sector during the 1980s, the government of Indonesia opened up the sector to foreign investors in the early 1990s (McCarthy and Cramb, 2009: 114–117). Half of the land bank allocated for the sector was offered to foreign private estates. Further enticements were offered, including generous fiscal incentives, streamlined procedures for licensing, the initiation of a privatization programme, the reduction of income tax and the removal or minimization of existing impediments to FDI (Rajenthran, 2002: 2–29). For example, Government Regulation No. 45/1996 accorded FDI from specific sectors, especially agribusiness, with tax holidays. The tax holiday policy was designed as an instrument to encourage investment into priority areas such as palm oil and underdeveloped regions (Rajenthran, 2002: 29). Other reforms of particular importance to foreign investors included the equal treatment of foreign and domestic investors and streamlined application procedures for the approval of investments (Lipsey and Sjoholm, 2011: 55).

However, Indonesia still maintained restrictions on the entitlements of foreign investors on land rights and usage. As part of the FIL, foreign entities can register a limited company (*perseroan terbatas* or PT) in Indonesia as either a private or public company (Rajenthran, 2002: 21). But, the Basic Agrarian Law No. 5 of

1960 only allows three out of 11 types of land rights for foreign investors: the Right of Building (*Hak Guna Bangunan*), the Right to Use (*Hak Pakai*) and the Right to Cultivation (*Hak Guna Usaha* or HGU). The HGU allows the usage of state-owned land for agriculture, fishing or ranching over 30 years. Normally, the bearer of the HGU must be an Indonesian legal entity, however in a joint venture company, the Indonesian partner may grant the use of the land to its foreign partner (Rajenthran, 2002: 15). Furthermore, Indonesian policy stipulated that all medium and large foreign entities may participate in the Indonesian economy only through joint ventures (with at least 20 per cent equity) with domestic small-scale entities (Rasiah *et al.*, 2010: 338–340). This meant that most foreign investments in the oil palm sector had to enter Indonesia as joint-ventures with local firms (Surya [I9] and Akbar [I10], 2010).

Despite these restrictive policies, the sector attracted considerable investment from overseas, primarily Malaysia and to a lesser extent Singapore. For example, the early 1990s saw the first entry of investments from companies like Malaysia's Kuala Lumpur Kepong (KLK) (Kuala Lumpur Kepong Berhad, 2010) and Singapore's Wilmar International (Compliance Advisor Ombudsman, 2009: 3). Such companies established joint ventures with local partners, and then proceeded to 'take over' smaller plantation companies as their subsidiaries. By 1996, 45 Malaysian firms and several other Singaporean ones along with their Indonesian partners had been able to secure land banks in Indonesia totaling approximately 1.3 million hectares (Othman, 2003: 245–255). This opening was short lived, however, as the amount of foreign investor interest was so overwhelming that domestic companies complained that they had to compete with these foreigners for land. The Indonesian government was obliged to accede to the requests of these powerful local companies and closed the oil palm sector to foreigners in 1997 (WALHI and Sawit Watch, 2009: 1–5).

The AFC was a watershed in Indonesia and the region in terms of foreign investments in the oil palm sector. When the AFC hit Indonesia in 1997, many Indonesian plantation companies suffered financial difficulties (Interviewee M41, 2010). With International Monetary Fund (IMF) structural reforms demanding the opening of Indonesian markets to FDI, foreign investment flowed into the economy, particularly into lucrative extractive and resource-intensive sectors, such as agribusiness and oil palm plantations (Marinova, 1999: 77). The opening up of forest concessions to foreign companies (a reversal of the earlier policy, discussed above) was therefore part of the conditionalities that came with IMF assistance to Indonesia after the AFC (Mathew [M8], 2010). As part of the conditionalities, foreign investors could purchase companies to salvage and improve them for continued development through the application of new technology and the increase of production, marketing or exports (Rajenthran, 2002: 22–23). During this period, Indonesia also reintroduced the tax holiday scheme via Presidential Decree 7/1999 to further encourage foreign investment (Rajenthran, 2002: 29). Furthermore, government regulations in 1998 allowed foreign entities to sell raw materials directly to Indonesian entities to be used in their production processes, and also sell their finished products in Indonesia through a foreign distributor. With Indonesia's huge potential market size of more than 240 million consumers, domestic market penetration was indeed attractive to these foreign investors (Rajenthran, 2002: 30).

Therefore, in the aftermath of the AFC, states in the region that were less severely affected by the crisis, such as Malaysia and Singapore, began increasing outgoing FDI to neighbouring countries, and a large part of this went to Indonesia (Marinova, 1999: 77). Regional plantation companies once again flocked into Indonesia around the turn of the millennium, on the invitation of the Indonesian government to help take over financially distressed and failed Indonesian plantation companies (Interviewee M28, 2010). These firms were attractive to foreign investors due to their low prices (after conversion into foreign currencies), the country's new openness to mergers and acquisitions and Indonesia's favourable long-term prospects after the crisis (Rajenthran, 2002: 22–23). An example of such a takeover was Malaysian-based KLK who acquired 95 per cent of PT Adei Plantation and Industry (PT API), which owned 27,760 hectares of plantation land in Riau in 1997 (WALHI *et al.*, 2009: 5–9). As Figure 3.1 details, by 2004, around 2.7 million hectares of oil palm plantations in Indonesian were held by foreign investors. Total oil palm plantations in Indonesia that year was around 3.32 million hectares (FAOSTAT, 2012), meaning that 81 per cent of Indonesia's oil palm plantations involved foreign investments, with Malaysia and Singapore being the largest investors (around 25 per cent) (WALHI *et al.*, 2009: 5).

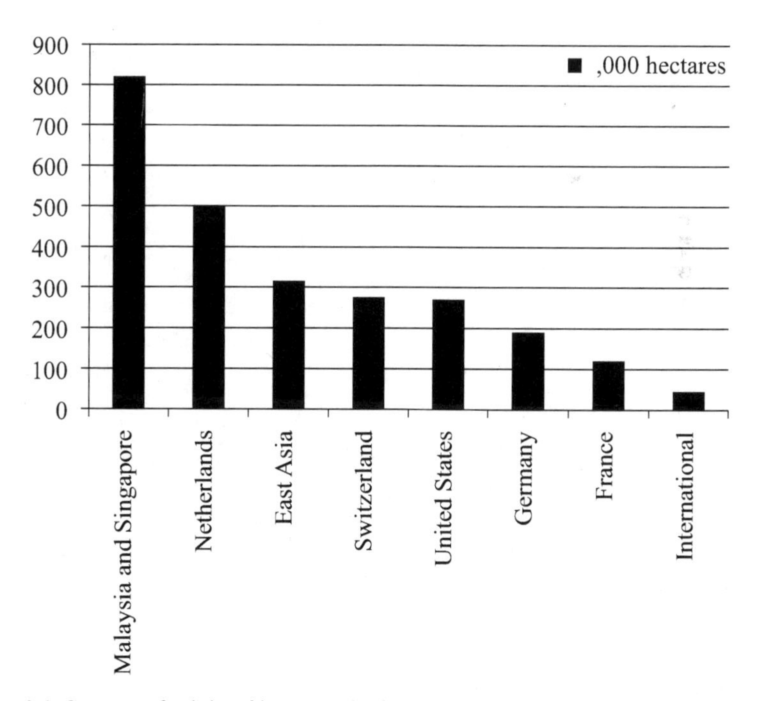

Figure 3.1 Country of origin of investors in the oil palm sector in Indonesia, 2004

Source: Adapted from WALHI and Sawit Watch, 2009

Due to the fact that the size of sovereign land that was involved in such deals was unprecedented, there was substantial government-to-government involvement from both sides in these investment arrangements (Interviewee M24 and Interviewee M25, 2010; Interviewee M28, 2010). The government of Indonesia thus executed bilateral investment treaties with Malaysia and Singapore for specific agricultural purposes (Rajenthran, 2002: 46), including for oil palm plantations. Although the FIL outlined the general FDI framework on a national level, these bilateral treaties were designed for the specific states, setting out the rights, obligations and liabilities of Indonesia with the particular investor state. Generally, these treaties outline provisions for most-favoured-nation status, national treatment, fair and equitable treatment, adequate and effective compensation,and dispute resolution mechanisms (Rajenthran, 2002: 46). For example, as part of an Indonesian-Malaysian bilateral investment treaty in 1997, *the Indonesian government pledged to specially allocate 1.5 million hectares to Malaysian investors for the development of oil palm estates* (Casson, 2002: 228–243).

This openness to FDI in Indonesia, especially to regional firms, has continued in recent years. For example, in 2007, Indonesia introduced the New Investment Law No. 25/2007 to reinvigorate investment, create jobs and reduce poverty. As part of this new law, foreign investors were allowed to obtain land rights of a longer tenure. The previous regulations discussed above granted investors the HGU for only 30 years; the new investment law extends the lease allowance up to 60 years for the first business cycle, which then can be extended for another 35 years (Caroko *et al.*, 2011: 8). Today, the allowance for foreign ownership of Indonesian plantations is set at a maximum of 95 per cent[2] (Taylor and Supriatna, 2014).

Indonesia also actively adopted ASEAN-level policies and initiatives to further promote economic regionalization. For example, Indonesia executed the ASEAN Hanoi Declaration of 1998 by agreeing to offer 'additional special privileges to qualified ASEAN investors'. This included a corporate income tax exemption for a minimum of three years, or a 30 per cent allowance on corporate income tax, duty-free imports of capital goods, domestic market access, foreign personnel employment, prompt customs clearance and a minimum 30-year leasehold period for land. All new investments approved under FIL that were expanding their projects to produce similar products were also entitled to import duty and levy exemptions (Rajenthran, 2002: 30). Furthermore, with the implementation of the Framework Agreement on Enhancing ASEAN Economic Corporation, Indonesia accorded national treatment (in terms of admission, establishment, acquisition and expansion) and most-favoured-nation status to all ASEAN member state investors in 2010; allowed entry to all economic sectors for ASEAN states; and opened its borders to free flow of capital, skilled labour, professional expatriates and technology from members (Rajenthran, 2002: 47). This encouraged investment inflow from the neighbouring Malaysia and Singapore and the further regionalization and integration of the oil palm plantation sector in particular. A trend quickly developed within the sector where regional investors, Malaysian and Singaporean in particular, overwhelmingly outnumbered investors from other countries (see Figure 3.1) (Marinova, 1999: 77).

Research has shown that there have been significant positive spillovers on the Indonesian economy as a result of increased regionalization, especially in the oil palm plantation sector. In terms of productivity, technology spillovers have benefited domestic plantation firms. Furthermore, the increased competition has encouraged domestic plantation firms to compete to secure market share and survival (Lipsey and Sjoholm, 2011: 49–51). The government of Indonesia however declared another moratorium on foreign investment in the sector in 2011, so as to give more market opportunities to local businesspeople. In the follow up to this moratorium, the Indonesian Forestry Minister Zulkifli Hasan called on national businesspeople who wish to participate in the oil palm business to take the opportunity to do so, as 'there was still plenty of land for the purpose' (Del Gallego, 2011).

However, Malaysian, Singaporean and other foreign investors had already managed to establish a significant presence in the Indonesian oil palm plantation sector by this time. With the relaxation of foreign investment barriers in this sector and the deepening of investment links between regional governments over the years there has been an increasing number of joint ventures and significantly higher levels of economic regionalization and interdependence within this sector (Hurrell, 1995: 23). Latest figures indicate that Malaysian and Singaporean investments control about half of all Indonesian oil palm plantations, a drastic increase from the 25 per cent held by Malaysian and Singaporean investors in 2004 (see Figure 3.1 above) (Adnan, 2013; Down to Earth, 2007; Maruli, 2011; PalmOilHQ, 2009). These companies operate alongside other large, powerful local companies that control significant land banks, like Bakrie Sumatra Plantations (BSP), Duta Palma, Astra Agro, Makin Group, and Musim Mas (Van Gelder, 2004: 32). Malaysian investments have an investment value of US$702.4 million and Singaporean investments in the sector amount to $112.2 million (Sawit Watch, 2008: 9).

As discussed above, Malaysia and Singapore have played an important role in the Indonesian palm oil industry over the last two decades (WALHI and Sawit Watch, 2009: 1–5). To further illustrate the extent of economic regionalization in the sector, the following sections discuss in detail the motivations and circumstances of Malaysian and Singaporean plantation investments into Indonesia respectively. These sections detail the high levels of government involvement in the process of the outward movement of firms to neighbouring countries in the region, especially Indonesia. This resulted in a situation where the Malaysian and Singaporean governments had substantial vested interests in their plantation firms operating in Indonesia. As the chapter continues to show, this explains why states often can be seen to defend their firms operating in Indonesia when faced with accusations of causing haze-producing fires.

Malaysian outward investments to Indonesia

Prior to the 1970s, Malaysia's outgoing regional investment was insignificant (Goh and Wong, 2011: 508). However beginning from the 1990s, the Malaysian government encouraged GLCs and private firms to venture abroad (Goh and Wong, 2011: 499–501), especially to other developing countries in the region (Carney and Dieleman, 2011: 122). This was to encourage the long-term development of successful Malaysian multinationals so that they could play a part in the regional and global production network, as stated in the Third Industrial Master Plan and the Ninth Malaysia Plan (*Rancangan Malaysia Ke-9*) (Goh and Wong, 2011: 499-501).

In conjunction with this, firms were encouraged to participate in investment promotion missions abroad organized by the government, which were often led by Malaysian prime ministers (Rasiah *et al.*, 2010: 347–348). In fact, there were specific incentives offered to Malaysian firms to invest abroad, particularly those in sectors that were no longer domestically competitive (Goh and Wong, 2011: 499–501), such as oil palm and other land-intensive and labour-intensive sectors. These incentives can be broadly categorized into four areas: 1) tax exemption, tax incentives and special funds, 2) investment guarantee agreements, 3) trade and investment missions and 4) institutional support (Tham, 2007: 64).

First, the Malaysian government since 1991 offered various forms of tax breaks to Malaysian firms investing abroad (Tham, 2007: 64). This included tax abatements on income earned abroad (Carney and Dieleman, 2011: 122; Rasiah *et al.*, 2010: 347–348) and tax deductions for 'pre-operating expenses' (Haji Mat Zin, 1999: 470). Second, the Malaysian government negotiated investment guarantees with 65 countries in the 1990s (Rasiah *et al.*, 2010: 347–348; Tham, 2007: 65), including with Indonesia on oil palm (Casson, 2002: 228–243). Third, trade and investment promotion missions were undertaken by the Malaysian Industrial Development Authority (MIDA) to promote investment abroad under its cross-border investment section (Tham, 2007: 65). Fourth, the Export-Import Bank of Malaysia Berhad (EXIM Bank) was established in 1995 to provide institutional support through medium- and long-term credit to Malaysian outward investors as well as foreign buyers of Malaysian goods (Sim, 2006: 490–491; Tham, 2007: 65–66).

While the Malaysian External Trade Development Corporation (MATRADE) was tasked to officially provide market information and FDI advisory services for companies planning to invest outwards (Tham, 2007: 65), the Malaysian government further assisted with governmental networks and ties to host countries such as Indonesia, which provided knowledge and access to local markets, distribution systems, connections around local bureaucracy and business systems, as well as potential business partners and even financing (Sim, 2005: 47–48).

Complemented by other push factors (for example, low labour cost advantage in host countries, saturation of the domestic Malaysian market, the need to enhance export-competitiveness in third-country markets, and to exploit the domestic market potential in other countries) (Tham, 2007: 44), these incentives contributed towards a sharp increase in outward investment from Malaysia in the late 1990s, especially to neighbouring countries (Goh and Wong, 2011: 508). Malaysia's outward FDI rose from a low of $146 million in 1980 to $3.4 billion in 1997, with a further increase to $3.8 billion in 2007 (Goh and Wong, 2011:

508), mostly concentrated in the Southeast Asian region (Sim, 2005: 40–41). In 2007, Malaysian FDI outflows surpassed inflows for the first time, and this trend continued in the next couple of years. As explained above, a major motivation for this, especially in the natural resources sector, was that Malaysia's rapid development in the 1970s onwards resulted in an increasingly tight labour market and rising labour costs, coupled with a dwindling land supply (Sim, 2005: 38). Therefore, Malaysian firms established production bases in host countries such as Indonesia to reap the benefits of economies of scale and lower prices due to their larger populations and abundant lands (Goh and Wong, 2011: 508). At the same time, the more advanced Malaysian firms functioning in countries such as Indonesia brought along with them knowledge of labour-intensive processes, appropriate technology and flexible production, allowing them advantages over local firms (Sim, 2005: 43). Malaysian investments in Indonesia were especially prominent in the oil palm sector, as detailed below.

Malaysian plantation companies in Indonesia

As discussed previously, Malaysia was the largest producer of palm oil until it was overtaken by Indonesia in 2008 (*Bernama*, 2010; Jarvis *et al.*, 2010: 2–12; McCarthy, 2010: 822–844; Reuters, 2011; World Growth, 2011: 4–13). While Malaysia possesses a distinct advantage in capital and technology over its neighbouring competitor Indonesia, available arable land in the relatively smaller and less-forested Malaysia quickly dwindled (World Growth, 2011: 16). Malaysia has limited opportunity for expansion through land conversion due to developing concerns of eco-certification standards and particular land use restrictions (Interviewee M41, 2010; *New Straits Times*, 2006). For example, Malaysia has pledged to keep 50 per cent of its forest cover at several international conferences, including the Commonwealth Heads of Government Meeting 1989, the Rio Earth Summit 1992, the Copenhagen Climate Conference in 2009 and most recently at RIO+20 in 2012[3] (Embas, 2012: 3). United Nations (UN) sources estimated that by 1992, Malaysia only had 56.2 per cent land area under forest cover (Bankoff and Elston, 1994: 13–14), leaving not much space available for further expansion (Hameiri and Jones, 2013: 471; Interviewee M41, 2010; *New Straits Times*, 2006; Tarigan [I23], 2010). In relation to this, the Malaysian government has stopped new forest land from being opened up for crops including oil palm, restricting planting to logged-over land zones for agriculture only (Malaysian Palm Oil Council, 2006: 10). This situation was exacerbated further by the labour scarcity in Malaysia (Interviewee M41, 2010; *New Straits Times*, 2006: 221–242; Tarigan [I23], 2010) and the fact that yields on Malaysian plantations are decreasing (World Growth, 2011: 16). All of these factors resulted in a stagnating oil palm sector in Malaysia, with a growth of production of only 2–3 per cent each year (UOB Kay Hian, 2011: 7).

These reasons, coupled with a limited domestic market, induced Malaysian investors to venture out into developing countries with potentially large and untapped markets, plentiful labour and land resources, and costs that are still relatively low (Haji Mat Zin, 1999: 470). In response to these limitations, the Malaysian government announced that it had acquired land in Indonesia, Papua New Guinea (105,000 hectares) and Brazil (100,000 hectares) for continued oil palm development (Koh and Wilcove, 2008: 67–68). With advantageous policies in Indonesia as discussed above, the abundant lands in Indonesia have been an important prospect for expansion and investment for the Malaysian oil palm sector since the 1990s. Malaysia is now the biggest investor in the Indonesian oil palm plantation sector (Lipsey and Sjoholm, 2011: 55). Currently it is estimated that there are 162 plantations having linkages to Malaysia companies, making up almost half of Indonesia's palm land bank. In addition, Malaysian-linked investments, through shareholding and direct investments, are estimated to control some 500,000 more hectares of land in Sumatra and Kalimantan that have yet to be converted into plantation land (WALHI *et al.*, 2009: 5). This total area is around double the total land bank used for oil palm plantations in Malaysia (Interviewee M28, 2010).

The Malaysian oil palm industry was, and still is, generally populated by GLCs or private companies in close association with the Malaysian government (Norhashim and Ab. Aziz, 2005: 31–45). Due to this, the Malaysian government was highly involved in facilitating the entry of major Malaysian companies in Indonesia (Abdul Mutalib [M42], 2010), as discussed in the previous section. As a result, most Malaysian companies that ventured out to Indonesia to run plantations there were already well-established GLCs or major conglomerates in their home state. Major Malaysian investors in the Indonesian oil palm plantation industry include: Sime Darby, Tabung Haji Plantations (THP), KLK, Genting Plantations and IOI Corporation Berhad (IOI). Sime Darby and THP are prominent Malaysian GLCs, while Genting Plantations, KLK and IOI are owned by powerful and well-connected Chinese-Malaysian tycoons. Four of these companies are in the top 50 list of largest companies in Malaysia; Sime Darby at seventh place, Genting at ninth, KLK at twentieth and IOI at fiftieth (Gomez, 2009: 375–377).

With an abundance of land in the post-colonial era (late 1950s onwards), the Malaysian government had established GLCs with specific focus on the natural resource sector. For example, shortly after independence, the Malaysian government facilitated stock purchases of previously private, foreign-owned plantations to be converted into GLCs (Naguib and Smucker, 2009: 100–110). Leadership of these GLC were normally awarded to prominent Malays who were politically well-connected (Lim and Stern, 2003: 33–35). A good example of this was when the government-run Permodalan Nasional Berhad (PNB, the national capitalization agency) bought out almost 8 million shares of the United Kingdom's Guthrie Corporation and acquired control over about 80,645 hectares of Malaysia's oil palm plantations. Guthrie, together with another GLC, Golden Hope Plantations, merged with Sime Darby in 2007 to form Malaysia's largest oil palm plantation company.

Over the years, PNB and other government entities have retained a substantial stake in Sime Darby,[4] maintaining the Malaysian government's control over the company (Greenpeace, 2007: 16–39). The Malaysian GLC Amanah Saham Trustee Berhad is the largest shareholder with a total stake of 37.3 per cent, followed by the government's Employees Provident Fund (EPF) with 14.1 per cent stake, and PNB owning 12.2 per cent stake (UOB Kay Hian, 2011: 1). On the board of Sime Darby sit former prolific Malaysian politicians such as former Deputy Prime Minister of Malaysia Tun Musa Hitam, and former Chief Secretary to the Malaysian Government Tan Sri Samsudin Osman (Sime Darby, 2011). Its chief executive officer (CEO) is Datuk Mohd Bakke Salleh, who is also chairman of another GLC, Bank Islam (Adnan, 2010), which is said to be an important financier for Sime Darby and other Malaysian plantation companies (Surya [I9] and Akbar [I10], 2010).

The close relationship and vested interests (Hicken, 2011: 290–306) existing between Sime Darby and the Malaysian government were strengthened over the years as Sime Darby assisted the Malaysian government in their developmental goals, by supporting 'national causes' through the undertaking of economically risky but strategically attractive projects (Tay, 2003: 51–53). For example, when the Sarawak Land Development Board (SLDB), the government agency that was put in charge of plantation development in Sarawak, was making substantial losses and carried major liabilities in 1987, Sime Darby stepped in to assist the state government by buying over the management of SLDB and all its plantation assets, including more than 24,000 hectares of oil palm in 13 estates (McCarthy and Cramb, 2009: 113–119). Sime Darby successfully turned the financial situation of these estates around before handing them over to a government-owned company, Sarawak Plantation Services (Ministry of Land Development Sarawak, 2011). This relationship has been said to render Sime Darby 'almost untouchable'. For example, interviewees who were in close contact with Malaysian NGOs related a conversation they had with officials from the Human Rights Commission of Malaysia in reference to Sime Darby. These officials told them that 'it is very difficult for us to discuss Sime Darby's actions, because the government is so involved with them' (Surya [I9] and Akbar [I10], 2010).

Another prominent Malaysian GLC operating in Indonesia is THP[5] (Surya [I9] and Akbar [I10], 2010). THP is 71 per cent owned by the government-run Lembaga Tabung Haji (TH Plantations Berhad, 2014). A notable director is Dato' Noordin bin Md Noor, who has been active in the Malaysian political scene since 1976, holding various important positions in the Malaysian ruling party's United Malay National Organization youth wing (TH Plantations, 2010). With Sime Darby and THP being the major Malaysian players in the Indonesian oil palm plantation sector, it can be considered that up to 70 per cent of the finance capitals of Malaysian plantations in Indonesia are managed by the Malaysian government, drawing a direct link between these businesses and government interests (Surya [I9] and Akbar [I10], 2010).

Even the non-GLC Malaysian companies operating in Indonesia enjoy close connections with the Malaysian government. These companies are usually headed by elite Chinese Malaysians, who rose to prominence through subcontracting of government contracts from powerful Malays in an 'Ali-Baba' arrangement where the Malay 'Ali' receives the contract through connections, then subcontracts it to the Chinese 'Baba' (Naguib and Smucker, 2009: 100–110, Norhashim and Ab. Aziz, 2005: 31–45). These Chinese Malaysians eventually built up their own connections themselves among the Malay elite, and built their companies into major Malaysian conglomerates with prominent Malay and Chinese directors.

For example, on the board of KLK[6] sits Tan Sri Dato' Thong Yaw Hong, the former secretary general of the Malaysian Treasury and later chairman of the EPF (Kuala Lumpur Kepong Berhad, 2010). The EPF also holds a 12.2 per cent stake in the company (UOB Kay Hian, 2011: 40). Another example is the board of IOI,[7] which includes Datuk Hj Mohd Khalil B Dato' Hj Mohd Noor (a Malay), formerly the secretary of the government's Foreign Investment Committee of Malaysia (IOI Group, 2011). Yet another example is the Board of Directors of Genting Plantations,[8] which is populated by many Malay former military officers such as retired Lt. Gen. Dato' Haji Abdul Jamil bin Haji Ahmad; retired Gen. Tan Sri Mohd Zahidi bin Hj Zainuddin; and retired Lt. Gen. Dato' Abdul Ghani bin Abdullah. Another director, Tan Sri Mohd Amin bin Osman, was formerly the director of the Malaysian Police Special Branch (Genting Plantations Berhad, 2010).

Due to the vested interests between these companies and elites in the Malaysian government, the state had a particular interest in maintaining the well-being of these countries' operations in Indonesia (Abdul Mutalib [M42], 2010). Therefore, as explained above, most of the Malaysian companies' investments into the Indonesian oil palm plantation sector were facilitated by the Malaysian government, through government-to-government arrangements with Indonesia (Interviewee M24 and Interviewee M25, 2010; Interviewee M28, 2010). Beyond facilitating entry, the Malaysian government was also especially active in establishing and funding industry promotional groups and lobby groups to further support the ongoing operations of these firms once established in Indonesia. These groups were important in not only defending the general interests of the sector as explained next, but also particularly in protecting Malaysian firms from prosecution over haze-causing fires in Indonesia, as is discussed further in the chapter.

State support for established Malaysian firms in Indonesia

To further facilitate economic regionalization and to uphold its vested interests in the oil palm sector, the Malaysian government was especially active in lending its support to the continued advancement of the Malaysian oil palm plantation firms in Indonesia. For this purpose, the Malaysian government set up lobby groups, collectively sponsored by both the government and private sector (Interviewee M44, 2012). This included the Malaysian Palm Oil Association (which has industry membership and looks out for the interests of plantation owners); the Malaysian Palm Oil Board (a regulatory body focusing on research); and the Malaysian Palm Oil Council (MPOC) (a government-legislated company focusing on marketing and promotion of palm oil as a commodity). These groups are collectively known as 'MPOABC' (Harun [M49] *et al.*, 2012; Interviewee M53 and Interviewee M54, 2012; MPOA, 2011; MPOB, 2011; MPOC, 2011).

The MPOC has been especially active in supporting the causes of Malaysian investments in Indonesia (Harun [M49] *et al.*, 2012; Interviewee M53 and Interviewee M54, 2012; MPOA, 2011; MPOB, 2011; MPOC, 2011). It is a company legislated by the government tasked with the promotion and expansion of the palm oil market for Malaysian companies operating in Malaysia and overseas, by enhancing the image of palm oil and creating better acceptance of palm oil through awareness of various technological and economic advantages and environmental sustainability (MPOC, 2011). It has ten regional offices (Interviewee M53 and Interviewee M54, 2012) and is funded partly by a 'cess' (special tax) from the sale of palm oil by the industry (Harun [M49] *et al.*, 2012). It also functions as a watchdog and is responsible for countering 'misinformation' and what is regarded as unfair allegations from parties that view palm oil in a negative light (Harun [M49] *et al.*, 2012). It does this by engaging directly with international governments and NGOs through trade missions, dialogues and conferences. It also has a Communications Unit that monitors international news and developments with regards to palm oil, especially negative ones, and if necessary, do 'damage control' by producing and dispersing 'correct' information and new findings through various channels, including on YouTube (Interviewee M53 and Interviewee M54, 2012).

The links between MPOC and Malaysian investments in Indonesia are clear. For example, Dato' Lee Oi Hian, the CEO of KLK, is also chairman of the MPOC Board of Trustees (WALHI *et al.*, 2009: 5–9). On the Board of Trustees is also Dato' Lee Yeow Chor,[9] a director of IOI (IOI Group, 2011). The CEO of MPOC is Tan Sri Datuk Dr Yusof Basiron, who sits on the board of the two big Malaysian plantation GLCs operating in Indonesia, Sime Darby and THP (Sime Darby, 2011; TH Plantations, 2010). As explained by interviewees, these board members are especially important in determining the activities of MPOC both locally and abroad (Interviewee M53 and Interviewee M54, 2012). The MPOC is also very closely linked to the Malaysian Ministry of Plantation Industries and Commodities (Interviewee M53 and Interviewee M54, 2012), the primary body of the Malaysian government involved in brokering the entry of Malaysian firms into Indonesia. Indeed, the MPOC *has been known to represent the Ministry at the international level and speak on its behalf* (Basiron, 2010).

The MPOC invests heavily in lobbying and advertising on behalf of Malaysian palm oil investments (Wahid *et al.*, 2004: 1–8). It is often the first agency that identifies trade barriers against palm oil and undertakes appropriate counteractions (Interviewee M53 and Interviewee M54, 2012). For example, it is currently actively involved in fighting against what it regards as the 'unfair' labelling of palm oil products in various countries (Interviewee M45 *et al.*, 2012). In Australia, the Food Standards Amendment (Truth in Labeling – Palm Oil) bill was proposed in 2011 requiring the listing of palm oil as an ingredient in all food products, while other oils could remain to be listed as 'vegetable oil'. The MPOC argued that this was discriminatory treatment towards Malaysian-owned oil palm operations (Suharto, 2011: 1; Van Noordwijk *et al.*, 2011: 2) and a type of trade barrier (Interviewee M45 *et al.*, 2012). In response to this bill, a delegation from MPOC including its CEO, Tan Sri Datuk Dr Yusof Basiron (who, as mentioned above sits on the board of Sime Darby and THP, both important players in the Indonesian oil palm sector), appeared before an Australian House Standing Committee on Economics public hearing in August 2011 (Basiron, 2011c: 10), and was successful in convincing the Parliament to repeal the bill. Interviewees also detailed how MPOC even brought Senator Xenofon, the senator that proposed the bill, to Malaysian-owned plantations to view conditions on the ground to appease the senator. As a result, palm oil was no longer subject to discriminatory treatment as being the only vegetable oil distinctly labelled on Australian products, as all other oils (such as soybean oil and rapeseed oil) would also be similarly labelled (Interviewee M53 and Interviewee M54, 2012).

It has also been reported that MPOC has filed a complaint to the World Trade Organization against what they claim to be 'discriminatory' restrictions on biofuel imports under the European Union Renewable Energy Directive 2010 (Adnan, 2012), which they argue imposes arbitrary sustainability criteria that limited Malaysian producers' ability to export to Europe (Basiron, 2011b: 51 Roberts, 2011: 54). The MPOC also actively promotes palm oil produced by Malaysian companies (locally and abroad) as being more sustainable than others (i.e. Indonesia's). The MPOC has also been known to 'bad mouth' crude palm oil (CPO) produced by Indonesian companies, in the hope that foreign governments would prefer to buy CPO from Malaysian companies operating in Indonesia instead (Surya [I9] and Akbar [I10], 2010). And, despite the UK Advertising Standards Authority banning an MPOC commercial promoting Malaysian palm oil as 'sustainable since 1917' (on the grounds that that Malaysian facilities in Indonesia were found to be operating below industry sustainability standards) (WALHI and Sawit Watch, 2009: 1–5), the MPOC lobby continues to tour Europe and other markets to convince decision makers, buyers and consumers that Malaysian palm oil, including that produced in Indonesia, is environmentally sustainable (Raman *et al.*, 2008: 3–5). Furthermore, an interviewee explained that MPOC also funds World Growth, an international pro-palm oil lobby group that argues that the commercialization of palm oil is a good way to alleviate poverty among forest-dwelling communities, while ignoring and denying its environmental consequences (Interviewee M44, 2012).

The Malaysian government also proposed and sponsored the creation of the Jakarta-based lobby group, the Association of Oil Palm Plantation Investors of Malaysia in Indonesia (APIMI) in 1999, specifically to promote and protect the interests of Malaysian palm oil operations in Indonesia (Abdul Mutalib [M42], 2010). With funding from the Malaysian government, APIMI has a dedicated office and staff in the Jakarta central business district, and serves as the liaison between the governments of Malaysia and Indonesia over palm oil matters. The Malaysian ambassador to Indonesia is APIMI's chairman and the Malaysian economic counsellor at the Indonesian Embassy is its patron (APIMI, 2010). APIMI boasts membership of all 18 Malaysian companies operating in Indonesia, and currently has Sime Darby as the head of the board (Abdul Mutalib [M42], 2010).

On the Malaysian government's invitation, APIMI is among the few selected industry lobby groups that are allowed to attend yearly bilateral economic talks between Malaysia and Indonesia. It also functions as a direct link between Malaysian plantation investors in Indonesia and the Malaysian top leadership. Any arising oil palm issues raised by APIMI members can be forwarded by APIMI directly to the Malaysian Prime Minister's Department (PMD) and dealt with there. For example, the executive secretary of APIMI that was interviewed explained that APIMI recently requested through the PMD to reduce the CPO tax applied by the Indonesian government to Malaysian investors from 15 per cent to 10 per cent. The PMD is now directly negotiating this matter with the Indonesian government, and according to the executive secretary, is approaching agreement (Abdul Mutalib [M42], 2010). With encouragement from the Malaysian government, APIMI was also instrumental in establishing the Indonesia-Malaysia Palm Oil Group in 2010, created to further facilitate industry relations between the countries (Abdul Mutalib [M42], 2010).

Because of this governmental support and endorsement, APIMI and its corporate members have enjoyed an elevated role in the Indonesian business community. APIMI has been able to directly raise its concerns to the Indonesian leadership on issues affecting Malaysian investments in Indonesia. For example, in 2000, APIMI was able to directly raise the issue of native customary rights (NCR) land during a private meeting with the president. NCR issues were proving problematic to Malaysian companies that attempted to open up land that local communities claimed ownership of. As a result of this direct request, the Indonesian president gave Malaysian investors his personal assurance that their rights would be protected against overlapping claims of NCR land ownership by locals (Onn, 2000). Therefore, it can be said that the Malaysian government used its influence through APIMI to obtain special treatment for Malaysian firms. Apart from (soon to be) preferential taxation, Malaysian companies also receive preferential treatment on land rights, and as will be shown further in the chapter, also receive leniency on legal action relating to fire-producing haze.

This section has argued that the vested interests that exist between the Malaysian government and Malaysian oil palm plantation companies operating in Indonesia have encouraged substantial involvement of the state in order to ensure the well-being of these firms there (Abdul Mutalib [M42], 2010). This has extended beyond the facilitation of the initial entry of these firms to Indonesia, but also continued long after these firms were established and operating. Through organizations such as MPOC and APIMI, companies that venture into Indonesia still maintain strong links with Malaysia, their home state. This has been especially useful when confronted with high-profile regional problems such as the haze, as discussed further in this chapter. The next section discusses similar high levels of government facilitation that can be observed with Singaporean plantation firms operating in Indonesia.

Singaporean outward investments to Indonesia

The Singaporean government holds strongly to the belief that the economic structure of the state should not be left solely to the market (Yeung, 2011: 630). Singapore felt it was important to develop its indigenous economic capabilities that could tap into the growth potential in other countries (Blomqvist, 2000: 26; Yeung, 2011: 638), especially those within the region. By encouraging local firms to expand business and investment outward into the Southeast Asian region (which was dubbed the 'second wing' or 'external economy') Singapore's regionalization drive became a central strategy for economic growth (Blomqvist, 2000: 26; Hamilton-Hart, 2005: 186; Pereira, 2005: 386).

Regionalization ventures by Singapore firms were cited as early as the 1960s and 1970s (Goh *et al.*, 2001: 24–30), but the beginnings of Singapore's strong interventionist style towards regional investment can be traced back to the 1980s. These early efforts were known locally as 'government directed dynamic comparative advantage' (Ellingsen *et al.*, 2006: 4–34), stemming from the realization that Singapore faced serious physical limitations such as natural resources and manpower. Therefore, the government attempted to deliberately restructure and upgrade its economy by relocating labour intensive and other unsophisticated production to countries with an appropriate comparative advantage for such production (Blomqvist, 2000: 25–26).

Further facilitation and encouragement of outward regional investment by the government actively increased from the early 1990s onwards, with a regionalization policy promulgated as part of Singapore's Strategic Economic Plan (SEP) in 1991: 'Regionalization 2000' ((Blomqvist, 2000: 26; Rasiah *et al.*, 2010: 346–347,). As communicated in official statements on the issue, 'going regional is part of our [Singapore's] long-term strategy to stay ahead. It is to make our national economy bigger, our companies stronger, and some of them multinational' (Goh *et al.*, 2001: 24–30). Furthermore, such regionalization 'would allow Singapore to retain its status as a regional headquarters even as its firms were going offshore in search of either lower costs or to service clients in the region' (Haggard and Low, 2002: 313). In the larger context, this strategy was also seen as a way to cultivate and nurture political ties with Singapore's neighbours in ASEAN, given that these ties have sometimes been problematic (Blomqvist, 2000: 26).

Like Malaysia, Singaporean GLCs were encouraged to become the key drivers of regionalization either on their own or through partnerships with other companies (Blomqvist, 2000: 27; Sim, 2006: 490–491). In Singapore, the Directorship and Consultancy Appointments Committee under the Finance Ministry appoints the boards of directors and management of GLCs, and these appointments draw heavily from Singapore's civil service (Haggard and Low, 2002: 317). Due to this, like Malaysia as well, the Singaporean government was highly interested and involved in facilitating the entry of Singaporean companies to other states in the region. Accordingly, the government provided generous incentives to speed up the regionalization of local entrepreneurs, by way of tax incentives, grants, finance schemes and training (Blomqvist, 2000: 27; Sim, 2005: 34–37).

For example, the Economic Development Board (EDB), Singapore's leading development agency, became the main tool for the Singaporean government in its efforts to facilitate the regionalization of its economy. The services provided by the EDB included carrying out centralized marketing, assisting with feasibility studies, establishing of government-to-government committees and bilateral business councils, and dispatching overseas missions (Blomqvist, 2000: 26–27). The EDB also provided management training for Singaporean companies extending their operations in the region. In 2000, it awarded aid to 18 companies under its Overseas Enterprise Incentive and trained 147 Singaporean managers under a regionalization scheme (Hamilton-Hart, 2005: 188). Another programme was also launched in 2001 to train up to 500 Singaporeans to be 'Asian business experts' and to widen their networks in the region, focusing on creating a core of future business leaders who have 'strong links' in the region (Hamilton-Hart, 2005: 188).

Furthermore, the state also took on the role of entrepreneur by proactively setting up business opportunities overseas and establishing institutional frameworks such as the Singapore-Johor-Riau growth triangle for Singaporean firms to tap into (Sim, 2006: 490–491). As a result, Riau is currently a hotbed for Singaporean investment, including for oil palm. The Singapore government also sought assurances from neighbouring countries such as Malaysia and Indonesia at both the local and central government level for preferred treatment of Singaporean businesses (Rasiah *et al.*, 2010: 346–347). It also established trade and cultural offices in these neighbouring countries to further facilitate this, for example, the Jakarta trade and cultural office that opened in 1961 (Rahim, 2009: 153). The government also made available international schools for the children of Singaporean expatriates at certain host countries. And, as an additional push factor, the government deliberately increased wages in Singapore in order to squeeze out labour intensive, low-productive industries, inducing them to move to other locations (Blomqvist, 2000: 26–27).

A particularly important role that the Singaporean government played in regional investment promotion was the role of active facilitator for investment. Once a Singaporean company displays interest in expanding its operations overseas, the government will provide it with strategic information on the host country's business and investment environment, including home country contributions and other information that can be used as leverage. The government also often helps in introducing business contacts abroad and in facilitating access to key government officials in the host country (Goh *et al.*, 2001: 42).

Therefore, the laws of economics that encouraged Singaporean firms to look outwards to overcome local physical limitations such as natural resources and manpower (Blomqvist, 2000: 26–27) have been further supported by strong government encouragement and facilitation. This resulted in a significant increase of outward FDI from Singapore in the mid-1990s. Like in Malaysia, Singaporean firms expanding their operations outwards also focused on neighbouring countries, with an excess of 60 per cent of all new investment going to countries within the region in 1995 (Goh *et al.*, 2001: 24–30). This trend has continued, and latest figures show that Singapore is the biggest Southeast Asian source of investment in the region, still accounting for up to half of the region's FDI (Rajan, 2007: 218). In Indonesia in particular, Singapore is the fourth largest investor, after the US, Japan and Hong Kong, with more than $3.2 billion worth of investments there (Rahim, 2009: 170).

The Singaporean government has specifically targeted the agricultural sector for reform, which had been languishing due to pressures of land scarcity, high labour costs and small-scale operation. Indonesia in turn is complementary to Singapore as a large, labour-abundant but capital-scarce economy where primary commodity exports continue to perform an important role (Hamilton-Hart, 2009: 262–264). Therefore, the Singaporean government encouraged their agribusiness companies to invest overseas in more labour- and land-intensive production of all types of foodstuffs and cash crops (Neville, 1992: 241–254). With this government encouragement, Singaporean companies embraced the plantation boom in the region and established significant land holdings for cash crops, especially in Indonesia, mostly through joint ventures with local companies (Thee, 2006: 60–61). Therefore, while Singapore may not have the experience and expertise that Malaysia has with natural resource industries, Singaporean involvement in Indonesia's natural resource sectors is still significant (Ghani [S6], 2010), with agriculture and agriculture-related manufacturing (including CPO processing[10]) consisting of 33 per cent and 5 per cent of Singapore's investment in Indonesia respectively (Thee, 2006: 60–61). A large percentage of this includes investments in the oil palm sector.

Singaporean plantation companies in Indonesia

Although Singapore's foray into the oil palm plantation business does not go as far back as Malaysia's (Pereira, 2005: 386), from the 1990s Singaporean businesspeople were urged by their government to invest in Indonesia's oil palm plantations to take advantage of booming regional markets (*The Straits Times*, 1997). Singaporean companies have thus also ventured out to invest in the Indonesian oil palm plantation sector on the encouragement and the support of their government (Pereira, 2005: 386). Therefore, despite its lack of arable land and expertise advantages as compared to Malaysia as discussed above, Singapore is a major player in the region's oil palm sector as well (Thee, 2006: 60–61). Today, most of the global trade in Indonesian palm oil is handled by traders based in Singapore (Greenpeace, 2007: 3), and Singapore is also a major palm oil processing hub[11] (Lawrence [I38], 2011, Lee [S20], 2010). Singapore's home-grown Wilmar International[12] is the largest palm oil producer in the world and an important player in the Indonesian oil palm plantation sector (Creagh and Chatterjee, 2010; Grant, 2008).

A notable regionalization trend with Singaporean investments in the region, and in the oil palm sector specifically, is the phenomenon known as 'round-tripping' (Carney and Dieleman, 2011: 116). Round-tripping refers to capital outflows shifted offshore into special-purpose entities that subsequently divert the funds back to the origin economy. Reasons for doing this vary, including to take advantage of Singapore's stronger currency (Lopez, 1995), more secure property rights regimes, rules-based regulations (Hamilton-Hart, 2005: 181) and inward foreign investment incentives (Carney and Dieleman, 2011: 116); to benefit from the bigger and more sophisticated capital markets in Singapore; and because of the ease of obtaining funding and equipment (Arif [I41], 2011; Ghani [S6], 2010; Yansen [I43], 2011). Because of these reasons, Singapore is often viewed as a 'safe haven' for Indonesian investors who are anxious about an unreliable government at home or simply wanting to avoid tax liabilities (Hamilton-Hart, 2005: 181). This practice is usually done by Sino-Indonesian investors, including those involved in the natural resource sectors, most notably oil palm. In fact, figures by the investment bank Merrill Lynch show that up to a third of investors with assets totalling in excess of $1 million in Singapore have Indonesian origins. Altogether, these entities had combined assets of $87 billion as of 2007 (Chua, 2008: 57).

Reflecting this, Singapore generally does not publish trade statistics between these two countries, partly in order to avoid close scrutiny of this 'round-tripping' practice (Hamilton-Hart, 2005: 181; Hamilton-Hart, 2009: 257–264). This was based on a bilateral agreement between Indonesia and Singapore made in 1974. However, pressured by allegations of a lack of transparency from some Indonesian officials, Singapore published trade statistics with Indonesia for the first time in more than 30 years in 2004. Despite this, opinion remains that Singapore's bilateral trade statistics continue to conceal certain activities (Rahim, 2009: 167–168) in the interests of these companies based in Singapore.

Examples of companies practising 'round-tripping' include Sinar Mas and the Salim Group, among the biggest Indonesian conglomerates. While these companies were already to a certain extent shifting investments to Singapore before the crisis (for example, the Salim Group began establishing headquarters in Singapore by the early 1990s) (Sato, 2004: 30–31), the aftermath of the AFC saw intensified shifting of operations and funds across the border (Rahim, 2009: 167), taking advantage of Singapore's removal of the 40 per cent foreign ownership limit for investments in 1999 (Haggard and Low, 2002: 315). They currently control listed plantation companies in Singapore, namely Golden-Agri Resources (GAR)[13] and Indo Agri[14] respectively, and have put second-generation family members in charge of managing the round-tripping of their group's activities, alongside local Singaporean directors. Such companies are a good reflection of the regionalization of the oil palm sector in Southeast Asia, where plantation companies cannot be easily identified with a specific national home base (Carney and Dieleman, 2011: 116; Rukmantara [I45], 2011).

State support for established Singaporean firms in Indonesia

Singapore's hands-on approach in facilitating investment resulted in a complex web of linkages between the plantation sector and the government. The government is a major stockholder in many Singaporean corporations (Haley, 1996:

22–25; Lim and Stern, 2003: 36–38), and the boards and executive posts of these companies are often staffed with current and former civil servants, military officers or members of parliament (MPs) who are, by definition, part of the ruling People's Action Party (Case, 2003: 253–258). For example, on Wilmar's Board of Directors sits Chua Phuay Hee, a former senior figure in the Monetary Authority of Singapore, and Yeo Teng Yang who was also a senior officer at the Monetary Authority and Ministry of Finance, as well as ambassador of Singapore to the European Community. Other notable figures on Wilmar's Board are Leong Horn Kee and Kuok Khoon Ean. Leong served at the Singaporean Parliament for 22 years, was formerly a senior figure with the Ministry of Trade and Industry and the Ministry of Finance. Kuok in turn served on various government-run statutory bodies such as the Sentosa Development Corporation, the Singapore Trade Development Board, the Singapore Tourism Board and the Singapore Management University (Wilmar, 2010). Indo Agri's chairman is Edward Kee Kwong Foo, a veteran of the Singapore Administrative Service who served, among other positions, as Singaporean ambassador to Indonesia during which he received Indonesia's highest civilian honour, the Bintang Jasa Utama (First Class). On its Board also sits Lim Hock San, a former senior official at the Port of Singapore Authority and the Civil Aviation Authority of Singapore (Indo Food Agri Resources, 2010). And on GAR's Board sits Lew Syn Pau, who served as a member of the Singaporean Parliament for 13 years, as a representative of the ruling party (Golden-Agri Resources Ltd, 2010).

These linkages have fused corporate plantations with the dominant party and the state bureaucracy in what can be depicted as deep elite 'cohesion' (Case, 2003: 253–258). However in this respect, information on Singaporean government engagement with the Indonesian government on behalf of Singapore-based companies is sparse (Neville, 1992: 241–254). As noted previously, Singapore is famously non-transparent in terms of corporate disclosures, and secrecy of government-business relations is a norm in Singapore (Rodan, 2004: 483). As mentioned earlier in this chapter, it is known that there is a bilateral treaty between Singapore and Indonesia on plantation investments (Rajenthran, 2002: 46), but the contents of this treaty have not been made public. However, Singaporean government support and protection of their home companies have been visible in other aspects of dealings in the sector, specifically on dealing with negative backlashes that has affected the sector due to haze. The following subsection addresses this, in the context of both the Malaysian and Singaporean governments.

Dealing with backlash as a result of haze

This book argues that the economic regionalization of the Southeast Asian oil palm plantation sector is a major driver of transboundary haze and an important factor in its persistence. As discussed in Chapter 2, fire is widely used by large-scale commercial plantations in Indonesia as a cost-effective way to clear land in preparation for planting oil palm (Colfer, 2002: 318; Interviewee I21, 2010;

Maitar [I12], 2010; Moore [I5], 2010; Surya [I9] and Akbar [I10], 2010). This has been identified as a primary source of haze in the region (Page *et al.*, 2009: 893). As discussed above, the process of economic regionalization focused on Malaysian and Singaporean plantation interests in Indonesia, forming a sector populated with a mix of local and foreign companies. Evidence presented briefly in the previous chapter and more extensively in Chapter 4 shows that the practice of land-clearing using fire is not limited to local plantation firms but is often carried out by Malaysian and Singaporean firms operating in Indonesia as well (Rukmantara [I45], 2011; Tan [S7], 2010).

Other foreign companies, like those from the Netherlands, Switzerland and the United States, also own substantial amounts of plantation land in Indonesia, as detailed in Figure 3.1. However, these other foreign companies have only very rarely been linked to fire and other environmental misconducts in Indonesia. Differences of attitudes between Southeast Asian firms and these other foreign firms have been noted by several interviewees (Interviewee I48, 2011; Rolland [I50], 2011). With the Southeast Asian culture of natural resource exploitation as discussed in Chapter 2, investors from within the region are more likely to abuse the environment for profit.

With years of persistent haze, the regional and global public has become increasingly aware of the complicity of local, Malaysian and Singaporean plantation companies in causing the haze problem (Chee [M27], 2010; Ramakrishna [M20], 2010; Singh [M18], 2010). A flurry of local and foreign NGO publications focusing on the misconduct of oil palm plantations[15] received significant attention both locally and internationally (Stone, 2007; WALHI *et al.*, 2009; Wakker, 2005). Backlash from this increased awareness posed some serious threats to the regional oil palm industry. For example, at the regional level, civil society and the media, especially in Malaysia and Singapore, became increasingly vocal in voicing their dissatisfaction in having to suffer the haze year after year, and began to demand real proactive action from their governments (Ho, 1997; Interviewee S4 and Interviewee S5, 2010; Interviewee S18, 2010; Interviewee I25, 2010; Lim [S13], 2010; *New Straits Times*, 1997b).

At the international level, a shift in consumer concerns towards sustainability encouraged governments to tighten sustainability requirements of imported CPO and palm kernel oil (PKO). For example, the United States' Environment Protection Agency began to label products containing palm oil as being very low in greenhouse gas savings (Interviewee M45 *et al.*, 2012), reducing the attractiveness of these products among environmentally concerned consumers. New Zealand also announced that it will begin imposing tariffs on CPO products, due to sustainability concerns (Harun [M49] *et al.*, 2012). The World Bank also has proposed imposing strict sustainability certifications on international investment in oil palm plantations, which also has the potential to reduce the development and expansion of the sector (Basiron, 2011a: 16). Also, bad publicity had the potential to affect oil palm plantation investments in other countries as well, especially since Malaysia and Singapore had substantial palm oil investments outside Indonesia too (Koh and Wilcove, 2008: 67–68), as mentioned previously.

To further facilitate economic regionalization and to uphold their vested interests in the sector, Malaysian and Singaporean governments were active in lending their support to the continued well-being of the their firms in Indonesia, going beyond the mere facilitation of entry of these firms into Indonesia. For example, as explained earlier in this chapter, the Malaysian government facilitated the establishment of lobby groups to protect the interests of their firms in Indonesia (Interviewee M44, 2012). Similar efforts were seen with the issue of haze-producing fires. The export-oriented nature of the sector meant that the role and influence of home governments in appeasing regional and global concerns was especially important for the continued profitability of the sector. Therefore, with CPO and PKO exports facing such serious economic threats as discussed above, Malaysian and Singaporean governments were often observed visibly stepping in to use their influence and resources to provide protection and defend their firms operating in Indonesia when faced with such external pressures.

A common reaction among Southeast Asian states, especially during the early haze years, was a combination of denial and downplay of the source and severity of the haze (McLellan, 2001: 253). The word 'haze' itself, adopted unanimously by states in the region at the ASEAN level, has been recognized to be euphemistic and thus inappropriate for describing such a man-made problem. Semantically, the term normally denotes a *naturally occurring* climatic condition in which visibility is affected, for example 'heat haze'. A more appropriate term would have been 'smoke'. At the time, there was already awareness that the phenomenon was caused by human-induced fires, however the choice of the word 'haze' by states to describe the events is indicative of how Southeast Asian states preferred to frame the issue (McLellan, 2001: 254) by diverting attention away from the human and especially commercial drivers of the problem. This is detailed further in Chapter 5 on ASEAN engagement over the haze. Detailed responses by Malaysian and Singaporean governments are explored below to illustrate in detail the extent of the involvement of these governments in upholding the interests of their firms in Indonesia throughout the regionalization process.

The Malaysian government's response

When referring to transboundary haze, official Malaysian government communication preferred to classify haze as not caused by humans, and therefore 'no one was to blame' (McLellan, 2001: 254). Over the years, government spokespersons pointed to various sources for the haze, ranging from eruptions of Mount Galunggung in Java, Indonesia (*Sunday Mail*, 1982) and Mount Pinatubo in the Philippines (*New Straits Times*, 1991). Later, fault was extended to local car emissions, the open burning of rubbish (*Malay Mail*, 1990) and pollution from local factories as a possible cause of haze (*Malay Mail*, 1977). In 1990, as the public began to realize that the smell of the haze was redolent of burning wood, Malaysia absurdly named bush fires in far-away Australia as one of the sources of the haze (Lau, 1990). When at last the Malaysian government acknowledged forest fires in Indonesia producing the smoke haze, it still did not identify large-scale plantations as the major source of these fires (Dauvergne, 1994: 499), instead pointing towards small-scale shifting cultivation by forest-dwelling peoples, the actions of whom were largely outside of the control of state mechanisms (*New Straits Times*, 1985).

Furthermore, the Malaysian Education Ministry was said to have barred academic researchers from talking to the media on 'sensitive issues that could distort the country's good image', like the haze (Zainal Abidin [M38], 2010). For example, an academic from Universiti Putra Malaysia who was interviewed lamented that 'the government banned my research! Dr Mahathir was not happy with it, so they did not let me circulate it … because they did not want the public to find out how bad the haze was for their health' (Zainal Abidin [M38], 2010). Consequently, concerns about the haze negatively affecting citizen health were dismissed by the Malaysian government. Since the first appearance of the haze in 1982, the Ministry of Science, Technology and Environment (MSTE) frequently reassured the public that haze particles were non-toxic and not active, and therefore not hazardous to health (Nayar *et al.*, 1990). Even after the Health Ministry acknowledged the increase of haze-related diseases, public health advisories frequently advised the public to merely 'not breathe too vigorously' while outdoors (Foong, 1994). Furthermore, in June 1999, the Malaysian Cabinet directed the Malaysian Meteorological Service to use the Official Secrets Act 1972 to withhold the dissemination of daily Air Pollution Index (API) updates to the public, as it 'did not want irresponsible parties to take advantage of the situation and exaggerate conditions' (*New Straits Times*, 2005a). The Act allows a minister to mark any document 'secret' for an unlimited period of time[16] (Article 19 and CIJ, 2007: 38).

Economic losses as a result of the haze were also underplayed in Malaysia. Local economic analysts were reported in the newspapers saying that the ten-day emergency that was declared in Sarawak because of the haze (as mentioned in Chapter 1) would not have any immediate effect on the economy[17] (Ngiam and Tawie, 1997). However when the economic impact grew increasingly harder to deny, the Malaysian government reacted defensively by clamping down on haze-related news. For example, when questioned by opposition representatives in Parliament, ministers repeatedly denied that they had any details on the amount of economic losses as a result of the haze from 2000 onwards (Parliament of Malaysia, 2010), despite independent research having already been done on the matter (Mohd Shahwahid and Othman, 1999).

Also, at the early stages of the haze, a spokesperson from the Malaysian Ministry of Culture and Tourism insisted that the haze was not affecting tourist arrivals to the country (Kang, 1997). In connection to this, the Information Ministry was reported to have warned TV stations not to blow the haze problem out of proportion, or they could have their licenses revoked (McLellan, 2001). When irrefutable figures of the drop of tourist arrivals surfaced, the government blamed this drop on outdated coverage of haze by foreign media (*Business Times*, 1997a), based on distortions of local media reports. In fact, the Information Ministry lobbied this matter so avidly that it managed to get an apology and compensation (in the form of airtime promoting Malaysia) from the American network CNN for its supposedly 'less-than fair' reports on the haze (*New Straits Times*, 1997a).

In addition to this self-censorship (Interviewee M44, 2012), the Malaysian government's reactions towards allegations of burning by Malaysian companies in Indonesia have been generally defensive. For example, Malaysian official figures often grossly underestimate the amount of land owned by Malaysian investments in Indonesia to give the impression that their contribution to the haze could not be that drastic. For instance, based on data presented by the Malaysian Ministry of Plantation Industries and Commodities to the Parliament in December 2005, Malaysian investors only controlled some 890,000 hectares of land bank in Indonesia at the time. However, according to estimates based on media reports and independent sources from that period, the total land bank held by Malaysian investors in Indonesia was about double the official amount; closer to 1.7 to 2 million hectares (WALHI *et al.*, 2009: 5). Now of course, this figure would be much higher (WALHI and Sawit Watch, 2009: 1–5,; WALHI *et al.*, 2009: 5). A recent study by Aidenvironment in 2014 estimated that Malaysian companies hold a land bank of 1.8 million hectares throughout Indonesia (Aidenvironment, 2014).

Despite this, the topic of Malaysian companies' burning activities in Indonesia was avidly discussed in the Malaysian media in 1997 (Sharif [M21] and Abdul Hathi [M22], 2010). Following a list provided by the Indonesian government that was said to have identified the top 35 smoke-emitting plantations in Indonesia as of Malaysian origin (Interviewee M44, 2012) there was an initial acceptance of responsibility by the Malaysian government during the late 1990s, with Malaysia affirming that companies guilty of burning would face consequences. This however was not coupled with any concrete remedial steps.

For example, the then Prime Minister Mahathir Mohamed advised those companies to take remedial action fast in response to these allegations by Indonesia (Sharif [M21] and Abdul Hathi [M22], 2010). However, when asked if any legal action would be taken towards companies who admit to burning, the Natural Disaster Management and Relief Committee Chairman said that 'the government is not fond of prosecuting people' (*Business Times*, 1997b), implying that no action would be taken. The chairman later held closed-door meetings with the firms involved, where 31 companies, (Emmanuel and Yusoff, 1997) reportedly including major players like Sime Darby and KLK (Interviewee M44, 2012), pledged financial assistance to help lessen Indonesia's burden in tackling the haze problem. The companies were asked to contribute about $1.4 million towards this cause. The names of the companies, and the specific sums the companies had pledged were not disclosed, but sources said that some companies had pledged upwards of $30,000 (Emmanuel and Yusoff, 1997). It was later reported that the government had yet to receive any of the funds pledged by these companies, but no further action was taken to pursue the matter (*Business Times*, 1997b).

Legal action by Indonesia against a Malaysian plantation firm (KLK's subsidiary PT API, which is discussed at length in the next chapter) in 2001, and its resulting negative media backlash, invited an even more defensive Malaysian response in the following years. Frequent reports by Indonesian authorities and NGOs of Malaysian companies suspected of burning were quickly dismissed and denied by Malaysian authorities (Interviewee M17, 2010; Nagulendran [M34] and Interviewee M35, 2010; *New Straits Times*, 2006), citing lack of evidence from Indonesia (Hajramurni and Sangadji, 2006). For example, in 2005, in response to a statement by the Indonesian Forestry Minister that ten Malaysian companies were involved in open burning activities in Indonesia (*Bernama*, 2005), both the Malaysia Department of Environment and the Malaysian Ministry of Plantation Industries and Commodities denied having any information of wrongdoings (*New Straits Times*, 2005b). And in 2006, Minister for Plantation Industries and Commodities Peter Chin blatantly denied having received any official statement from the Indonesian government that Malaysian companies were involved in open burning, despite news of this in both the Malaysian and Indonesian press. He argued that these allegations were baselessly made by NGOs with 'hidden agendas' (*Bernama*, 2006; Interviewee M11, 2010). An interviewee explained that at another meeting between the Malaysian government and industry that year, all companies denied conducting open burning. The interviewee noted that 'the Malaysian government accepted this denial at face value' (Interviewee M17, 2010) and did not pursue the matter further.

More recently in 2009, in response to Indonesia's concerns, Minister Chin merely 'reminded' Malaysian companies operating there to 'continue' to practice zero burning within their plantations (*Bernama*, 2009). When questioned in Parliament in 2010, the new Minister for Plantation Industries and Commodities Bernard Giluk Dompok again insisted that all Malaysian companies in Indonesia have been following Indonesian rules and regulations. He said that he had also recently visited some Malaysian plantations there and had observed that 'all is well' (Parliament of Malaysia, 2010). The Malaysian government either does not take any harsh action upon guilty firms or denies all allegations of guilt coming from the Indonesians. Complementing this, the Malaysian Palm Oil Council (MPOC) continues to insist that 'zero-burning is strictly enforced', 'forests are not converted for oil palm expansion' and that environmental impact assessment (*analisis mengenai dampak lingkungan* or AMDAL) studies 'ensure wise development' (Raman *et al.*, 2008: 3–5) in all Malaysian-owned plantations, including those in Indonesia.

Furthermore, several interviewees noted that it has become increasingly difficult to prosecute Malaysian plantation firms in Indonesia (Bratasida [I36], 2010; Satyawan [I20], 2010). As mentioned above, an interviewee explained that Sime Darby was regarded as 'almost untouchable' because of its close relationship with the Malaysian government (Surya [I9] and Akbar [I10], 2010). Another interviewee explained how a Malaysian-owned plantation was brought to court recently, but for some reason the case was 'stopped from continuing on to a higher court' (Satyawan [I20], 2010). It was implied that there had been some direct intervention by the Malaysian government to protect their firms from prosecution (Bratasida [I36], 2010; Satyawan [I20], 2010).

Of late, interviewees have also noted that due to APIMI's influence, special agreements have been reached with the Indonesian government in regards to how to handle allegations of open burnings on Malaysian oil palm plantations. As explained by APIMI's executive secretary, it has been agreed that if fires are detected on Malaysian plantations, no immediate administrative or legal action would be taken (Abdul Mutalib [M42], 2010), despite the fact that Indonesian law stipulates that those companies found guilty could face heavy sanctions, revocation of their licenses or prosecution (Tan, 1997). Instead, the incident would be reported to APIMI, who would then communicate it back to the PMD in Malaysia, which would instruct the involved plantation headquarters in Malaysia to merely 'report back on the situation' (Abdul Mutalib [M42], 2010). These reports hardly ever received any follow-up by either the Malaysian or Indonesian governments (Abdul Mutalib [M42], 2010; Interviewee M28, 2010; Kamaruddin [M26], 2010). This makes it increasingly harder for Malaysian plantation companies to be reprimanded for misconduct in their operations in Indonesia. Similar patterns of response can be observed from the Singaporean government on behalf of their firms operating in Indonesia, as detailed below.

The Singaporean government's response

The Singaporean government also displayed behaviour similar to their Malaysian counterparts when faced with haze pressures. Despite heightened public anxiety over the haze episodes beginning from 1972 (*The Straits Times*, 1972), Singaporean Pollution Control Department (PCD) spokespersons maintained that there was no need for public alarm over the situation. The reason given was because the haze was not photochemical[18] in nature, and thus was not dangerous to health and did not increase pollution levels in Singapore. Public speculation that the haze might be radioactive was quelled by the Singaporean authorities (*The Straits Times*, 1972) and the PCD declared that it was not dangerous to be outdoors (Nathan, 1991). Reports in 1984 stated that the levels for all air pollutants in Singapore were generally within the World Health Organization standards and the United States Environmental Protection Agency Primary Standards (Singaporean Government, 1985: 228). The Ministry for the Environment maintained that eye irritation and a slight odour in the air was nothing to be concerned about (*The Straits Times*, 1982). Even during the worst haze episode in the region in 1997, the then Environment Minister Yeo Cheow Tong maintained that most Singaporeans would be able to cope with the haze without any equipment such as purifiers or filters (Parliament of Singapore, 1998a).

Singaporean journalists who were interviewed said that, throughout the haze episodes, they were instructed not to write or speculate about the sources and causes of the haze[19] (Interviewee M23, 2010; Interviewee S19, 2010; Lee [S20], 2010). Instead, the Singaporean government overwhelmingly blamed slash-and-burn agriculture for the haze, with little mention of large-scale plantation fires. The then Singaporean Minister of Environment and Water Resources Dr Yaacob Ibrahim was quoted as saying that the haze persists because 'having to get farmers to change their livelihoods, to adopt new clearing methods, will take time'

(Parliament of Singapore, 2006). This view was echoed later by the Minister of Foreign Affairs George Yeo. He stated that an important strategy to address fires was to teach small-scale farmers the techniques to overcome their problems of daily life in a way that was less deleterious to the environment (Parliament of Singapore, 2010a).

Despite this denial of the severity of the haze, Singaporean plantation firms operating in Indonesia suffered particularly badly economically due to the backlash from haze and environmental sustainability concerns. Under pressure from NGOs and bad publicity, major companies normally receiving CPO or PKO supplies from these firms boycotted or threatened to boycott their products due to the environmentally unsustainable farming practices such as open burning (*Jakarta Post*, 1999). For example, companies such as Burger King, Unilever and Nestlé cancelled their supplier contracts with Singapore-listed GAR subsidiaries, unless and until land clearing by fire was stopped (*Jakarta Post*, 2010; Subejo, 2010). These contracts that were suspended were worth $33 million (Subejo, 2010). The World Bank Group's International Finance Corporation also froze funding of Singapore-based Wilmar's palm oil-related development projects valued at $132 million in September 2009, after allegations by environment NGOs that Wilmar ignored social and environmental impact laws, with specific reference to laws on land clearing (Roberts, 2011: 57).

Reactions of the Singaporean government in response to these industry reactions have also been similar to the Malaysian response. On the face of things, Singapore seemed to be willing to reprimand their companies. Ministry of Environment staff were reported to have called up the directors of Singaporean plantation companies to remind them to observe the no-burning policy or face legal consequences (Interviewee M1, 2010; Khalik, 2000). Furthermore, subsequent ministers for the environment vowed that the Singaporean government would not protect any Singaporean company that is found guilty (Interviewee S14 and Interviewee S15, 2010; Khalik, 2000). However, when two Singaporean companies were identified by Indonesian authorities in 1998 as having used fire to clear land (*The Straits Times*, 1998), Singaporean officials were said to have denied the allegations because of supposed lack of proof from Indonesia (Interviewee S14 and Interviewee S15, 2010).

Repeated requests by opposition MPs for the Singaporean government to monitor Singaporean investments in Indonesia for burning were also thrown out (Parliament of Singapore, 2010b). Reasons given ranged from the government not having any information on which companies in Singapore were involved in plantation investments (Parliament of Singapore, 2007) to Indonesia not cooperating in providing Singapore with this information (Parliament of Singapore, 1998b). However, as discussed in the previous paragraph, the Singaporean government obviously had this information as they had announced earlier that they managed to 'call them up to remind them' (Interviewee M1, 2010; Khalik, 2000). Singapore's reluctance to attach environmental requirements or codes of conduct on Singaporean investments overseas was justified by the minister for the environment on economic grounds. The minister argued that 'it is important that we separate trade from other matters like environment. It is a position that the World Trade Organization adopts. I would be very reluctant to depart from that position' (Parliament of Singapore, 2000). However, the minister's answer did not address the real issue concerning control over commercial investments and activities in another state. Overall, much like Malaysia, the Singaporean government (at least up to the mid-2013 haze episode[20]) also largely refused to acknowledge their firms' role in the Indonesian fires. This attitude of denial and defensiveness by the home government further complicates efforts to reprimand Singaporean companies for unsustainable conduct in their operations in Indonesia.

Conclusion

As detailed in the introductory chapter, economic arguments relating to foreign debt pressure have previously been offered as a major explanation for the persistence of haze. Scholars such as Gellert (1998: 81) and Marinova (1999: 72) note that Indonesia was forced to open their natural resource sectors to foreign investors as part of the conditionalities of the IMF loan package that Indonesia accepted in the aftermath of the AFC. Given that Indonesia's competitive advantages were in natural resources, FDI flowed into extractive and resource-intensive sectors, such as oil palm plantations (Marinova, 1999: 77). These scholars argued that this influx of foreign investments essentially drove forest degradation and fires. Indeed, the IMF conditionalities did open doors for foreign investments. However, this does not explain why the foreign investors that did enter the sector (mostly Malaysian and Singaporean ones) were able to conduct themselves with impunity in the face of open burning allegations. This chapter has shown that an important explanatory point for this is the fact that economic regionalization in Southeast Asia, while largely market driven, is also actively facilitated by both home and host states.

The above discussion has thus established that a combination of market-led and state-facilitated factors have resulted in a regionalized and highly integrated Southeast Asian oil palm sector, with relatively free movement of investment into Indonesia and 'most favoured nation' and 'national treatment' of foreign investors, especially Malaysian and Singaporean ones, once established. This has led to a concentration of foreign plantation firms, especially from Malaysia and Singapore, in Indonesia. These Malaysian or Singaporean companies that have ventured outwards to Indonesia have often been either GLCs or well-established plantation companies in their home state, often with government elites having vested interests in them. This chapter proposed that these vested interests were an important motivator for home state involvement and facilitation to ensure the well-being and continued profitability of these plantation firms in Indonesia. This explains why Malaysian and Singaporean government facilitation of the regionalization process of their firms to Indonesia was not limited to brokering entry for these firms, but has included using their influence and resources to defend their firms operating in Indonesia when faced with accusations of open-burning misconduct there. These governments have been observed ardently attempting to appease regional and global environmental concerns by downplaying the severity of haze, while at the same time denying the complicity of their firms in the Indonesian fires. This, coupled with local patronage politics as detailed in the next chapter, provides layers of protection to these companies and allows them to elude legal action and burn with impunity, while continuing to prioritize cost effectiveness and profit over regional environmental concerns.

Notes

1 Parts of this chapter have appeared in Varkkey (2013).
2 Recently, a new draft bill was drawn up by members of Indonesia's Parliament looking to restrict foreign ownership to no more than 30 per cent (from the current 95 per cent), to give more ownership opportunities to the local sector. However, this bill has been met by resistance from within the sector, and also among financial advisors. Industry commentators have opined that this restriction would hinder the flow of overseas capital needed to develop and modernize the industry, and also negatively affect the investment atmosphere in Indonesia (Taylor and Supriatna, 2014). This bill, if passed, would have interesting impacts on the sector, which will be of great interests to researchers and analysts in the future.
3 Indonesia, by contrast, made no such pledges.
4 Sime Darby is Malaysia's largest transnational corporation (TNC) as listed on the Malaysian bourse (Yeoh *et al.*, 2011b: 14). It has also been ranked as the world's biggest TNC in agribusiness industries according to the UN's *World Investment Report* (UNCTAD, 2009: 124). The 2007 merger of three major Malaysian plantation companies, Sime Darby, Golden Hope Plantations and Kumpulan Guthrie established Sime Darby as the world's largest plantation company by land bank (Tan and Oetomo, 2011: 5), with 850,000 hectares of land worldwide (UOB Kay Hian, 2011) and the potential to produce 8 per cent of global oil palm output (UNCTAD, 2009: 126). Plantations are Sime Darby's most important sector, contributing 62 per cent of total revenue to the company in 2011 (Tan, 2011: 1). Its Indonesia operations make up around 35 per cent of its total planted land for oil palm (UNCTAD, 2009: 126). Today, Sime Darby is the largest foreign company operating in the Indonesian oil palm sector and the largest exporter of palm oil from Indonesia (Saravanamuttu [S23], 2010).
5 Tabung Haji was launched in 1963 and began as the Malaysian Muslim Pilgrims Savings Corporation. Tabung Haji diversified and increased its investment activities in various sectors such as plantations, commerce, construction, property development and manufacturing. THP's first overseas venture in Indonesia was with PT Multi Gambut in Riau, Indonesia, to operate an oil palm plantation and processing facilities. It holds a 70 per cent equity in PT Multi Gambut and its investment totals $256 million (Haji Mat Zin, 1999: 492–496). Today, THP owns and manages 200,000 hectares of plantation land mainly on peatlands in Riau, Sumatra (*The Star*, 2007) through the joint venture, PT TH Indo Plantations, which it bought over for $5.8 million. In 2010, Tabung Haji Plantations produced a total revenue of $117.2 million (TH Plantations, 2010).
6 KLK is the world's seventh biggest TNC in agribusiness industries (UNCTAD, 2009: 124). It is Malaysia's third largest plantation company by market capitalization (Yeoh *et al.*, 2011b: 13). KLK was incorporated in Malaysia in 1973. It expanded its plantation business to Indonesia from the 1990s. KLK now has a plantation land bank of more than 250,000 hectares in Malaysia and Indonesia, with more than half of that in Indonesia (139,126 hectares). In Indonesia, its total assets are valued at $368.4 million, mostly located in Medan, Pekanbaru and Belitung in Sumatra, as well as

Sampit and Tanjung Redeb in Kalimantan (Kuala Lumpur Kepong Berhad, 2010). A significant holding is PT Adei Plantation and Industry, which was established under a joint venture with prominent Indonesian lawyer Al Hakim Hanafiah, with 27,760 hectares of land (Saharjo *et al.*, 2003: 3). In 2010, KLK obtained revenue of $1.06 billion in palm products, contributing 81 per cent of its profits. KLK is currently converting former rubber plantations and plantation reserves to oil palm in North Sumatra (Kuala Lumpur Kepong Berhad, 2010) and other areas in Indonesia, targeting to open up 25,000 hectares over the next two years (Yeoh *et al.*, 2011a: 30).

7 IOI is the world's 44th biggest TNC in agribusiness industries (UNCTAD, 2009: 124). It is the biggest Malaysian oil palm group that is listed on the Kuala Lumpur Stock Exchange (Milieudefensie, 2010: 6). IOI started out as a real estate firm in 1982, and grew to be involved in various sectors including property, manufacturing and plantations. Its plantations division has developed into an integrated operation involved in the entire value chain of oil palm production. IOI's plantation division is the most important and profitable division of the Group, contributing 55 per cent of its operating profit, or US$ 110.5 million. The group has a total of 82 estates, with 5 per cent of this total in Indonesia (IOI Group, 2011). IOI extended its activities to Indonesia in 2005 (UNCTAD, 2009: 127), where it now holds a total land bank of 172,000 hectares in Indonesia (Milieudefensie, 2010: 6). Its associate company in Indonesia is PT Bumitama Gunajaya Agro Group, and this company has planted approximately 6,000 hectares of oil palm to date and is planning to plant a further 27,000 hectares over the next few years, with plans to bring total acreage in Indonesia to more than 35,000 hectares by 2014 (IOI Group, 2011).

8 Genting Plantations is a 54.6 per cent owned subsidiary of Genting Berhad, one of Malaysia's biggest multinationals (Genting Plantations Berhad, 2010). Genting Plantations commenced operations in 1980, and now owns a combined area of 228,300 hectares of plantation land in Malaysia and Indonesia (Genting Group, 2014). In Indonesia, Genting Plantations formed a joint venture with the Sepanjang Group, and this group has been Genting Plantation's partner for all projects in West Kalimantan, namely the Ketapang Estates, Sanggau Estates and Kapuas Estates. Through these joint ventures, Genting currently holds a total plantable land bank of 80,000 to 90,000 hectares there, of which over 32,000 has been planted. Genting is currently expanding its planted land bank at a rate of 10,000 to 11,000 hectares annually (Yeoh *et al.*, 2011a: 34). In 2010, Genting Plantations undertook its maiden harvesting of oil palm fruits in Indonesia, a ceremony that was attended by local dignitaries and customary heads. This first harvesting delivered revenue of $288.3 million (Genting Plantations Berhad, 2010).

9 Dato' Lee is also a council member of the Malaysian Palm Oil Association (Milieudefensie, 2010: 7).

10 Palm oil usually has to be processed before export as CPO. Sometimes, economic indicators list these processed products under 'manufacturing', instead of agriculture.

11 This is largely owing to Finnish oil refiner, Neste Oil's recently built world's largest biodiesel plant. Neste Oil wanted to take advantage of Singapore's technological advantages and close proximity to raw materials (Neste Oil, 2010; World Growth, 2011: 4–8).

12 Wilmar International is headquartered in Singapore and is one of Asia's leading agribusiness groups. It is the 21st biggest TNC in agribusiness industries (UNCTAD, 2009: 124) and handles about 25 per cent of international palm oil output (Zakaria *et al.*, 2007: 14). Wilmar was founded in 1991 as a palm oil trading company and now is the world's largest palm oil refiner (Tan and Oetomo, 2011: 6) and one of the largest oil palm plantation owners and biodiesel manufacturers (Profundo, 2007: 1; Richardson, 2010: 69; UNCTAD, 2009: 127,). The company is spearheaded jointly by Kuok Khoon Hong, the nephew of Malaysian billionaire Robert Kwok, and Martua Sitorus (one of Indonesia's richest persons) (Profundo, 2007: 3), who has been instru-

mental in the development of the group's business operations in Indonesia (Profundo, 2007: 1). Wilmar is one of the largest oil palm plantation owners in the world, second only to Malaysia's Sime Darby (Tan and Oetomo, 2011: 5), with a total land bank of 604,130 (Zakaria *et al.*, 2007: 5) and a planted area of 493,000 hectares in 2010 (Greenpeace, 2007: 42). About 75 per cent of the total planted area is located in Indonesia with the remaining 25 per cent in East Malaysia. Wilmar's activities in Indonesia began since 1991, where it started to manage oil palm plantations in Sumatra, in the provinces of West Sumatra, South Sumatra and Riau (Compliance Advisor Ombudsman, 2009: 3). Wilmar plans to increase its land bank at a yearly rate of 15,000 hectares (Zakaria *et al.*, 2007: 20). It also runs 18 palm and lauric oil refining plants in Indonesia with a total capacity of 9.6 million tonnes per year (Nature, 2007: 3), making it the largest palm oil producer in Indonesia (Saravanamuttu [S23], 2010) and the world (Poynton, 2014). Due to this, Wilmar in effect controls 30 per cent of the global market share in oil palm processing (UOB Kay Hian, 2011: 36). Sale of this palm oil has produced a yearly turnover of US$ 5.3 billion (Profundo, 2007: 1). Wilmar plans to invest $900 million to build more processing facilities in Indonesia (Reuters, 2011; *The Straits Times*, 2011). Wilmar also recently acquired a 20 per cent stake in the Singapore-listed Kencana Agri, which owns a total of 185,888 hectares land bank in Sumatra, Kalimantan and Sulawesi, of which 46,713 have been planted (Kencana Agri, 2010).

13 Listed on the Singapore Stock Exchange since 1999, GAR and its subsidiaries (PT Sinar Mas Agro Resources and Technology or PT SMART) form the second largest integrated oil palm company in the world (Yeoh *et al.*, 2011a: 14). The Board of Directors of the company mainly consists of members of the rich Indonesian Widjadja family (Cochraine, 2010), Franky Oesman Widjadja, Muktar Widjadja and Frankle Widjadja, alongside prominent Singaporeans (Golden-Agri Resources Ltd, 2010). The Widjadja family controls 50 per cent stake in the company (UOB Kay Hian, 2011: 32). Through its subsidiaries, GAR manages 142 oil palm estates in Indonesia, cultivating around 1.65 million hectares of plantations in Indonesia and producing about 11 per cent of palm oil in Indonesia (Greenpeace, 2007: 37–42). GAR reaped a total revenue of more than $3.5 billion, net profit of $1.4 billion and core net profit of $387 million in 2010. It is currently the largest landholder in Indonesia and has an aggressive plantation expansion plan to maintain this lead. It has grown its oil palm plantation area by over a third since 2008 (Golden-Agri Resources Ltd, 2010). In 2010, GAR expanded its planted area by around 15,200 hectares through new plantings (Maitar, 2008: 1), and this was followed by another 8,000 hectares in 2011 (UOB Kay Hian, 2011: 32). It has plans to develop another 2.8 million hectares of land all over Indonesia (Maitar, 2008: 1).

14 The Salim Group's food-related enterprises were its most lucrative sector, and round-tripping to Singapore was an attempt to retain control of these enterprises during the aftermath of the AFC and its related racially fuelled (anti-Chinese) bank run and riots (Sato, 2004: 34). Indo Agri is the Salim Group's overseas enterprise in Singapore (Sato, 2004: 35). It is listed on the main board of the Singapore Stock Exchange (Indo Food Agri Resources, 2010) and is also among the largest plantation owners in Indonesia. Like Wilmar and Golden Agri Resources, Indo Agri is known to be headed by a Singaporean and Indonesian cohort (Tarigan [I23], 2010). Axton Salim, a member of the Salim family, is a director (Indo Food Agri Resources, 2010). Indo Agri's sole asset, of which it owns 72 per cent, is Salim Ivormas Pratama, a major plantation company in Indonesia (Oetomo and Sandianto, 2011: 1). Through this company it controls a land bank of over 549,287 hectares in Medan, Pekanbaru and Palembang in Sumatra, and Pontianak in Kalimantan, of which 35,566 remain unplanted (Richardson, 2010: 57). This makes it owner of the second largest nucleus oil palm plantation area among all Indonesian CPO producers (Oetomo and Sandianto, 2011: 1). It plans to expand its plantations by 15,000 to 20,000 hectares per

year (UOB Kay Hian, 2011: 32), and it achieved this in 2011 when it opened up 15,041 hectares for planting. In 2010, the company reported revenue of $1.05 billion (Indo Food Agri Resources, 2010).

15 Other than open burning, other misconducts that oil palm plantation companies have been blamed for include deforestation, loss of orangutan habitat, land conflicts, problems with smallholders, brutality and illegal operations (WALHI *et al.*, 2009).

16 Only in 2005, after six years of NGO pressure for the figures to be released, were they again available to the media and the public (Mathews [M33], 2010; *New Straits Times*, 2005a).

17 The government was later forced to admit that Sarawak suffered economic losses of $340 million during the emergency (Tawie, 1997).

18 A 'photochemical smog' is the chemical reaction of sunlight and various chemicals in the atmosphere producing smoke that can be very dangerous to human health. The PCD argued that the haze did not contain any reactive chemicals.

19 Press freedom in Singapore is relatively low. All media is owned by the Singaporean government. Singapore is ranked 150 out of 180 countries in the Press Freedom Index 2014. Malaysia ranked slightly better at 147, while Indonesia ranked among the highest in Southeast Asia at 132 (Reporters Without Borders, 2014). The Singaporean government used their control over the press to limit unsavoury information on haze issues.

20 Singapore's tone in responding to the haze and alleged involvement by Singaporean companies showed a significant shift from its usual responses during the mid-2013 haze episode. This shift may have been triggered by critical-level PSI recordings of more than 400 in July that year, the highest ever recorded by the island nation. While Singaporean-listed companies operating in Indonesia such as First Resources, Indofood Agri Resources, Wilmar and GAR once again denied their complicity in causing haze-producing fires (Kwok and Feng, 2013), Singapore's reaction to these denials was markedly different from the past. Instead of taking them at face value, the Singaporean Parliament passed the 'Transboundary Pollution Bill' on 5 August 2014, which would provide for criminal and civil liability for any Singaporean or non-Singaporean entity causing or contributing to transboundary haze pollution in Singapore. The bill makes it a criminal offence when an entity engages in conduct or authorizes any conduct that causes or contributes to haze in Singapore. Under the bill, companies found guilty of causing haze could be fined up to S$100,000 (approximatley US$72,220) for each day they pollute, with the maximum aggregate amount being S$2 million (US$1,444,373) (*Malay Mail*, 2014). The bill is unique for its application of extra-territoriality; it covers the operations of all Singaporean and non-Singaporean entities whose activities outside of Singapore contribute to haze pollution in the city-state. It is also the first of its kind in the region and the world, as there is currently no other law anywhere else that allows a state to prosecute corporations in other states for such transgressions (*Channel NewsAsia*, 2014b). To complement the bill, particularly to help in the identification of errant parties, current Singaporean Minister for Environment and Water Resources Dr Vivian Balakrishnan has also been at the same time very vocal in pushing for Indonesia to share with Singapore digitized land-use maps and concession maps of fire-prone areas that cause transboundary haze, under the ASEAN Sub-Regional Haze Monitoring System (further discussed in Chapter 5) (*Channel NewsAsia*, 2014a). The bill will now go to the president who will then sign it into law. The effectiveness of this new bill, however, will have to be tested in courts in the fullness of time before any conclusions can be drawn about whether Singapore's stance has truly shifted in terms of acknowledging the role of their firms in the fires.

References

Abdul Mutalib [M42], N. H. 22 July 2010. *RE: Executive Secretary, Association of Plantation Investors of Malaysia in Indonesia.*

Adnan, H. 2010. Sime's Bakke has vast expertise. *The Star*, 15 June 2010.

Adnan, H. 2012. Cries of EU biofuel discrimination grows louder. *The Star*, 25 January 2012.

Adnan, H. 2013. Helping to clear the haze Eight Malaysian-owned firms under Indonesian probe. *The Star*, 25 June 2013.

Aidenvironment 2014. Malaysian Overseas Foreign Direct Investment in Oil Palm Land Bank: Scale and Sustainability Impact. Amsterdam: Aidenvironment.

Apimi 2010. *About Us*. Jakarta. Available: www.uiccm.com/apimi/index.php/7-about-us/2-about-apimi [accessed 6 October 2010].

Arif [I41], J. 4 November 2011. *RE: Forest Campaigner, Greenpeace Southeast Asia.*

Article 19 and CIJ 2007. *A Haze of Secrecy: Access to Environmental Information in Malaysia*. Kuala Lumpur.

Bankoff, G. and Elston, K. 1994. *Environmental Regulation in Malaysia and Singapore*, Perth, University of Western Australia Press.

Barber, C. V. 1998. Forest resource scarcity and social conflict in Indonesia. *Environment*, 40, 4.

Basiron, Y. 2010. *Testimony of Dr Yusuf Basiron Chief Executive Officer of the Malaysian Palm Oil Council (MPOC) to the Hearing of the Senate Community Affairs Committee (Truth in Labelling – Palm Oil) Bill 2010*. Kuala Lumpur: Malaysian Palm Oil Council.

Basiron, Y. 2011a. A fair trade approach for promoting food security and ensuring supply sustainability in oils and fats trade. *Journal of Oil Palm and the Environment*, 2, 15–24.

Basiron, Y. 2011b. Preparing the palm oil industry for the opportunities and challenges of tomorrow. *Global Oils and Fats*. Kuala Lumpur: Malaysian Palm Oil Council.

Basiron, Y. 2011c. 'Truth' held hostage. *Global Oils and Fats Magazine*. Kuala Lumpur: Malaysian Palm Oil Council.

Beeson, M. 2004. Southeast Asia. *In:* Payne, A. (ed.) *The New Regional Politics of Development*. Hampshire: Palgrave Macmillan.

Bernama 2005. No M'sian firms involved in open burning in Sumatra. *Bernama Daily Malaysian News*, 12 August 2005.

Bernama 2006. Don't carry out open burning, Abdullah tells Malaysian companies. *Bernama Daily Malaysian News*, 12 January 2006.

Bernama 2009. Malaysian seeks help of its oil palm planters in Riau to prevent haze. *Bernama Daily Malaysian News*, 9 August 2009.

Bernama 2010. Palm oil sector to become larger contributor to GDP. *Bernama Daily Malaysian News*, 30 March 2010.

Blomqvist, H. C. (ed.) 2000. *Development Policies of Singapore: Dynamics of Internationalism versus Regionalisation*, Swedish School of Economics and Business Administration.

Bratasida [I36], L. 29 July 2010. *RE: Assistant Minister of Global Environmental Affairs and International Cooperation, Ministry of Environment.*

Breslin, S. and Higgott, R. 2003. New regionalism(s) in the global political economy. Conceptual understanding in historical perspective. *Asia Europe Journal*, 1, 167–182.

Business Times 1997a. Drop in tourism earnings expected. *Business Times*, 15 November 1997.

Business Times 1997b. Govt yet to get financial aid pledged by 31 firms. *Business Times*, 1 October 1997.

Carney, M. and Dieleman, M. 2011. Indonesia's missing multinationals: Business groups and outward direct investment. *Bulletin of Indonesian Economic Studies*, 47, 105–26.

Caroko, W., Komarudin, H., Obidzinski, K. and Gunarso, P. 2011. *Policy and institutional frameworks for the development of palm oil-based biodiesel in Indonesia*. Working Paper. Jakarta: Center for International Forestry Research.

Case, W. 2003. Interlocking elites in Southeast Asia. *Comparative Sociology*, 2, 249–267.

Casson, A. 2002. The political economy of Indonesia's oil palm sector. *In:* Colfer, C. J. and Resosudarmo, I. A. P. (eds) *Which Way Forward? People, forests and policymaking in Indonesia*. Singapore: Institute of South East Asian Studies.

Channel Newsasia 2014a. Haze Monitoring System's full operation faces obstacle: Balakrishnan. *Channel NewsAsia*, 2 April 2014.

Channel Newsasia 2014b. Up to S$100.000 fine for every day if transboundary haze. *Channel NewsAsia*, 7 July 2014.

Chee [M27], T. Y. 14 April 2010. *RE: Manager, Global Environment Center.*

Chua, B. H. 2008. Singapore in 2007: High wage ministers and the management of gays and elderly. *Asian Survey*, 48, 55–61.

Cochraine, J. 2010. Growing pains. *Post Magazine*. United Kingdom.

Colfer, C. J. P. 2002. Ten propositions to explain Kalimantan's fires. *In:* Colfer, C. J. and Resosudarmo, I. A. P. (eds) *Which Way Forward? People, forests and policymaking in Indonesia*. Singapore: Institute of Southeast Asian Studies.

Compliance Advisor Ombudsman 2009. Complaint from Communities in Kalimantan and Civil Society in relation to activities of the Wilmar Group of Companies. *Final Ombudsman Assessment Report*. Jakarta: Multilateral Investment Guarantee Agency.

Creagh, S. and Chatterjee, N. 2010. Interivew Update 1 – Indonesia may cancel permits to save forests. Reuters, 18 August 2010.

Dauvergne, P. 1994. The politics of deforestation in Indonesia. *Pacific Affairs*, 66, 497–518.

Del Gallego, M. 2011. Govt temporarily stops allowing foreign investment in oil palm sector. *Food and Agriculture, News, Policy and Finance*, 16 may 2011, p.18 July 2011.

Down to Earth 2007. *Oil Palm Plantation Expansion in Indonesia*. Down to Earth – International Campaign for Ecological Justice in Indonesia.

Ellingsen, G., Likumahuwa, W. and Nunnenkamp, P. 2006. Outward FDI by Singapore: A different animal? *Trnasnational Corporations*, 15, 1–34.

Embas, D. U. 2012. Statement by the Honourable Dato' Sri Douglas Unggah Embas, Minister of Natural Resources and Environment, Malaysia. *In:* Environment, M. O. N. R. A. T. (ed.). *Rio De Janeiro: The United Nations Conference on Sustainable Development*, 22 June 2012.

Emmanuel, T. and Yusoff, S. 1997. 31 firms pledge financial help. *New Straits Times*, 27 September 1997.

Faostat 2012. Area Harvested of Oil Palm Fruit in Indonesia – 1961–2012. Geneva: Food and Agriculture Organization of the United Nations.

Foong, P. Y. 1994. Lee: Don't breathe vigorously outdoors. *The Star*, 10 September 1994.

Gellert, P. K. 1998. A brief history and analysis of Indonesia's forest fire crisis. *Indonesia*, 65.

genting group 2014. *Genting Plantations Berhad*. Kuala Lumpur. Available: www.genting.com/groupprofile/genp.htm [accessed 15 August 2014].

Genting Plantations Berhad 2010. *Annual Report*. Kuala Lumpur: Genting Plantations Berhad.

Ghani [S6], A. 17 May 2010. *RE: former Straits Times Press Reporter.*

Goh, M. L., Sikorski, D. and Wong, W. K. 2001. Government policy for outward investment by domestic firms: The case of Singapore's regionalization strategy. *Singapore Management Review*, 1, 23–42.

Goh, S. K. and Wong, K. N. 2011. Malaysia's outward FDI: The effects of market size and government policy. *Journal of Policy Modeling*, 33, 499–508.

Golden-Agri Resources Ltd 2010. *Annual Report.* Singapore: Golden Agri-Resources Ltd.

Gomez, E. T. 2009. The rise and call of capital: Corporate Malaysia in historical perspective. *Journal of Contemporary Asia*, 39, 345–381.

Grant, R. 2008. High hopes. *Telegraph Magazine.* London.

Greenpeace 2007. *How the Palm Oil Industry is Cooking the Climate.* Jakarta: Greenpeace.

Haggard, S. and Low, L. 2002. State, politics, and business in Singapore. *In:* Gomez, E. T. (ed.) *Political Business in East Asia.* New York: Routledge.

Haji Mat Zin, R. 1999. Malaysian reverse investments: Trends and strategies. *Asia Pacific Journal of Management*, 16, 469–496.

Hajramurni, A. and Sangadji, R. 2006. KL supports plan to sue companies for forest fires. *The Jakarta Post*, 13 October 2006.

Haley, U. C. V. 1996. Singapore incorporated: Reinterpreting Singapore's business environment through a corporate metaphor. *Management Decision*, 34, 17–28.

Hameiri, S. and Jones, L. 2013. The politics and governance of non-traditional security. *International Studies Quarterly*, 57, 462–473.

Hamilton-Hart, N. 2005. The regionalization on Southeast Asian businesses: Transnational networks in national contexts. *In:* Pempel, T. J. (ed.) *Remapping East Asia: The Construction of a Region.* Ithaca: Cornell University Press.

Hamilton-Hart, N. 2009. Indonesia and Singapore: Structure, politics and interests. *Contemporary Southeast Asia*, 31, 249–271.

Harun [M49], M. H., Omar [M50], W., Hashim [M51], Z. and Jantan [M52], N. M. 20 January 2012. *RE: Tropical Peat Insitutute Unit, Malaysian Palm Oil Board.*

Hicken, A. 2011. Clientelism. *Annual Review of Political Science*, 14, 289–310.

Hiratsuka, D. 2006. *Outward FDI from an Intraregional FDI in ASEAN: Trends and Drivers.* Discussion Paper, 2006. Institute of Developing Economies, 1–16.

Ho, W. F. 1997. The Big Haze – Indonesian plantations' denial 'incredulous'. *The Straits Times*, 2 October 1997.

Hurrell, A. 1995. Explaining the resurgence of regionalism in world politics. *Review of International Studies*, 21, 331–358.

Indo Food Agri Resources 2010. *Annual Report.* Singapore: Indo Food Agri Resources.

Interviewee I21. 16 July 2010. *RE: Telapak.*

Interviewee I25. 20 July 2010. *RE: Channel NewsAsia.*

Interviewee I48. 30 November 2011. *RE: Fauna Flora International.*

Interviewee I49. 1 December 2011. *RE: Leuser Foundation.*

Interviewee M1. 4 March 2010. *RE: Ministry of Natural Resources and the Environment.*

Interviewee M11. 24 March 2010. *RE: Ministry of Foreign Affairs.*

Interviewee M17. 1 April 2010. *RE: Department of Environment.*

Interviewee M23. 9 April 2010. *RE: Universiti Kebangsaan Malaysia.*

Interviewee M24 and Interviewee M25. 12 April 2010. *RE: a major Malaysian plantation corporation.*

Interviewee M28. 14 April 2010. *RE: TH Plantations.*

Interviewee M41. 11 May 2010. *RE: Ministry of Plantation Industries and Commodities.*

Interviewee M44. 5 January 2012. *RE: Global Environment Center.*
Interviewee M45, Interviewee M46, Interviewee M47 and Interviewee M48. 17 January 2012. *RE: Plantation Sustainability Department, Sime Darby.*
Interviewee M53 and Interviewee M54. 26 January 2012. *RE: Malaysian Palm Oil Council.*
Interviewee S4 and Interviewee S5. 14 May 2010. *RE: National Environment Agency.*
Interviewee S14 and Interviewee S15. 19 May 2010. *RE: Ministry of Environment and Water Resources.*
Interviewee S18. 26 May 2010. *RE: Conservation International.*
Interviewee S19. 26 May 2010. *RE: Straits Times Press.*
IOI Group 2011. *Annual Report.* Malaysia: IOI Group.
Jakarta Post 1999. Dealing with the haze. *Jakarta Post*, 7 August 1999.
Jakarta Post 2010. Comment: Burger King to stop buying palm oil. *Jakarta Post*, 9 September 2010.
Jarvis, D., Richmond, N., Phua, K. H., Pocock, N., Sovacool, B. K. and D'agostino, A. 2010. Palm oil in Southeast Asia. *Asian Trends Monitoring Bulletin*, 4, 9–14.
Johnston, M. 2005. *Syndromes of Corruption: Wealth, Power and Democracy*, New York, Cambridge University Press.
Kamaruddin [M26], H. 13 April 2010. *RE: Lecturer, Faculty of Law, UKM.*
Kang, S. L. 1997. Tourism arrivals unaffected, says ministry. *Business Times*, 17 September 1997.
Katzenstein, P. J. 1997. Introduction: Asian regionalism in comparative perspective. *In:* Katzenstein, P. J. and Shiraishi, T. (eds) *Network Power: Japan and Asia.* Ithaca: Cornell University Press.
Kencana Agri 2010. *Annual Report.* Singapore: Kencana Agri.
Khalik, S. 2000. Haze – S'pore won't protect guilty firms. *The Straits Times*, 6 April 2000.
Koh, L. P. and Wilcove, D. S. 2008. Oil palm: Disinformation enables deforestation. *Trends in Ecology and Evolution*, 24, 67–68.
Kuala Lumpur Kepong Berhad 2010. *Annual Report.* Ipoh: Kuala Lumpung Kepong Berhad.
Kwok, J. and Feng, Z. 2013. Haze update: Palm oil companies listed in Singapore deny using fire to clear land. *The Straits Times*, 23 July 2013.
Lau, P. P. 1990. Australian fires behind haze afecting the whole country. *The Star*, 27 August 1990.
Lawrence [I38], P. 27 November 2011. *RE: Researcher, Ecostrategy.*
Lee [S20], P. O. 26 May 2010. *RE: Fellow, Regional Economic Studies, Institute for South East Asian Studies.*
Lim [S13], M. A. 18 May 2010. *RE: Manager, Policy Research, Singapore Institute of International Affairs.*
Lim, L. Y. C. and Stern, A. 2003. State power and private profit: The political economy of corruption in Southeast Asia. *Asian-Pacific Economic Literature*, 16, 18–52.
Lipsey, R. E. and Sjoholm, F. 2011. Foreign direct investment and growth in East Asia: Lessons for Indonesia. *Bulletin of Indonesian Economic Studies*, 47, 35–63.
Lopez, L. 1995. Corporate Foryas into Singapore. *Business Times*, 27 July.
Maitar [I12], B. 2 July 2010. *RE: Forest Campaign Team Leader, Greenpeace-Southeast Asia.*
Maitar, B. 2008. Sinar Mas: Indonesian palm oil menace. *Briefing.* Jakarta: Greenpeace.
Malay Mail 1977. Haze over Klang Valley. *Malay Mail*, 28 October 1977.
Malay Mail 1990. Pollution the cause of the haze. *Malay Mail*, 15 September 1990.

Malay Mail 2014. Singapore approves bill to fine companies that cause air pollution. *Malay Mail*, 5 August 2014.
Malaysian Palm Oil Council 2006. *Oil Palm: Tree of life*, Kuala Lumpur, Malaysian Palm Oil Council.
Marinova, N. 1999. Indonesia's Fiery Crises. *Journal of Environment and Development*, 8, 70–81.
Maruli, A. 2011. Half of RI's oil palm plantations foreign-owned. *Antara Magazine*. Jakarta: Financial Times Information Limited.
Mathew [M8], K. G. 20 March 2010. *RE: former Plantation Manager, Sime Darby Plantation.*
Mathews [M33], P. 19 April 2010. *RE: former Assistant Director General, Institute for Strategic and International Studies.*
McCarthy, J. and Cramb, R. A. 2009. Policy narratives, landholder engagement, and oil palm expansion on the Malaysian and Indonesian frontiers. *The Geographical Journal*, 175, 112–123.
McCarthy, J. F. 2010. Process of inclusion and adverse incorporation: oil palm and agrarian change in Sumatra, Indonesia. *The Journal of Peasant Studies*, 37, 821–850.
Mclellan, J. 2001. From denial to debate – And back again! Malaysian press coverage of the air pollution and 'haze' episodes, July 1997–July1999. *In:* Eaton, P. A. R., M (ed.) *Forest Fires and Haze in Southeast Asia*. New York: Nova Science Publishers.
Milieudefensie 2010. *Milieudefensie's Response to IOI's rebuttal in Substance*. Jakarta: Milieudefensie.
Ministry Of Land Development Sarawak 2011. *SLDB*. Sarawak: Ministry of Land Development.
Mohd Shahwahid, H. O. and Othman, J. 1999. Malaysia. *In:* Glover, D. and Jessup, T. (eds) *Indonesia's Fires and Haze: The Cost of Catastrophe*. Singapore: Institue of Southeast Asian Studies.
Moore [I5], P. F. 27 June 2010. *RE: Project Manager, IUCN-WWF Project Firefight Southeast Asia.*
MPOA 2011. *About MPOA*. Kuala Lumpur. Available: www.mpoa.org.my/v2/index.php?option=com_content&view=article&id=19&Itemid=27 [accessed 13 December 2011].
MPOB 2011. *About MPOB*. Kuala Lumpur. Available: www.mpob.gov.my/ [accessed 13 December 2011].
MPOC 2011. *About MPOC*. Kuala Lumpur. Available: www.mpoc.org.my/Corporate_Profile.aspx [accessed 13 December 2011].
Naguib, R. and Smucker, J. 2009. When economic growth rhymes with social development: The Malaysia experience. *Journal of Business Ethics*, 89, 99–113.
Nagulendran [M34], K. and Interviewee M35. 20 April 2010. *RE: Deputy Under Secretary, Ministry of Natural Resources and Environment and officer.*
Nathan, D. 1991. Change in the wind direction will help clear haze over Singapore. *The Straits Times*, 2 October 1991.
Nature 2007. Focus on surfectants. *Nature*, 3.
Nayar, I., Chua, E., Azmin, Y. and Hamid, F. 1990. Visibility alert. *Malay Mail*, 28 August 1990.
Neste Oil 2010. *Annual Report*. Finland: Neste Oil.
Neville, W. 1992. Agribusiness in Singapore: A capital-intensive service. *Journal of Rural Studies*, 8, 241–255.

New Straits Times 1985. 10-km visibility in Sabah due to haze. *New Straits Times*, 24 July 1985.
New Straits Times 1991. Pinatubo's ash falling in Sabah and Sarawak. *New Straits Times*, 18 June 1991.
New Straits Times 1997a. CNN to make amends for biased coverage. *New Straits Times*, 27 November 1997.
New Straits Times 1997b. EPSM wants haze constituents to be made public. *New Straits Times*, 25 September 1997.
New Straits Times 2005a. Clearing the air. *New Straits Times*, 11 August 2005.
New Straits Times 2005b. Malaysian firms also to blame. *New Straits Times*, 12 August 2005.
New Straits Times 2006. Burning of fences. *New Straits Times*, 19 December 2006.
Ngiam, D. and Tawie, S. 1997. No immediate impact on economy seen from closure. *New Straits Times*, 20 September 1997.
Norhashim, M. and AB. AZIZ, K. 2005. Smart partnership or cronyism? A Malaysian perspective. *International Journal of Sociology and Social Policy*, 25, 31–48.
Oetomo, T. and Sandianto, A. 2011. Long SIMP and short IEAR. *Indonesia and Singapore Plantation Sector.* Jakarta: Credit Suisse.
Onn, O. 2000. M'sian investors still in a fix over expansion plan. *Bernama*, 19 June 2000.
Othman, J. 2003. Linking agricultural trade, land demand and environmental externalities: Case of oil palm in South East Asia. *ASEAN Economic Bulletin*, 20, 244–55.
Page, S., Hoscilo, A., Wosten, H., Jauhiainen, J., Silvius, M., Rieley, J., Ritzema, H., Tansey, K., Graham, L., Vassander, H. and Limin, S. 2009. Restoration ecology of lowland tropical peatlands in Southeast Asia: Current knowledge and future research directions. *Ecosystems*, 12, 888–905.
Palmoilhq 2009. *Indonesia still on the radar for Malaysian palm oil planters*. Cairns. Available: www.palmoilhq.com/PalmOilNews/indonesia-still-on-the-radar-for-malaysian-palm-oil-planters/ [accessed 10 October].
Parliament of Malaysia 2010. DR 2.11.2010 (House of Senate). Kuala Lumpur.
Parliament of Singapore 1998a. *ASEAN Environment Ministers' Meeting (Progress towards addressing problems of fires and haze pollution) (1998-04-02)*. Singapore.
Parliament of Singapore 1998b. *Haze pollution (motion) (1998-06-30)*. Singapore.
Parliament of Singapore 2000. *Fires in Indonesia (2000-03-13)*. Singapore.
Parliament of Singapore 2006. Haze situation (Update) (2006-11-14). Singapore.
Parliament of Singapore 2007. *Indonesia's export ban on sand and soil products (2007-02-12)*. Singapore.
Parliament of Singapore 2010a. *Haze and forest fires (Commitment from Indonesia) (2010-11-22)*. Singapore.
Parliament of Singapore 2010b. *Tackling transboundary haze (2010-11-22)*. Singapore.
Pempel, T. J. 2005. Introduction: Emerging webs of regional connectedness. *In:* Pempel, T. J. (ed.) *Remapping East Asia: The construction of a region*. Ithaca: Cornell University Press.
Pereira, A. 2005. Singapore's Regionalization Strategy. *Journal of Asia-Pacific Economy*, 10, 380–396.
Poynton, S. 2014. Wilmar's 'no deforestation' goal could revolutionise food production. *The Guardian*, 29 January.
Profundo 2007. *Buyers and Financiers of the Wilmar Group*. Amsterdam: Milieudefensie.
Rahim, L. Z. 2009. *Singapore in the Malay World*, New York, Routledge.
Rajan, R. S. 2007. Intra-developing Asia FDI flows: Magnitudes, trends and determinants.

In: Soesatro, H. (ed.) *Deepening Economic Integration in East Asia – The ASEAN Community and Beyond.* Economic Research Institute for ASEAN and East Asia.

Rajenthran, A. 2002. *Indonesia: An Overview of the Legal Framework of Foreign Direct Investment.* ISEAS Working Papers: Economics and Finance. Singapore: Institute of Southeast Asian Studies.

Ramakrishna [M20], S. 7 April 2010. *RE: Coordinator, Malaysian Environmental NGOs.*

Raman, M., Van Schaik, A., Richter, K. and De Clerck, P. 2008. *Malaysian Palm Oil – green gold or green wash? A comment on the sustainability claims of Malaysia's palm oil lobby, with a special focus on the state of Sarawak.* Kuala Lumpur: Friends of the Earth.

Rasiah, R., Gammeltoft, P. and Jiang, Y. 2010. Home government policies for outward FDI from emerging economies: Lessons from Asia. *International Journal of Emerging Markets*, 5, 333–357.

Reporters Without Borders 2014. *Press Freedom Index 2014.* USA.

Reuters 2011. Update 1 – Wilmar to invest $900 mln in Indonesia palm oil product plants. Reuters, 7 February 2011.

Richardson, C. L. 2010. *Deforestation due to Palm Oil Plantations in Indonesia. Towards the Sustainable Production of Palm Oil.* Nimbin, Australia: The Palm Oil Action Group

Roberts, J. M. 2011. How Western environmental policies are stunting economic growth in developing countries. *Journal of Oil Palm and the Environment*, 2, 48–62.

Rodan, G. 2004. International capital, Singapore's state companies and security. *Critical Asian Studies*, 36, 479–499.

Rolland [I50], D. 7 December 2011. *RE: Former staff of Rimbunan Hijau.*

Rosser, A. 2007. Escaping the resource curse: The case of Indonesia. *Journal of Contemporary Asia*, 37, 38–58.

Rukmantara [I45], A. 14 November 2011. *RE: Former environmental journalist, Jakarta Post.*

Saharjo, B. H., Danny, W., Moore, P. F. and Simorangkir, D. 2003. Convicting forest and fire offences: A case study of the legal process in Riau, Indonesia. *Project Fire Fight.* Jakarta.

Saravanamuttu [S23], J. 7 June 2010. *RE: Visiting Senior Research Fellow, Institute for South East Asian Studies.*

Sato, Y. 2004. The decline of conglomerates in post-Soeharto Indonesia: The case of Salim Group. *Taiwan Journal of Southeast Asian Studies*, 1, 19–43.

Satyawan [I20], L. S. 16 July 2010. *RE: Lecturer, Forest Fire, Department of Silviculture, Institute Pertanian Bogor.*

Sawit Watch 2008. Satu Dekade Bersama Sawit Watch. *Editorial.* Bogor: Sawit Watch.

Scott, J. C. 1972. Patron-client politics and political change in Southeast Asia. *American Political Science Review*, 66, 91–113.

Sharif [M21], R. and Abdul Hathi [M22], J. S. 8 April 2010. *RE: Director, ASEAN-Malaysia National Secretariat, Ministry of Foreign Affairs.*

Sim, A. B. 2005. An exploratory study of internationalization strategies of emerging Malaysian multinational companies. *Journal of Asia-Pacific Business*, 6, 27–48

Sim, A. B. 2006. Internationalization strategies of emerging Asian MNEs – Case study evidence on Singaporean and Malaysian firms. *Asia Pacific Business Review*, 12, 487–505.

Sime Darby 2011. *Annual Report.* Kuala Lumpur: Sime Darby.

Singaporean Government 1985. Singapore country paper: Air pollution monitoring in Singapore. *ASEAN/EC Workshop/Seminar on Air Pollution Monitoring.* Bangkok.

Singh [M18], G. 2 April 2010. *RE: Chairman, Center for Environment, Technology and Development.*

Stone, R. 2007. Can palm oil plantations come clean? *Science*, 317, 1491.

Subejo. 2010. Dimming international faith in Indonesian CPO. *Jakarta Post*, 1 April 2010.

Suharto, R. 2011. *Food Standards Amendment (Truth in Labellling – Palm Oil) Bill 2010.* Jakarta: Indonesian Palm Oil Commission.

Sunday Mail 1982. Encounter of the hazy kind. *Sunday Mail*, 12 September 1982.

Surya [I9], M. T. and Akbar [I10], A. 30 June 2010. *RE: Deputy Directors, Wahana Lingkungan Hidup Indonesia.*

Tan [S7], A. K. J. 17 May 2010. *RE: Vice Dean, Faculty of Law, NUS.*

Tan, E. 1997. Jakarta probes into 18 firsm with Malaysian shareholders. *New Straits Times*, 19 September 1997.

Tan, T. M. 2011. May inventories rebounded 23 per cent/YoY to 16-month high- bearish for palm oil prices. *Malaysia Palm Oil Sector.* Kuala Lumpur: Credit Suisse.

Tan, T. M. and Oetomo, T. 2011. Back to Basics – Who, what and how? *Asia Palm Oil Sector.* Kuala Lumpur: Credit Suisse.

Tarigan [I23], A. 16 July 2010. *RE: Executive Director, Sawit Watch.*

Tawie, S. 1997. Sarawak lost RM1 billion during 10-day emergency. *New Straits Times*, 6 October 1997.

Tay, S. S. C. 2003. Corruption after the crisis: Governance, Asian values, and international instruments. *In:* Tay, S. S. C. and Seda, M. (eds) *The Enemy Within: Combating Corruption in Asia.* Singapore: Eastern University Press.

Taylor, M. and Supriatna, Y. 2014. Indonesia lawmakers draft bill to slash foreign ownership of plantations. Reuters, 15 August 2014.

TH Plantations 2010. *Annual Report.* Kuala Lumpur: TH Plantations.

TH Plantations Berhad 2014. *Shareholdings*. Kuala Lumpur. Available: www.thplantations.my//shareholdings.php [accessed 15 August 2014].

Tham, S. Y. 2007. Outward foreign direct investment from Malaysia: An exploratory study. *Südostasien Aktuell – Journal of Current Southeast Asian Affairs*, 26, 44–72.

Thee, K. W. 2006. The surge of Asian NIC investment into Indonesia. *Bulletin of Indonesian Economic Studies*, 27, 55–87.

The Star 2007. Environmental Hazard. *The Star*, 11 December 2011.

The Straits Times 1972. Haze gets worse. *New Straits Times*, 14 October 1972.

The Straits Times 1982. Why haze might have hurt eyes yesterday. *The Straits Times*, 26 September 1982.

The Straits Times 1997. S'pore firms urged to invest in Indonesia. *Straits Times*, 20 February 1997.

The Straits Times 1998. President unhappy with Singapore, says AWSJ. *The Straits TImes*, 5 August 1998.

The Straits Times 2011. Wilmar to invest $1.2b in Indonesian plants. *Straits Times*, 8 February 2011.

UNCTAD 2009. TNCs and agricultural production in developing countries. *World Investment Report 2009: Transnational Corporations, Agricultural Production and Development.* Geneva: UNCTAD.

UOB Kay Hian 2011. Plantation Sector: Peak production growth is over; upgrade to market weight. Change of Recommendation. *Regional.* Kuala Lumpur: Regional Research Team, UOB Kay Hian.

Van Gelder, J. W. 2004. *Greasy palms: European buyers of Indonesian palm oil.* Castricum: Friends of the Earth.

Van Noordwijk, M., Dewi, S., Khasanah, N., Ekadinata, A., Rahayu, S., Caliman, J. P., Sharma, M. and R., S. 2011. *Estimating carbon footprint from biofuel production rom oil palm: methodology and results from 2 pilot areas in Indonesia*. Jakarta: World Agroforestry Centre, SMARTRI, AsianAgri, Indonesia Palm Oil Commission.

Varkkey, H. 2013. Malaysian investors in the Indonesian oil palm plantation sector: Home state facilitation and transboundary haze. *Asia Pacific Business Review*, 19, 381–401.

Vernon Henderson, J. 1994. Where does an industry locate? *Journal of Urban Economics*, 35, 83–104.

Wahid, M. B., Abdullah, S. N. A. and Henson, I. E. 2004. Oil palm – Achievements and potential. 'New directions for a diverse planet'. *Proceedings of the 4th International Crop Science Congress*. Brisbane: Australian Agronomy Conference.

Wakker, E. 2005. *Greasy Palms: The social and ecological impacts of large-scale oil palm plantation development in Southeast Asia*. Indonesia: AIDEnvironment.

WALHI and Sawit Watch 2009. Memorandum: Issues Surrounding Malaysia Palm Oil Investments and Plantation Operations in Indonesian Palm Oil Industry. WALHI and Sawit Watch.

WALHI, Sawit Watch and CELCOR 2009. Malaysian Palm Oil and Logging Investments and Operations. *Factsheet*. WALHI, Sawit Watch and CELCOR.

Wilmar 2010. *Annual Report*. Singapore: Wilmar.

World Growth 2011. The economic benefit of palm oil to Indonesia. Virginia: World Growth.

Yansen [I43]. 9 November 2011. *RE: Tropical Ecologist, University of Bengkulu*.

Yeoh, S., Chan, Y. J. and Srinath, A. 2011a. Supply side support in 2012; Top picks – Wilmar and Sime Darby. *ASEAN Plantations*. Kuala Lumpur: J. P. Morgan.

Yeoh, S., Srinath, A. and Chan, Y. J. 2011b. ASEAN plantations: Downside risks and opportunities; a look at 2008/2009. *Asia Pacific Equity Research*. Kuala Lumpur: J. P. Morgan.

Yeung, H. W. C. 2011. From national development to economic diplomacy? Governing Singapore's sovereign wealth funds. *The Pacific Review*, 24, 625–652.

Zainal Abidin [M38], A. 29 April 2010. *RE: Deputy Director, Pusat Tenaga Malaysia*.

Zakaria, A., Theile, C. and Khaimur, L. 2007. *Policy, practice, pride and prejudice: Review of legal, environmental and social practises of oil palm plantation companies of the Wilmar Group in Sambas District, West Kalimantan (Indonesia)*. Netherlands: Milieudefensie.

4 Regionalization and patronage politics[1]

As mentioned earlier in this book, scholars have noted two distinct drivers of regionalization in the Southeast Asian context: the role of the state as facilitator and similar patronage cultures (Sim, 2006: 490–491). Chapter 3 dealt with the first driver: that of the role of the state as facilitator of regionalization of the oil palm sector and also discussed how this tied in with open burning and haze. This chapter addresses the second driver, the role of cultural familiarity (Sim, 2006: 499–500), particularly the culture of patronage that is common among many countries in Southeast Asia. This chapter is divided into four sections. The first section of this chapter offers a brief review of the patronage literature. The second section explores patronage linkages that exist between local, Malaysian and Singaporean plantation companies, with Indonesian government elites. The third and fourth sections discuss how these patronage linkages have been instrumental in weakening state capacity to make and implement effective policies related to land use and fires, enabling companies to develop fire-prone peatlands and to use fire as a cost-effective way to clear land, with little fear of prosecution. This cost-cutting has enabled extraordinarily high profits in the sector year after year, with plantations delivering an average of 47 per cent earnings growth in 2011 (Di, 2011: 1). This chapter identifies patronage as a common business culture among Southeast Asian states, and shows that patronage politics has not only been instrumental in encouraging the regionalization of the sector but also has been an important driver of transboundary haze.

Patronage politics

Patronage politics can be defined as:

> a special case of dyadic (two-person) ties involving an instrumental friendship in which an individual of higher socioeconomic position (patron) uses his[2] own influence and resources to provide protection or benefits, or both, for a person of lower status (client) who, for his part, reciprocates by offering general support and assistance, including personal services, to the patron.
>
> (Scott, 1972: 92)

Patronage relationships are 'amorphous, latent, elusive, and ubiquitous' (Scott, 1972: 92–113). As an extension of the simple dyadic patronage link, patronage politics refers to the overall pattern of patronage linkages joining the actors in a given area or community (Scott, 1972: 92–113).

Patrons and clients are almost exclusively motivated by material gain (Kurer, 1996: 645–661). In this way, patronage politics can be seen as 'a form of domination that is used by modern political and economic elites to channel resources for their own benefit' (Gunes-Ayata, 1994: 17–26). This is why they are usually regarded as disreputable, if not illegal, by parties external to this relationship (Eisenstadt and Roniger, 1995: 209–233).

According to Kurer (1996: 645–661), 'patrons and clients have an interest in replacing collective with private goods, and one way of accomplishing this is to override bureaucratic procedures and allocate resources not according to bureaucratic norms (or set policies) but on the basis of political interest'. An important contemporary resource base available to a potential patron is indirect, office-based property (Scott, 1972: 92–113). This involves office holders who hold discretionary powers over scarce values such as employment, promotion, assistance, welfare, licensing and permits (Scott, 1972: 92–113). For example, an office-holding patron can offer privileges to property rights to generate economic rent, or income-earning opportunities such as licenses to generate an income above opportunity costs (Kurer, 1996: 645–661). This is illustrated clearly later in this chapter, where well-connected plantation companies in Indonesia are able to obtain privileged rights to choice parcels of land for development of oil palm plantations (Rukmantara [I45], 2011; Suwarsono [I3], 2010; Tarigan [I23], 2010,), despite contrary laws and policies that exist. It is this combination of potentially open access to markets with the continuous semi-institutionalized attempts to limit free access that is the crux of the patronage politics model (Eisenstadt and Roniger, 1995: 209–233).

An excellent way for a political leader to stay in power is to ensure that he is always surrounded by loyal followers. Hence, he may calculate that some inefficiency in the system is a small price to pay for said loyalty. Patronage 'allows leaders to build a team of public managers who share the leaders' policy agenda and who can be trusted not to sabotage or delay important programs' (Brinkerhoff and Goldsmith, 2004: 163–182). In such conditions, there often arise situations of 'mutual hostage' relations, which Enderwick (2005: 129) describes as situations 'where the principal partners (politicians and business leaders) become locked into a situation of mutual dependency, where change by one threatens the well-being of the other'. Such mutual hostage relations severely restricts state capacity to create or uphold effective policies, as powerful patrons in the government or administration are locked into making policy choices that reflect the interests of their client, with little consideration of the interests of the society at large.

One of the main things that differentiate patronage politics from a one-off bribe is the ongoing nature of the relationship. Patronage politics is essentially a reiterated interaction, with each side making decisions about their behaviour today in the anticipation of future interactions. Repeated interaction bring with them the right of each partner to expect favoured treatment from the other (Gunes-Ayata, 1994: 17–26). This continued reciprocity that establishes and solidifies the patronage relationship creates trust, loyalty and affection between patrons and clients (Eisenstadt and Roniger, 1995: 209–233).

Patronage arrangements also generate 'expectations and hope, the individual's feeling of being protected, of being able to depend on some 'patron', be it an individual or an organization' (Gunes-Ayata, 1994: 22). When the client has an emergency (perhaps needing a loan or a good word with the police or administration), he knows he can rely on his patron for assistance. The patron, in turn, rests assured that 'his people' will support his designs when needed (Kurer, 1996: 645–661). As discussed later in the chapter, this has often been why illegal commercial open burning cases have very rarely found their way to court (Rukmantara [I45], 2011).

Patronage politics is blamed for 'stifling popular participation, subverting the rule of law, fostering corruption and collusion, and a host of other political and economic ills' (Brinkerhoff and Goldsmith, 2004: 163–182). In this way, it weakens state capacity by restricting accountability, autonomy, transparency and the ability to organize around common and enduring interests (Garcia-Guadilla, 2002: 91–106). It is a classic free-rider (collective action) problem: what might be rational at the society level makes less sense at the individual level and disincentivises people to go along with changes in patronage systems that would benefit the majority. Patrons disregard the long-term interest and focus on helping their clients; anyone outside the favoured group can expect little from the government (Larson and Soto, 2008: 218–226). As this chapter notes, the haze is a good example of the manifestation of free-rider attitudes within the sector, with patrons in the Indonesian government being obliged to disregard the long-term interest of society for a haze-free atmosphere, focusing instead on helping their clients maximize profitability in the oil palm plantation sector (Larson and Soto, 2008: 218–226). Furthermore, it is notoriously hard to destroy or dismantle patronage networks because these networks support the needs and interests of many individuals. Therefore, elites are highly motivated to block, dilute or slow down any form of legislative or policy amendments that would threaten the informal relationships from which they so greatly benefit (Brinkerhoff and Goldsmith, 2004: 163–182).

Patronage politics has been an important part of the culture of business in many Southeast Asian countries. The following subsection discusses the similar trends of patronage politics that exist historically throughout the region. This perspective is useful for this chapter in proposing that Malaysia, Singapore and Indonesia share many cultural similarities, especially in terms of patronage trends, which served as an advantage for Malaysian and Singaporean firms regionalizing their operations to Indonesia and integrating with the local economy, especially within the oil palm plantation sector.

Patronage politics in Southeast Asia

The prevalence of relationship-based instead of rules-based economies in Southeast Asia encourages the persistence of patronage types of relationships. Indeed, patronage politics has been a dominant characteristic of the societies in the region (Enderwick, 2005: 117–127), so much so that patronage ties are a legitimate, accepted, even expected part of the economic process here (Dauvergne, 1995: 89–98). Most countries in the Southeast Asian region display the three necessary conditions for patronage structures to flourish: 1) marked inequalities over the control of power, wealth and status in an authoritarian system that has been accepted as more or less legitimate; 2) the absence of firm, impersonal guarantees of physical security, status, position or wealth; and 3) the inability of the kinship unit to serve as an effective vehicle for personal security and advancement. In these ways, the general political structure of Southeast Asia has favoured the growth of patronage systems (Scott, 1972: 92–113). Traditional patronage politics in Southeast Asia was generally characterized by highly affectionate ties based on kinship, village or neighbourhood bonds. Loyalty, obligation, honour and non-material rewards supplemented material exchanges (Dauvergne, 1995: 75–76).

Patronage politics was especially prevalent in the natural resource sectors. During the colonial era, colonial authorities made natural resources and cash crops such as sugar, rubber and bananas as the economic backbone of many of these countries (Hurst, 1987: 170–171). These imperial links greatly increased the economic power and scope of the state, making it a key source to bind patronage ties through the selective dispersal of funds, licenses and career opportunities (Dauvergne, 1995: 75–76). Crops were all grown on cleared forest land, and control over large areas of land became a source of considerable wealth. With this, a land-owning elite emerged, generally consisting of people who were in good favour with the colonial authorities (Hurst, 1987: 170–171).

As Dauvergne (1995) and Ross (2001) have noted, traditional patronage politics in Southeast Asia has adapted to evolving economic, social and political structures and processes, especially during the shift from colonialism to independence (Dauvergne, 1995: 75–76). Political consolidation and increased power disparities that developed after independence enlarged the potential role of patronage clusters in the region. New resources for patronage, such as party and bureaucratic connections, development programmes and nationalized enterprises were created. New national leaders took over colonial tasks such as hiring, firing and promotion of civil servants, and the granting of contracts, licenses and permits, all of which could be used to create a personal following (Scott, 1972: 92–113). These patronage institutions were useful in rewarding supporters, buying off potential rivals and creating personal loyalties superseding administrative and ideological boundaries (Ross, 2001: 160).

Furthermore, access to natural resources such as land were officially 'nationalized' (Scott, 1972: 92–113). With this, local business elites were heavily promoted by governments, their state enterprises and business conglomerates bolstered by skewed process of state tendering, licensing, lending, privatizing and, in times of crisis, bailouts and re-nationalization (Case, 2003: 249–252). Patronage exchange became more specific and less personal. Patrons were less likely to maintain regular contact with a client and more likely to exchange tangible goods, such as a license for a 'political contribution' (Neher, 1994: 950). Patronage exchange became more monetized, calculations more explicit, and concern more centred on the tangible rate of return from the relationship than on its durability (Scott, 1972: 101–108). As a result, modern patronage politics became based less on blind or reflexive loyalty, obligation and honour (Brinkerhoff and Goldsmith, 2004: 163–182). For example, during Indonesia's New Order Era, President Suharto actively developed patronage institutions that created a stable set of incentives for military officers, many of whom had few or no personal links to him (Ross, 2001: 160). However, political patterns still represent diffuse personal and affectionate bonds when compared to contractual marketplace ties that are much more impersonal (Scott, 1972: 101–108).

This restriction of the allocation of economic resources and opportunity to the privileged elite, and the integration of government, business and banking to ensure that this elite group continues to enjoy considerable advantages, is popularly known as 'crony capitalism' (Enderwick, 2005: 117–127). For example, in exchange for support, governments were able to provide select individuals with credible guarantees that they would limit their predatory behaviour, protect property rights and maintain macroeconomic and political stability (Hamilton-Hart, 2007: 94). Through control over political parties and parliaments (Hadiz and Robison, 2005: 232), privately held companies with special connections to leaders obtained special status and were able to pursue mutually beneficial deals. They received state protection from or preference over other companies (Rose-Ackerman, 2008: 336–337). As a corollary, such 'special status' corporations often support 'national causes', whether through corporate largesse or by undertaking projects that are not economically viable in themselves but strategically attractive (Tay, 2003: 51–53). An example for this was discussed in the previous chapter in the Malaysian context, where Sime Darby stepped in to assist the Sarawak state government by buying over the management of Sarawak Land Development Board (SLDB) and all its plantation assets when they were making substantial losses and carrying major liabilities in 1987 (McCarthy and Cramb, 2009: 113–119). As a result, the interconnected web that linked corporate entities, family and top state leadership were thick and often tangled (Tay, 2003: 51–53).

At the same time, leaders are confronted by threats from those outside their patronage cluster. Therefore, in order to survive, leaders will follow strategies that undermine state capabilities and weaken state capacity. Ross (2001) and Dauvergne (1994, 1995) have observed these practices as conscious attempts by political elites to put into motion processes of institutional change that bring personal benefit, which may lead to institutional decay and collapse. To gain direct, exclusive and discretionary allocation rights to office-based property such as permits and licenses, these leaders dilute or dismantle state autonomy, change institutions that give others the right to influence allocation decisions, and create new constraints (such as burdensome regulations or spurious delays) on the asset's use (Ross, 2001: 35–36). To weaken challenges from various levels of the state, top leaders remove and shuffle agency elites. To maintain and increase power, they appoint loyal followers, close friends and family (Dauvergne, 1995: 68–77). To appease hostile groups (Dauvergne, 1994: 501–502) and to preserve stability, they make non-merit appointments to co-opt powerful business leaders. Surviving as a leader involves maintaining the intricate balance between restraining agencies sufficiently so they pose no threat to rulers, while allowing sufficient organization so the agencies can perform the tasks necessary for state and leader survival (Dauvergne, 1995: 68–77). Patronage therefore originates at the top political level (Kurer, 1996: 645–661).

When patronage originates at the highest levels, it is also likely to extend to the middle and lower levels (Rose-Ackerman, 2008: 330) of the bureaucracy, police and judiciary, and it contributes to widespread violations of state laws and regulations. This results in an overall weak bureaucracy paralyzed in its ability to create and carry out effective policy. Hence the rule of law and strong institutions are replaced instead by personal ties based on reciprocity (Case, 2003: 263; Tay, 2003: 39–54). At the administrative level, the exploitation of the 'spoils of government' by bureaucratic officials is often too strong a temptation to resist (Hicken, 2011: 290–306).

Lower-level patrons within the bureaucracy may themselves be clients of a more highly ranked patron, and the result is a pyramid of patronage ties (Kurer, 1996: 645–661); forming a patronage network to secure loyalty and control (Rajenthran, 2002: 6). If the bureaucracy is 'politicized' this way, it encourages officials to create red tape, resulting in a bureaucracy that is almost autonomous, corrupt, incompetent and ineffective and suffers from low legitimacy, with unfair distribution of scarce benefits that undermine the purpose of public programmes (Kurer, 1996: 645–661; Rose-Ackerman, 2008: 331). This can be observed, for example, when court verdicts are regularly sold to the highest bidders (Rajenthran, 2002: 5).

This makes it easy for well-connected clients to skirt, resist or even ignore state policies (Dauvergne, 1995: 89–98). Because of this, powerful businessmen with good patronage ties have no reason to fear punishment, and the law will be disregarded and wrong-doing may become the norm (Kurer, 1996: 645–661). Hence, some state agencies end up accommodating, assisting or even strengthening the practices that destroy natural resources (Dauvergne, 1995: 89–98). As they are very hard to suppress, and as they serve the interests of their network members, they continue to flourish (Lande, 1983: 438–450). As one interviewee expressed, 'in such environments without the rule of law and with weak government institutions, the big and the powerful tend to have disproportionate influence' (Moore [I5], 2010).

This web of state, corporations and family relationships has become part of the identity of many Southeast Asian nations (Tay, 2003: 51–53). For instance, Hadiz (2004: 697, 2007: 873) describes patronage in the Indonesian context as a system of mutually shifting and fluid coalitions of predatory networks, usually characterized by corruption and abuse of power. These predatory networks gained foothold in Indonesia primarily during Suharto's centralized New Order system. Through control over political parties and parliaments, via business alliances, and by engaging in various types of political violence, patrons have been able to gain ascendance over state institutions and its resources (Hadiz and Robison, 2005: 232) and remain protected by authoritarian means (Hadiz, 2007: 873). This book proposes that the fact that patronage politics has become such a dominant identity of these nations has been an important driver of regionalization in Southeast Asia, especially within the oil palm plantation sector. With similar patronage cultures in their home states, Malaysian and Singaporean companies were able to easily insert themselves into patronage networks in Indonesia (Tarigan [I23], 2010), further spurring economic regionalization in the sector.

Patronage politics as a driver of economic regionalization

Regionalization is often facilitated by cultural familiarity (Sim, 2006: 490–491). An important element in the selection of a destination country for outward investment is 'psychic distance'. A firm will usually be more willing to enter into a foreign market that is closer in terms of psychic distance, taking into consideration similarities in language, education, business practises, culture and industrial development (Sim, 2006: 490). Familiarity with cultures within the same region also lowers transaction costs associated with doing business. Similar cultural heritage and attitudes further encourages cooperation and trust between investors and locals in the host country (Terjesen and Elam, 2009: 1105–1106).

As discussed above, this sort of patronage politics has played an important and constant role in the business atmosphere of Southeast Asian countries such as Malaysia, Singapore and Indonesia (Enderwick, 2005: 117–127). While foreign firms that intend to enter into markets where patronage politics play an important role will often attempt to engage in similar practices as well (Enderwick, 2005: 126; Hamilton-Hart, 2005: 171), patronage networks are more easily built and managed across similar ethnic, cultural and linguistic contexts (Terjesen and Elam, 2009: 1105–1106). This is because internationalizing businesses tend to acquire characteristics and strategies that reflect the cultural and institutional contexts in which they are established (Hamilton-Hart, 2005: 171). Therefore, this chapter displays that Malaysian and Singaporean plantation companies have an advantage over other foreign firms when investing in Indonesia, because of their close psychic distance with each other, especially in terms of the culture of patronage in business practices. Hence, this has been an important driver for regionalization in this sector (Anshari [I42], 2011; Lawrence [I38], 2011). Because these Malaysian and Singaporean firms are already familiar with patronage practices at home, they are able to easily adapt and insert themselves into local patronage networks in Indonesia, hence effectively integrating into the Indonesian economy.

This has been further made possible by the development of patronage politics in modern times. As Dauvergne has previously argued, the spread of market capitalism (Dauvergne, 1995: 75–76), which included the opening up of markets to foreign investment as discussed in Chapter 3, has caused modern patronage exchanges to became more monetized, no longer relying on longstanding kinship bonds (Scott, 1972: 101–108). Dauvergne refers to this as 'modern patron-client relations'. This book adopts and extends Dauvergne's concept in the context of Malaysian and Singaporean plantation firms in Indonesia. Since patronage relations were no longer based on long-term loyalty, these new 'modern' relationships became quite businesslike (Aspinall and Van Klinken, 2011: 12). Hence, 'newcomer' firms from Malaysia and Singapore were able to also easily establish their own patronage relations with Indonesian elites. Therefore, culturally similar Malaysian and Singaporean[3] firms were not at a disadvantage for being foreign, and were able to insert themselves into these local patronage networks. Indeed, as the previous chapter detailed, home and host governments would often take the initiative to facilitate access to such contacts (as potential patrons) in host countries as well (Goh *et al.*, 2001: 42).

As this chapter will discuss, this has proven beneficial for Malaysian and Singaporean firms, as well as their host country Indonesia. In terms of the overall cost–benefit equation, even though patronage politics increases the cost of production for investors (since time and resources have to be spent in establishing and maintaining these relationships in order to acquire government permits or licenses to conduct investment) (Al-Sadig, 2009: 267; Lipsey and Sjoholm, 2011: 43–44), other country characteristics in Indonesia such as large markets and cheap labour make up for these negative costs (Lipsey and Sjoholm, 2011: 43–44). Furthermore, in the presence of rigid regulation and an inefficient bureaucracy such as in Indonesia, patronage politics may actually increase the efficiency of the bureaucracy by accelerating the decision-making process (Al-Sadig, 2009: 269; Rose-Ackerman, 2008: 328–330) and may, in turn, indirectly encourage incoming investment and economic growth in Indonesia (Al-Sadig, 2009: 269; Richardson, 2010: 51), especially from neighbouring countries.

This chapter will show that these patronage relationships served as useful protection for these firms, enabling them to conduct themselves on the ground in Indonesia with impunity. In this way, patronage politics can be seen as an important driver for haze in the region as well. The next section expounds on the patronage linkages that exist between Malaysian, Singaporean and Indonesian firms and the Indonesian government elite, which is useful in contextualizing the following discussions later in this chapter on how these companies were able to use these linkages to their advantage, with little concern for the impact of their operations on regional air quality.

Local patronage networks

Indonesia's political leaders have long used patronage to augment their authority (Ross, 2001: 159), hence Indonesia has been a popular case study for the examination of patronage networks on the ground for much of its modern political history. Scholars such as Aspinall and Van Klinken (2011) are among the recent contributors to the topic, demonstrating that in Indonesia, patronage is a form of state illegality[4] that is deeply 'entrenched' in various aspects of daily life, with patrons 'backing' (*beking* or *deking*) protection rackets, motorcycle thieves, pirates, drug dealers, prostitutes, illegal timber cutters and the like (Aspinall and Van Klinken, 2011: 5). Hence, the Indonesian state can be viewed as less of a bureaucratic machine, and more of a field of power characterized by competition and insecurity. Patronage is vital for the purchase of political protection or access from above, and political support or acquiescence from below, or to exclude rivals laterally. Therefore, patronage among elites in Indonesia is often connected simultaneously to the distribution of material resources and political opportunities (Aspinall and Van Klinken, 2011: 23–24). Seminal works on patronage networks in Indonesia have focused particularly on the military-based patronage networks that flourished on timber resources during Suharto's New Order era. These include writings by Crouch (1984), Robison (1986) and Ross (2001).[5] Similar patterns of patronage fuelling resource exploitation are visible in the Indonesian oil palm sector of present times, as described below.

Like the timber sector in its heyday, a central feature of the Indonesian oil palm sector also is the importance of patronage networks (Arif [I41], 2011; Rukmantara [I45], 2011; Surya [I9] and Akbar [I10], 2010; Syaf [I27], 2010), especially in terms of knowledge of (and access to) local markets and distribution systems, personal connections to local bureaucracy, potential business partners, associates and financing (Terjesen and Elam, 2009: 1105–1106). Indonesia's oil palm sector today also tends to be organized through personal and industry-based social networks and relationships (Sim, 2006: 491). With the particularly long time frames of the sector (with a crop rotation of about 20 to 30 years) firms often need to cultivate long-term patronage relationships throughout this period (Surya [I9] and Akbar [I10], 2010).

Therefore, it is common among the top tiers of Indonesian plantation firms to have 'functional directors' appointed to perform 'extra-economic functions' (Gomez, 2009: 10), and 'advisors' who are elected on a retainer basis. Indonesia adopts a two-tier management structure, consisting of a board of directors and a board of commissioners. Formally, the directors manage and represent the company while the commissioners supervise the directors (Rajenthran, 2002: 21). However, in reality, members of the board of commissioners (and sometimes also board of directors) are typically retired senior bureaucrats (*mantan*) who could act as intermediaries with the state and perform 'advisory and brokerage functions' on behalf of the company when needed (Anshari [I42], 2011; Arif [I41], 2011: Surya [I9] and Akbar [I10], 2010: Syaf [I27], 2010: Tarigan [I23], 2010). In other words, they are elected to the post by virtue of their connections.

This is an important element in patronage politics (Johnston, 2005: 21), and especially common in the oil palm sector (Arif [I41], 2011; Rukmantara [I45], 2011; Surya [I9] and Akbar [I10], 2010; Syaf [I27], 2010). For example, one of the directors of the Indonesian plantation company BSP is Bungaran Saragih, who formerly served as minister of agriculture under two Indonesian cabinets. A former minister of agriculture, Dr Anton Apriyantono, is also a commissioner for BSP (Bakrie Brothers, 2010). Also, chairman of the Bakrie and Brothers Group, parent company of BSP, is Aburizal Bakrie, who is also the chairman of the strong and influential political party in Indonesia, Golkar (Golongan Karyawan or the Party of the Functional Groups) (Syarif [I2], 2010; Yansen [I43], 2011). Aburizal Bakrie is said to have a close relationship with Ginandjar Kartasasmita, an Indonesian politician and former speaker of the Dewan Perwakilan Rakyat Daerah (DPRD, or Regional House of Representatives). He was also a former secretary general of the Indonesian president's Economic and Financial Resilience Council (Eklof, 2002: 235). In the case of the Indonesian plantation company Duta Palma, a 30 per cent ownership by the Indonesian military has meant that many prominent former military men have positions within the company (Gilbert, 2009: 2–3). For example, an interviewee detailed that a director at Duta Palma is on the staff of the Special Presidential Division of Social Communication, retired Major General Sardan Marbun (Arif [I41], 2011).

By virtue of being local, these local firms often also have 'home court advantages' by way of knowledge of regulations and laws, and relationships with important local players including governments, customers and other businesses. To be able to successfully compete in these markets, foreign companies should possess and exploit (Terjesen and Elam, 2009: 1105–1106) specialized knowledge of local business norms and practices. This book points out that Malaysian and Singaporean firms, familiar with the function of patronage networks at home and possessing cultural similarities with the Indonesian host state, understood the necessity of these connections (Anshari [I42], 2011; Ghani [S6], 2010; Interviewee I49, 2011; Syarif [I2], 2010; Tarigan [I23], 2010; Wiryono [I40], 2011) and had no qualms about adopting this patronage culture themselves. Interviewees explained how Malaysian and Singaporean firms were more likely to engage in patronage as compared to other foreign firms operating in the Indonesian oil palm plantation sector due to institutional inertia from behaviour in their home countries (because these companies were more likely to have engaged in patronage behaviour in their home states too) (Interviewee I49, 2011; Rolland [I50], 2011). Furthermore, these similarities have enabled even deeper regional integration of the sector, where Malaysian and Singaporean companies were able to take advantage of these conditions more effectively, compared to other foreign firms like Dutch or American ones (Interviewee I49, 2011). Indeed, one interviewee explained that there was a marked increase of patronage behaviour from the plantation PT Asiatic Persada when it was bought over by Singapore's Wilmar from Cargill, an American company, three years ago (Interviewee I47, 2011). Cultural similarities encouraged these Malaysian and Singaporean firms to also establish their own linkages with patrons by hiring or establishing relationships with prominent Indonesians (Surya [I9] and Akbar [I10], 2010; Wibisino [I44], 2011). These locals are then able to use their influence over politicians and the administration to ensure preferable outcomes for these foreign companies, in the same way that Indonesian companies do (Norhashim and Ab. Aziz, 2005: 31–45).

For example, the Singapore-listed GAR is said to have several important current and former government officials (Syarif [I2], 2010; Tarigan [I23], 2010) and other prominent individuals 'on the payroll' (Dieleman, 2010: 489; Dieleman and Sachs, 2006: 528–530; Dieleman and Sachs, 2008b: 278–279; Dieleman and Sachs, 2008a: 166–167; Pratono, 2009). GAR employed Ambassador Cameron Hume (Keen, 2010), a well-received former United States ambassador to Indonesia as an advisor (Rukmantara [I45], 2011). Also, on the board of GAR's subsidiaries are Rachmad Gobel, who enjoys direct access to the president as an advisor on the National Innovation Committee; Dr Susiyati B. Hirwan, a former director general at the State Finance Department (SMART Agribusiness and Food, 2010); and also a former senior staff member of the Ministry of Agriculture (Tarigan [I23], 2010). Also, NGOs that were interviewed told of the rumour that Agus Purnomo, the Indonesian special advisor to the Ministry of Environment and head of the Secretariat of the National Climate Change (hence making him a central figure on conservation and sustainability issues in Indonesia) (Syarif [I2], 2010) is being employed on a retainer basis by GAR (Surya [I9] and Akbar [I10], 2010). Anthony Salim, who helms the Salim Group (the parent company for Singapore's Indo Agri) also is said to enjoy close relations with the ruling government, having also held the position of secretary general of the president's Economic and Financial Resilience Council before Aburizal Bakrie (Eklof, 2002: 235), as discussed above.

Other examples are the Malaysian plantation firm Sime Darby, which as a matter of principle, is said to seek out eminent people in host countries to be a part of its board of directors (Haji Mat Zin, 1999: 483–484). The rationale for this is that these eminent people can further vouch for more strategically important people with whom Sime Darby can have strategic alliances with (Haji Mat Zin, 1999: 483–484). For example, Sime Darby hired as an advisor the former environment minister Emil Salim (no relation to the Salim Group), who famously promoted the idea that 'nature is purely something to be exploited' during his time in office (*Jakarta Post*, 1987). Sime Darby also recently appointed the powerful governor of the Indonesian Central Bank, Arifin Siregar, as a commissioner (Tarigan [I23], 2010).

Such appointments also occur at the local level, especially with the advent of decentralization, as is elaborated below. In Chapter 1, this book discussed Mayer's (2006: 213–214) previous work that argued that Indonesia's flawed decentralization policies in the late 1990s have driven haze-causing fires. She argued that the government's decentralization policies 'failed to anticipate effects of regional autonomy reforms, which limit the central government's ability to organize fire management on the ground' (Mayer, 2006: 213). This book agrees with Mayer's analysis but extends it further to include the element of patronage networks by applying McCarthy's (2002) framework of localized patronage structures to analyze how these networks have enabled well-connected plantation companies to better exploit the post-decentralization administrative confusion, further driving fires and haze.

For example, as the central government decentralized important aspects of licensing to the district level, district actors found themselves suddenly wielding huge local discretionary power (McCarthy *et al.*, 2012: 555–560). Hence, the role of local police chiefs (Interviewee M45 *et al.*, 2012), local (district and regency) governments, administrators and politicians became increasingly important (Interviewee I49, 2011; Lawrence [I38], 2011). In accordance with this increased importance, patrons have reconstituted themselves through new local alliances (Hadiz, 2004: 697–698). These elites at the district level act either directly as patrons or as brokers between local clients and patrons at higher levels (McCarthy, 2002: 81). In short, as Hadiz (2004: 711) succinctly puts it, 'decentralization is facilitating the emergence of more localized patronage networks that are relatively autonomous of central state authority'.

This book therefore proposes that decentralization processes have further encouraged predatory behaviour by shifting some of the incentives and opportunities for patronage and corruption from the central to the subnational level (Lee [S20], 2010), where local parliaments also become sites of corrupt deal making in which legislators collude with officials and businesspeople to override policies in favour of their business allies, by directing contracts or licenses their way (Aspinall, 2010: 20–23). Here, revenue-oriented local officials and elites take advantage of decentralization by establishing their very own local fiefdoms sustained by decentralized corruption (Syarif and Wibisana, 2007: 31; Widianarko, 2009: 1) and high-level local politicians can use their influence to collect kickbacks from private firms (Rose-Ackerman, 2008: 331).

In these ways, decentralization impedes coordination (Samsul *et al.*, 2007: 13) and exacerbates incentives for officials at different levels to 'overgraze' the common resource base, creating new networks of patronage (Fan *et al.*, 2009: 14–32). Indeed, a larger number of administrative or government tiers is correlated with higher corruption and patronage (Fan *et al.*, 2009: 14–32). With poor supervision of local politicians and bureaucrats especially after decentralization, state capacity is further weakened as these officials are no longer bound to abstract rules and regulations. Rather, their decisions and actions depend on bargaining and deals between implementers, other state officials and strongmen outside the state (Kurer, 1996: 645–661). This situation was acknowledged by an Indonesian official at a national forum for investors and local officials, who admitted that 'doing business out of Jakarta required a firm and committed relationship with the *Bupatis* [head of regencies]' (Lawrence [I38], 2011).

Indeed, an interviewee from a major plantation company described these local strongmen 'like kings, who can make your life miserable if you do not have a good relationship with them' (Interviewee M45 *et al.*, 2012). Business interests that previously only maintained patronage relationships with officials from the central government were now cultivating patronage networks with leaders and officials at the local level as well (Lew [M6] and Interviewee M7, 2010; Tan, 2004: 178–179). Plantation companies began to elect as part of their staff local strongmen, their relatives (Surya [I9] and Akbar [I10], 2010; Wibisino [I44], 2011), retired three- or four-star generals, police chiefs or relevant ministry staff. These individuals would be hired as managers, special 'community relations officers' (*Hubungan Masyarakat* or *HuMas*) (Peters [I1], 2010) or 'government relations officers' (Rowland [I39], 2011) to cultivate healthy patronage links at the local level (Peters [I1], 2010; Rukmantara [I45], 2011; Wibisino [I44], 2011). For example, an interviewee who has many years of experience working in the natural resources sectors in Papua, Indonesia professed that he was in high demand among companies because of his close personal friendships to ministers and *Bupatis* (Rolland [I50], 2011).

GAR has been said to be particularly active in recruiting instrumental individuals at the local level. For example, GAR is said to have funded political campaigns of hopefuls and keep them on a retainer basis once they have been elected to the DPRD (Syaf [I27], 2010). This creates the earlier discussed 'mutual hostage' situation (Interviewee I49, 2011; Tarigan [I23], 2010; Yansen [I43], 2011) where there is a mutual indebtedness between the parties, a common criteria of patronage relations (Enderwick, 2005: 129). For example, an interviewee explained how GAR was said to have employed three members of the DPRD in Tanjung Jabung Barat where GAR has substantial landholdings. This is said to include Slamet Riyanto, a former senior staff at the Jambi provincial forestry and plantation office (*Jakarta Post*, 2006c), who later was elected to the DPRD. Others were said to include a member of the Prosperous Justice Party (Partai Keadilan Sejahtera), Aziz Rahman (who was given leave while serving on the DPRD) and Megawati Sihotang, a member of the Indonesian Democratic Party (Partai Demokrasi Indonesia) and DPRD representative (Syaf [I27], 2010).

Some of these individuals have been implicated by Indonesian law. For example, former governors of North Sumatra and Riau have been jailed because they were exposed for having 'unlawful connections' (vested interests) with oil palm companies (Syarif [I2], 2010; Yansen [I43], 2011). Indonesia Corruption Watch has identified and are currently investigating several *Bupatis* in West and Central Kalimantan that also have vested interests in plantations (Arif [I41], 2011). However, because patronage politics is so widespread that it is almost the norm (Dauvergne, 1995: 89–98), these cases are the minority. Even with anti-corruption efforts that intensified after the fall of President Suharto, recent reports indicate new setbacks in terms of state capacity to investigate and prosecute corruption claims, as the police force, the Parliament and the attorney general's office often obstruct the work of the anti-corruption commission (Lipsey and Sjoholm, 2011: 55). For example, on multiple occasions, the Supreme Court has blocked the regulation that would create a joint investigating team to look into complaints pertaining to patronage influences in courts (Rajenthran, 2002: 50).

Therefore, across the board in the Indonesian oil palm plantation sector, local, Malaysian and Singaporean plantation companies have individuals who have the ability to meet easily with ministries, *Bupatis* and governors to maintain patronage-type relationships (Arif [I41], 2011; Surya [I9] and Akbar [I10], 2010; Syaf [I27], 2010). Individuals are expected to appeal to the administration on the company's behalf should any problems arise (Arif [I41], 2011) and help to quietly 'settle' any disputes, including through informal influence with the local and central government (Arif [I41], 2011; Interviewee M28, 2010). Once the political connections were made, these companies face few constraints from the local and central state framework (Johnston, 2005: 46). For example, an interviewee detailed that when Rimbunan Hijau, a Malaysian company operating in Papua faced administrative troubles for clearing land outside their concessions, the company requested a staff member known for his 'connections' and native Papuan kinship bonds to meet the local ministry to get all required documentation, which he was able to obtain by virtue of said bonds (Rolland [I50], 2011).

Indeed, for a former senior government or military official, holding such a post by virtue of their former position is usually the 'ultimate goal' after retirement, and often even while these officials are in office, they will be maintaining relationships with companies in the hopes of securing such a post after retirement (Rukmantara [I45], 2011; Syaf [I27], 2010; Syarif [I2], 2010). As one interviewee observed, 'why otherwise would they put former important government people, with little or no business expertise in the sector, in their management?' (Arif [I41], 2011). As a result, there is an extraordinary amount of support for oil palm expansion from higher-level local officials, largely due to the patronage links cultivated within the sector (Colfer, 2002: 314). Government agencies are thus 'captured' by industry interests (McCarthy and Zen, 2010: 155–171), 'not by gaining control over the policy making process and perverting it to its private benefit *per se*, but rather by tying the state's hands in ways that make it difficult for the state to effectively regulate business activity' in the sector (Wederman, 2002: 57). This is a classic description of reduced state capacity and policy paralysis. An NGO coalition known as the Anti-Plantation Mafia argues that patronage networks have been especially higher than average in the Indonesian oil palm plantation sector compared to other sectors in Indonesia because they involve a high level of illegal activity, for example through illegal licensing and land clearing (Arif [I41], 2011).

Therefore, patronage networks are especially important in this sector to protect these commercial interests (Arif [I41], 2011; Syarif [I2], 2010). The following subsections discuss outcomes on the ground that illustrate this weak state capacity and policy paralysis. Failure of the government to uphold effective policies can be seen first in the illegal release of peatlands to powerful companies, and second in illegal commercial fires that have been largely ignored by the authorities, despite clear regulations. Both these outcomes have been identified as major drivers of haze in the region. This chapter shows that all these outcomes have been possible due to the patronage networks that exist within the Indonesian oil palm plantation sector.

Patronage networks and land licensing

Aspinall (2010), Barr (1998), Mayer (2006), McCarthy *et al.* (2012), Rajenthran (2002) and Richardson (2010) have previously identified land licensing as a form of resource that can be tapped for patronage purposes. Barr's (1998: 1–3) early work on the shifting dynamics of control of Indonesia's timber sector had discussed the preferential allocation of plywood licenses to members of the

Indonesian Wood Panel Association (Apkindo), an association that was controlled by Bob Hasan, a well-known associate of President Suharto.

This trend has continued until today, where we see oil palm plantation companies cultivating patronage relationships, often from a very early stage, for similar purposes (Interviewee I49, 2011). Patronage influences in the sector are especially important in obtaining licenses and property rights for the opening of plantation land, one of the earliest stages involved in the process of establishing plantations. Influential actors in the sector are often able to obtain rights to environmentally sensitive land not normally released for conversion, such as peatlands (Interviewee I49, 2011; Wibisino [I44], 2011). This is an important criterion of patronage relations, where privileges to property rights and licenses differ from 'free market' exchange, i.e. differ from outcomes strictly following the law (Eisenstadt and Roniger, 1995: 209–233), as has been discussed earlier in this chapter. Patronage influence in licensing has therefore resulted in a situation where most of the oil palm plantation land in Indonesia is controlled largely by only around ten (Chalil, 2008: 24) local and foreign conglomerates (Moore [I5], 2010). Hence, patronage networks have encouraged the unsustainable use of fire-prone peatlands in Indonesia by encouraging disreputable allocation of resources (peatland), and by guiding state decision making towards the short-term interests of exploiters (Johnston, 2005: 25).

This section discusses the procedures of land licensing in the Indonesian oil palm plantation sector and analyzes the role that patronage plays in policy paralysis at this level. It first reviews the Indonesian laws concerning licensing, especially those pertaining to the licensing of peatlands for conversion. The second subsection then discusses Indonesia's decentralization laws, and how this has complicated licensing matters. The third subsection argues that because of these issues, both local and foreign oil palm plantation companies have been able to make use of their patronage ties to obtain rights to land, often including the fire-prone peatlands. The final subsection discusses the latest attempt by the Indonesian government to address these land-licensing issues, which continues to favour the interests of commercial plantation companies, and hence has also met with limited success.

Indonesian policy on land use and licensing

Forest policy in Indonesia is based on the Constitution of 1945 (Article 33), which mandates the state to manage Indonesia's natural resources, 'for the benefit of the people' (Abdullah, 2002). In addition, Act No. 5/1990 and Act No. 41/1999 on Biodiversity Conservation are the main references for the management of forest resources in Indonesia (Masripatin *et al.*, 2009: 2–3). These regulations reflect the country's philosophy of forest management that accommodates the need to optimally utilize forest resources while conserving said resources to assure multiple benefits in a sustainable way (Masripatin *et al.*, 2009: 2–3). To ensure this, the government of Indonesia fosters and controls local private sector and foreign investment licensing in forestlands (Rajenthran, 2002: 10). Indonesian forests are divided into four main functional categories (Anshari [I42], 2011): production forest (*hutan produksi*), convertible forest (*hutan konversi*); protection forest (*hutan lindung*); and conservation forest (*kawasan konservasi*). Convertible production forest (*hutan produksi konversi* or HPK) can be converted to other non-forest uses, like oil palm. The majority of the HPK is found in the lowlands of Indonesia, including peatlands (Masripatin *et al.*, 2009: 2–3).

As previously discussed, the conversion of peat often directly (through land clearing) or indirectly (through the drying-out of peat) leads to haze-producing fires. Peatlands are often an attractive land for oil palm plantations for several reasons. First, there is often valuable timber on these lands that can be harvested and sold to provide additional funding to developers (Stone, 2007: 1491). Second, peatlands are usually 'empty' in terms of communities, enabling companies to avoid conflicts with increasingly vocal and empowered local communities (Wibisino [I44], 2011). Third, peatlands are often located deep inside forested areas or coasts, far away from administrative centres. These secluded areas would enable plantations to conduct their activities with minimal monitoring by authorities (Anshari [I42], 2011; Casey [I46], 2011; Rukmantara [I45], 2011; Wibisino [I44], 2011). Fourth, demand for peatlands is increasing with the decreasing availability of other drylands around Indonesia (Greenpeace, 2007: 2). As a result, a disproportionate and unsustainable amount (Interviewee I18, 2010) of peatlands has been converted or has been earmarked for conversion into plantations (Greenpeace, 2007: 18; Kaat and Silvius, 2011: 3; Silvius and Kaat, 2010: 13–23; Wicke *et al.*, 2011: 194–200). Once cleared and dried, even if these lands are not deliberately burned, they are often highly fire-prone (*Jakarta Post*, 1994).

While the Forestry Ministry has the ability to redesignate forestland as HPK as explained above, the exceptional nature of peatlands and impacts of peatswamp forest fires as explained in Chapter 2 justified special legislation restricting development on peatlands (Anshari [I42], 2011). Combined, these policies very clearly render the issuance of plantation concessions on peatlands across Indonesia as wholly forbidden (PanEco Foundation, 2008: 1). However, as the following section expounds, the advent of decentralization in Indonesia has raised new tensions between the central and local governments that have produced grey areas in the licensing process for land. This, coupled with protection from their patrons, has made it easier for plantation companies to skirt regulations to obtain land, as is discussed below.

Decentralization complicating the land licensing process

As previously argued by Mayer (2006: 213–214) Indonesia's flawed decentralization policies in the late 1990s failed to anticipate the effect of internal regional autonomy reforms that, among others, have complicated the land licensing process. Decentralization had also caused serious confusion about who actually has the rightful authority to grant approvals for land use redesignation and plantation development at the local level, and the exact process of how these approvals should be legally carried out (Mayer, 2006: 213–214). Although the central government maintains decision-making power on 'policies on natural resources utilization' (Article 7 of the Regional Autonomy Law No. 22/1999), the management of these policies per se remains with the regional governments (Article 10 of the RAL) (Rajenthran, 2002: 17). For example, the law states that the 'local government has the authority to manage natural resources occurring in its jurisdiction and shall be responsible to secure environmental sustainability in accordance with laws and regulations' (Richardson, 2010: 30). Before decentralization, evaluation of the AMDAL was done at the ministerial level. With decentralization, AMDAL evaluation has come under local government capacity (Widianarko, 2009: 1–6). Therefore, the Environmental Act No. 23/1997 and its subordinate regulations have been rendered ineffective by decentralization (Widianarko, 2009: 1–6).

Furthermore, with decentralization, newly empowered regional authorities were also now able to grant various new and additional types of regionally administered plantation license rights to cooperatives, individuals and companies (Mayer, 2006: 213–214). With specific reference to natural resources, decentralization has empowered the regencies to administer the governance of 'capital investments' of their natural resources (Rajenthran, 2002: 17), to promote regional development (Lee [S20], 2010; Mohd Kassim [M3], 2010) and encourage private companies to be committed to their investments (Richardson, 2010: 33–34). In particular, Government Regulation No. 6/1999 granted district governments the authority to issue small-scale timber concession licenses (Obidzinski and Barr, 2003: 17) to individuals, cooperatives or corporations owned by its citizens for areas up to 100 hectares (Palmer and Engel, 2007: 2132–2136) within production or conversion forests identified for reclassification, including into oil palm plantations (Syarif [I2], 2010). Following that, the National Deregulation Policy Package of 2003 granted greater authority to local governors, allowing them to grant permits to convert forests to plantations to a maximum of 1,000 hectares (Richardson, 2010: 33–34). This was encouraged by the fact that with decentralization, local governments were responsible for a big part of their own administrative budgets. Issuing new plantation permits and licenses presented a quick and easy way to fill regional government coffers (Duncan, 2007: 711–724; McCarthy *et al.*, 2012: 555–560). Local administrations have taken advantage of this; for example research by Zakaria *et al.* (2007) in the regency of Seruyan in Central Kalimantan noted that 'colours on the land use map of the regency quickly changed from green "Production Forest" to orange "HPK" or land available for conversion into plantations' soon after decentralization (Zakaria *et al.*, 2007: 62).

However, Central Forestry Law No. 41/1999 and its implementing instrument, Government Regulation 34/2002 on the Management, Exploitation and Use of Forest Areas, maintains central government competence in the granting of concession licenses (Tan, 2004: 178–179). This meant that the authority areas of different agencies remained vague (McCarthy and Zen, 2010: 155–171), which created a great deal of confusion, as various levels of government disagreed with the interpretations of the laws (White III, 2007: 51–63). Although theoretically, any conversion of primary forests into plantation land must obtain Ministry of Forestry approval, regional governments only rarely bother complying with this (Richardson, 2010: 33–34).

Essentially, the decision to release HPK from the forest estate is based on industry proposals but subject to ministerial approval (Masripatin *et al.*, 2009: 2–3). For forestry and agricultural matters, the Ministry of Forestry processes the initial application of both local and foreign approvals (Rajenthran, 2002: 10). The licensing process of obtaining land for plantation purposes thus is a lengthy and complicated procedure, involving various levels of governance in Indonesia, and it allows for high-handed bureaucratic intervention (Rajenthran, 2002: 14) at both the central and local level (Interviewee S14 and Interviewee S15, 2010; Lew [M6] and Interviewee M7, 2010). The procedure is outlined as follows:

1 Obtain a technical recommendation for investment in plantation business from the Directorate General of Plantations (central level);
2 If the investment is foreign, obtain a foreign investment approval from the Indonesian Capital Coordinating Board, and duly establish a company approved for foreign investment (central level);
3 Obtain a recommendation from the relevant regional government institution stating that the intended area for plantation development is in accordance with the regional zoning plan determined by the regional government (district level);
4 Obtain a location permit to commence land acquisition (central level);
5 Conduct the land acquisition;
6 Apply for HGU land title (central level);
7 Conduct an AMDAL study, and obtain the AMDAL approval from the regional government (regional level);
8 Prepare a business plan for the company;
9 Obtain a plantation business permit (*izin usaha perkebunan* or IUP) (regional level);
10 Commence the seeding and planting of plantation plants.

(United Plantations, 2008: 7)

As described above, lengthy and complicated 'red tape' is often deliberately incorporated into bureaucratic procedures to present more opportunities for 'intervention' (Kurer, 1996: 645–661; Rose-Ackerman, 2008: 331). Hence, instead of strengthening state capacity, these procedures effectively weaken it instead. As the following subsection expounds, this ten-step procedure is often skipped or overlooked by well-connected companies and their patrons in power, often resulting in parcels of fire-prone peatlands being illegally released to plantation companies.

The role of patronage in obtaining licenses for peatlands

For a host of local officials, the new decentralized laws and procedures presented opportunities to 'cut in' into a previously Jakarta-centred lucrative 'industry' of licensing rents (Hunt, 2010: 187–190; Lim and Stern, 2003: 23–26; Palmer and Engel, 2007: 2132–2136; Tan, 2004: 178–179; White III, 2007: 51–63). Therefore, opportunities for patronage politics exist at various central and local levels. As one interviewee observed, 'Indonesia is dominated by big business, and the bureaucracy is so corrupted that it is easy' (Moore [I5], 2010) for these well-connected clients to take advantage of this. Oil palm plantation companies, both local and foreign, have indeed done so, using their influence and resources to obtain the rights to large, secluded tracts of land that will not be easily subjected to administrative scrutiny, with little concern if this land is restricted due to peat or not (Rukmantara [I45], 2011; Suwarsono [I3], 2010; Tarigan [I23], 2010). As a result, it was reported in 2005 that in Riau, only 5 out of 36 concessions were issued according to the above ten-step procedure (Harahap, 2008).

An important step in this process that is often skipped by well-connected companies is the AMDAL requirement (Interviewee I18, 2010). Optimally, under a system with strong state capacity, the AMDAL process should be the step where land with peat is detected and licenses are denied. Indeed, the positive outcome for the AMDAL review process should be the main prerequisite for the minister or governor to issue a permit of environmental feasibility, which can be then used to obtain an IUP (step nine above) (Milieudefensie, 2010a: 2). However, because these well-connected companies often gain 'special' approvals (Arif [I41], 2011) to proceed with land opening before the AMDAL is carried out (Zakaria *et al.*, 2007: 72), peat is often included in these parcels, rendering all policies restricting development on peat impotent.

For example, the NGO Borneo People's Contact reported that five plantation companies in Kalimantan had engaged in patronage activities at both the local and higher levels of government to obtain permits (*Jakarta Post*, 2011). Indonesia's Duta Palma reportedly began operations in West Kalimantan without any of the four key land use and land use change permits as listed above, including the AMDAL. Locals were of the opinion that Duta Palma was able to operate with such impunity due to its strong military connections (Gilbert, 2009: 2–3). And Malaysia's IOI reportedly received 'special approval' from the Ministry of Forestry to open up parts of their concessions in West Kalimantan before the AMDAL process was completed (Milieudefensie, 2010a: 6).

Singapore's Wilmar was reported to have started land clearing on plantations containing peat in West Kalimantan before the approval of AMDAL, because of 'special permission' from the governor (Zakaria *et al.*, 2007: 72). Likewise, GAR was also reported to have conducted land clearing before AMDAL was completed on six of its concessions in Central Kalimantan. They reportedly obtained special 'in-principle business permits' from the governor and local officials to enable them to do so (Reksoprodjo, 2010: 2). One interviewee explained that GAR often obtains these special licenses in exchange for GAR's contributions in funding election campaigns of local leaders (Interviewee I49, 2011). This is an example of the 'mutual hostage' situation, when each party is indebted to the other (Interviewee I49, 2011). Sometimes these corrupt patrons who give out these special allowances do get caught. For example, an East Kalimantan mayor was found guilty for issuing permits not in accordance with procedure for a project that would turn a 1 million hectare forest along the Indonesia-Malaysia border into oil palm plantations (*Jakarta Post*, 2006b). However, these cases are rare.

As a result, despite ample regulations restricting palm oil development on peatlands, up to 25 per cent of concessionaires deviate from this rule and plant on deep peat anyway (Silvius and Kaat, 2010: 21). Today, over a quarter of all oil palm concessions in Indonesia are located on peat (see Table 2.1) (Greenpeace, 2007: 2–33; Kaat and Silvius, 2011: 3; Silvius and Kaat, 2010: 13; Wicke *et al.*, 2011: 194–200) and more than 50 per cent of new plantations are planned within these peatland areas (Greenpeace, 2007: 2–33; Silvius and Kaat, 2010: 13), as detailed in Chapter 2. For a country that has such extensive policies restricting development on peatland, this outcome shows convincing evidence of policy paralysis due to the undue influence of powerful elite groups in the society.

This situation is especially serious in Riau on Sumatra Island, where a third of all palm oil concessions are situated on peat. Furthermore, local governors in Riau collectively have plans to expand oil palm plantations by 3 million hectares. The 2007 draft of the new provincial land use plan shows that hundreds of thousands of hectares of peatlands have been designated for conversion, the majority of this consisting of large tracts of tropical peatlands, which were until recently forested areas (Greenpeace, 2007: 2–33). Many major plantation companies have been found to have obtained licenses for peatlands in Riau. For example, an investigation by Greenpeace reported that Indonesian companies Duta Mas, Astra Agro and Musim Mas have all acquired land on peat. According to the report, Duta Palma was found to hold five concessions on very deep strata of peat ranging from 3.5 to 8 metres, with a total area of 55,000 hectares. Musim Mas also has a concession on deep peat in Riau, with an estimated area of 30,600 hectares, in some areas over 4 metres deep. Astra Agro has two concessions on peatlands in Riau, with an estimated total area of 20,000 hectares. Greenpeace reported that foreign companies were no exception. The study detailed that GAR has six concessions on peatlands in Riau, with an estimated total area of over 54,000 hectares. Wilmar has three concessions on peatlands there, with an estimated total area of over 29,000 hectares (Greenpeace, 2007: 3–56). Other reports detailed that Indo Agri has a concession on peat in Riau, with an estimated total area of 8,500 hectares; 70 per cent (19,432 hectares) of PT API's (a subsidiary of KLK) land in Riau is on peatsoil (Saharjo *et al.*, 2003: 3); and most of THP's 200,000 hectares of allocated plantation land there is on peatsoil as well (*The Star*, 2007). In the neighbouring province of Jambi, companies such as BSP, Sime Darby, Makin Group and GAR also reportedly operate on peatlands (Munadar *et al.*, 2010: 1).

Peat areas in Borneo Island's Kalimantan are quickly being converted into oil palm plantations as well due to illegal licensing (Arif [I41], 2011). It has been reported that 307,515 hectares of peat in Kalimantan has already been illegally converted to plantations (Gunarso *et al.*, 2013: 29). Malaysia's IOI reportedly has five concessions on peat in West Kalimantan (with one consisting of 88 per cent peat) (Milieudefensie, 2010b: 18) and one concession on peat in Central Kalimantan, with an estimated area of 3,000 hectares of peatlands. The Malaysian Sime Darby also reportedly has a concession on peat in Central Kalimantan, with an estimated area of 1,600 hectares (Greenpeace, 2007: 3–56). Singapore's Wilmar reportedly has peatlands in four concessions in West Kalimantan and 12 in Central Kalimantan (Greenpeace, 2007: 21; Zakaria *et al.*, 2007: 56–74). In Central Kalimantan, Singapore's GAR was reported to have 1,880 hectares of oil palm developments on peat, while in West Kalimantan, this figure was 1,330 hectares (Reksoprodjo, 2010: 2). The Greenepace study also reported that Indonesia's Musim Mas has four concessions on peat, and Astra Agro has seven concessions on peat in Central Kalimantan (Greenpeace, 2007: 21).

This is clearly at odds with many of these companies' policies on the environment. For example, GAR's Forest Conservation Policy claims that all of their operations observe the conservation of high-carbon stock forests and a zero-deforestation footprint (Reuters, 2011), and includes pledges to stop all development on peat regardless of depth (Golden-Agri Resources Ltd, 2010). Wilmar's sustainability commitments include not establishing plantations on high conservation value forests, primary forests or peatlands less than 3 metres deep (Greenpeace, 2007: 53; Richardson, 2010: 69; Zakaria *et al.*, 2007: 5). Sime Darby has also made public commitments not to develop on peat (Interviewee M44, 2012), and IOI's corporate social responsibility statements clearly pronounce that it does not develop on any peat (Milieudefensie, 2010a).

According to the previously discussed Indonesian law, all plantation land on peat is essentially illegal (Anshari [I42], 2011; Surya [I9] and Akbar [I10], 2010). This means that more than a quarter of all oil palm plantation land in Indonesia is illegal. However, even though by law, if existing or pending plantation licenses relate to deep peat, such licenses should be revoked under provisions of Presidential Decree 32/1990, Minister of Agriculture's Instruction to the Governors of Indonesia No. 301/TU.210/M/12/2001, Government Regulation 26/2008 and Ministry of Agriculture Regulation 14/2009 (PanEco Foundation, 2008: 1; Wibisino *et al.*, 2011: 15), no plantations have had their licenses revoked on these ground as yet. It has been argued that one reason for this is that decentralization has resulted in the power to rescind operating licenses being granted to the local sectoral agencies such as the Department of Industry and Trade (Dinas Perindustrian dan Perdagangan) and the Plantation Agency (Dinas Perkebunan), which do not have environmental or conservation responsibilities, but have a primary interest in supporting regional development (McCarthy and Zen, 2010: 155–171) and thus are easily swayed by clients on developmental grounds.

Therefore, this chapter points out that these well-connected plantation companies have been allowed to act with such impunity because of the patronage networks that they maintain with both the local and central governments, which have resulted in weak state capacity and a lack of bureaucratic oversight. In these ways, the resource-rich Indonesian landscape has produced and encouraged a culture of 'grab and greed' at both the central and district level (Brown, 2006: 995–991). For example, as discussed above, many of these companies enjoy direct access to the President (Surya [I9] and Akbar [I10], 2010) and also local governors (Syaf [I27], 2010) through their advisors and staff, and other companies such as Sime Darby or have powerful former ministry staff in their employ (Tarigan [I23], 2010). As several interviewees explained, the influence of these individuals are often instrumental in acquiring such land permits and licenses (Arif [I41], 2011; Surya [I9] and Akbar [I10], 2010; Syaf [I27], 2010), and also in 'settling' any disputes that might arise (Arif [I41], 2011; Interviewee M28, 2010).

Because of this, powerful plantation companies with good patronage ties have no reason to fear punishment and the law will often be disregarded (Kurer, 1996: 645–661). This fosters a culture of impunity (Dauvergne, 1995: 89–98) among well-connected elites in the sector. As a result, massive amounts of fire-prone peat are now exposed to conversion and development into plantations, further driving the haze. In short, patronage politics within the Indonesian oil palm plantation sector have been very influential in the management, or mismanagement, of peatlands there. Hence, despite Indonesia having very clear policies limiting the use of peatsoil, its peatlands continue to be exploited to fuel the growth of the sector. There have been recent governmental efforts to address this issue, the most notable being the United Nations Collaborative Programme on Reducing Emissions from Deforestation and Forest Degradation in Developing Countries (REDD). However, the influence of patronage has also limited the effectiveness of this programme, as the following section expounds.

REDD and peatland regulation

The latest and most high-profile development regarding peatland regulation in Indonesia (Rowland [I39], 2011) is the REDD programme (Butler *et al.*, 2009: 67–73; Richardson, 2010: 88). Under the programme, Norway pledged $1 billion to Indonesia in 2009 (Butler *et al.*, 2009: 67–73) in exchange for a two-year moratorium on primary forests and peatlands (Arif [I41], 2011; Surya [I9] and Akbar [I10], 2010; Syaf [I27], 2010) in order to identify which parts of the Indonesian peatlands are safe for further development (Maitar [I12], 2010, Syaf [I27], 2010; Syarif [I2], 2010). As part of this agreement, the Indonesian government agreed to establish a degraded land database, providing the necessary information to identify areas of land acceptable for the establishment of economic activity, including oil palm plantations (World Growth, 2011: 4–13). After a delayed start, the moratorium commenced in May 2011 with Presidential Instruction No. 10/2011 (Rondonuwu, 2011).

However, the REDD scheme has many inherent weaknesses. It has been argued that the REDD moratorium was watered down due to inherent political and private interests (Rondonuwu, 2011; Simamora, 2011) bolstered by patronage networks (Syarif [I2], 2010; Tarigan [I23], 2010). As discussed above, patronage connections often guide state decision making (Johnston, 2005: 25) as elites are highly motivated to block, dilute or slow down any form of legislative or policy amendments that would threaten the informal relationships from which they so greatly benefit (Brinkerhoff and Goldsmith, 2004: 163–182). Therefore, webs of patronage networks can result in a situation of 'state capture', where certain sectors mould the state and influence the policy-making environment (Ascher, 1998: 37–61). Hence, the resulting weakened state capacity affects the ability of the state to not only implement policy, as detailed in the earlier sections, but also to create or modify them (Knutsen, 2013: 2; Skocpol, 1985). In this way, the political influence of those who gain economically from exploitation activities can thwart proposals for environmental reform. The state finds itself without the autonomy or indeed the motivation to pursue policies that do not reflect the short-term interests of the exploiters (Ascher, 1998: 37–61).

For example, some interviewees note the irony that Agus Purnomo, earlier mentioned as rumoured to be closely associated with GAR (Surya [I9] and Akbar [I10], 2010), is a central figure in REDD implementation in his capacity as the Indonesian special advisor to the Ministry of Environment and head of the Secretariat of the National Climate Change. Furthermore, illustrating the close relationship between government and industry, the president himself met personally with, and promised major players and the sector's lobby group, the Indonesian Palm Oil Association (Gabungan Pengusaha Kelapa Sawit Indonesia or GAPKI[6]), that he would ensure that their interests would be accommodated through REDD (Simamora, 2011) prior to the start of the moratorium. This is an example of the weakening of the president's capacity to make policy decisions. One interviewee also told how Joko Supriyono, a director at Astra Agro and also secretary general of GAPKI was able to use his formidable influence with the government in getting a weaker moratorium passed (Interviewee I48, 2011).

As a result of all this, the government decided that as part of REDD, existing plantation investment projects (including those on peatlands) already approved by the Indonesian government will not be affected by the moratorium (Kuala Lumpur Kepong Berhad, 2010). Also, the moratorium was set for only two years, an extremely short timeframe in contrast with the long time horizons of the sector. This period of time has been argued by environmentalists as too short to bring about any significant improvement on the situation of peatlands in Indonesia (Arif [I41], 2011; Interviewee I47, 2011; Tarigan [I23], 2010). Furthermore, the Indonesian government has yet to clarify areas that are 'sensitive' and areas that are not, resulting in many 'grey areas' of ambiguous land (Interviewee M55, 2012). Also, several interviewees argued that the reason for the delayed implementation of the moratorium was so that central and local governments could release a large amount of primary forests and peatlands to selected well-connected companies before the moratorium came into force (Arif [I41], 2011; Syaf [I27], 2010). Indeed, just before the moratorium was passed in May 2011, the Ministry of Forestry was said to have released several thousand hectares of land in Central Kalimantan, including primary forests and peatlands, to the well-connected Duta Palma, GAR and Wilmar (Arif [I41], 2011), which an interviewee estimates would meet their supply of land for at least the next two years while the moratorium is in force (Interviewee M44, 2012).

Under the REDD, however, there is a proposed land-swap mechanism (Wibisino [I44], 2011), where the government will purportedly encourage those who hold existing permits in areas of primary forests or deep peat to swap them for replacement permits on degraded lands. Additionally, these permit holders will also be compensated accordingly, based on the size of their concessions (Richardson, 2010: 88). This is good news for Indonesia's peatlands. However, this mechanism is purely voluntary and no major plantation company has engaged in land swaps as yet (Wibisino [I44], 2011). It remains to be seen if this land swap mechanism would be considered as a cost-effective option for the companies involved.

Furthermore, environmentalists operating in the field have discovered that district governments are already breaking the moratorium due to patronage pressures from companies (Interviewee I49, 2011; Syaf [I27], 2010; Syarif [I2], 2010). For example, the governor of Aceh, Irwandi Yusof, was recently reported to have continued to release licenses for peatlands in his regency despite the moratorium and was brought to court by a local NGO on that account (Interviewee I49, 2011). Therefore, it remains to be seen if the REDD moratorium will be any more effective than previous regulations restricting the use of peatlands for plantation purposes.

The contradiction here between governmental restrictions on land for plantations and governmental goals for continued expansion of the sector to reach a CPO output of 40 million tonnes per year by 2020 (Boer *et al.*, 2012: 4; Hameiri and Jones, 2013: 471) (as discussed in Chapter 2) has not been lost. An interviewee detailed how Joko Supriyono, a director at Astra Agro as mentioned above, in fact pointed this out to environmental NGOs to argue that in order for the government's goals to be achieved, companies 'had no choice' but to continue establishing plantations on restricted areas (Interviewee I48, 2011). Indeed, research has shown that strategies of commercial plantations to increase productivity have primarily focused on expansion of new land, rather than replanting or research and development (Suharto, 2011: 20).

The influence of patronage can once again be seen in ensuring that any changes of licensing procedures remain firmly to the advantage of these powerful groups. This highlights the pertinent problem with peatland management in Indonesia. Policies that have been shaped for conservation purposes often do not stand up against economic interests especially when both patrons and clients stand to gain economically. If expansion continues into these areas, especially on peatlands, the persistence of haze is extremely likely. As explained above, converted peatlands are highly fire-prone and the fires on peat produce exceptionally sooty and thick smoke that travel across national boundaries creating regional haze. While this subsection has shown how patronage politics has played an important part in land acquisition at the early stages of plantation expansion, patronage politics continues to be important throughout the lifetime of the plantations. It is especially important when it comes to the deliberate use of fire for land-clearing purposes on plantations, as the following section expounds.

Patronage networks and haze-producing fires

Patronage relationships often also extend well beyond the licensing stage. A key criteria of patronage politics is the ongoing nature of the relationship, in contrast to one-off bribery (Hicken, 2011: 290–306). This is especially necessary with the Indonesian oil palm plantation sector. With oil palm, often plantation companies do not clear and plant the whole land parcel at once. They also constantly apply and receive approval for new land licenses in different areas. Furthermore, as mentioned above, crop rotation occurs every 20 to 30 years. This means that, land clearing for new plantings or replacement plantings often occur continually over time, not just once during the land lease. As discussed above, many plantation companies have used fire as a cost-efficient way to clear land (Interviewee M36, 2010; Then [M14], 2010). Therefore, long-term patronage relationships have to be cultivated so that patron protection can be relied upon throughout this period of time (Surya [I9] and Akbar [I10], 2010) to protect their clients from the repercussions of their actions. Because of the long timeframes of the sector and the continuous process of land clearing, it is important for companies to maintain ongoing patronage relationships to enable them to conduct unscrupulous land clearing with impunity (Surya [I9] and Akbar [I10], 2010; Syarif [I2], 2010), far beyond just the licensing stage discussed above.

The first subsection discusses the importance of ongoing patronage networks within the sector, in the context of weakening the capacity of the state to effectively curb the use of fire for land clearing. It reviews the Indonesian laws concerning land clearing, especially those pertaining to the use of fire. The second subsection then discusses how weaknesses of these laws provide strategic advantages to these firms to get away with open burning. The third subsection goes on to discuss burning laws in the context of decentralization, and how this decentralization (and the decentralization of patronage networks) has further complicated effective enforcement of these laws. Subsection four gives examples of how various well-connected Indonesian, Malaysian and Singaporean plantation companies have, with the assistance of their patrons, managed to escape investigation and conviction of open burning allegations. The final subsection discusses recent revisions to burning laws and how despite this, burning laws still cannot be implemented effectively due to patronage influence.

Indonesian policy on land clearing and fire

The Basic Agrarian Law 1960, Presidential Decree No. 23/1980, Law No. 12/1992 on Agriculture, and Law No. 23/1997 on Environmental Management set the main environmental legislative policies for Indonesia (Rajenthran, 2002: 25). The central Environment Impact Management Agency (Badan Pengendalian Dampak Lingkungan) is tasked with the nationwide development and implementation of policies on environmental and pollution management (Rajenthran, 2002: 25).

As explained in Chapter 2, plantations often use fire in preparation for planting because it is on average 40 times cheaper than mechanical land clearing

(Salim, 2007), it is a fast way to clear unwanted weeds and grass (Interviewee I21, 2010; Maitar [I12], 2010; Moore [I5], 2010; Surya [I9] and Akbar [I10], 2010), it gives a shot of fertilizer to the soil and it reduces the risk of pests (Zakaria *et al.*, 2007: 25). Previous research has shown that commercial burning for land clearing has been proven to be responsible for up to 80 per cent of the haze-causing fires in Indonesia (Richardson, 2010: 22). While fires on peatlands produce the thickest and sootiest smoke haze, burning of all types of forestlands also contribute to the regional haze.

Commercial land clearing by use of fire has been illegal in Indonesia since 1997 (Cho, 1994). Due to rising concerns of haze that year, a Presidential Decree called for the banning of all slash-and-burn style land clearing activities across the country (*Jakarta Post*, 1997), which was supported by the new Environmental Management Act (EMA) No. 23/1997 (Dauvergne, 1998: 13–17; Syarif and Wibisana, 2007: 20; Zakaria *et al.*, 2007: 24). Most notably the EMA 1997 stated that fire ignition is a 'corporate crime' and not a 'personal crime' (Saharjo *et al.*, 2003: 8). It incorporated the principle of strict liability (McCarthy and Zen, 2010: 155–171; Syarif and Wibisana, 2007: 20; Zakaria *et al.*, 2007: 24), which means that the burden of proof is placed on the firm responsible for the fire (Arif [I41], 2011). This applied the 'presumption of guilt' clause that compels a plantation owner to prove that any fire on his land was not his doing and that he had taken all necessary actions to prevent or stop it (Arif [I41], 2011; Parliament of Singapore, 1999), thus shifting the burden of proof to the plantation owner. This applies to both intentional burning and fire outbreaks due to neglect (Syarif and Wibisana, 2007: 20; Zakaria *et al.*, 2007: 24).

Several other laws were put into place after 1997 to complement the Environmental Act No. 23. Most notably, Government Regulation No. 4/2001, Law 18/2004 Concerning Crop Estates and Ministry of Agriculture Regulation No. 26/2007 (Syarif and Wibisana, 2007: 20; Zakaria *et al.*, 2007: 24) Concerning the Guidance on Estate Enterprise Permit provided regulation for the control of pollution or other environmental damage from forest and land fires. The regulation details the obligations of those who control certain land areas (such as oil palm plantations) to prevent fires and any associated pollution or environmental damage. They are obliged to use satellite images to monitor fire outbreaks and report back to the Governor's Office, district head and mayor twice a year. Alongside this, they are also responsible to prepare the necessary fire prevention and fire control equipment and facilities, and to monitor and report these prevention activities to the governor or mayor of the respective areas (Syarif and Wibisana, 2007: 20; Zakaria *et al.*, 2007: 24). And, in the event of fires, they have the immediate obligation to bring said fires under control and subsequently to rehabilitate the resulting damaged area (Hedradjat [I14], 2010; Surya [I9] and Akbar [I10], 2010; Tarigan [I23], 2010,). Overall, there are around 19 presidential and ministerial decrees that deal specifically with forest fires that supplement these basic laws (Bowen *et al.*, 2001: 60).

If fires were found on plantation land, the law allowed the Ministry of Environment to seal off burned lands by setting up a police line around them, pending an investigation (Rukmantara, 2006a). If found guilty, penalties for commercial open burning based on these regulations range from a minimum of a five-year jail term and a fine of $5,000 and to a maximum of a 15-year jail term and a fine of $1 million (Syarif and Wibisana, 2007: 20). These penalties could be doubled for individuals or groups or companies that intentionally start fires (Abdullah, 2002: 6–7). The Ministry of Agriculture Decree No. 357/Kpts/HK.350/5/2002 on Guidance Regarding the Licensing of Plantation Businesses (Syarif and Wibisana, 2007: 20; Zakaria *et al.*, 2007: 24) and the Ministry of Agriculture Regulation No. 26 Concerning the Guidance on Estate Enterprise Permit furthermore stipulates that any plantation investor found to clear land using fire may face administrative sanctions, including revocation of its IUPs (McCarthy and Zen, 2010: 155–171; Syarif and Wibisana, 2007: 20; Zakaria *et al.*, 2007: 24). However, there remain inherent weaknesses in these laws that enable companies to get away with burning (Yansen [I43], 2011).

Weaknesses in the burning laws complicating enforcement

Several serious weaknesses within the laws give plantation companies strategic advantages to get away with burning (Yansen [I43], 2011). For example, even though it is illegal to burn the land, there is no legal restriction to plant on burned land (*Jakarta Post*, 2006d). Therefore, if plantations escape being caught during the burning, no retrospective action can be taken. Also, existing policies on insurance schemes have been shaped to benefit plantations; insurance schemes guarantee refunds for fire damaged plants without investigation into the source of the fire (Jhamtani, 1998: 366). And as explained above, the EMA 1997 incorporated the principle of strict liability whereby the burden of proof should lie with the company responsible for the pollution. However, efforts to operationalize the principle of strict liability of land owners for fire has never been put into place (McCarthy and Zen, 2010: 155–171). An interviewee provided an example of how patronage networks functioned at the parliamentary level, by explaining that provisions for the operationalization of this principle was continuously blocked in Parliament by parliamentarians sympathetic to powerful plantation interests, due to influence from well-connected individuals in the sector and from the lobby group GAPKI (Interviewee I25, 2010). This is a clear example of patronage relationships weakening the capacity of the states to effectively implement laws, resulting in policy paralysis when laws exist but cannot be operationalized.

Therefore, companies that were setting the fires still had to be caught red-handed (Parliament of Singapore, 1998), or evidence such as matches and oil jerrycans had to be found at the site of the crime (Interviewee I25, 2010; Surya [I9] and Akbar [I10], 2010). This was difficult to do (*Jakarta Post*, 2005a; Parliament of Singapore, 1998; Rukmantara [I45], 2011; Wibisino [I44], 2011) because current laws do not allow for police to take action against land burners on the spot or collect evidence in the field (Interviewee I25, 2010; *Jakarta Post*, 2006e). Furthermore, an interviewee, based on personal experience, professed that if a company maintained a good relationship with the police, it would receive adequate warning before the police came (Rolland [I50], 2011) so that evidence could be cleared. The police also would not search for evidence of burning thoroughly (Anshari [I42], 2011; Arif [I41], 2011).

Taking advantage of this loophole, concessionaires have developed further tactics to avoid being caught. As one interviewee explained, this included burning on weekends or during Friday prayers, so that when police or officials detect fires and approach the company office, 'no one will be around for confrontation' (Udiansyah [I15], 2010). Interviewees also tell how plantation companies often trespass and burn villager's land beside their concessions and let the fires spread to their land as a way to circumvent laws (Interviewee I25, 2010; Syarif [I2], 2010). Other interviewees explained that companies often hired subcontractors (Arif [I41], 2011; Lim [S13], 2010; Moore [I5], 2010; Rowland [I39], 2011) or locals to burn the forests. For example, NGOs interviewed said that they have met locals who admitted to receiving money from plantations such as Duta Palma and GAR to burn plantation land on the pretence that it is for their own personal purposes (Surya [I9] and Akbar [I10]; 2010, Syaf [I27], 2010, Anshari [I42], 2011; Udiansyah [I15], 2010). It is more economical for companies to hire villagers to burn their land, because 'if the villager gets caught and put in jail, it is cheaper for the company to just pay compensation to his family' (Tarigan [I23], 2010). Sometimes, even the companies themselves will call the police to 'catch' these hired perpetrators (Surya [I9] and Akbar [I10], 2010), leaving behind conveniently burned land to conduct new planting.

For example, three smallholders were jailed in East Kalimantan in 1997 for allegedly causing forest fires (Saharjo, 1999: 142). And in 2000, two 'arsonists' from South Sumatra, believed to have been hired as scapegoats by the concessionaire (Interviewee I25, 2010; Udiansyah [I15], 2010), were sentenced to jail for 20 months for allegedly setting fire to concession lands (Saharjo *et al.*, 2003: 1). One interviewee in fact had personal experience of this, where he had to take the fall (including jail time) for a major Malaysian company's illegal activities (Rolland [I50], 2011). Local policy makers and prosecutors predictably will tend to side with the commercial plantation companies in such cases instead of these few implicated smallholders and locals, who usually lack powerful political backers (Hameiri and Jones, 2013: 471). This is due to the stronger pecuniary incentives offered by clients in these commercial companies, which, as detailed above, is not only a source of personal enrichment for local patrons but also political enrichment, as a way to bring development to the areas under their administration to ensure continued support from the larger community. On top of all this, many interviewees pointed out that decentralization of government authority in Indonesia had rendered top-down implementation of fire policies obsolete.

Decentralization complicating enforcement of burning laws

As part of the decentralization laws, Act No. 22/1999 (replacing a 1974 act on regional government and a 1979 act on local government, and later replaced by Act No. 32/2004) concerning regional government, environment issues were no longer under central control but became the responsibility of regency[7] governments (Richardson, 2010: 30; Syarif and Wibisana, 2007: 8–14; Widianarko, 2009: 1–6). In effect, in 2002, the role of the Environment minister as the head of the Environmental Impact Management Agency was dissolved, reducing the Environment Ministry's authority to the mere functional coordination of environmental matters among ministries and departments (Interviewee M44, 2012; Widianarko, 2009: 1–6).

This resulted in situations where certain regional administrations take the issue of burning less seriously than others (Hedradjat [I14], 2010; Suwarsono [I3], 2010), and sometimes provincial laws contradicted central laws (Hariri [I30] and Ardiansyah [I31], 2010; Krezdorn [I32], 2010; Udiansyah [I15], 2010). For example, NGOs that were interviewed explained that there is a law in Riau that allows open burning for plantations of up to 2 hectares (Hariri [I30] and Ardiansyah [I31], 2010), so long as a regional-level permit has been granted (ADB-ASEAN in Severino, 2006: 114), despite national zero-burning laws (Parliament of Singapore, 2000). Also, local authorities involved in patronage relationships with oil palm plantation companies continue to use this confusion of the laws as an excuse for why they have not brought any plantation companies to court, saying that only the Ministry of Forestry had the administrative right to revoke operating permits of errant companies holding forest concessions (*Jakarta Post*, 2000).

As one interviewee explained, 'these complicated conditions on the ground further encouraged patronage politics' (Kamaruddin [M26], 2010). Uncertainty with the complex web of environmental laws as a result of decentralization has compromised law enforcement on fire issues, especially over whether the central government or local government is responsible for fire-related crimes (Wootliff, 2009). It has also obscured the rights and obligations of local and central agencies, enabling and encouraging individual officials to apply illegitimate discretion and favouritism in making their decisions on whether or not to uphold laws (McCarthy and Zen, 2010: 155–171). As a result, these officials are weakened in their capacity to carry out official policy, as they are no longer bound to abstract rules and regulations. Rather, their decisions and actions are guided by patronage relationships (Kurer, 1996: 645–661). Indeed, in 2004, two local Riau administrators were questioned by central police for aiding and abetting the fire crimes (*Jakarta Post*, 2004b), however, again such cases were in the minority, and patronage networks that bolster illegal burning among large plantation companies often go undetected.

Therefore decentralization has been a welcome development for plantation companies, and many major plantation companies have been establishing relationships with local *Bupatis* (Moore [I5], 2010). As one plantation manager expressed, 'operations will be much smoother and more efficient if companies can deal straight with the *Bupati*' (Sandker *et al.*, 2007: 37–40), inferring that patronage networks can be established and maintained more easily at the local level to protect their interests. As a result, open burning becomes the norm (Moore [I5], 2010) as major plantation companies with good patronage ties have no reason to fear punishment, as burning laws are often disregarded by the administration itself (Kurer, 1996: 645–661). Thus, major plantation companies were able to continue to conduct large-scale open burning for land clearing, often undetected or if caught, unsuccessfully charged (Arif [I41], 2011; Casey [I46], 2011; Syarif [I2], 2010; Yansen [I43], 2011).

For example, in 2006, the NGO Wahana Lingkungan Hidup Indonesia (The Indonesian Forum for the Environment) identified 106 plantations belonging to various major plantation companies to be responsible for open burning and haze (Rukmantara, 2006b). Indeed, an interviewee witnessed the process of land clearing on plantation lands in Indonesia (Interviewee M15, 2010). In 2005 to 2007, a Greenpeace study reported that hotspots were detected on five Astra Agro concessions in Riau, two of which were on peatlands. One peat concession of Musim Mas there was also found to have had hotspots. In Central Kalimantan 73 hotspots were detected on three of Sime Darby's concessions and 188 hotspots on three Musim Mas concessions (Greenpeace, 2007: 42).

NGOs often face difficulty or indifference when they report these incidences to the local authorities (Chee [M27], 2010; Ramakrishna [M20], 2010; Singh [M18], 2010; Stone, 2007). NGOs also often find their attempts to investigate burnings on plantation land blocked by local police (Interviewee I6, 2010). For instance, when local NGOs wanted to enter an Aceh plantation to confirm fires on the plantation, they found their path blocked by district police (Interviewee I49, 2011). Other NGO representatives that were interviewed related an incident by a West Kalimantan governor who bluntly denied that two major companies had burned forests in the province to expand their estates, even though proof was shown with satellite data. They implied that his denial was due to the close relationship cultivated between the governor and those companies (Albar [I17], 2010). Furthermore, junior-level civil investigators have also noted the absence of authorisation to conduct investigations on burning activities as requested by these NGOs from their superiors, who they suspect have been influenced by their clients to do so, as a hindrance to their enforcement efforts (Abdullah, 2002: 30). The weaknesses of governmental capacity to implement the burning laws, as explained above, coupled with these complications that arose with decentralization, have resulted in most commercial open-burning cases going uninvestigated or uncharged (Arif [I41], 2011; Casey [I46], 2011; Simamora, 2010; Syarif [I2], 2010; Yansen [I43], 2011).

Well-connected firms escaping investigation and conviction

Many Indonesian, Malaysian and Singaporean firms have been able to evade official investigation by the Indonesian government despite repeated indicators of open burning.[8] For example, Indonesia's Duta Palma is said to be one of the companies with the worst track record (Interviewee I47, 2011), but has never officially been scrutinized. Greenpeace investigations in Riau have reported serious breaches of Indonesian law on Duta Palma plantations, especially illegal, intentional and systematic land clearing using fire. From January 2006 to 2007, fires were detected several times inside 12 of Duta Palma concession areas. Planting of oil palm seeds often takes place immediately after burning, which Greenepace argues proves that the fires were deliberate (Greenpeace, 2007: 30–43). Similarly in West Kalimantan, the Rainforest Action Network (RAN) found evidence of burning on Duta Palma concessions in April 2009 (Gilbert, 2009: 2; Laurance *et al.*, 2010: 379). According to the RAN report:

> foreboding clouds of black smoke hang over Semunying Jaya [the village], reminding the villagers that the clearing continues. After the chainsaws and bulldozers, Duta Palma labourers pour diesel fuel over the felled forest and sets it ablaze, lighting fires that smoulder for days.
>
> (Gilbert, 2009: 2)

Incidences of burning have been reported to various authorities by NGOs and village heads, but no legal action has resulted (Greenpeace, 2007: 30–43). As RAN argues, it is Duta Palma's connections within the Indonesian military that allow Duta Palma to operate with such impunity (Gilbert, 2009: 2).

Similarly, Astra Agro also reportedly escaped allegations without any official investigation. Greenpeace found hotspots on seven Astra Agro concessions between 2006 to 2007 (Greenpeace, 2007: 42), and Astra Agro was also reported to be using fire to clear land in the protected Leuser Ecosystem area in Aceh (Richardson, 2010: 68). However, as with previous accusations against them, Astra Agro denied charges that the fires were deliberately lit, maintaining that they were instead mainly the work of slash-and-burn farmers and log smugglers who try to destroy the evidence of their activities by burning stumps (WALHI *et al.*, 2009: 5–9). Again, no action from the authorities was recorded.

Other similar cases were with plantations of Malaysian companies such as THP and IOI. An interviewee from the Global Environment Centre (GEC) explained that THP was known to have burned about 20,000 hectares of land in Sumatra in 1997, which was identified as being the main source of smoke travelling to Singapore that year (Interviewee M44, 2012). More recently, Greenpeace detected 234 hotspots on five of IOI's concession between 2006 and 2007 (Greenpeace, 2007: 21), and Milieudefensie, another NGO, found that newly opened plantations in West Kalimantan belonging to Malaysia's IOI in 2009 had a significant increase in fire hotspots in freshly cleared land (Milieudefensie, 2010a: 12). It was found that before the beginning of land-clearing activity in preparation for planting in 2009, there were zero hotspots in the concession, however several concentrations of hotspots occurred in newly cleared areas. As the Milieudefensie report notes 'although the concentrated occurrence of fire hotspots in newly cleared plantation development areas alone does not represent hard evidence that IOI subsidiaries practice intentional open burning, few alternative causes could be determined' (Milieudefensie, 2010b: 18). As noted above, plantation owners are known to set fire onto land to clear the remaining stumps after valuable timber has been removed.

This is at odds with IOI's self-imposed strict 'zero burning policy on planting or replanting and on waste management' (Milieudefensie, 2010b: 18). IOI claims that their zero-burning policy was designed to completely overcome haze pollution normally associated with land clearing using slash-and-burn methods, and to return organic matter to the soil (Milieudefensie, 2010b: 18). When confronted by Milieudefensie, IOI reiterated their commitment to zero burning and insisted that the fires were actually due to paddy farmers on their concessions that burn after cultivation and deer hunters that burn to encourage new vegetation that attract deer. However, Milieudefensie argued instead that if paddy farmers and hunters were the cause of these hotspots, then there should have been fire hotspots in earlier years as well, which was not the case for the years 2007 and 2008 (Milieudefensie, 2010a: 12). Furthermore, according to Indonesian law, concession owners are responsible for fires on their concessions regardless of origin (Hedradjat [I14], 2010; Surya [I9] and Akbar [I10], 2010; Tarigan [I23], 2010). However, despite these arguments, no further investigations were carried out by the local government and IOI's plantations were not held accountable for the localized haze that was caused by fires in their concession areas in 2009.

The Singaporean based GAR also similarly escaped any official scrutiny. In 2005 to 2007, Greenpeace detected hotspots on six of their concessions in Riau, three of which were located on peatlands. In Central Kalimantan during the same period, 322 hotspots were detected on five of their concessions (Greenpeace, 2007: 42). In Papua in 2008, the Greenpeace investigation team again found evidence of land burning to prepare land for oil palm plantations on GAR concessions (Maitar, 2008: 2). In 2009, GAR was reported to have started fires on its concessions in Central Sumatra (Richardson, 2010: 62). However, GAR strongly denied these accusations by reaffirming that they have a zero-burning policy since 1997 for land preparation (GAR and SMART, 2013), in accordance with the ASEAN Policy on Zero Burning (Golden-Agri Resources Ltd, 2010; Reksoprodjo, 2010: 2). According to GAR, all their land clearing happens through manual methods such as bulldozing and stacking of trees, to prevent air pollution, preserve the soil structure and retain nutrients in the soil through the decomposition of biomass (Golden-Agri Resources Ltd, 2010). A former GAR plantation manager that was interviewed insisted that 'there have always been budget allocations for mechanical clearing on plantations' (Peters [I1], 2010). However, interviews with senior officers at the Indonesian Ministry of Environment revealed evidence dismissing the argument. They found that such companies' budget reports for land clearing are often 'very low, and did not match the expenses required for mechanical clearing' (Interviewee I7 and Interviewee I8, 2010). GAR also claimed that most hotspots and burnings on their concessions occurred before land preparation and were probably caused by slash-and-burn activity by the local villagers (Reksoprodjo, 2010: 2). Again, no official action was taken by the authorities. Notably, the high-profile hiring of Ambassador Hume as advisor, as mentioned above, occurred soon after Greenpeace's accusations made the news. Pundits have argued that Ambassador Hume was taken on board in hopes that he could assist in smoothing over these controversial NGO allegations due to his good connections with the Indonesian administration (Keen, 2010).

Indo Agri also had similar experiences. Indo Agri has a zero burning policy on the clearing of plantation estates. According to this policy, fully mechanized methods are deployed for the felling and stacking of trees during replanting and land clearing (Indo Food Agri Resources, 2010). However, an Indo Agri plantation was heavily criticized by NGOs for its alleged association with the 1997–1998 forest fires and illegal land clearing (Casson, 2006). In 2005 and 2006, fire hotspots were reportedly detected in four of Indo Agri's concessions in Riau, one of which was on peatlands (Greenpeace, 2007: 42; Walhi, 2010: 5). Despite repeated requests by NGOs for further official investigations, the government refused to take any action (Casson, 2006).

When authorities did conduct investigations, these investigations tend to often disappear into thin air (Udiansyah [I15], 2010) and very rarely reached the stage where companies are penalized (Witular, 2005: 624). Government agencies seem to prefer the persuasive approach to law enforcement rather than resorting to legal procedures when confronting plantation offenders (Gunawan, 1997). The Ministry of Forestry in fact had announced that the government did not plan to impose any penalties for land clearing but would merely continue to 'urge parties to stop the habit' (*Jakarta Post*, 2005b), despite zero burning regulations. Interviewees at the Ministry of Environment explained that usually if fires are detected, the company will merely be sent a show cause letter and the local authorities will be asked to go over to check the premises. However, only if fires are detected multiple times will court proceedings be even considered (Interviewee I7 and Interviewee I8, 2010). These reactions are weak compared to the officially sanctioned punishments described above, which involve serious fines and jail time.

For example, in the period of 1997 to 1998, 176 forest concessions and plantation companies operating mainly in Sumatra and Kalimantan were accused of using fire to clear land and were issued warnings by the government. The authorities investigated 13 companies, and five were taken to court (Saharjo *et al.*, 2003: 2), including one Malaysian-owned company (Interviewee M17, 2010). However, no company or individual was penalized (Parliament of Singapore, 1997). In 1999, 22 companies were identified for causing fires in their concession areas. Three were investigated, three others warned and two received light sanctions from the Ministry of Forestry. None of them were taken to court. In 2000, five companies in North Sumatra and one in West Kalimantan were investigated for similar offences, but again this did not culminate in court cases. In Riau, four plantation companies received first warnings from the Ministry of Forestry and one company received a second warning. The IUPs of the four plantation companies were revoked temporarily (Saharjo *et al.*, 2003: 2), but quickly reinstated.

In 2001, five plantation companies operating in Riau were taken to court for using fire to clear their concession areas (Saharjo *et al.*, 2003: 2). Two cases were dismissed due to 'difficulties in collecting evidence' (Bratasida [I36], 2010), while two others are pending indefinitely (Saharjo *et al.*, 2003: 2). In 2004, the Ministry of Environment handed over the names of five companies together with evidence to the national police to investigate further (*Jakarta Post*, 2004a), since the Ministry is not mandated to carry out legal investigation and enforcement

(Nguitragool, 2011: 372). However nothing came out of the police investigation. That same year, one company was brought to court over evidence that it had issued 12 letters, each ordering the clearing of 100 hectares of land using slash-and-burn methods at $70 per hectare. This provided proof that the fires were organized. However, this company was also not successfully prosecuted (Santoso and Naomy, 2004). And in 2006, an interviewee related a case where she, as an academic specializing in forest fires, was asked to assist in investigations for a suspected burning case in Central Kalimantan (Satyawan [I20], 2010). During investigations, they found evidence of oil in jerrycans, proof that the areas were purposefully and systematically burnt. The company representatives said that the fire spread from the villages, but the villages were found to be one hour away, too far to have caused the fires. The case was brought to court, but was later dropped for 'unknown reasons' (Satyawan [I20], 2010), most likely due to the close relationship that the company had with certain administrators.

An example of such inconclusive investigations includes plantations owned by Wilmar. Wilmar also claims to have a strict zero-burning policy in place as part of their sustainability commitments (Compliance Advisor Ombudsman, 2009: 3; Greenpeace, 2007: 53; Richardson, 2010: 69; Zakaria *et al.*, 2007: 5). Greenpeace found in 2006 to 2007 that in Central Kalimantan, 1,130 hotspots were detected on seven of Wilmar's concessions (Greenpeace, 2007: 21). Milieudefensie's study on three of Wilmar's plantations in West Kalimantan presented evidence that illegal burning was carried out with the purpose of clearing land. A total of 3,800 hectares of burning land were detected as occurring simultaneously while land clearing was underway. It was very likely that the smoke from these fires was a major contributor to the August 2006 episode of haze in the region. Outbreak of these fires was reported by Wilmar to the wrong authorities or not reported at all, and the freshly burnt land was quickly planted over with new palms. Milieudefensie had alerted the provincial Environmental Monitoring Agency and an official investigation team was formed. The team found Wilmar guilty of intentionally and systematically setting fire to the land with the intention to clear it for further plantation development. They also found that Wilmar companies did not have the required capacity to prevent and fight fires on their land (Guswanto [I28], 2010; *Jakarta Post*, 1994; Syaf [I27], 2010) including watch towers, water pumps and fire-fighting squads (Zakaria *et al.*, 2007: 25–26) as required by law (Syarif and Wibisana, 2007: 20; Zakaria *et al.*, 2007: 24). The team filed three lawsuits against Wilmar in the district courts in November 2006. However, it was reported that the investigating team only charged Wilmar for smaller fires of only around 30 hectares and not bigger ones which were detected earlier. It was reported that, like other companies, Wilmar did not deny that these fires took place, but instead blamed neighbouring plantations and local farmers for starting them. These arguments were found to be flawed as no new oil palm plantings were affected by these supposed 'accidental' fires. However, as is typical with most court cases involving well-connected oil palm plantations, these cases have never been brought to court, the official reason given being 'limited human resources' to do so (Zakaria *et al.*, 2007: 25–26).

Malaysia's KLK is one of the few companies that have ever been successfully prosecuted for open burning in Indonesia thus far (Surya [I9] and Akbar [I10], 2010; Syaf [I27], 2010; Syarif [I2], 2010). A KLK subsidiary plantation, PT API, was found guilty for illegal burning under the EMA 1997 in 2001 (Saharjo *et al.*, 2003: 2). KLK claims to be enforcing a zero-burning policy in all its new planting and replanting activities to prevent smoke pollution and carbon dioxide emissions so as to maintain the air quality of surrounding areas (Kuala Lumpur Kepong Berhad, 2010). When fires broke out within PT API during the haze season of 2000, the Riau Provincial Justice Team conducted a field investigation that indicated that PT API was responsible for the fires (Saharjo *et al.*, 2003: 2). While the company blamed smallholders, investigators dismissed this excuse as the fires were on PT API's land concession, and PT API was responsible regardless of who started them.[9] Indeed, interviewees detailed how investigators found the company's planning book, which showed that plans to open the land matched the schedule of the fires. Also, the company's budget report for land clearing was very low, which did not match the expenses required for mechanical clearing (Interviewee I7 and Interviewee I8, 2010).

The case was handed to the public prosecutor, who prepared the indictment and took the company to court. After a long trial process, the company was found guilty in October 2001. The general manager of the company, Mr C. Gobi, was sentenced to a two-year imprisonment and the company was fined $27,600. However, on 11 February 2002, the High Court reduced the sentence to eight months and the fine to $11,000 on appeal by the company (Saharjo *et al.*, 2003: 2), on the grounds that the element of 'deliberate' or 'intentional' burning could not be proven, as required by the EMA (Syarif and Wibisana, 2007: 31). The Supreme Court then upheld this decision at the end of 2002 (Saharjo *et al.*, 2003: 2). However, the prosecutors were not happy with the decision, as in their view, the ruling was too lenient (Syarif and Wibisana, 2007: 31). Indeed, this ruling was far below the minimum jail term and fine as stipulated under the EMA 1997. As mentioned above, penalties for commercial open burning based on the EMA should start at a minimum of five year jail terms and a fine of $5,000 (Syarif and Wibisana, 2007: 20). This most likely could have been because of undue influence on the courts by prominent Indonesian lawyer Al Hakim Hanafiah who is in partnership with KLK over PT API (Saharjo *et al.*, 2003: 3). Another of PT API's general managers was again found guilty for causing forest fires in 2014, and the sentence is currently suspended pending appeal (*The Star*, 2014).

While PT API is the only commercial palm oil company that so far has been successfully prosecuted, another case that deserves mention occurred in January 2014. An Indonesian court found PT Kallista Alam guilty of burning large areas of protected peat forests in Tripa to establish oil palm plantations. The company was instructed to pay $9.4 million in compensation and $20.8 million to restore the affected areas. The case remains under appeal (Gartland, 2014), so its final outcome is unclear at time of writing. However, the lack of similar cases like this that have been successfully brought to court over the years underlines the problems related to prosecutions in the sector.

Hence, with patronage, patrons are encouraged to protect their clients from the repercussions of their actions instead of upholding law. This weakens the power of the state in terms of law enforcement, where national laws against the use of fire are rendered useless in the face of powerful economic interests. Therefore, well-connected companies are able to continue to use fire as a cost-efficient way to clear land while disregarding its serious environmental and socioeconomic implications.

Ineffective revisions of burning laws maintains status quo

The latest revisions to the Indonesian environmental law attempt to address the confusions and uncertainties that limit the effective implementation of burning laws in Indonesia, as discussed earlier. The new EMA of 2009 attempts to integrate and harmonize central, provincial and district governments' responsibilities on environmental management (Syarif, 2010: 8–10). It also tightens laws and penalties for commercial open burning. Under the EMA 2009, every person is prohibited from using fire for land clearing purposes, and whosoever intentionally breaches the standards of environmental damage by committing acts that violate the ambient air, water and sea water shall be criminally liable to imprisonment (a minimum of three to a maximum of ten years) and fines (a minimum of $330,000 to a maximum of $1.1 million) (Syarif, 2010: 16–17). If the act is found to cause injury or death, this can be increased to a maximum of 15 years imprisonment and $1.7 million. For cases of negligence, fines and imprisonments are set at a maximum of three years or $330,000. If the order for burning can be traced back to an individual (or the leader of the company), that individual is criminally liable for the act. If the perpetrator is a company, imprisonment and fines will be increased by one third of the maximum penalty (Syarif, 2010: 16–17). However, despite these revisions, the Ministry of Environment still does not have any power to coerce other central or local agencies to comply with any requirements or expectations. Thus, the implementation of the abovementioned laws will still mainly hinge on the willingness of these agencies to enforce them (Syarif, 2010: 8–10).

As a result, fires continue to be detected on the concessions of major plantation companies to the present day. Outgoing President Susilo Bambang Yudhoyono himself recently estimated that 70 per cent of these fires were lit by such landowners wanting to clear ground for more plantations (Vidal, 2014). In 2011, there was illegal commercial land clearing by fire in Jambi, Riau and West Kalimantan, Central Kalimantan and South Sumatra (Arif [I41], 2011; Interviewee I48, 2011; Surya [I9] and Akbar [I10], 2010; Tarigan [I23], 2010), including, as interviewees detailed, on Duta Palma (Interviewee I48, 2011) and Makin Group plantations (Syaf [I27], 2010). However, most companies did not receive any serious negative backlash from this. Some companies only received a warning letter from the local governments (Arif [I41], 2011), while others were slapped with a token small fine (Casey [I46], 2011; Interviewee I48, 2011), and no further action was taken (Interviewee I48, 2011).

Powerful companies with good patronage ties therefore have no reason to fear punishment (Kurer, 1996: 645–661). Indeed, very few big industry players or their related businesses have been successfully prosecuted in court (*Jakarta Post*, 2006a; Udiansyah [I15], 2010). Hence, well-connected plantation companies often act like they are above the law. For example, according to Indonesian law as detailed above, plantations are obliged to monitor and report fire outbreaks twice yearly to the Governor's Office, district head, the mayor and other technical institutions. However, an interviewee from Greenpeace said this is not happening (Interviewee S19, 2010). Also, many concessionaires have been found to have flouted the legal requirement of keeping fire-fighters and equipment ready on their plantations (Syaf [I27], 2010). Furthermore, the Ministry of Environment was particularly constrained because it is only able to *monitor* companies, and not actually enforce any of the regulations. Former Environment Minister Sarwono complained that throughout the haze crises, many plantation owners simply ignored the concerns raised by his Ministry with regards to fire control, often inferring that their political connections would protect them against any action that the Ministry would decide to take against them (Dauvergne, 1998: 13–17). As a result, environmental regulations on burning are flouted with impunity.

Conclusion

This chapter has identified two major drivers of transboundary haze: first, through the unsustainable conversion of fire-prone peatlands into plantation land, and second, through illegal commercial open burning to prepare land for planting. Well-connected local and foreign plantation companies are able to get away with both of these activities due to their strong patronage networks within the sector. Haze is a result of corporate decisions made to ensure cost effectiveness and competitiveness within the sector. As Cotton (1999: 341–342) has argued previously in the context of logging concessionaires, this chapter pointed out that patronage politics in the context of oil palm plantation companies has affected state autonomy and policy choices, resulting in weak state capacity and policy paralysis within the oil palm plantation sector. This analysis refines the previously proffered arguments by scholars such as Eaton and Radojevic (2001: 248), Aiken (2004: 74) and Thompson (2001: 17) that focus on flawed public policy as the major explanation for haze. While the above discussion has shown that some Indonesian policies related to fires and haze are to some extent flawed, other policies are in fact quite stringent; however even these stringent ones are susceptible to policy paralysis in the hands of opportunistic patrons and clients. This chapter has shown that patronage networks within the sector are an important explanation for the continued haze, despite stringent policies.

As explained above, ruling elites took the interests of these well-connected companies seriously because industry support was important in maintaining their political power base. Therefore, due to the overwhelming influence of local patronage networks, this chapter noted that there seems to be no political will within Indonesia to seriously address the fire and haze problem. For example, despite the drastic toll on the regional environment, the Indonesian environment minister admitted that the fires were at most fifth on the national agenda (Hudiono, 2003; Satyawan [I20], 2010). As elaborated through examples throughout the chapter, specific use of bureaucratic instruments by the elites in favour of their clients has compromised and undermined the rational-legal capacity of the state to deal with the problem. As one interviewee succinctly put it, 'everybody understands the problem and what needs to be done, but the problem lies with the strong linkages between powerful stakeholders and different levels of government' (Interviewee S18, 2010).

Therefore, the persistence of the haze can be explained as a case of public officers misusing positions and resources of public office by giving priority to their own self-interest or to a client's interest at the expense of public interest. As such, it becomes obvious that a free-rider problem exists. While haze costs the Indonesian society up to 4.5 per cent of Indonesia's GDP, as discussed in Chapter 2, the 7 per cent GDP that the oil palm industry contributes to the Indonesian economy (see Figure 2.6) takes priority because the patronage system within this sector means that the government would not necessarily make decisions based on what is rational at the level of society, but instead would make decisions that would benefit the well-connected minority. Therefore, well-connected clients unfairly multiply their income and investments while environmental costs are all ultimately passed on to the Indonesian and Southeast Asian societies in the form of the haze.

This chapter and the previous chapter collectively have discussed the two distinct drivers of regionalization in the Southeast Asian context: the role of the state as facilitator and similar patronage cultures. It has shown that these factors have also been important drivers of regional haze. In this sense, this book notes that the regional haze is driven by the economic regionalization of Indonesian, Malaysian and Singaporean commercial oil palm plantation actors, focusing their activities in Indonesia. The high levels of government facilitation encouraging regional integration of this sector, coupled with the ubiquitous atmosphere of patronage on the ground in Indonesia, have enabled both local and foreign companies to carry out their operations with impunity. Despite clear links being drawn between the activities of these companies and transboundary haze, plantation companies have not viewed the transnational effects of haze and its mitigation as a priority, and have continued with business-as-usual. As discussed in Chapter 1, this is unsurprising, as economic regionalization does not presuppose any specific impact on relations between states within the region. Instead, most haze mitigation activities have been ASEAN-level projects. While the *source* of the haze has its roots in intense economic regionalization in the oil palm sector, ASEAN states have elected for *solutions* that were rooted in political regionalism. However, as the following chapter expounds, the nature of ASEAN regionalism has allowed patronage politics to wield influence at the ASEAN level, ensuring that ASEAN's organizational capacity is also weakened, which results in ASEAN initiatives that continue to favour corporate interests, which further explains the persistence of the haze.

Notes

1 Parts of this chapter have appeared in Varkkey (2012, 2013a, 2013b).
2 Much of the patronage politics literature is written in gendered language, referring to patrons and clients as generally male. Of course, this may not be the case in reality. However, for the purposes of this book, the gendered language is largely maintained in line with the literature.
3 While this book acknowledges that Singapore consistently has scored among the highest in the world in Transparency International's Corruption Perceptions Index (tied with Norway at fifth in the latest list in 2013), it notes that this perception may not be entirely accurate, especially in terms of regional oil palm investments, based on evidence presented throughout this book (Transparency International, 2013).
4 Aspinall and Van Klinken's concept of state illegality relates to the idea that although it is the state that defines what is legal and illegal, in reality state officials themselves are frequently implicated in various kinds of illegality. Sometimes, these illegalities serve useful functions to certain sectors of society, and as a result, such illegality is sometimes viewed as legitimate by these sectors of society.
5 During this era, the central government's budgetary allocations for the military (and their timeliness in supplying these funds) were not able to meet the Indonesian military's revenue needs (Crouch, 1984: 84; Robison, 1986: 255). At the same time, the better-capitalized, more experienced Chinese businessmen and foreign investors (Ross, 2001: 161) were facing difficulties in securing governmental contracts and needed access which military officers could provide. This situation encouraged military elites to engage in tripartite joint ventures with these businessmen and investors (Crouch, 1984: 84–85). These elites often sat as directors on the boards of these companies (Robison, 1986: 256), but usually did not contribute any capital or managerial skills. However, they were able to exert direct corporate control over strategic sectors of the economy (Robison, 1986: 258) by offering their partners access to the central bureaucracy to obtain government licenses, credit, tax breaks, contracts, monopoly concessions, exemptions from onerous regulations and even personal protection (Crouch, 1984: 82; Ross, 2001: 161). This was especially rampant in the forestry industry, particularly timber. The military was very successful in obtaining logging concessions for their business partners, in return for a share of the profits generated from its exploitation and some management experience for their own enterprises (Robison, 1986: 256; Ross, 2001: 161). And even though only a small percentage of these companies met the conditions of their concessions (including restrictions on the sizes and numbers of trees, replanting requirements, royalties and the setting up of sawmills), little or no action was taken upon those who did not, thanks to their strong military backing (Crouch, 1984: 86). This resulted in virtually unrestrained exploitation and export of logs in the 1970s (Robison, 1986: 257), during which timber became Indonesia's second major export after oil (Crouch, 1984: 86). These arrangements were not only a source of revenue for the military but officers also found it as a handy way to increase their own political power, personal wealth, and to facilitate their personal entry into the Indonesian capitalist class. Hence, the military had a deep vested interest in perpetuating the conditions conducive to this sort of limited access to markets and resources, to facilitate their own accumulation of capital and the generation of profits (Robison, 1986: 255–258).
6 GAPKI membership is made up of 382 local and foreign commercial plantations (GAPKI, 2010).
7 Rural city, one step lower than province in Indonesia.
8 While foreign firms that intend to enter into markets where patronage politics plays an important role will often attempt to engage in similar practices (Enderwick, 2005: 129; Hamilton-Hart, 2005: 171), these firms will usually continue to display distinctive features of their home country in their business dealings in the new host country

(Doremus *et al.*, 1999: 1999). Hence, other foreign countries, like those from the Netherlands, Switzerland and the USA that also operate in Indonesia, have generally not been able to fully integrate themselves into local patronage networks, a largely Asian characteristic (Enderwick, 2005: 129). Because of this, they do not have the liberty to act with impunity on the ground, and thus have only very rarely been linked to fire and other environmental damage in Indonesia (Interviewee I48, 2011; Rolland [I50], 2011).

9 This pattern of commercial plantations blaming smallholders for starting fires is fairly common. Companies usually either say that fires on their land spread from neighbouring independent smallholder estates, or that smallholder running estates on their concessions under the 'nucleus-plasma' scheme started the fires. However these excuses are questionable, because as mentioned above, plantation companies have been known to trespass and burn villager's land beside their concessions and let the fires spread to their land as a way to circumvent laws (Interviewee I25, 2010; Syarif [I2], 2010). And, for the case of plasma estates, the plantation company is responsible for all activity on their concession land (Interviewee I7 and Interviewee I8, 2010). Hence, it is the legal responsibility of the company to educate the farmers linked to their plantations to not use fire and to ensure that this rule is upheld.

References

Abdullah, A. 2002. *A Review and Analysis of Legal and Regulatory Aspects of Forest Fires in South East Asia.* Jakarta: Project Fire Fight South East Asia.

Aiken, S. R. 2004. Runaway fires, smoke-haze pollution, and unnnatural disasters in Indonesia. *Geographical Review*, 94, 55.

Al-Sadig, A. 2009. The effects of corruption on FDI inflows. *Cato Journal*, 29, 267–269.

Albar [I17], I. 13 July 2010. *RE: Head, Directorate of Forest Fire Control, Ministry of Forestry.*

Anshari [I42], G. Z. 9 November 2011. *RE: Center for Wetlands People and Biodiversity, Universitas Tanjungpura.*

Arif [I41], J. 4 November 2011. *RE: Forest Campaigner, Greenpeace Southeast Asia.*

Ascher, W. 1998. From oil to timber: The political economy of off-budget development financing in Indonesia. *Indonesia*, 65, 37–61.

Aspinall, E. 2010. The Irony of Success. *Journal of Democracy*, 21, 20–34.

Aspinall, E. and Van Klinken, G. 2011. The state and illegality in Indonesia. *In:* Aspinall, E. and Van Klinken, G. (eds) *The State and Illegality in Indonesia.* Leiden: KITLV Press.

Bakrie Brothers 2010. *Annual Report.* Indonesia: Bakrie Brothers.

Barr, C. M. 1998. Bob Hasan, the rise of Apkindo, and the shifting dynamics of control in Indonesia's timber sector. *Indonesia*, 65, 1–36.

Boer, R., Nurrochmat, D. R., Ardiansyah, M., Hariyadi, Purwawangsa, H. and Ginting, G. 2012. Indonesia: Analysis of implementation and financing gaps *Project Report.* Bogor: Center for Climate Risk and Opportunity Management, Bogor Agricultural University

Bowen, R., Bompard, J. M., Anderson, I. P., Guizol, P. and Gouyon, A. 2001. Anthropogenic fires in Indonesia: A view from Sumatra. *In:* Eaton, P. and Radojevic, M. (eds) *Forest Fires and Haze in South East Asia.* New York: Nova Science Publishers.

Bratasida [I36], L. 29 July 2010. *RE: Assistant Minister of Global Environmental Affairs and International Cooperation, Ministry of Environment.*

Brinkerhoff, D. W. and Goldsmith, A. A. 2004. Good governance, clientelism, and patrimonialism: New perspectives on old problems. *International Public Management Journal*, 2004, 2, 163–182.
Brown, R. A. 2006. Indonesian corporations, cronysim, and corruption. *Modern Asian Studies*, 40, 953–992.
Butler, R. A., Lian, P. K. and Ghazoul, J. 2009. REDD in the red: Palm oil could undermine carbon payment scheme. *Conservations Letters*, 2, 67–73.
Case, W. 2003. Interlocking elites in Southeast Asia. *Comparative Sociology*, 2, 249–267.
Casey [I46], M. 22 November 2011. *RE: Writer, Associate Press.*
Casson, A. 2006. Decentralisation, forests and estate crops in Kutai Barat District, East Kalimantan. *In:* COOKE, F. M. (ed.) *State, Communities and Forests in Contemporary Boreno.* Canberra: The Australian National University E Press.
Chalil, D. 2008. An Empirical Analysis of Assymetric Duopoly in the Indonesian Crude Palm Oil Industry. PhD thesis, University of Sydney.
Chee [M27], T. Y. 14 April 2010. *RE: Manager, Global Environment Center.*
Cho, Y. 1994. *Effects of Indonesia Forest Fire.* Available: www1.american.edu/TED/indofire.htm [accessed 8 August 2014].
Colfer, C. J. P. 2002. Ten propositions to explain Kalimantan's fires. *In:* Colfer, C. J. and Resosudarmo, I. A. P. (eds) *Which Way Forward? People, forests and policymaking in Indonesia.* Singapore: Institute of Southeast Asian Studies.
Compliance Advisor Ombudsman 2009. *Complaint from Communities in Kalimantan and Civil Society in relation to activities of the Wilmar Group of Companies.* Final Ombudsman Assessment Report. Jakarta: Multilateral Investment Guarantee Agency.
Cotton, J. 1999. The 'haze' over Southeast Asia: Challenging the ASEAN mode of regional engagement. *Pacific Affairs*, 72, 331–351.
Crouch, H. 1984. *Domestic and Political Structures and Regional Economic Cooperation,* Singapore, Institute of Southeast Asian Studies.
Dauvergne, P. 1994. The politics of deforestation in Indonesia. *Pacific Affairs*, 66, 497–518.
Dauvergne, P. 1998. The political economy of Indonesia's 1997 forest fires. *Australian Journal of International Affairs*, 52, 13–17.
Dauvergne, P. J. M. 1995. Shadows in the Forest: Japan and the politics of timber in Southeast Asia. Doctor of Philosophy thesis, University of British Columbia.
Di, S. 2011. Tread Cautiously. *Indo Plantations Sector Outlook.* Jakarta: CLSA Asia Pacific Markets.
Dieleman, M. 2010. Shock-imprinting: External shocks and ethnic Chinese business groups in Indonesia. *Asia pacific Journal of Management*, 27, 481–502.
Dieleman, M. and Sachs, W. 2006. Oscillating between a relationship-based and a market-based model: The Salim Group. *Asia Pacific Journal of Management*, 23, 521–536.
Dieleman, M. and Sachs, W. 2008a. Reluctant internationalization: The case of the Salim Group. *In:* Suryadinata, L. (ed.) *Ethnic Chinese in Contemporary Indonesia.* Singapore: Institute for South East Asian Studies.
Dieleman, M. and Sachs, W. M. 2008b. Economies of connectedness: Concept and application. *Journal of International Management*, 14, 270–285.
Doremus, P. N., Keller, W. W., Payly, L. W. and Reich, S. 1999. *The Myth of the Global Corporation*, Princeton, Princeton University Press.
Duncan, C. R. 2007. Mixed outcomes: The impact of regional autonomy and decentralization on indegenous ethnic minorities in Indonesia. *Development and Change*, 438, 711–733.
Eaton, P. and Radojevic, R. 2001. *Forest Fires and Regional Haze in Southeast Asia*, New

York, Nova Science Publishers, Inc.
Eisenstadt, S. N. and Roniger, L. 1995. Patron-client relations as a model of structuring social exchange. *In:* Eisenstadt, S. N. (ed.) *Power, Trust, and Meaning: Essays in Sociological Theory and Analysis.* Chicago: The University of Chicago Press.
Eklof, S. 2002. Politics, business, and democratization in Indonesia. *In:* Gomez, E. T. (ed.) *Political business in East Asia.* New York: Routledge.
Enderwick, P. 2005. What's bad about crony capitalism? *Asian Business and Management*, 4, 117–132.
Fan, S., Lin, C. and Treisman, D. 2009. Political decentralization and corruption: Evidence from around the world. *Journal of Public Economics*, 93, 14–34.
Gapki 2010. *About: Introduction*. Available: www.gapki.or.id/ [accessed 19 August 2011].
GAR and SMART 2013. *GAR and SMART Firmly Commit to Zero Burning Policy*. GAR Holding Statement. Singapore: Golden Agri.
Garcia-Guadilla, M. P. 2002. Democracy, decentralization, and clientelism: New relationships and old practises. *Latin American Perspectives*, 29, 90–109.
Gartland, A. 2014. Palm oil company fined millions for burning Sumatran rainforest. *ENS Newswire*, 12 January 2014.
Ghani [S6], A. 17 May 2010. *RE: former Straits Times Press Reporter.*
Gilbert, D. 2009. *Duta Palma's Filthy Supply Chain: A case study of a palm oil supplier in Indonesi*a. San Francisco: Rainforest Action Network.
Goh, M. L., Sikorski, D. and Wong, W. K. 2001. Government policy for outward investment by domestic firms: The case of Singapore's regionalization strategy. *Singapore Management Review*, 23–42.
Golden-Agri Resources Ltd 2010. *Annual Report*. Singapore: Golden Agri-Resources Ltd.
Gomez, E. T. 2009. The rise and call of capital: Corporate Malaysia in historical perspective. *Journal of Contemporary Asia*, 39, 345–381.
Greenpeace 2007. *How the Palm Oil Industry is Cooking the Climate*. Jakarta: Greenpeace.
Gunarso, P., Hartoyo, M. E., Agus, F. and Killeen, T. J. 2013. Oil Palm and Land Use Change in Indonesia, Malaysia and Papua New Guinea. *Reports from the Technical Panels of the 2nd Greenhouse Gas Working Group*. Roundtable on Sustainable Palm Oil.
Gunawan, T. S. 1997. Environmental campaign ruled by forest fires. *Jakarta Post*, 26 December 1994.
Gunes-Ayata, A. 1994. Clientelism: Premodern, modern, postmodern. *In:* Roniger, L. and Gunes-Ayata, A. (eds) *Democracy, Clientelism, and Civil Society.* London: Lynne Rienner Publishers.
Guswanto [I28]. 26 July 2010. *RE: Senior Administrator of Research and Development, Meteorology, Climatology and Geophysics Agency.*
Hadiz, V. R. 2004. Decentralization and democracy in Indonesia: A critique of institutionalist perspectives. *Development and Change*, 35, 697–718.
Hadiz, V. R. 2007. The localization of power in Southeast Asia. *Democratization*, 14, 873–892.
Hadiz, V. R. and Robison, R. 2005. Neo-liberal reforms and illiberal consolidations: The Indonesian paradox. *Journal of Development Studies*, 41, 220–241.
Haji Mat Zin, R. 1999. Malaysian reverse investments: Trends and strategies. *Asia Pacific Journal of Management*, 16, 469–496.
Hameiri, S. and Jones, L. 2013. The politics and governance of non-traditional security. *International Studies Quarterly*, 57, 462–473.

Hamilton-Hart, N. 2005. The regionalization on Southeast Asian businesses: Transnational networks in national contexts. *In:* Pempel, T. J. (ed.) *Remapping East Asia: The Construction of a Region.* Ithaca: Cornell University Press.
Hamilton-Hart, N. 2007. Government and private business: Rents, representation and collective action. *In:* McLeod, R. H. and Macintyre, A. (eds) *Indonesia: Democracy and the promise of good governance.* Singapore: Institute of Southeast Asian Studies.
Harahap, R. 2008. Govt urged to review forest concessions in Riau. *Jakarta Post*, 14 May 2008.
Hariri [I30], D. and Ardiansyah [I31], I. 27 July 2010. *RE: WWF-Indonesia.*
Hedradjat [I14], N. 8 July 2010 2010. *RE: Director of Crop Protection, Ministry of Agriculture.*
Hicken, A. 2011. Clientelism. *Annual Review of Political Science*, 14, 289–310.
Hudiono, U. 2003. RI missing out on ASEAN haze agreement: Activist. *Jakarta Post*, 3 December 2003.
Hunt, C. 2010. The costs of reducing deforestation in Indonesia. *Bulletin of Indonesian Economic Studies*, 46, 187–192.
Hurst, P. 1987. Forest destruction in South East Asia. *Ecologist*, 17, 170–174.
Indo Food Agri Resources 2010. *Annual Report.* Singapore: Indo Food Agri Resources.
Interviewee I6. 27 June 2010. *RE: formerly of Greenpeace-South East Asia.*
Interviewee I7 and Interviewee I8. 28 June 2010. *RE: Ministry of Environment.*
Interviewee I18. 14 July 2010. *RE: National Council on Climate Change.*
Interviewee I21. 16 July 2010. *RE: Telapak.*
Interviewee I25. 20 July 2010. *RE: Channel NewsAsia.*
Interviewee I47. 28 November 2011. *RE: Burung Indonesia.*
Interviewee I48. 30 November 2011. *RE: Fauna Flora International.*
Interviewee I49. 1 December 2011. *RE: Leuser Foundation.*
Interviewee M15. 29 March 2010. *RE: former Environmental Reporter, The Star.*
Interviewee M17. 1 April 2010. *RE: Department of Environment.*
Interviewee M28. 14 April 2010. *RE: TH Plantations.*
Interviewee M36. 28 April 2010. *RE: Lecturer, Monash University Sunday Campus.*
Interviewee M44. 5 January 2012. *RE: Global Environment Center.*
Interviewee M45, Interviewee M46, Interviewee M47 and Interviewee M48. 17 January 2012. *RE: Plantation Sustainability Department, Sime Darby.*
Interviewee M55. 31 January 2012. *RE: Maybank Investment Bank.*
Interviewee S14 and Interviewee S15. 19 May 2010. *RE: Ministry of Environment and Water Resources.*
Interviewee S18. 26 May 2010. *RE: Conservation International.*
Interviewee S19. 26 May 2010. *RE: Straits Times Press.*
Jakarta Post 1987. Indonesia's environment. *Jakarta Post*, 24 September 1987.
Jakarta Post 1994. Kalimantan, Sumatra forest fires turn into blaming game. *Jakarta Post*, 3 October 1994.
Jakarta Post 1997. When haze becomes hazier. *Jakarta Post*, 11 September 1997.
Jakarta Post 2000. Riau authorities fed up with continuing forest fires. *Jakarta Post*, 20 July 2000.
Jakarta Post 2004a. Government prepares lawsuits against firms over fires. *Jakarta Post*, 25 June 2004.
Jakarta Post 2004b. Haze endures despite rainfall. *Jakarta Post*, 28 June 2004.
Jakarta Post 2005a. Govt moves against firms responsible for forest fires. *Jakarta Post*, 13 August 2005.

Jakarta Post 2005b. Malaysia and Indonesia agree to battle fires, haze. *Jakarta Post*, 12 August 2005.

Jakarta Post 2006a. A bad neighbour. *Jakarta Post*, 10 October 2006.

Jakarta Post 2006b. New Depok mayor questioned in corruption case. *Jakarta Post*, 15 March 2006.

Jakarta Post 2006c. Pests devastate Jambi harvests. *Jakarta Post*, 16 June 2006.

Jakarta Post 2006d. Smothering Kalimantan waits for rains. *Jakarta Post*, 2 November 2006.

Jakarta Post 2006e. Stricter law urged to tackle haze. *Jakarta Post*, 16 October 2006.

Jakarta Post 2011. Groups suspect graft in plantations. *Jakarta Post*, 7 June 2011.

Jhamtani, H. 1998. *Forest and land fires in Indonesia: An evaluation of factors and management efforts.* International cross sectoral forum on forest fire management in South East Asia, 1998 Jakarta. National Development Planning Agency, Indonesia.

Johnston, M. 2005. *Syndromes of Corruption: Wealth, Power and Democracy,* New York, Cambridge University Press.

Kaat, A. and Silvius, M. 2011. *Impacts of biofuel demands on carbon dioxide emissions from peatlands*. Jakarta: Wetlands International.

Kamaruddin [M26], H. 13 April 2010 2010. *RE: Lecturer, Faculty of Law, UKM.*

Keen, M. 2010. Sinar Mas intends to regain image. *Climate Action*, 14 December 2010.

Knutsen, C. H. 2013. Democracy, state capacity, and economic growth. *World Development*, 43, 1–18.

Krezdorn [I32], R. 27 July 2010. *RE: Programme Director, German Technical Coperation.*

Kuala Lumpur Kepong Berhad 2010. *Annual Report.* Ipoh: Kuala Lumpung Kepong Berhad.

Kurer, O. 1996. The political foundations of economic development policies. *Journal of Development Studies*, 32, 645–668.

Lande, C. H. 1983. Political clientelism in political studies: Retrospect and prospects. *International Political Science Review*, 4, 435–454.

Larson, A. M. and Soto, F. 2008. Decentralization of natural resources governance regimes. *Annual Review of Environment and Resources*, 33, 213–239.

Laurance, W. F., Koh, L. P., Butler, R., Sodhi, N. S., Bradshaw, C. J. A., Neidel, J. D., Consunji, H. and Vega, J. M. 2010. Improving the performance of the Roundtable on Sustainable Palm Oil for Nature Conservation. *Conservation Biology*, 24, 377–381.

Lawrence [I38], P. 27 November 2011. *RE: Researcher, Ecostrategy.*

Lee [S20], P. O. 26 May 2010. *RE: Fellow, Regional Economic Studies, Institute for South East Asian Studies.*

Lew [M6], S. and Interviewee M7. 18 March 2010. *RE: Peatland Programme, Global Environment Center.*

Lim [S13], M. A. 18 May 2010. *RE: Manager, Policy Research, Singapore Institute of International Affairs.*

Lim, L. Y. C. and Stern, A. 2003. State power and private profit: the political economy of corruption in Southeast Asia. *Asian-Pacific Economic Literature*, 16, 18–52.

Lipsey, R. E. and Sjoholm, F. 2011. Foreign direct investment and growth in East Asia: Lessons for Indonesia. *Bulletin of Indonesian Economic Studies*, 47, 35–63.

Maitar [I12], B. 2 July 2010. *RE: Forest Campaign Team Leader, Greenpeace-Southeast Asia.*

Maitar, B. 2008. Sinar Mas: Indonesian palm oil menace. *Briefing*. Jakarta: Greenpeace.

Masripatin, N., Rufi'ie, Ginoga, K., Gintings, N., Siregar, C. A., Sugardiman, R., Wibowo, A., Darmawan, W. S., Rahman, S., Maryani, R., Pribadi, A., Nurfatriani, F., Puspasari,

D., Imamnudin, R. and Pradjadinata, S. 2009. *National Strategy: Reducing Emissions from Deforestation and Forest Degradation in Indonesia, Readiness Phase Draft – August 2009*. Jakarta: Ministry of Forestry.

Mayer, J. 2006. Transboundary perspectives on managing Indonesia's fires. *The Journal of Environment and Development*, 15, 202–233.

McCarthy, J. and Cramb, R. A. 2009. Policy narratives, landholder engagement, and oil palm expansion on the Malaysian and Indonesian frontiers. *The Geographical Journal*, 175, 112–123.

Mccarthy, J. and Zen, Z. 2010. Regulating the oil palm boom: Asessing the effectiveness of environmental governance approaches to agro-industrial pollution in Indonesia. *Law and Policy*, 32, 153–179.

McCarthy, J. F. 2002. Power and interest on Sumatra's rainforest frontier: Clientelist coalitions, illegal logging and conservation in the Alas Valley. *Journal of Southeast Asian Studies*, 33, 77–106.

McCarthy, J. F., Gillespie, P. and Zen, Z. 2012. Swimming upstream: Local Indonesian production networks in 'globalized' palm oil production. *World Development*, 40, 555–569.

Milieudefensie 2010a. *Milieudefensie's Response to IOI's Rebuttal in Substance*. Jakarta: Milieudefensie.

Milieudefensie 2010b. *Too green to be true: IOI Corporation in Ketapang District, West Kalimantan*. Amsterdam: Milieudefensie.

Mohd Kassim [M3], Z. 8 March 2010. *RE: Assistant Director General (Operations), Fire and Rescue Department*.

Moore [I5], P. F. 27 June 2010. *RE: Project Manager, IUCN-WWF Project Firefight Southeast Asia*.

Munadar, A., Ruth, D. and Putra, A. 2010. Rejection REDD Plus program Australia-Indonesia in Jambi. *Position Paper*. Jambi: Regional Executive WALHI Jambi.

Neher, C. D. 1994. Asian style democracy. *Asian Survey*, 34, 949–961.

Nguitragool, P. 2011. Negotiating the haze treaty. *Asian Survey*, 51, 356–378.

Norhashim, M. and Ab. Aziz, K. 2005. Smart partnership or cronyism? A Malaysian perspective. *International Journal of Sociology and Social Policy*, 25, 31–48.

Obidzinski, K. and Barr, C. M. 2003. *The Effects Decentralization on Forests and Forest Industries in Berau District, East Kalimantan,* Bogor Barat, Center for International Forestry Research.

Palmer, C. and Engel, S. 2007. For better or for worser? Local impacts of the decentralization of Indonesia's forest sector. *World Development*, 35, 2131–2149.

Paneco Foundation 2008. *Vanishing Tripa: The continuous destruction of a unique ecosystem by palm oil plantations*. Banda Aceh: PanEco Foundation.

Parliament of Singapore 1997. Haze (1997-10-07). Singapore.

Parliament of Singapore 1998. Haze pollution (motion) (1998-06-30). Singapore.

Parliament of Singapore 1999. Fires and haze from Indonesia (1999-05-04). Singapore.

Parliament of Singapore 2000. Fires in Indonesia (2000-03-13). Singapore.

Peters [I1], E. 13 April 2010. *RE: Sinarmas Group*.

Pratono, H. 2009. *Indonesia oil palm plantation*. Surabaya: Universitas Surabaya. Available: http://30205z.blogspot.com/2009_04_01_archive.html [accessed 9 August 2011].

Rajenthran, A. 2002. *Indonesia: An overview of the legal framework of foreign direct investment.* ISEAS Working Papers: Economics and Finance. Singapore: Institute of Southeast Asian Studies.

Ramakrishna [M20], S. 7 April 2010. *RE: Coordinator, Malaysian Environmental NGOs.*
Reksoprodjo, F. 2010. Independent verification reveals Greenpeace claims are exaggerated or wrong. *Press release.* Jakarta: SMART Agribusiness and Food.
Reuters 2011. Indonesia's SMART says Unilever resumes palm oil buys. *Reuters*, 18 October 2010.
Richardson, C. L. 2010. *Deforestation due to palm oil plantations in Indonesia. Towards the Sustainable Production of Palm Oil.* Australia.
Robison, R. 1986. *Indonesia: The Rise of Capital*, Sydney, Allen & Unwin.
Rolland [I50], D. 7 December 2011. *RE: Former staff of Rimbunan Hijau.*
Rondonuwu, O. 2011. Indonesia divided over forest moratorium, misses Jan start. *Reuters*, 6 January 2011.
Rose-Ackerman, S. 2008. Corruption and government. *International Peacekeeping*, 15, 328–343.
Ross, M. L. 2001. *Timber Booms and Institutional Breakdown in Southeast Asia*, Cape Town, Cambridge University Press.
Rowland [I39], I. 3 November 2011. *RE: Tropical Forest Conservation Manager, The Royal Society for the Protection of Birds.*
Rukmantara [I45], A. 14 November 2011. *RE: Former environmental journalist, Jakarta Post.*
Rukmantara, A. 2006a. 'We must do more to educate people about open burning'. *Jakarta Post*, 4 September 2006.
Rukmantara, T. A. 2006b. New Borneo fires raise haze threat. *Jakarta Post*, 14 August 2006.
Saharjo, B. H. 1999. The role of human activities in Indonesian forest fire problems. *In:* Suhartoyo, H. and Toma, T. (eds) *Impacts of Fire and Human Activities on Forest Ecosystems in the Tropics*. Samarinda, Indonesia: Tropical Forest Research Center, Mulawarman University.
Saharjo, B. H., Danny, W., Moore, P. F. and Simorangkir, D. 2003. *Convicting forest and and fire offences: A case study of the legal process in Riau, Indonesia.* Project Fire Fight. Jakarta.
Salim, E. 2007. *The Haze: Economic and social ramifications*. ISEAS Regional Outlook Forum 2007. Singapore: Institute of South East Asian Studies.
Samsul, Firman, Muhib, Syarwani, Helmi, Nurdin and Zakaria 2007. *The Golden Crop? Palm oil in post-tsunami Aceh.* Aceh: Eye on Aceh.
Sandker, M., Suwarno, A. and Campbell, B. M. 2007. Will forests remain in the face of oil palm expansion? Simulating change in Malimau, Indonesia. *Ecology and Society*, 12.
Santoso, P. and Naomy, P. C. 2004. More firms probed over Riau fires. *Jakarta Post*, 26 June 2004.
Satyawan [I20], L. S. 16 July 2010. *RE: Lecturer, Forest Fire, Department of Silviculture, Institute Pertanian Bogor.*
Scott, J. C. 1972. Patron-client politics and political change in Southeast Asia. *American Political Science Review*, 66, 91–113.
Severino, R. C. 2006. *Southeast Asia in Search of an ASEAN Community: Insights from the former ASEAN Secretary-General.* Singapore: ISEAS.
Silvius, M. and Kaat, A. 2010. Peat swamp forests and palm oil. Powerpoint Presentation. Indonesia.
Sim, A. B. 2006. Internationalization strategies of emerging Asian MNEs – Case study evidence on Singaporean and Malaysian firms. *Asia Pacific Business Review*, 12, 487–505.

Simamora, A. P. 2010. Government eyes owners of unlicensed mines, plantations. *Jakarta Post*, 23 September 2010.

SimamorA, A. P. 2011. SBY vows to protect palm oil interests. *Jakarta Post*, 26 March 2011.

Singh [M18], G. 2 April 2010. *RE: Chairman, Center for Environment, Technology and Development.*

Skocpol, T. 1985. Bringing the state back in. *In:* Evans, P. B., Rueschemayer, D. and Skocpol, T. (eds) *Bringing the State Back In.* Cambridge: Cambridge University Press.

Smart Agribusiness and Food 2010. *Annual Report.* Jakarta: SMART Agribusiness and Food.

Stone, R. 2007. Can palm oil plantations come clean? *Science*, 317, 1491.

Suharto, R. 2011. *Sustainable Palm Oil Development in Indonesia.* Jakarta: Indonesia Palm Oil Commission.

Surya [I9], M. T. and Akbar [I10], A. 30 June 2010. *RE: Deputy Directors, Wahana Lingkungan Hidup Indonesia.*

Suwarsono [I3]. 24 June 2010 2010. *RE: Researcher, Remote Sensing Applications and Technology Development Center, Indonesian National Institute of Aeronautics and Space.*

Syaf [I27], R. 24 July 2010. *RE: Director of Conservation Information, Wahana Informasi.*

Syarif [I2], L. M. 24 June 2010. *RE: Chief, Cluster of Security and Justice Governance, Kemitraan Partnership.*

Syarif, L. M. 2010. The source of Indonesian environmental Law. *IUCN Academy of Environmental Law*, 1.

Syarif, L. M. and Wibisana, A. G. 2007. *Strengthening legal and policy frameworks for addressing climate change in Asia: Indonesia. Asian Environmental Compliance and Enforcement Network.* United States: United States Environment Programme.

Tan, A. K. J. 2004. Environmental laws and institutions in Southeast Asia: A review of recent developments. *Singapore Year Book of International Law*, 177–192.

Tarigan [I23], A. 16 July 2010. *RE: Executive Director, Sawit Watch.*

Tay, S. S. C. 2003. Corruption after the crisis: Governance, Asian values, and international instruments. *In:* Tay, S. S. C. and Seda, M. (eds) *The Enemy Within: Combating corruption in Asia.* Singapore: Eastern University Press.

Terjesen, S. and Elam, A. 2009. Transnational entrepreneurs' venture internationalization strategies: A practice theory approach. *Entrepreneurship Theory and Practice*, 1093–1116.

The Star 2007. Environmental Hazard. *The Star*, 11 December 2011.

The Star 2014. M'sian jailed over forest fires. *The Star*, 14 September 2014.

Then [M14], S. 28 March 2010. *RE: Environmental Reporter, The Star.*

Thompson, H. 2001. Crisis in Indonesia: Forests, fires and finances. *Electronic Green Journal*, 1, 1–19.

Transparency International 2013. *Corruption Perceptions Index 2013 Results.* Transparency International.

Udiansyah [I15]. 28 July 2010. *RE: Faculty of Forestry, Lambung Mangkurat University.*

United Plantations 2008. *United Plantations response to unjust and wrongful allegations by Greenpeace.* Jakarta: United Plantations.

Varkkey, H. 2012. Patronage politics as a driver of economic regionalisation: The Indonesian oil palm sector and transboundary haze. *Asia Pacific Viewpoint*, 53, 314–329.

Varkkey, H. 2013a. Oil palm plantations and transboundary haze: Patronage networks and land licensing in Indonesia's Peatlands. *Wetlands*, 33, 679–690.

Varkkey, H. 2013b. Patronage politics, plantation fires and transboundary haze. *Environmental Hazards*, 12, 200–217.
Vidal, J. 2014. Indonesia's forest fires feed 'brown cloud' of pollution choking Asia's cities. *The Guardian*, 22 March.
WALHI 2010. Kebakaran Hutan: Bunus Tahunan Oengelolaan Hutan Yang Salah Kaprah. Powerpoint Presentation. Indonesia.
WALHI, Sawit Watch and CELCOR 2009. Malaysian Palm Oil and Logging Investments and Operations. *Factsheet.* WALHI, Sawit Watch and CELCOR.
Wederman, A. 2002. Development and corruption: The East Asian paradox. *In:* Gomez, E. T. (ed.) *Political Business in East Asia.* New York: Routledge.
White III, A. J. 2007. Decentralized environmental taxation in Indonesia: A proposed double dividend for revenue allocation and environmental regulation. *Journal of Environmental Regulation*, 19, 43–69.
Wibisino [I44], I. T. C. 10 November 2011. *RE: Wetlands International.*
Wibisino, I. T. C., Silber, T., Lubis, I. R., Rais, D. S., Suryadiputra, N., Silvius, M., Tol, S. and Joosten, H. 2011. *Peatlands in Indonesia's National REDD+ strategy*. Bogor: Wetlands International.
Wicke, B., Sikkema, R., Dornburg, V. and Faaij, A. 2011. Exploring land use changes and the role of palm oil production in Indonesia and Malaysia. *Land Use Policy*, 28, 193–206.
Widianarko, B. 2009. *Democratization, Decentralisation and Environmental Conservation in Indonesia.* Asia-pacific NGO Environmental Conference. Kyoto.
Wiryono [I40]. 8 November 2011. *RE: Forestry Department, University of Bengkulu.*
Witular, R. A. 2005. Govt vows to prosecute 10 firms over forest fires. *Jakarta Post*, 16 August 2005.
Wootliff, J. 2009. Blaze and haze in nation's forests must be stamped out for good. *Jakarta Post*, 16 June 2009.
World Growth 2011. *The Economic Benefit of Palm Oil to Indonesia.* Virginia: World Growth.
Yansen [I43]. 9 November 2011. *RE: Tropical Ecologist, University of Bengkulu.*
Zakaria, A., Theile, C. and Khaimur, L. 2007. *Policy, Practice, Pride and Prejudice: Review of legal, environmental and social practises of oil palm plantation companies of the Wilmar Group in Sambas District, West Kalimantan (Indonesia).* Netherlands: Milieudefensie.

5 The regionalism of haze mitigation at the ASEAN level[1]

Southeast Asian states have largely elected to address the issue of transboundary haze through collaboration at the regional level through ASEAN, with limited success. This chapter shows that the regionalism of haze mitigation through ASEAN initiatives have failed to curb haze because of the undue influence of patronage networks in the oil palm plantation sector. The ASEAN model of regionalism, which emphasizes national sovereignty and self-determination (Interviewee A7, 2010; Narine, 1998a: 555; Smith, 2004: 418; Zainal Abidin [M38], 2010), has allowed member states to shape collective mitigation initiatives at the ASEAN level in accordance with the interests of political and economic elites. This has weakened ASEAN's capacity to create and enforce haze mitigation efforts that serve collective regional interests. Nesadurai (2008: 237) has argued that 'the ASEAN Way is often only strictly adhered to and enforced by states in areas where crucial economic interests are affected'. The previous chapters have demonstrated that maintaining current practices in the region's oil palm plantation sector is indeed an area of crucial economic interest for the states concerned, both in its contribution to GDP, and as a source of patronage for the ruling elite. This chapter therefore argues that the states involved have chosen to adhere to the ASEAN Way when dealing with the haze to preserve crucial economic interests. At the ASEAN level, this has resulted also in a sort of paralysis where haze initiatives instead protect elite corporate interests, preserve state sovereignty and deflect responsibility for the haze issue (Tan [S7], 2010; Yahaya [M13], 2010).

This chapter thus elucidates the effects of these patronage networks on the regionalism of haze mitigation at the ASEAN level. It is divided into three sections. The first section introduces the concept of political regionalism. It notes that, while regionalism has been viewed in the literature as an important strategy for resolving common environmental problems (as proven by the European experience with acid rain), the ASEAN model of regionalism, with its selective use of the ASEAN Way principles by member states, has not been conducive to this. This model inherently weakens organizational capacity to create and uphold effective regional initiatives and agreements. The second section reviews the ASEAN haze initiatives, arguing that states *chose* to adhere to the ASEAN Way principles while shaping these initiatives. As a result, these initiatives have largely been ineffective in curbing haze, but effective in protecting the interests of the business elites. Special focus is given here on the influence of patronage politics on Indonesia's decision not to ratify the ASEAN Agreement on Transboundary Haze Pollution (ATHP) for more than ten years, and how Indonesia's non-ratification has seriously limited the capacity of ASEAN to enforce the ATHP effectively during this time. The third section then focuses on the Malaysian and Singaporean Adopt-A-District programmes in Indonesia, as part of the ASEAN initiatives. These programmes again show the influence of patronage politics; initiatives on the ground rarely engage with commercial plantations, and do not scrutinize their activities. As a whole, this chapter demonstrates that ASEAN is not the appropriate forum to effectively carry out haze mitigation, because the ASEAN style of regionalism weakens the organization's capacity to enforce agreements and encourage conducive regional cooperation, as it allows for undue influence from the region's political and economic elites.

Political regionalism

This book uses the varieties of regional integration as a lens through which the failure of ASEAN and regional governments to effectively mitigate haze can be analyzed. 'Regionalization', as explained previously, often refers to bottom-up economic processes of integration (Breslin and Higgott, 2003: 177) that lead to comparably higher levels of economic interdependence within that region (Hurrell, 1995: 334). A high level of economic regionalization can be observed in the Southeast Asian oil palm plantation sector, with Malaysian and Singaporean companies pooling investments and operations in Indonesia alongside local companies. A combination of home government protection and local patronage networks has allowed local and foreign companies to act with impunity in their operations to maximize profit, but with the side effect of transboundary haze.

However, as awareness of the source and dangers of smoke haze spread, Southeast Asian governments increasingly came under pressure from the public and civil society at the national, regional and international levels to address the haze issue, as discussed in Chapter 3 (Ho, 1997; Interviewee S4 and Interviewee S5, 2010; Interviewee S18, 2010; Interviewee I25, 2010; Lim [S13], 2010; *New Straits Times*, 1997). There is an assumption in the literature that as the demand for regional cooperation increases (in this case, the demand for haze mitigation by civil society) because of deepening economic regionalization, it will be matched by a 'supply' of appropriate regional institutions (Jayasuria, 2004). Hence, in 1997, the Myanmar foreign minister who chaired Environmental Affairs at ASEAN at the time suggested that the haze should be addressed at the ASEAN level separately from other environmental issues (Interviewee A2, 2010) due to its transboundary nature, its extreme impact on society and its close relation to natural resource management (Interviewee A7, 2010; Mat Akhir [A1], 2010). ASEAN member countries unanimously supported this as an opportunity to address civil society's concerns (Interviewee A2, 2010). This marked the start of the 'regionalism' of haze mitigation at the ASEAN level (Interviewee A2, 2010).

To reiterate, regionalism refers to top-down, state-led cooperative projects that emerge from intergovernmental dialogues and treaties (Breslin and Higgott, 2003: 177). This type of political regionalism focuses on regional interstate cooperation, involving the negotiation and creation of interstate regimes or agreements (Hurrell, 1995: 336–337). Regionalism may involve the creation of formal institutions, but it can often be based on a much looser structure, involving patterns of regular meetings with some rules attached, together with mechanisms for preparation and follow up. Such innovative arrangements can serve many purposes: to secure welfare gains, to promote common values or to solve common problems arising from intensified regional interdependence (Hurrell, 1995: 336–337). Political regionalism therefore 'involves a set of social functions that is concerned with making collective choices among people delineated by geographical proximity and other shared notions of sameness' (Boas, 2000: 415–416).

The regionalism of transboundary environmental issues

The regionalism of environmental issues has been viewed in the literature as an important strategy for resolving common environmental problems. Regionalism scholars argue that action at the regional level *should* be able to help streamline national policy positions around a joint regional position, and thus better facilitate the establishment and implementation of such multilateral agreements (Koh and Robinson, 2002: 1–2). For example, scholars such as Hurrell (1995: 336–337) and Koh and Robinson (2002: 1–2) have argued that regional systems of environmental management can be an important complement to national governance in solving common regional environmental problems. As Campbell (2005: 218) argues:

> Environmental regionalism is often viewed as a more feasible, effective, and democratic approach for addressing environmental problems that transcend national boundaries … Primarily because a small number of countries are involved, regionalism is seen as more likely to facilitate participation and represent the interests of all the parties … Regional commonalities such as geography, culture, values, and economic and political systems, combined with a smaller number of countries needed for consensus, will make agreement easier to reach.

Indeed, there have been examples of other regional environmental issues that, through the process of regionalism, have been successfully mitigated (Tay, 2008: 60). The most prominent example of this is the regionalism of the acid rain issue at the European Union (EU) level. Scholars such as Sliggers and Kakebeeke (2004) and Wettestad (2002: 32) have presented this as a successful example of what can be achieved through intergovernmental cooperation on transboundary environmental issues. A brief review of the European experience with transboundary acid rain, and reasons given in the literature for its comparative success, is discussed here.

In the 1960s, European scientists revealed a worrying relationship between heightened sulphur emissions in continental Europe and increased acidification of lakes in Scandinavia. Acid rain was found to have harmful effects on ecosystems, infrastructure and also human health in the region. In response to these acute problems, European policy makers established a regional platform for European air pollution abatement, with secretariat services provided by the United Nations Economic Commission for Europe. As a result, the 1979 Convention on Long-Range Transboundary Air Pollution (CLRTAP) was signed early on by all the 34 European governments and the European Economic Community (Johannessen, 2009). When the CLRTAP was created, only two of its signatories regarded acid rain as a serious problem (Levy, 1992: 16). Also, all CLRTAP initiatives and decisions were taken by the countries themselves (Campbell, 2005: 224), and therefore there was a highly uneven implementation of the CLRTAP among signatories.

From this weak start, it has been argued that the eventual success of the CLRTAP is linked directly to the Convention being absorbed into the EU framework. When the European Economic Community evolved into the EU,[2] the EU's Commission took over jurisdiction from the United Nations on air pollution control policy. Thus, the CLRTAP was integrated into the EU's 1998 Clean Air for Europe (CAFE) programme to integrate air pollution policies among member states (Wettestad, 2002: 336). CAFE's aims were to 'develop a long-term, strategic and integrated policy to protect against the effects of air pollution on human health and the environment' (Wettestad, 2002: 32) by integrating member states' policy objectives, harmonizing activities and sharing problem and solution frames (Tuinstra, 2008). These developments changed the ways in which certain CLRTAP policies were implemented.

For example, before 1987, environmental directives usually required consensus, but qualified majority decisions was allowed for policy making under the 1987 Single European Act (Wettestad, 2002: 38–39). Qualified majority voting under this act saw both the surrender of individual states' decision-making power and the centralization of decision-making systems. This enabled decisions at the regional level to be implemented without consensus under the centralized supranational agents (Yoshimatsu, 2006: 120). Essentially this means that within the EU, the Commission is identified as a unitary space and the key actor that contributes to the shaping of the region as a whole, in terms of the creation and deployment of policy instruments, the initiation of dialogue and the provision of resources (Rosamond, 2004: 74). Hence, the main role of the Commission is to set agendas and initiate policy (Wettestad, 2002: 38–39). The strong top-down component to the supranational EU strengthened the organizational capacity of the Commission, enabling the Commission to dictate policy to laggards (Grennfelt and Hov, 2005). It also plays a key role in ensuring that EU legislations are followed through (Wettestad, 2002: 38–39). The EU's supranational nature allowed hard law policies to be imposed upon member states in the larger interest of the community. Furthermore, EU regionalism fosters early, rapid and, when necessary, robust intervention by the Commission when faced with non-compliance (Christoph, 2005). In short, in the process of European regionalism, formal rules and regulations, and the power granted to the Commission to wield them has played an important role in ensuring compliance from member states (Kim, 2011: 414).

Therefore, when absorbed into CAFE, the Commission held the initiative to carry out CLRTAP initiatives instead of the member states. With this new jurisdiction, the Commission quickly added binding air emission limitations to the CLRTAP in eight separately negotiated treaties known as protocols (Campbell, 2005: 224). This made the CLRTAP the first enforceable legally binding instrument to deal with problems of air pollution on a broad regional basis (Eaton and Radojevic, 2001). For example, the CLRTAP originally worked on consensus, but within CAFE the Commission makes the final decisions and is also responsible for the final policy proposal. Also, while monitoring and inventory efforts within the CLRTAP were originally on a voluntary basis, within CAFE, all members had to participate and to deliver compliance by a set date (Tuinstra, 2008: 35). Because of these developments, Europe has achieved more than 60 per cent reductions in the emissions of sulfur, nitrogen oxides, volatile organic compounds, heavy metals and persistent organic pollutants (Eaton and Radojevic, 2001: 336).

The physical parallels of the European transboundary acid rain problem and the regional haze in Southeast Asia are immediately apparent. Here were two anthropogenic pollution problems that originated from economic activity in particular states in the region, but with effects that were felt more severely in neighbouring states. Therefore, scholars such as Florano (2004, 2003: 127–147), Syarif (2007) and Karim (2008) suggested that the regionalism of haze mitigation should be helpful in addressing the Southeast Asian haze, much in the same way that the regionalism of the acid rain issue were successful in Europe. For example, Syarif (2007) dedicated an entire chapter in his doctoral thesis to comparatively evaluating ASEAN haze management with air pollution policies in Europe. He proposes the EU model as a possible model for future ASEAN environmental cooperation, both generally and on the haze issue in particular. Karim (2008) also describes the CLRTAP as an encouraging example for ASEAN and haze mitigation, and proposes that ASEAN nations could learn from the experience of the ATHP, especially in terms of overcoming collective action problems. Florano (2004) even notes that haze management should be easier in ASEAN because compared to Europe's acid deposition where pollutants mix together easily while being transported by air, the exact locations of fires or hotspots and 'smoke plumes' could be easily detected through technology available at the ASEAN Specialized Meteorological Centre (ASMC).

However, the outcomes of haze mitigation at the ASEAN level are in stark contrast to Europe's acid rain experience. Although serious transboundary haze problems in Southeast Asia have encouraged significant levels of regional cooperation, the initiatives adopted here to address the issue have largely been ineffective (Campbell, 2005: 230) in mitigating haze. This chapter proposes that scholars such as Florano (2003: 127–147, 2004), Syarif (2007) and Karim (2008), who assume that the regionalism of haze mitigation in Southeast Asia should be successful because regionalism of the acid rain issue has been successful in Europe, overlook a very important point. These scholars do not engage with current debates in the literature on whether there is indeed a single model of regionalism. This chapter sides with scholars such as Murray (2010: 318), Yoshimatsu (2006: 136) and Kim (2011: 426) who argue that there is no single model of regionalism. It further notes that not all models of regionalism are conducive to *effective* regionalism. As Hurrel (1995: 336–337) points out, high levels of regionalism are no guarantee of the effectiveness of solving common problems.

These scholars argue that the *model* of regionalism is an important determinant of whether the regionalism process is effective in solving regional problems or not. The EU's model of regionalism is characterized by supranational institutions and the *pooling* of sovereignty. In ASEAN, the *maintenance* of national sovereignty remains the focus of regionalism. Therefore, the ASEAN model of regionalism differs from the EU, owing to different emphases on sovereignty (Kim, 2011: 422; Murray, 2010: 311–313). This difference means that some forms of transnational coordination and cooperation are simply more feasible in Europe than they are in Southeast Asia (Beeson, 2007: 25). Therefore, the European regionalism model cannot simply be copied in Southeast Asia (Kim, 2011: 429). For example, this explains why, despite ASEAN initiatives eventually also adopting legally binding elements such as the CLRTAP (as explained below), haze continues to persist. The following section discusses the ASEAN style of regionalism, noting that this model has generally not been conducive in collectively addressing Southeast Asian environmental issues.

The ASEAN model of regionalism and the environment

ASEAN was established in 1967 with five founding members: Indonesia, Malaysia, Singapore, the Philippines and Thailand. ASEAN now consists of ten member states in the Southeast Asian geographical region, with subsequent members in order of membership being Brunei Darussalam, Vietnam, Laos, Myanmar and Cambodia. ASEAN was founded primarily with the purpose of accelerating economic growth, social progress and cultural development in the region (ASEAN Secretariat, 2009). These goals are expressed in various ASEAN treaties including its founding document, the 1967 Bangkok Declaration, the 1971 Declaration of the Zone of Peace, Freedom and Neutrality, the 1976 Treaty of Amity and Cooperation in Southeast Asia (Katanyuu, 2006: 827), the 2003 Second Declaration of ASEAN Concorde (Severino, 2006: 85–90) and most recently the 2007 ASEAN Charter (Koh, 2008: 16). These documents also prescribe approaches to regional engagement, known collectively as the ASEAN Way, a set of behavioural and also procedural norms. These include the pursuit of consensus; the sanctity of sovereign rights and the related concept of non-interference; the principles of sensitivity and politeness; non-confrontational negotiation processes; behind-the-scenes discussions; an emphasis on informal and non-legalistic procedures; and flexibility (Kivimaki, 2001: 16).

As discussed in the introductory chapter, a common explanation for the persistence of the haze is the limitations posed by the ASEAN Way of regional governance as explained in the previous chapter. Scholars such as B. Tan (2005: 3–4), Tay (2002: 74), Yahaya (2000: 49), Nguitragool (2011: 357) and Chang and Rajan (2001: 666) have argued that while regional environmental governance can be instrumental in finding solutions to collective action problems, this model of ASEAN cooperation does not work when dealing with environmental challenges such as fires and haze. Scholars have argued that because the ASEAN Way is too deeply engrained in the process of regional governance in ASEAN, member states cannot imagine ASEAN functioning any other way (Kamaruddin [M26], 2010; Lew [M6] and Interviewee M7, 2010; Nagulendran [M34] and Interviewee M35, 2010; Syarif [I2], 2010). Severino (2006: 85–90) has described the ASEAN Way as a 'doctrine'; something ideological and therefore to be adhered to at all costs. Therefore, Aggarwal and Chow (2010: 282–286) insist that ASEAN states 'undoubtedly desire the elimination of the haze problem', but were unable to balance this with their stronger desire to comply with the broader ASEAN Way norms, especially those of non-interference and decision making based on consensus.

These scholars argue that the persistence of the haze can be explained by the fact that the ASEAN organization is too tightly bound to these norms as guidance devices for decision making (Kratochwil, 1984: 705, 1989: 9; Narine, 1998b: 15–33). They argue that due to the *necessarily* strict adherence to the ASEAN Way, environmental problems in ASEAN, such as the haze, are approached through the non-interference principle. This impedes collective problem-solving methods when dealing with natural resource issues, as other states are not allowed to pressure members into acting in accordance with collective interest (Tan, B., 2005: 3–4). Because of this, it is argued that ASEAN states struggle to draw a line between respecting their neighbouring government's right to self-determination and cooperatively mediating the region's haze problem (Tan, B., 2005: 3–4). Therefore, ASEAN has emphasized policy pronouncements and rhetoric over actual implementation of effective haze mitigation efforts (Chang and Rajan, 2001: 666), largely rendering them ineffective.

This book finds these arguments flawed. States do not blindly follow the ASEAN Way principles due to some deeply ingrained 'habit'. In fact, there have been instances where the ASEAN Way has been deliberately ignored in order for member states to pursue narrow understandings of their self-interests (Narine, 1998a: 555). Indeed, research by Nischalke (2000: 104) into 20 distinguishable foreign-policy initiatives provides evidence of only moderate compliance to the ASEAN Way. While 13 of the initiatives have observed the prescribed pattern of consensus seeking and consultation, at least seven have not observed the organization's procedural norms. Furthermore, no ASEAN member state had any serious reservations about the policy outcomes in these seven cases, despite them being contrary to the ASEAN Way. Good examples are Singapore's decision to offer the United States access to some of their military facilities in 1995, and the Australian–Indonesian security agreement in the same year. Singapore's consultation with its regional neighbours was inconclusive, and Indonesia's was non-existent. However, no ASEAN member raised any reservations to these cases, despite ASEAN's collective aspirations for regional security autonomy, manifest in the ZOPFAN (Zone of Peace, Freedom and Neutrality) declaration of 1971 (Nischalke, 2000: 95–104). This illustrates how an ASEAN state can choose to *not* adhere to the ASEAN Way in order to preserve crucial economic interests, without suffering any consequences (Nischalke, 2000: 94).

This chapter points out that in the same way, states *choose* to adhere to the ASEAN Way if it is in their interests to do so. This is the crux of the ASEAN model of regionalism. As detailed above, while the EU model of regionalism is characterized by the pooling of sovereignty, the ASEAN model is characterized by its maintenance of national sovereignty (Kim, 2011: 422; Murray, 2010: 311–313). This chapter shows that this difference in emphases of sovereignty explains why environmental regionalism in Europe has been successful, while environmental regionalism in Southeast Asia has not. While the main drivers of EU are its supranational institutions, the main drivers of the ASEAN organization are member states (Narine, 1998a: 555; Interviewee A7, 2010; Smith, 2004: 418; Zainal Abidin [M38], 2010). Unlike the European Commission, the ASEAN Secretariat has been deliberately denied the resources and mandate necessary to carry out such a responsibility (Kim, 2011: 422), and continues to be subordinate to national secretariats (Beeson, 2007: 237; Solingen, 2005: 49). Hence, the ASEAN organization has an inherently weak capacity to act in the regional interest. As one interviewee put it, action in ASEAN depends 'not on the Secretariat, but on the country leaders' and representatives (Zainal Abidin [M38], 2010). This ASEAN model of regionalism therefore enables member states to control the scope, depth and speed of regionalism in ASEAN, which best suits their national interests (Kim, 2011: 416). Therefore, while decision making in the EU is geared towards the collective interest, decision making in ASEAN is shaped according to the interests of its member states (Interviewee A7, 2010). Hence, states are free to decide whether or not to adhere to ASEAN Way norms, depending on whether it is in their best interests to do so. Instead of being a limiting effect on state behavior, the ASEAN Way can be better explained as tools for political action that states can selectively use in line with their interests (Khoo, 2004: 42).

Upholding the ASEAN Way when necessary shields states from having to commit joint tasks that they find politically difficult (going against dominant national interests), administratively challenging or simply not important enough (according to their national priorities). In keeping with the norms of non-interference, member states can stress the primacy of national laws, policy making and implementation (Elliott, 2003: 32–40). In keeping with procedural voluntarism, members can avoid legally binding agreements. This clause, along with sovereignty concerns, has also resulted in a lack of capacity of central institutions in ASEAN to uphold compliance or any credible mechanisms for settling disputes in an objective and binding manner (Severino *et al.*, 2005). This complicates the application of multilateral pressure and collective problem-solving methods (Tan, B., 2005: 3–4). The non-interference clause also enables governments to exclude any issue they consider to be politically sensitive from ever being discussed at the ASEAN level (Nesadurai, 2008: 555). As a result, these principles provide members with substantial autonomy in determining to what extent they would carry out regional environmental agendas, even those that they have already agreed to initially (Nesadurai, 2008: 227). Indeed, as an institution centred around the promotion of economic cooperation and prosperity among its members (Smith, 2004: 418), environmental objectives are therefore often overlooked in the pursuance of these economic goals.

Furthermore, as discussed in the previous chapter on patronage politics, the relationship between key economic actors and national political elites in Southeast Asia is traditionally very close (Nesadurai, 2003: 239). The extensive patron-client relationships prevalent within the region's forestry and agricultural industry (Aggarwal and Chow, 2010: 278–282) have meant that many political parties in power have direct links to natural resources (Resosudarmo [I26], 2010). This situation encourages elites to favour arrangements that ensure domestic and regional political economic stability and market access to these natural resources (Solingen, 1999: 31–46), while providing a lack of incentives for effective regional environmental conservation. This book therefore demonstrates that the protection of these elite interests was more important than responding to environmental issues through ASEAN (Cotton, 1999: 341–342).

As a result, ASEAN developed into an elite-centred framework of regionalism (Ferguson, 2004: 396), where (elite) economic growth takes precedence over social development and environmental protection (Nesadurai, 2008: 229). States were unwilling to antagonize domestic interests by applying prohibitive national- or regional-level environmental law, especially when such natural resource interests are so closely intertwined with a leader's political power base (Aggarwal and Chow, 2010: 278–282; Boas, 2000: 415). Member states sought to protect the interests of the political and economic elites by maintaining their 'power of veto' (by denying such a mandate to its Secretariat, as discussed above) over effective policy innovation at the ASEAN level (Cotton, 1999: 341–342). Therefore, member states were free to pick and choose instances where they would strictly follow the ASEAN Way or ignore it, as long as it was in the interests of the members' political and economic elites.

Hence, with national priorities skewed to elite interests connected with national resources, ASEAN initiatives have thus far had a strong preference in the observation of the ASEAN Way where protection of the regional environment is concerned (Abdullah, 2002: viii). Indeed, the protection of the environment within ASEAN was largely seen as something that would threaten economic growth, development and social cohesion of most of the member states (Jones and Smith, 2002: 101). The application of the ASEAN Way has enabled members to retain a great degree of domestic policy autonomy (Nesadurai, 2008: 233) over environmental matters. Hence, ASEAN operates not from any set of strict legal procedure like the EU but instead by creating sequential issue-by-issue ad-hoc coalitions (Pempel, 2005: 11). Declarations and agreements adopted at the ASEAN level usually articulate mere 'principles' for regional environmental cooperation but rarely include guidelines for national environmental practice that could be construed as 'intervention' (Elliott, 2003: 29). Therefore, ASEAN environmental initiatives have relied on voluntary cooperation, non-binding agreements and a weak institutional infrastructure (Campbell, 2005: 216) emphasizing aspirational policy pronouncements and rhetoric over actual implementation (Chang and Rajan, 2001: 661–667).

This rhetoric has had no observable impacts on the intergovernmental policy practices of the ASEAN members and have failed to transform their trade and investment patterns (Kim, 2011: 412). Greater priority has thus been attached to economic growth than to health and environmental protection in ASEAN (Campbell, 2005: 220). While member states recognized that they had common environmental problems, their material interests in addressing them arose from the importance of domestic economic progress and development. Therefore, it was more important for these states to maintain the availability of, and access to, natural resources (Elliott, 2003: 29–35) such as timber and forest products to be used in the pursuit of development. As a result, mechanisms that could improve the effectiveness of ASEAN in regional environmental governance were never operationalized. For example, a regional body on the environment, suggested in the 1987 Jakarta Resolution to undertake policy recommendations and monitor environmental quality (Elliott, 2003: 32–40) still has not been established. In this way, adherence to the ASEAN Way provides an avenue for member states to pursue their national interests with minimal resistance, while ensuring that the regional atmosphere is healthy and supportive. As a result, effective cooperative regional arrangements over environmental issues at the ASEAN level have been problematic (Elliott, 2000, 2001, 2003; Karim, 2008). These problems of course extend to haze mitigation activities at the ASEAN level, which the following section discusses.

The ASEAN Way in ASEAN-level haze-mitigation initiatives

Efforts to address the Southeast Asian haze have overwhelmingly originated from the ASEAN level (ASEAN Secretariat, 1995: 1–5; Letchumanan [A6], 2010; Severino, 2006: 112–114; Yahaya, 2000: 45). Some scholars viewed this as a strategic move within the institutional space to construct a post-Westphalian form of multilevel governance, by shifting or 'rescaling' governance of this issue from the Indonesian state apparatus into regional modes of governance to serve regional agendas (Hameiri and Jayasuria, 2011: 20; Hameiri and Jones, 2013: 468). Hameiri and Jones (2013: 469) envisioned this ASEAN-level collaboration over haze as 'an internationally based regulatory framework, which set the agenda for national and subnational regulatory and enforcement agencies, aspiring towards a complex form of multilevel governance'. Indeed, regional collaboration over the haze became very high profile and was pegged as the earliest example of ASEAN cooperation over transboundary issues (Elliott, 2003: 32–40; Interviewee A2, 2010). Several scholars and agencies have praised ASEAN haze mitigation efforts. For example, the United Nations Environment Programme (UNEP) hailed the ASEAN Way of haze collaboration (enshrining sovereignty and non-interference) as a pioneering achievement that could become a global model for handling transboundary issues (Severino, 2006: 112–114). It was envisioned that there would be an increasing emphasis of cooperative measures (carrots, like those prescribed in the ASEAN Way) instead of sanctions and strict state responsibility (sticks) as guidance devices for actions among other regions and in other international environmental regimes in the future (Tay, 2002: 53–73). Scholars also argued that soft law agreements, as are prevalent in ASEAN haze initiatives, saved time as ASEAN was able to immediately get the cooperation of Indonesia, which would have been unlikely under the threat of sanctions (Cotton, 1999: 344–347; Florano, 2004: 1–12). Solingen (2005: 40) noted that such informal agreements could better facilitate cooperation because they make fewer informational demands on the parties, can be negotiated quickly and can be rapidly modified as conditions change. These scholars further argued that these tactics enabled ASEAN to test and adjust their strategies without them being set in stone (Florano, 2004: 1–12), and have led to enhanced contact between officials and experts across ASEAN (Cotton, 1999: 344–347). Other scholars say it has been useful in attracting funding (Florano, 2004: 1–12; Mayer, 2006: 202–218) and technical assistance, as once a regional machinery is established based on local volunteerism, contributions from the international community would be expected to pour in[3] (Florano, 2004: 1–12). In this sense, ASEAN haze collaboration can be seen as providing symbolic diplomatic rather than legal pressure on culprits (Mayer, 2006: 202–218), which have been viewed positively by the scholars and agencies mentioned here.

However, despite these positive reviews, the regionalism of haze mitigation has failed to bring about meaningful results, and the haze persists as a regional pollution problem year after year (Campbell, 2005: 216). While scholars such as Koh and Robinson (2002: 1–2) have argued that such regionalism should be able to help streamline national policy positions around a joint regional position, and thus better facilitate the establishment and implementation of such multilateral agreements as mentioned above, other scholars have argued that high levels of political regionalism in Southeast Asia are no guarantee of the effectiveness of solving such common problems (Hurrell, 1995: 336–337). Powerful opponents (both patrons and clients) operating at the national and local levels have severely limited the degree of regionalism of the practical operation of regional and state apparatuses over haze (Hameiri and Jones, 2013: 468). With member states being the main drivers of the organization, these states were able to shape the (albeit high levels of) regionalism of haze mitigation to privilege economic actors in the region's oil palm plantation sector that are close allies of the political elite (Nesadurai, 2003: 239). Hence, instead of generating emergency or extraordinary responses as would be expected, ASEAN governance over haze remains considerably constrained (Hameiri and Jones, 2013: 468).

Accordingly, this chapter will show that states have elected to adhere to ASEAN Way principles as a way to reassert their authority and their right to self-determination over the haze issue, resulting in the continuing haze. More importantly, this enables them to continue to protect their crucial economic interests in the regional oil palm plantation sector (Campbell, 2005: 216). Therefore, the regionalism strategy of addressing haze through ASEAN unsurprisingly fails to deliver environmentally positive results.

Through a chronological examination of ASEAN haze initiatives, the following discussion argues that the observance of the ASEAN Way principles of sovereignty, non-interference and economic development above all have resulted in outcomes that were largely ineffective in curbing haze, but effective in protecting the interests of the business elites and further encouraging the unscrupulous practices of the region's oil palm plantation industry. In short, this section points out that these cooperative agreements that were produced have been deliberately designed by member states to protect national economic interests and preserve state sovereignty, while deflecting responsibility on the haze issue (Tan [S7], 2010; Yahaya [M13], 2010).

ASEAN haze initiatives, 1985–2003

As explained earlier, the ASEAN Way principles, especially the principles of non-interference and non-legalistic procedures, are often strictly adhered to and enforced by states in areas where crucial economic interests are affected (Nesadurai, 2008: 237). The economic importance of the oil palm sector to member states, coupled with the importance of the clients populating this sector to elite patrons in the government (Ferguson, 2004: 396), meant that this sector was one of crucial economic importance to Indonesia, Malaysia and Singapore. This book therefore argues that ASEAN states were pressured by civil society to act upon the haze, but at the same time also faced economic pressures from the region's oil palm plantation sector. Therefore, states had to address both concerns from civil society and the economic elite by engaging at the ASEAN level over haze, but in a way that would maintain the status quo of privileging economic actors in the oil palm plantation sector that are close allies of the political elite. This chapter shows that to do this, ASEAN states chose to largely adhere to the ASEAN Way in regards to haze cooperation at the ASEAN level. Therefore, ASEAN initiatives on haze have essentially resulted in outcomes that protect national economic interests, preserve state sovereignty and deflect responsibility for the haze issue (Tan [S7], 2010; Yahaya [M13], 2010), instead of actually reducing or eradicating haze.

ASEAN as an organization began to acknowledge haze as a regional concern in 1985, with the adoption of the Agreement on the Conservation of Nature and Natural Resources, which specifically referred to air pollution and 'transfrontier environmental effects' (ASEAN Secretariat, 1995: 1–5). This was followed over the years by other agreements with references to transboundary pollution, such as the 1990 Kuala Lumpur Accord on Environment and Development and the 1992

Singapore Resolution on Environment and Development (ASEAN Secretariat, 1995: 1–5). Indeed, the 1992 Singapore Resolution identified such transboundary pollution as a major environmental concern and in the same year, ASEAN environment ministers agreed to streamline policy directions and establish technical and operational cooperation, with special reference to haze (Tay, 2008: 60). Following this, the first Workshop on Transboundary Pollution and Haze in ASEAN Countries was held in Balikpapan, Indonesia in September 1992, specifically addressing the haze as an individual problem in the region (see Figure 5.1) (ASEAN Secretariat, 1995: 1–5). The first informal ASEAN Ministerial Meeting on the Environment in Kuching, Sarawak in 1994 marked the beginnings of a more visible effort by the ASEAN member countries to address the continuous problem of the haze. Here the ministers agreed to 'enhance cooperation to manage natural resources and control transboundary pollution within ASEAN, to develop an early warning and response system, and to improve the capacity of member countries in these areas' (Yahaya, 2000: 45).

In 1995, member states agreed to adopt an ASEAN Cooperation Plan on Transboundary Pollution (Severino, 2006: 112). The plan described broad strategies and policies to manage transboundary atmospheric pollution and other forms of transboundary pollution (Severino, 2006: 112), including a number of concrete measures to prevent and respond to the fires and haze, such as the promotion of zero-burning practices, the deployment of ground forces to prevent and detect forest fires and the establishment of national focal points (NFPs) (Nguitragool, 2011: 363). These NFPs were envisioned to strengthen regional coordination by disseminating forestry and peatland governance standards designed by experts in the region and developing and coordinating domestic agencies to prevent and suppress fires (Hameiri and Jones, 2013: 469). As a follow up to this plan, the ASEAN senior officials on the Environment Meeting established a Haze Technical Task Force (HTTF) with the objective of implementing the mechanisms detailed in the Cooperation Plan (Severino, 2006: 112). It outlined the haze mitigation efforts to be made at both national and regional levels (Tay, 1998: 204). The ministers also agreed to develop a regional fire-danger rating system and a common air-quality index (Tay, 2002: 60). Member states furthermore agreed to exchange technology and knowledge on forest fire prevention and mitigation, and to create a cooperative mechanism for combating these fires (Tay, 1998: 204).

At the suggestion of the ASEAN chair of Environmental Affairs (Interviewee A2, 2010) in 1997, the ASEAN Ministerial Meeting on Haze was established. This marked the beginning of the specific regionalism of haze mitigation at the ASEAN level, with the haze being given a special status of importance in the organization, separate from other transboundary environmental issues. The Meeting formulated the Regional Haze Action Plan (RHAP) under the HTTF to provide further commitments and detail to the Cooperation Plan (Quadri, 2001). In the spirit of the ASEAN Way, the RHAP was designed to overcome the haze problem with concerns of culture, economy and individual governments in mind (Abdullah [M43], 2011). It was a soft-law, non-binding instrument that stood on three pillars:

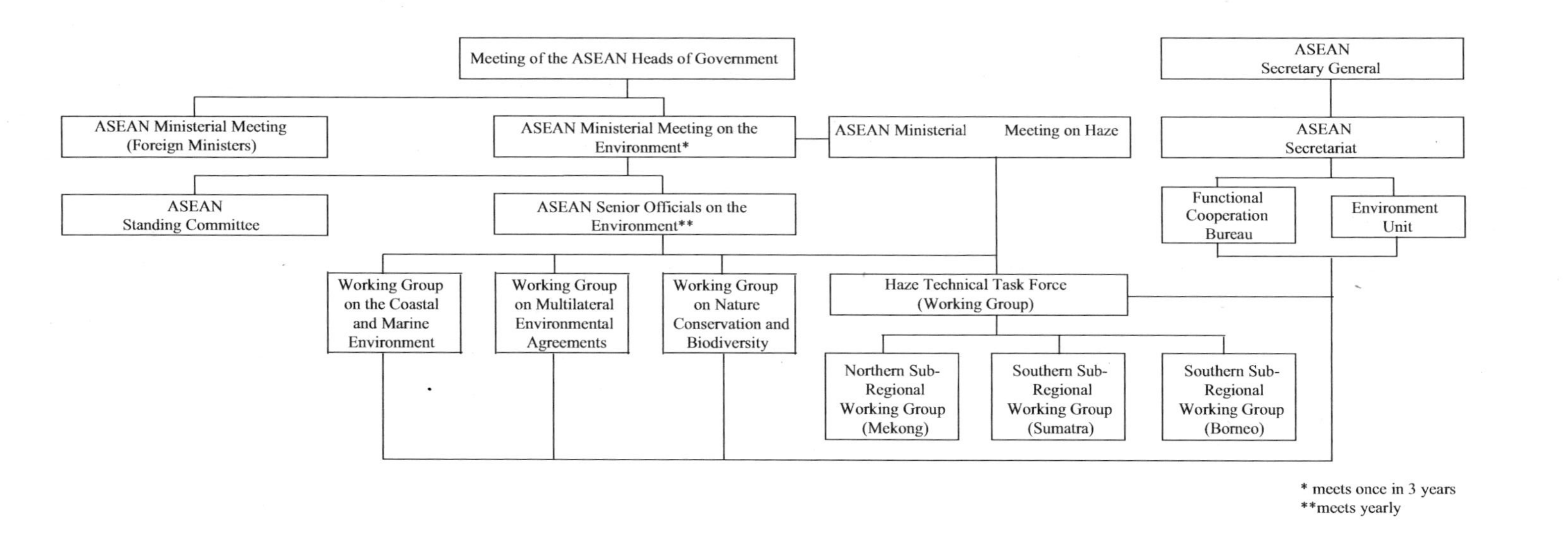

Figure 5.1 Organizational structure of ASEAN environmental and haze cooperation

Source: Adapted from ASEAN Secretariat, 2002a

the spirit of voluntarism, the no-fault finding rule and the offering of assistance based on capability and expertise (Florano, 2004: 5). Under the RHAP, member parties were obliged to develop their own guidelines, plans and other measures to prevent and monitor fires that could cause transboundary haze pollution.

The plan was sectioned into three parts. The first required member states to develop national plans based on the regional plan (Jones, 2006: 437). The second sought to strengthen the regional surveillance function of the ASMC in Singapore, which includes using satellite data to deliver daily updates on hotspots, and to monitor and anticipate forest fires and increased pollution levels (Hameiri and Jones, 2013: 470; Jones, 2006: 437). The third focused on the enhancement of fire-fighting capability (Jones, 2006: 437). It also established an ASEAN Policy on Zero Burning. These guidelines for zero burning, however, were not meant to be prescriptive and controlled burning continued to be allowed for 'specific situations' (ASEAN Secretariat, 2003b: 1–23). Other aspects emphasized in the RHAP included the identification and mobilization of resources, the exchange of information and the development of markets for biomass and agricultural wastes, which are otherwise disposed of by burning (Nguitragool, 2011: 365). Furthermore, it solidified the breakdown of haze mitigation roles at the ASEAN level according to the country's expertise (Yahaya, 2000: 46): Malaysia for prevention, Singapore for monitoring and Indonesia for fire-fighting (Woon, 2002: 135).

In 1998, the ASEAN Summit in Vietnam issued the Hanoi Plan of Action that called for full implementation of the RHAP by 2001 (Yahaya, 2000: 46). It established a mechanism to pool fire-fighting resources for regional operations (Tay, 2008: 60). Specifically, it established two Sub-Regional Fire-Fighting Arrangements (SRFA) for Borneo and the Sumatra/Riau provinces in Indonesia under the RHAP to facilitate the movement of resources from one member country to the other in order to mitigate the haze problem (Yahaya, 2000: 48). To complement the SRFA, a SRFA Legal Group was established in 2000 to examine the legislative and enforcement issues in the region related to curbing forest and land fires (Jones, 2006: 437).

An ASEAN Peatland Management Initiative (APMI) was proposed at the nineth ASEAN Ministerial Meeting on Haze in 2002. This initiative was to complement the SRFA initiatives with a special focus on addressing issues of fire prevention and control in the region's peatlands. The initiative was established in collaboration with the Global Environment Centre (GEC), an NGO focusing on peatland conservation in the region. The goals of the APMI are:

> to promote sustainable management of peatlands through collective efforts and enhanced cooperation among ASEAN Member Countries towards achieving local support and sustaining livelihood options, regional benefits through reduced risk of fire and its associated haze and contributing globally in minimizing impacts of climate change [as a result of carbon release from peatlands].
>
> (ASEAN Secretariat, 2003a: 1)

On top of these plans and agreements, other ASEAN initiatives on the haze include detailed operational procedures for monitoring, assessment and joint emergency response; the formation of a regional network made up of NFPs; an inventory of fire-fighting resources and training mechanisms; simulation exercises for joint emergency response between countries; and demonstration sites for the benefit of farmers, smallholders and shifting cultivators (ASEAN Secretariat, 2004). As mentioned above, the political impetus for these initiatives were that states came increasingly under pressure from the public and civil society at the national, regional and international levels to address the haze issue as awareness of the source and dangers of smoke haze spread (Ho, 1997; Interviewee S4 and Interviewee S5, 2010; Interviewee S18, 2010; Interviewee I25, 2010; Lim [S13], 2010; *New Straits Times*, 1997). However, this plethora of plans and projects over the decades failed to break the persistent cycle of haze in the region.

In the regionalism literature, binding agreements, an institutionalized system and the sectoral integration of policies are often singled out as some of the most important factors that render the regionalism process a success (Murray, 2010: 319; Shelton, 2003: 552). A close observance of these early ASEAN initiatives on haze however reveals that these ASEAN Way-compliant initiatives rarely contained these important factors for success. For example, the 1998 Cooperation Plan on Transboundary Pollution and its complementary HTTF were found to be much less formal or binding than comparable documents in other regions such as Europe for curbing transboundary harm (Tay, 2008: 60). The plan was largely a listing of general actions that governments *ought* to take to prevent and mitigate forest fires (Severino, 2006: 112). The lack of explicit operational directives rendered it ineffective, and member countries were again thrown into crisis-management mode with the advent of the most serious haze of the region in 1997 to 1998 (Tay, 2008: 60). Likewise, the 1998 RHAP continued to focus on national plans and capabilities instead of regional initiatives (Tay, 1998: 205). Like the Cooperation Plan, the RHAP exemplified a soft-law approach and was also not a legally binding agreement (Tay, 2008: 60). It was left to the governments concerned to decide what was to be included in their national plans, with the freedom to bypass or equivocate on matters raised in the RHAP (Jones, 2006: 438). There were no mechanisms under the plan for any member country to ensure that the other member countries fulfilled their obligations (Parliament of Singapore, 1998a).

As a result, most of the ASEAN initiatives on haze since were useful in generating a massive amount of information on the haze (Severino, 1999) but not much in terms of effective implementation of haze mitigation activities. The focus on national plans and the lack of legally binding documents ensured that states were largely free to pick and choose regional initiatives that best suited their narrow economic national interests. For example, the RHAP established the role of the ASMC[4] as the region's mapping, imaging and forecasting provider for fires and haze. However, the Malaysian government used sovereignty arguments to strongly oppose the use of satellite data for haze monitoring purposes at the regional level during the early years of the haze (Campbell, 2005: 222). Also, meteorological officials from Indonesia's Lembaga Penerbangan dan Antariksa Nasional (Indonesian National Institute of Aeronautics and Space) who were interviewed said that Indonesian ministries also used similar arguments to explain their lack of acceptance of ASMC data. Indonesia preferred to use its own, less-advanced meteorological data for fire mapping and haze monitoring (Haryanto [I16], 2010; Roswiniarti [I13], 2010). In respect of Indonesia's sovereignty, ASEAN could not insist on Indonesia's use of ASMC data. This choice of inferior fire mapping by Malaysia and Indonesia of course enables many local and foreign plantation companies in Indonesia to avoid scrutiny of fire activities on their land. Furthermore, even though the SRFA was meant to quickly facilitate the movement of fire-fighting resources from one member country to the other in the event of fires (Yahaya, 2000: 48), Indonesia was known to turn down or unnecessarily delay entry of regional fire-fighting teams even though all requirements for the activation of SRFA assistance were fulfilled (Hedradjat [I14], 2010; Syarif [I2], 201c). This way, Indonesia was able to avoid opening its doors to unwanted external scrutiny of its internal and commercial practises (Koh [S2], 2010; Tay [S12], 2010).

Therefore, the outcomes of these early ASEAN initiatives have largely been ineffective in providing long-term, workable solutions for transboundary haze. Instead, in the spirit of the ASEAN Way, they have enabled the practices of the regional oil palm sector to continue. The current stage of ASEAN cooperation over the haze stands at the implementation of the ATHP, which was brought into force in 2003 (see Figure 5.2) (ASEAN Secretariat, 2004). However, as the following subsection shows, this agreement also suffers from the similar fate as these earlier ASEAN initiatives and is, as one scholar describes, a 'blind and toothless paper tiger' (Florano, 2003: 142).

The 2003 Agreement on Transboundary Haze Pollution

Before the ATHP, member states generally avoided legally binding agreements on environmental and haze matters (Elliott, 2003: 32–40). However, the 1997–1998 haze episode, which was the most severe the region had seen, sparked renewed

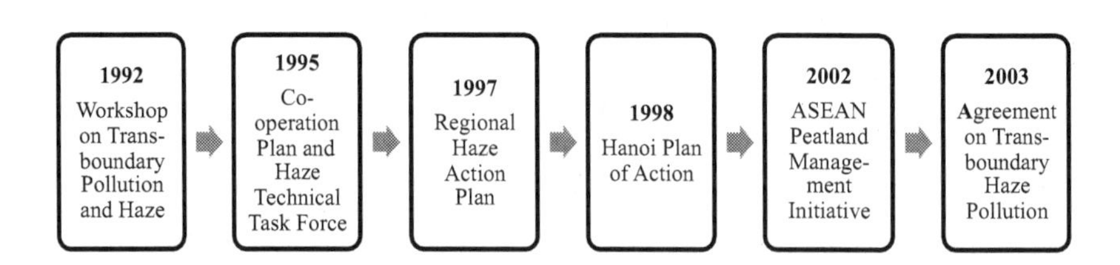

Figure 5.2 ASEAN initiatives relating directly to haze

outcry from the public and civil society (Letchumanan [A6], 2010). This backlash prompted member states to agree to establish a legally binding mechanism to address haze (Letchumanan [A6], 2010) and appease civil society. Therefore, in 2001 the ATHP was proposed to provide legally binding support for the RHAP (Florano, 2003: 132–133). Hence, the ATHP is notable for being one of the few legally binding ASEAN environmental agreements to be entered into force (ASEAN Secretariat, 2004).

In Jones' (2004: 66) assessment, the Agreement conforms to the regular format of international treaties concerning public policy and its management. The Agreement comprises a preamble, definition of terms, overall objective, statement of principles, obligations of the signatory states, financial and institutional arrangement for implementing the Agreement, obligations of ratification by signatory states and a reference to protocols that detail the procedures of implementation (Jones, 2004: 66). Several international principles and customary international law have been adopted into the Agreement's legal framework, including the obligation to not cause environmental harm, the precautionary principle, the duty to cooperate, the principle of good neighbourliness, sustainable development, notification and information, public participation and prevention (Nurhidayah, 2012: 15).

The Agreement's stated objective, under Article 2, is 'to prevent and monitor transboundary haze pollution as a result of land and/or forest fires which should be mitigated, through concerted national efforts and intensified regional and international cooperation' (ASEAN Secretariat, 2002a: 4). The treaty upholds states' sovereign right to exploit their own resources as they see fit, in the pursuit of their own developmental and environmental policies (ASEAN Secretariat, 2002a: 4), among other international law principles as stated above (Article 3) (Florano, 2003: 132–133). Article 5 of the ATHP also calls for the establishment of an ASEAN Coordinating Centre for Haze in Indonesia, and a supporting ASEAN Haze Fund, for the purposes of 'facilitating cooperation and coordination among the parties in managing the impact of land and/or forest fires in particular haze pollution arising from such fires' (ASEAN Secretariat, 2002a: 6).

Four rounds of negotiations for the ATHP were held between March 2001 and September 2001 (Nguitragool, 2011: 367). Negotiations were concluded and the ATHP was signed by the ten member states in 2002 in Kuala Lumpur (ASEAN Secretariat, 2002b). Over the years, additional arrangements have been added on to the ATHP framework, the most recent of which was during the 15th Meeting of the Sub-Regional Ministerial Steering Committee on Transboundary Haze Pollution, where environment ministers from Indonesia, Malaysia, Singapore, Brunei and Thailand launched the ASEAN Sub-Regional Haze Monitoring System (HMS), which involved government-to-government sharing of concession maps on an ad-hoc basis to further facilitate cooperation over haze (Woo, 2013).

Interviewees explained that with the entry into force of the ATHP in 2003, the Working Group on Haze was elevated to the ministerial level, with a Conference of the Parties held on an annual basis. Under the working group were the

Northern and Southern Ministerial Steering Committees (MSCs), supported by their respective Technical Working Groups (see Figure 6.1) (Interviewee A4 and Interviewee A5, 2010). The Technical Working Groups were tasked to develop the Comprehensive ASEAN Plan of Action (POA) on Transboundary Haze Pollution (ASEAN Secretariat, 2007: 6). The resulting POA included a cooperation mechanism for members to help Indonesia prevent haze by controlling fires, creating early warning systems, offering mutual assistance and sharing technology and information (Khalik, 2006).

Furthermore, a Panel of Experts (POE) was established to support the implementation of the POA. According to the Agreement, the POE 'may be utilised when taking measures to mitigate the impact of land and/or forest fires or haze pollution arising from such fires, and also for the purpose of relevant training, education and awareness-raising campaigns' (ASEAN Secretariat, 2002a: 10). This meant that the POE was to offer rapid independent assessment and recommendations for resource mobilization. It was meant to empower regional experts to overcome national and local resistance (Hameiri and Jones, 2013: 468). These experts were to be deployed to the fire sites and would provide their report and recommendations to governments (Interviewee A4 and Interviewee A5, 2010).

The fact that the ATHP is legally binding was hoped to be a positive step forward in terms of effective regionalism. As noted above, legally binding arrangements are largely regarded in the literature as a more effective type of agreement, as it is one of the most common and traditional ways for inducing targeted actors to change their behaviour (Murray, 2010: 319; Shelton, 2003: 552), and of guarding against the risk of another party's nonperformance of a cooperative arrangement (Shelton, 2003: 73). This gradual move from non-binding to binding instruments was similar to the progression that occurred with the CLRTAP. As discussed earlier, the CLRTAP originally worked on consensus, and monitoring of acid rain was on a voluntary basis (Tuinstra, 2008: 35). Unsurprisingly, there was a highly uneven implementation of the CLRTAP among signatories during its early years (Wettestad, 2002: 336). However, the CLRTAP eventually became legally binding with the addition of binding air emission limitations to the Convention, and this was largely credited for its success (Campbell, 2005: 224; Eaton and Radojevic, 2001). Therefore, scholars were hopeful as this similar progression was observed in ASEAN: from a plethora of non-legally binding instruments such as the HTTF and the RHAP, to the legally binding ATHP. By virtue of being legally binding, scholars hoped that there would be a strengthening of ASEAN's capacity to enforce haze mitigation initiatives, as the ATHP would be able to help streamline national policy positions around the joint position of the RHAP and facilitate its implementation (Koh and Robinson, 2002: 1–2). Other scholars noted that this was a positive reflection of the willingness of states to put aside the taboo of interference in one another's affairs (Jones, 2006: 439–440; Smith, 2000: 42–43).

However, effective implementation of these mechanisms does not entirely rely on whether these initiatives are binding or non-binding (Koh and Robinson, 2002: 1–2). As discussed above, due to the different models of regionalism that exist in

Europe and Southeast Asia, not all forms of transnational coordination and cooperation that are feasible in Europe would be feasible in Southeast Asia (Beeson, 2007: 25). The binding mechanisms of the CLRTAP were effective in compelling European states to adhere to air emission limitations because the European model of regionalism is characterized by the pooling of sovereignty (Kim, 2011: 422; Murray, 2010: 311–313). Hence, European states were compelled to act in the region's *common* interests, despite only two signatories regarded acid rain as a serious *national* problem (Levy, 1992: 16). The model of ASEAN regionalism in turn is characterized by the maintenance of national sovereignty (Kim, 2011: 422; Murray, 2010: 311–313). Therefore, states were compelled to ensure that the ATHP, even when legally binding, still observed the national interests of the states, as opposed to the collective regional interest.

Again, member states did this by closely adhering to the spirit of the ASEAN Way. This ensured that the ATHP, while legally binding, was a highly watered down document that continued to protect national economic interests, preserve state sovereignty and deflect responsibility on the haze issue (Tan [S7], 2010; Yahaya [M13], 2010). This resulted in a treaty that, although technically legally binding, was 'vague and lacking in various hard-law instruments such as strong dispute-resolution and enforcement mechanisms. Important provisions, including those for developing preventive measures (both legislative and administrative), and a national emergency response, are left to member parties to interpret and apply' (Nguitragool, 2011: 357). Furthermore, unlike other similar treaty regimes, the ATHP did not include any provisions for dispute settlements through international courts or other arbitration tribunals (Tan, A. K., 2005: 664). As Article 27 of the Agreement states, 'any dispute between Parties as to the interpretation or application of, or compliance with, this Agreement or any protocol thereto, shall be settled amicably by consultation or negotiation' (ASEAN Secretariat, 2002a: 17). A. K. Tan (2005: 664) argues that this wholly pre-empts the 'enforcement of compliance through legal principles of state responsibility and international liability'. Hence, the ATHP did not significantly differ from the RHAP in either substance or in demands for member parties to make policy changes (Nguitragool, 2011: 365). This watering-down process, where the costs of cooperation for concerned parties are greatly lowered (Nguitragool, 2011: 368), is visible in the negotiation process leading up to the finalization of the ATHP, as is explained in the following paragraphs.

ASEAN Secretariat staff who were interviewed explained that due to the negative backlash from the haze issue, Secretariat representatives avidly argued the case for interference and the issue of consent of the receiving state for assistance during meetings leading up to the finalization of the ATHP. However, as the main drivers of the ASEAN organization are member states and not the Secretariat (Interviewee A7, 2010), member states had the final say and chose to prioritize sovereignty concerns over ensuring practical progress on the ground. Hence, the Secretariat was very limited in its organizational capacity to determine the direction of negotiations or to push for more stringent outcomes. Therefore, it was decided that ASEAN initiatives would strictly observe the norm of non-interference, and that assistance would only be upon the request or consent of the receiving state (Interviewee A4 and Interviewee A5, 2010; Mat Akhir [A1], 2010). As Article 12 states, 'assistance can only be employed at the request of and with the consent of the requesting Party, or, when offered by another Party or Parties, with the consent of the receiving Party' (ASEAN Secretariat, 2002a: 9).

Furthermore, ASEAN staff who were interviewed pointed out that issues that were deemed too 'sensitive' were not discussed at all during negotiations (Interviewee A7, 2010; Interviewee A4 and Interviewee A5, 2010; Mat Akhir [A1], 2010). For example, even though there was an unspoken understanding that commercial plantation burning was the major source of haze, the issue of illegal burning by local and foreign plantation companies was never raised during discussions leading up to the ATHP (Balamurugan [M40], 2010). An NGO representative who was interviewed also expressed this, stating that 'if ASEAN *really* wanted to address the haze problem', the issue of plantations and transnational business would have had to be inserted into the ATHP as well (Maitar [I12], 2010). As a result of these negotiations, the ATHP provided only weak legal enforcement as it relies on the cooperation of its parties through self-regulation and decentralized operations, despite being legally binding (Florano, 2003: 132–133).

For example, the strict observance of the non-interference norm within the ATHP (that dictates that assistance will only be activated upon request from the receiving state) (Interviewee A4 and Interviewee A5, 2010; Mat Akhir [A1], 2010) rendered important new elements such as the POE ineffective. Because of the non-interference requirements, there were very specific guidelines for deployment. In addition to approval by Indonesia, the POE team leader has to be Indonesian, and there has to be evidence of more than 250 hotspots over a period of two days (Interviewee A4 and Interviewee A5, 2010). As a result, the POE was very much paralysed. It was deployed only three times: to Indonesian provinces between August and October 2006 (Prasiddha, 2009). Furthermore, when deployed, the POE was subjected to serious pressure from local officials. For example, when the POE was deployed to Kalimantan, the provincial governor urged the Panel not to recommend the deployment of regional fire-fighting teams, instead insisting on the use of local capacities. At other times, the POE's reports were doctored under pressure from government officials in efforts to shield their institutional failures from external scrutiny (Hameiri and Jones, 2013: 471).

Indonesia also on several occasions denied or delayed entry of the POE, the latest of which was in 2009, even though all criteria for activation had been fulfilled (Interviewee A7, 2010; Interviewee A4 and Interviewee A5, 2010). Again, this enabled Indonesia to avoid opening its doors to unwanted external scrutiny (Koh [S2], 2010; Tay [S12], 2010).

Just like the other haze initiatives before it, non-interference was strictly adhered to with the ATHP as a way to ensure that crucial economic interests of the involved states were preserved. In this case, the ATHP was adopted using a very loose, vague expression of the doctrine of state responsibility (Syarif, 2007). As a result, instead of offering solutions to the transboundary haze problem, engagement at the ASEAN level has served to protect the interests of the oil palm plantation sector and the well-connected elites that control it, while allowing the haze to persist. Such regionalism does not promote effective cooperation towards the regional collective good, and thus cannot be expected to produce environmentally positive results (Smith, 2004: 418). Instead, it often results in regional initiatives that merely privilege economic actors that are close allies of the political elite (Nesadurai, 2008: 237). As one scholar expresses, 'emphasizing regional solidarity and providing "assistance" instead of "intervention" is what ASEAN has the potential to do best' (Nguitragool, 2011: 377). This statement underlines the ASEAN's organizational capacity; while the ability to intervene would depict strong organizational capacity, providing mere assistance does not.

This functional adherence to the ASEAN Way to preserve the interests of the economic and political elite, which this book argues is the major reason for the persistence of haze, can be observed in more detail when examining the conduct of individual countries involved, namely Indonesia, Malaysia and Singapore, in response to ASEAN initiatives. Despite being the central country in the regional haze equation, Indonesia refused to ratify the Agreement for more than ten years. The following section discusses the motivations for Indonesia's non-ratification during this time, arguing that undue influence of patronage networks in the oil palm plantation sector was a major factor in Indonesia's decision.

Indonesia's non-ratification of the ATHP

Up until 16 September 2014, the ATHP remained ratified by only nine ASEAN states, with the Philippines being the ninth country to ratify in early 2010. The former secretary general of ASEAN who was interviewed lamented Indonesia's refusal to ratify the Agreement during this time. He argued that since all ten states had signed the Agreement in 2002, that meant that they all agreed to the spirit of the Agreement already, and 'Indonesia should have no reason to withhold ratification' (Ong [A3], 2010). Other interviewees argue that Indonesia signed the Agreement for political reasons, for the good image of the state within ASEAN (Nagulendran [M34] and Interviewee M35, 2010), without having any intention to actually ratify. They reasoned that due to the norms of non-interference, Indonesia had nothing to lose by signing the Agreement as member states and the Secretariat could not force it to subsequently ratify (Casey [I46], 2011; Nagulendran [M34] and Interviewee M35, 2010). The Indonesian side of the story shows a more revealing explanation as to why Indonesia signed the ATHP but refused to ratify it for so long.

The ATHP observes the 'ASEAN minus X' formula for ratification (Letchumanan [A6], 2010; Mat Akhir [A1], 2010; Ong [A3], 2010). This means that the Agreement could be called into force with a minimum number of ratifications, and not all members were required to ratify the Agreement. While this is now a standard feature in international environmental treaty law, ASEAN officials explained that the ATHP was one of the earliest ASEAN mechanisms that practiced this formula (Letchumanan [A6], 2010; Mat Akhir [A1], 2010; Ong [A3], 2010). The 'ASEAN minus X' formula enables individual member states to go further and faster individually 'without upsetting consensus' (Smith, 2004: 426). It helps protect member states from having to commit to joint tasks that they do not have the administrative capacity to carry out, or tasks that they find politically difficult due to dominant domestic interests (Nesadurai, 2008: 228).

Interviewees pointed out that during the ATHP negotiations, officials foresaw that some countries would probably not ratify the ATHP (Interviewee A4 and Interviewee A5, 2010; Letchumanan [A6], 2010). Therefore, the head of the ASEAN Environment Department who was interviewed explained that the Secretariat proposed that this formula be applied to the ATHP out of concern that 'countries that did not have such a large interest in the issue, like Laos, would not ratify' (Letchumanan [A6], 2010). Hence, Secretary-General Rodolfo Severino had suggested the Agreement to enter into force with only six ratifications. This was inserted into the Agreement under Article 29, which states that 'this Agreement shall enter into force on the sixtieth day after the deposit of the sixth instrument of ratification, acceptance, approval or accession' (ASEAN Secretariat, 2002a: 18). With this, in 2003, the ATHP became one of the few legally binding ASEAN environmental agreements to be entered into force (ASEAN Secretariat, 2004) with six ratifications. Incidentally, Laos did ratify the ATHP, while Indonesian continued to delay its ratification.

Despite the weakness of the ATHP in providing legal enforcement for the RHAP (Florano, 2003: 132–133), Indonesia, as the central country implicated in the haze due to its key role as the dominant host country in the region's oil palm plantation sector, still considered the ATHP a risk to its crucial economic interests. As the following discussion elucidates, Indonesia's non-ratification of the ATHP was important in maintaining the availability of and access to plantation land[5] (Elliott, 2003: 29–35) in Indonesia, to cater to its dominant domestic economic interests. This created the free-rider situation (Larson and Soto, 2008: 218–226) discussed in the previous chapter, extrapolated to the regional level. Even though ATHP ratification might have been rational at the regional level, it made less sense to the Indonesian political and business elites. This created disincentives for Indonesia to ratify the ATHP. Therefore, many interviewees believe that Indonesian non-ratification was due to a combination of national interests and patronage factors. As explained in Chapter 3, oil palm is a matter of crucial economic importance to the socioeconomic development of the state as a whole. At the same time, the Indonesian oil palm plantation sector is made up of a dense network of patronage relationships that need to be preserved by the Indonesian political elite (see Chapter 4) (Syarif [I2], 2010). Hence, formally regionalizing haze governance through the ratification of the ATHP directly threatened these patronage accumulation strategies (Hameiri and Jones, 2013: 471). This has resulted in many years of resistance to ratification at various levels in Indonesia, first at the ministerial level even before the treaty was elevated to Parliament for ratification, and second at the parliamentary levels itself, as discussed respectively in the subsections below. In these ways, the ATHP's 'ASEAN minus X' formula for ratification became a major stumbling block for the effectiveness of the ATHP (Letchumanan [A6], 2010; Mat Akhir [A1], 2010; Ong [A3], 2010).

Resistance at the ministerial level

At the ministerial level, the Ministry of Forestry provided a strong counterweight to the Ministry of Environment in ratification efforts at ASEAN. At the parliamentary level, the bill for the ratification at the ATHP repeatedly reached impasse (Keraf [I35], 2010). These are telling examples of how national interests and patronage politics intersect, resulting in regional outcomes that privilege economic actors that are close allies of the Indonesian political elite (Nesadurai, 2008: 237). As discussed briefly in the previous chapters, there is a dearth of mutual cooperation among Indonesia's domestic institutions (Nguitragool, 2011: 371), resulting in a certain hierarchy among government ministries in Indonesia.

The Ministries of Forestry and Agriculture are the more powerful ministries, with greater mandate, manpower and budgetary resources (Tan, 2004: 178–179). Even though the Ministry of Environment has been the engine of Indonesia's environmental diplomacy and holds the mandate to negotiate environmental treaties (including the ATHP) on behalf of Indonesia, its officials barely wield decision-making authority over land and forest policy at the central bureaucratic level (Nguitragool, 2011: 371). The Environment Ministry remains a junior ministry within the Indonesian government, lacking 'line responsibility'. This means the Ministry has limited influence on the ground, including any powers to force these other government ministries to comply with any requirements or expectations, or to enforce domestic laws (Hameiri and Jones, 2013: 469; Nguitragool, 2011: 371; Syarif, 2010: 8–10). For example, as explained in an earlier chapter, the mandate to prevent fires in forest and plantation areas is under the inspection role of the Ministries of Forestry and Agriculture. Therefore, the institutions with actual authority to prevent the haze disaster have been distant from the ASEAN processes[6] (Nguitragool, 2011: 372).

This reflects Indonesia's national priorities, where the utility of the forests and land as natural resources is viewed as more important than the preservation of the environment (Elliott, 2003: 29–35), In fact, the Environment Ministry has been described as 'constitutionally not a policy-implementation agency of the government' (Eaton and Radojevic, 2001: 244). For example, as discussed in the previous chapter, the Ministry of Forestry is in charge of the licensing of forest exploitation concessions to private companies (Interviewee I25, 2010), while the Ministry of Environment possesses only coordinating and supervisory functions (Tan, 2004: 178–179). As a result of this, interviewees explained that the Forestry and Agriculture Ministries have closer patronage dealings with plantation companies as compared to the Ministry of Environment, and have often cultivated close instrumental relationships with them (Interviewee I25, 2010; Surya [I9] and Akbar [I10], 2010). In contrast, the Ministry of Environment has limited authority and ability to mobilize support from influential actors. Therefore, while at ASEAN, often representatives from the Ministry of Environment attend haze-related meetings on behalf of the government, the Ministry has largely been unable to influence decision making in response to these regional outcomes at the domestic level (Nguitragool, 2011: 372), as explained in the following paragraphs.

According to the Indonesian ambassador to ASEAN who was interviewed, the ATHP was put together at the ASEAN level in a particularly rushed manner because of the urgent pressure from civil society at that time. The Environment Ministry officials who represented Indonesia in ATHP negotiations were not able to adequately discuss the Agreement with other Indonesian ministries before signing the Agreement along with other member states. The ambassador explained that this was why the treaty was signed by Indonesia at the ASEAN level: 'because the Environment Ministry *only* was agreeable to it' (Swajaya [I37], 2010). The Ambassador explained that if the other ministries were consulted prior to signing, 'the ATHP would have looked much different than what it is today' (Swajaya [I37], 2010). Therefore, it can be seen here that Indonesia signed the ATHP because the Indonesian representatives to ASEAN at the time consisted of Environment Ministry officials who were less influenced by national and patronage interests and had more of an interest in the regional environmental good.

However, other more influential Indonesian decision makers were said to be against the ATHP, especially the Forestry Ministry (Interviewee I25, 2010; Surya [I9] and Akbar [I10], 2010). For example, a former environment minister, Dr A. Sonny Keraf, was a state representative to ASEAN for the ATHP and was one of the initiators of the Agreement. He said that he was 'fully supportive of the Agreement', but problems arose when he brought the treaty back home to the other ministries (especially the Forestry Ministry) (Keraf [I35], 2010). As mentioned above, important individuals at the Forestry Ministry are said to have cultivated close patronage links with prominent players in the oil palm plantation sector (Interviewee I25, 2010; Surya [I9] and Akbar [I10], 2010). Furthermore, the Forestry Ministry also had a material interest in ensuring Indonesia's economic progress through maintaining the availability of, and access to, the country's lucrative natural resources (Elliott, 2003: 29–35), which the ATHP threatened to disrupt. Interviewees explained that despite this resistance, the Environment Ministry continued running socialization exercises among the other ministries to garner support of the ATHP (Bratasida [I36], 2010; Hariri [I30] and Ardiansyah [I31], 2010).

Resistance at the parliamentary level

In Indonesia, any international or regional treaty has to be enacted as a law. This involves a long and tedious series of meetings and public hearings in the House of Representatives[7] of the Indonesian Parliament (Hudiono, 2003). A former ASEAN Secretariat staff member who was interviewed pointed out that 'this parliamentary system and procedures are slowing down ratification' (Interviewee A2, 2010). Despite resistance from the Ministry of Forestry, the Ministry of Environment prepared the required preliminary procedures for parliamentary ratification of the ATHP and submitted a proposal to the State Secretariat and Ministry of Foreign Affairs in 2002 (Kurniawan, 2002). The environment minister called for the urgent ratification of the Agreement, noting that it did not involve sanctions (Hariri [I30] and Ardiansyah [I31], 2010; Maitar [I12], 2010) and would have more positive than negative effects on the country (Hedradjat [I14], 2010; Sijabat, 2007,). That year, the Environment Ministry and Indonesia's House of Representatives agreed to accelerate preparations for the ratification of the ATHP, stating that in principle, they had agreed to ratify the Agreement by mid-2003 at the latest (Hariri [I30] and Ardiansyah [I31], 2010; Maitar [I12], 2010). When this did not transpire, then President Susilo Bambang Yudhoyono and the Ministry of Forestry identified the pact as one of the most important bills to be passed in 2004 (Nguitragool, 2011: 373).

However, as the years went on, it was announced that the State Secretariat was still considering the matter (Sijabat, 2006). An interviewee argued that this delay was due to the influence that the powerful Forestry Ministry had over the State Secretariat (Interviewee I25, 2010). By 2005, the bill had still not been publicized in regions across the country according to procedure (Sijabat, 2006). In 2006, the State Secretariat finally allowed the ATHP bill to be considered among 78 bills the Parliament would debate that year. However, the Parliament decided to drop it from the agenda that year without explanation (Maulidia, 2006). In 2007, a working committee of 40 legislators from three commissions overseeing defence and foreign affairs, agriculture and forestry affairs and environment affairs presented their views on the ATHP, but did not come to an agreement (Parliament of Singapore, 2007; Sijabat, 2007). In 2009, the House of Representatives (Dewan Perwakilan Rakyat) highlighted the ASEAN Haze Agreement as one of the six priority bills to be ratified before their current term ended on 30 September (Parliament of Singapore, 2009). However, this did not transpire that year either (Letchumanan [A6], 2010), and until today, the treaty is still 'stuck at Parliament' (Nagulendran [M34] and Interviewee M35, 2010). Most recently, at the 15th Meeting of the Sub-Regional Ministerial Steering Committee on Transboundary Haze Pollution in Kuala Lumpur held in the aftermath of the June–July 2013 haze episode, the Indonesian Environment Minister Balthazar Kambuaya stated that he would once again push for Indonesia's parliamentary ratification of the ATHP. Subject to parliamentary approval, the minister was hopeful of ratification by early 2014 (Woo, 2013). This did not happen, but the pledge to eventually ratify the Agreement was picked up by the newly elected Indonesian President Joko Widodo. The president's choice of former Environment Minister Dr A. Sonny Keraf (who was closely involved in the negotiation process of the ATHP as detailed above) as his advisor (Leonal and Wulandri, 2014) possibly played a role in Indonesia's long-awaited ratification of the Agreement on 16 September 2014, but further in-depth research is needed to explain this turn of events.

Other than the influence of the Forestry Ministry, sector lobby groups also had an important role in blocking ratification in Parliament over the past decade. In the patronage culture of Indonesia, lobby groups operate less as disciplined collectives and more as clusters of personal relationships. In this system, these groups were mainly interested in personal benefits for particular members (Kurer, 1996: 657). These groups often lobby parliamentarians to structure parliamentary outcomes for the individual gain of their prominent members (Enderwick, 2005: 129) and block policies and treaties that might threaten their interests (Hamilton-Hart, 2007: 95). Indeed, the Indonesian Parliament has been described as the 'weakest state institution' in Indonesia (Deutsch and Sender, 2011) because of this undue private-sector influence.

The Indonesian Sustainable Palm Oil Commission and Indonesian Palm Oil Association (GAPKI) are examples of such powerful lobby groups, and are said to be influential in recommending and changing regulations in accordance to industry interests (Soeharto [I51], 2012). As some interviewees stated, 'GAPKI has the power and influence to mould the future of the Indonesian palm oil industry' (Interviewee M53 and Interviewee M54, 2012). GAPKI especially strongly lobbies for 'the preservation of their heritage and way of life', referring to the status quo of open burning operations in land clearing and the use of peatlands for plantations (Ong [A3], 2010). GAPKI has also often used the 'nationalism card' to influence parliamentarians not to ratify the ATHP, arguing that the Agreement would be an impingement on Indonesia's sovereign status (Caballero-Anthony [S3], 2010; Lee [S20], 2010; Quah [S24], 2010; Saravanamuttu [S23], 2010; Tay [S12], 2010). GAPKI was said to be against the Indonesian government ratifying the ATHP and accepting outside assistance because it was worried that member states would then be able to pressure the Indonesian government to take more serious action over the haze (Tarigan [I23], 2010). Interviewees explained that one major concern of GAPKI was the fact that the ATHP allowed for additional protocols, and GAPKI was worried that this may later on include enforcement and liability clauses related to peatlands and use of fire, which would threaten the sector's practices (Interviewee S1, 2010; Interviewee S21, 2010).

Many interviewees pointed out that GAPKI is controlled by powerful Indonesian individuals with close personal relationships with prominent MPs (Caballero-Anthony [S3], 2010; Interviewee S14 and Interviewee S15, 2010; Interviewee I25, 2010; Interviewee A4 and Interviewee A5, 2010; Lee [S20], 2010; Mat Akhir [A1], 2010; Ong [A3], 2010), and with vested interests in maintaining the status quo in the plantation industry (Caballero-Anthony [S3], 2010; Lee [S20], 2010; Quah [S24], 2010; Saravanamuttu [S23], 2010; Tay [S12], 2010). For example, the current secretary general of GAPKI, Joko Supriyono, who as mentioned earlier is also a director at the major Indonesian plantation company Astra Agro, is said to have formidable influence with the Indonesian government and Parliament due to his many years of experience in the sector, and was instrumental in shaping the outcomes of many sector-related policy decisions (Interviewee I48, 2011).

As an interviewee explained, this endemic patronage culture has meant that 'vested interests are playing a very strong role in hindering ratification' (Lee [S20], 2010). Oil palm business interests are considered so influential in Parliament that one interviewee went so far as to say that parliamentary debates on the ATHP are all just token, as given 'the strength of the concessions, and the lobbying in the Parliament and contributions both under and above the table of the plantation sector to the economy and to the elite, the ATHP will never get passed'[8] (Interviewee I25, 2010). Interviewees argued that parliamentarian statements and positions on the ATHP were made based on the need to appease their powerful backers or constituents who have investments in the plantation sectors (Interviewee A7, 2010; Swajaya [I37], 2010; Tarigan [I23], 2010).

As discussed above, the ASEAN Way principles are often called upon by states in areas where crucial economic interests and dominant domestic interests are affected (Nesadurai, 2008: 237). Therefore, due to national economic and development interests coupled with patronage concerns, many legislators came out against ratification of the ATHP (Hariri [I30] and Ardiansyah [I31], 2010; Sijabat, 2007). Hence, arguments presented at the Parliament against ratification have included quite feeble political instead of environmental concerns (Hariri [I30] and Ardiansyah [I31], 2010). For example, sovereignty concerns were raised with regard to fire-fighting assistance under the ATHP despite the Agreement already containing specific clauses preserving the sovereignty of states during such assistance, as was pointed out by the former Indonesian environment minister who was interviewed (Keraf [I35], 2010). For instance, parliamentarians and bureaucrats from local governments and local forestry institutions expressed concern that foreign firemen would use the knowledge they gain inside Indonesia wrongfully (Keraf [I35], 2010; Nguitragool, 2011: 374), especially related to matters of terrain and defense. In light of extensive patronage networks related to haze as explained in the previous chapters, these concerns were actually more related to the worry that felonious patronage activities in remote areas could become transparent and even exposed internationally (Nguitragool, 2011: 374). A Southeast Asian scholar who was interviewed explained that governments will always use things like sovereignty as an excuse, 'because they cannot just come out and say that they have vested interests' in the issue (Interviewee M36, 2010).

Parliamentarians further argued that the Agreement unfairly placed all responsibility of the haze on Indonesia (Sijabat, 2007). However, this was not the case as during negotiations, negotiators were very careful to word the Agreement in such ways that did not place blame on any particular country. For instance, Indonesia's Environment Ministry officials that participated in the negotiation process of the ATHP had already ensured that the Agreement used general rather than specific terms for this very reason. Contentious words included 'Borneo'[9] (the island consisting of Indonesia's Kalimantan and the Malaysian states of Sabah and Sarawak) replacing 'Kalimantan', and 'pollution' replacing 'transboundary pollution' (because Indonesia argued that the haze was not always transboundary) (Nagulendran [M34] and Interviewee M35, 2010). Furthermore, ASEAN cautiously added the term 'haze' (which, as discussed in Chapter 1, denotes a naturally occurring phenomenon) to the term 'smoke', thus referring to the phenomenon as 'smoke haze' in order to prevent criminalizing Indonesia (Nguitragool, 2011: 362). In fact, throughout the history of haze cooperation at the ASEAN level (as detailed above), other ASEAN members have never explicitly called upon Indonesia to take official responsibility for breaching its obligations to control its fires, or to incur any formal liability for the damage that the resulting haze has caused to neighbouring states (Tan, A. K., 2005: 657). Despite this neutral language, parliamentarians for many years still chose to view the Agreement as unfairly laying responsibility upon Indonesia.

Parliamentarians also argued that ASEAN members were selfishly pushing Indonesia to ratify without considering Indonesia's interests (Hedradjat [I14], 2010; Interviewee I18, 2010; Interviewee A7, 2010; Keraf [I35], 2010; Surya [I9] and Akbar [I10], 2010). This external pressure was regularly depicted as a conspiracy of sorts to impede Indonesia's development (Hameiri and Jones, 2013: 471). Parliamentarians argued that there was no 'balance of benefits' in the Agreement, and it would benefit other ASEAN members more (Budianto, 2008; Hameiri and Jones, 2013: 471; Hariri [I30] and Ardiansyah [I31], 2010; Haryanto [I16], 2010; Interviewee I18, 2010; Keraf [I35], 2010; Maulidia, 2006; Parliament of Singapore, 2010a; Satyawan [I20], 2010). In reality, the Indonesian people in Kalimantan and Sumatra closest to the source of the fires would benefit most from the treaty and the clean air that it was hoped it would bring (Parliament of Singapore, 2010a). As one interviewee put it, the interests that the parliamentarians had in mind did not include the social well-being of the people, but instead the economic interests and practices of the oil palm plantation sector that were at stake with the ATHP (Lee [S20], 2010).

They also argued that the legal consequences of ratification were heavy (Sijabat, 2007), as Indonesia would have to amend many of its regulations by adding clauses on controlled burning and zero-burning practices (Budianto, 2008), and also limit activity on peatlands. However, Indonesia already has all these provisions in their law (Interviewee I7 and Interviewee I8, 2010), as explained extensively in the previous chapter. Parliamentarians also said that the government did not have enough money and was not financially prepared to support the tighter monitoring that was required in the Agreement. Hence, they argued that ratification of the ATHP would be a burden to Indonesia financially (Albar [I17], 2010; *Jakarta Post*, 2006b; Udiansyah [I15], 2010; Widodo [I11], 2010), since fighting large-scale land and forest fires is an expensive and difficult task because the Indonesian archipelago is vast and the fires are largely peat-based (Nguitragool, 2011: 369). This stance ignores the widely recognized understanding that a state's economic level is not a pretext to discharge it from its international law obligations (Tan, 1999). Furthermore, interviewees explained that ratification would somewhat address this concern because this would allow Indonesia access to the Haze Fund that was set up with the ATHP (Interviewee S14 and Interviewee S15, 2010).

To further substantiate the case for non-ratification, parliamentarians noted that even without the Agreement, the state had still managed to reduce the number of hotspots in 2007 by more than 70 per cent (Hariri [I30] and Ardiansyah [I31], 2010). However, this reduction could be credited to the mild El Niño cycle, not action on the ground (Joedawinata [I33] and Sartono [I34], 2010). Furthermore, some parliamentarians argued that there was no real difference to Indonesia whether the Agreement was ratified or otherwise (Maitar [I12], 2010; Roswiniarti [I13], 2010), since it would not be faced with any sanctions anyway (Maitar [I12], 2010) and Indonesia already had the necessary laws and projects in place (Bratasida [I36], 2010) (contradicting the legal burden argument as stated above). Also, they argued that since there was already some cooperation happening anyway through earlier agreements and action plans, ratification was a mere unimportant formality (Swajaya [I37], 2010).

Interviewees explained that the Environment and Foreign Affairs Ministries have tried to convince parliamentarians to ratify the treaty first, and then add protocols for issues that they were concerned about later (Bratasida [I36], 2010; Interviewee A4 and Interviewee A5, 2010; Keraf [I35], 2010; Mat Akhir [A1], 2010). These ministries were worried that Indonesia would miss out on the benefits of the ATHP by delaying its ratification, especially on the opportunity to show diplomatic goodwill that was gained by signing the ATHP (Hudiono, 2003; Interviewee I24, 2010; Parliament of Singapore, 2010a; Satyawan [I20], 2010; Tarigan [I23], 2010; Yusuf [I19], 2010).

However, in recent years, parliamentarians stood their ground and insisted that they would only ratify the treaty if amendments according to their requests were made first. Indeed, as pointed out above, the Agreement allows for amendments. But according to ASEAN procedure, it would be prudent for Indonesia to ratify the Agreement first, and then seek amendments. As explained by a GEC representative who was present during ATHP negotiations, if the ATHP were to be modified first without Indonesia's ratification, the 'new' modified Agreement would need to then be ratified again by all countries, further delaying the process. If Indonesia ratified it first and then modifications were done, the changes would be automatically adopted into the Agreement without having to go through an additional round of ratification. Indeed, an interviewee detailed how Indonesia only formally raised these concerns to ASEAN after seven countries had already ratified the Agreement; so understandably, countries were reluctant to heed Indonesia's requests (Interviewee M44, 2012).

As no further progress in response to Indonesia's 'concerns' was made at ASEAN, Indonesia's parliamentary stalemate continued for many years (Keraf [I35], 2010). One interviewee pointed out that Indonesia was fully aware of this procedural issue that made modifications without universal ratification almost impossible, and argued that this was an intentional 'bluff' by Indonesia, who actually had no intention of ratifying the Agreement at all, with or without the required modifications (Interviewee M44, 2012). One NGO representative who was interviewed said that he heard that 'Indonesia will not ratify the treaty for at least another five to ten years'. This was because plantation companies were still in the process of opening land, and it was both in the national interests and the interests of clients that this process was not disrupted. In his view, 'once all the land in Indonesia is opened, only then would Indonesia be prepared to ratify the treaty'[10] (Syaf [I27], 2010).

Non-ratification limiting effectiveness of the treaty

Due to the non-interference norm, neither the weak ASEAN Secretariat, nor any member country could question or pressure Indonesia on the issue of ratification (Casey [I46], 2011; Nagulendran [M34] and Interviewee M35, 2010; Yahaya [M13], 2010). Besides, despite the severe socioeconomic effects of the haze,

Malaysian and Singaporean governments have been reluctant to pursue the matter of ratification with Indonesia due to their own vested interests in the Indonesian oil palm plantation sector. For example, Singapore reiterated publicly several times that it was Indonesia's sovereign right whether or not to ratify the treaty (Channel NewsAsia, 2006; Interviewee S4 and Interviewee S5, 2010; Tan, 2007). And as many interviewees reasoned, Malaysia was also careful not to pressure Indonesia for fear of Indonesia clamping down on Malaysia's extensive economic interests in the oil palm plantation sector there (Abdul Rahim [M16], 2010; Interviewee M36, 2010; Mathews [M33], 2010; Nuruddin [M10], 2010; Singh [M18], 2010).

Hence, even the legally binding ATHP has failed to produce effective results for haze mitigation in the region. As predicted, initiatives strategically shaped in the spirit of the ASEAN Way have resulted in an ATHP that still enhances the power of the national government (Hurrell, 1995: 336–337), protects crucial national economic interests (Nesadurai, 2008: 237), preserves state sovereignty and deflects responsibility on the haze issue (Tan [S7], 2010; Yahaya [M13], 2010). On top of the watering-down that the document experienced at the negotiation stage (Tan [S7], 2010; Yahaya [M13], 2010), Indonesia's self-interested non-ratification of the ATHP for more than a decade has been a major stumbling block for the effectiveness of the Agreement (Letchumanan [A6], 2010; Mat Akhir [A1], 2010; Ong [A3], 2010; Rukmantara [I45], 2011). This has been publicly expressed by several parties. For example, a top UN official stated at a conference in Singapore that Indonesia needed to ratify the ATHP to prove its commitment, political will and moral obligation in tackling climate change through fighting forest fires (*The Straits Times*, 2009). Opposition MPs in Singapore also voiced the futility of the ATHP unless Indonesia ratified it (Parliament of Singapore, 2010b). The many years of non-ratification by Indonesia has limited the effectiveness of the ATHP in four specific ways: in terms of fire-fighting, coordination, policy making and future directions of the Agreement,[11] as detailed below.

First, as part of the ATHP mechanism, if a serious forest fire was spotted by the ASMC, neighbouring states could activate fire-fighting services and move in, without having to write in to the receiving government to get diplomatic clearance for aircrafts and permission from local fire services for each new case (Khalik, 2006). However, interviewees explained that this clause was only applicable if both countries had ratified the treaty. Therefore, even with the ATHP in force, assistance still could not be deployed immediately without ratification by Indonesia (Interviewee A4 and Interviewee A5, 2010), hence effectively paralyzing this mechanism over the years. On both matters of the Panel of Experts and fire-fighting assistance, interviewees suggested that the real reason behind Indonesia's reluctance was because the fires were on plantation land of particular well-connected individuals, and the Indonesian government did not want outside parties, such as the POE, to be exposed to this fact (Interviewee A7, 2010; Interviewee A4 and Interviewee A5, 2010).

Second, non-ratification has also delayed the establishment of the ASEAN

Coordination Centre for Haze (Bratasida [I36], 2010) and its dedicated Secretariat (Interviewee M44, 2012). This Centre and its Secretariat would have been useful for coordinating information and cooperation efforts around the region (ASEAN Secretariat, 2002a: 6; Bratasida [I36], 2010). The Annex of the Agreement goes into the details of the Centre's visualized role, including to:

> a) Establish and maintain regular contact with the respective National Monitoring Centres regarding the data, including those derived from satellite imagery and meteorological observation, relating to land and/or forest fire, environmental conditions conducive to such fires; and air quality and levels of pollution, in particular haze arising from such fires;
> b) Facilitate co-operation and co-ordination among the Parties to increase their preparedness for and to respond to land and/or forest fires or haze pollution arising from such fires;
> c) Facilitate co-ordination among the Parties, other States and relevant organizations in taking effective measures to mitigate the impact of land and/or forest fires or haze pollution arising from such fires; and
> d) Respond to a request for or offer of assistance in the event of land and/or forest fires or haze pollution resulting from such fires by transmitting promptly the request for assistance to other States and organizations; and co-ordinating such assistance, if so requested by the requesting Party or offered by the assisting Party.
>
> (ASEAN Secretariat, 2002a: 23–24)

During negotiations, ministers reached agreement that the Centre and Secretariat would be established as soon as possible, and was set to be located in Riau, Sumatra. This was hoped to fuel more awareness and ownership of the fire problem in the Riau administration. An interviewee from the Indonesian Environment Ministry explained that 'in the spirit of sovereignty', Indonesia was granted substantial control over the Centre, for instance on selection of experts working in the Centre (Bratasida [I36], 2010). However the Centre and Secretariat have yet to be established, pending Indonesia's ratification of the treaty. As a result, the ASEAN Secretariat, with limited staff spread over many departments, still functions as an interim Secretariat for haze matters in the region, instead of a dedicated Secretariat under the Centre (Interviewee M44, 2012). In short, even thought the treaty is already in force and was ratified by almost all ASEAN countries many years ago, only with the ratification by Indonesia could the ATHP be fully implemented.

Third, due to Indonesia's non-ratification, interviewees admit that ASEAN-level initiatives have not been able to 'address sensitive issues' (Syaf [I27], 2010) such as influencing Indonesian forest policy and the implementation of laws (Udiansyah [I15], 2010; Widodo [I11], 2010). Article 9 of the Agreement calls for the development of 'appropriate policies to curb activities that may lead to land and/or forest fires' (ASEAN Secretariat, 2002a: 8), however this is only applicable to ratified states. So ASEAN's capacity to advise on appropriate fire and haze mitigation policies for Indonesia remained effectively non-existent during this time. Hence, an interviewee pointed out that the success of ASEAN-level initiatives is 'essentially dependent on the Indonesian government, not on ASEAN' (Interviewee S16, 2010). Therefore, while regional systems of environmental governance can be an important complement to environmental governance, efforts at the national level suffered (Koh and Robinson, 2002: 1–2), and like many previous ASEAN-level environmental initiatives discussed earlier in this book, haze mitigation at the ASEAN level has been ineffective.

Furthermore, despite not ratifying the ATHP, Indonesia still attended ATHP meetings, merely updating the status of ratification as 'still stuck in their Parliament'. Importantly, interviewees explained that while the Conference of the Parties meetings should only be open to parties of the ATHP, Indonesia has not only been attending as an observer, but has also been accorded the same privileges as a party of the Agreement in the spirit of ASEAN solidarity, for example, permission to speak (Interviewee A4 and Interviewee A5, 2010; Letchumanan [A6], 2010; Ong [A3], 2010). Indonesia also actively participates in more non-invasive ATHP activities, such as the Standard Operating Procedures for Monitoring, Assessment and Joint Emergency Response Document, which parties are requested to submit come the dry season (Interviewee A4 and Interviewee A5, 2010; Letchumanan [A6], 2010; Mat Akhir [A1], 2010; Ong [A3], 2010). As many ASEAN staff who were interviewed indicated, all countries were essentially operating as if the Agreement had been ratified by all parties (Interviewee A4 and Interviewee A5, 2010; Letchumanan [A6], 2010; Ong [A3], 2010).

In this way, Indonesia could legitimately obstruct any clause or provision that would lead to what it feels is an encroachment on its sovereignty (Nguitragool, 2011: 368). For example, at the most recent Meeting of the Sub-Regional Ministerial Steering Committee mentioned above, Indonesia successfully blocked a proposal to make concession maps publicly available under the HMS.[12] Publicly available maps would enable interested parties, like NGO groups and academic researchers, to independently monitor hotspots and fires. However, Indonesia argued that the maps could not be released to the public due to the country's Freedom of Information Law (of which Indonesia refused to make exemptions, even though the government is empowered to do so) (Hussain, 2013; Woo, 2013). Academic observers such as Azmi Sharom have noted a more sinister reason related to patronage linkages in the sector: 'Who owns this land, who this person is related to, how big his area is – once everything is transparent, then any transaction or ownership which is dubious will be open to public scrutiny' (interviewed by Hussain, 2013). As a result, it was agreed that these concession maps would only be shared between governments on an ad-hoc basis, significantly limiting the potential effectiveness of this initiative. Therefore, despite years of non-ratification, Indonesia in reality still managed to retain influence over the direction of haze action in the region during this time.

The observation of the ASEAN Way in haze initiatives has allowed Indonesia to assert its sovereign right in selectively adopting or ignoring elements of the ATHP in ways that protect its crucial economic interests (Nesadurai, 2008: 237).

These institutional practices that tend to reinforce sovereignty and non-interference also tend to limit innovation and prevent harsh criticism of Indonesia (Ortuoste, 2008: 252). The failure of Indonesia as a state and ASEAN as a regional organization to deal effectively with the fire and haze problem clearly demonstrates the powerful economic and political constraints, both at the regional level within ASEAN and at the national level within Indonesia, which severely impede the effectiveness of the ATHP (Tan, A. K., 2005: 720). Therefore, due to the ASEAN style of regional engagement that prioritizes national sovereignty, the organization's capacity to guide the negotiations, outcomes and implementation of the ATHP was seriously restricted. Instead, member states were able to strategically shape the ATHP to preserve national political and economic interests, in this case being the interests of the patrons and clients in the Indonesian oil palm sector. With the ATHP, state sovereignty is still of paramount importance, international action is still dependent on the consent of the state where the fires originate, and the mechanisms prescribed do not seem to be any more effective or sophisticated than earlier ASEAN-level haze mitigation efforts (Tan, A. K., 2005: 720). This further limits the effective regionalism of haze mitigation at the ASEAN level.

As seen throughout this chapter thus far, instead of offering solutions to the transboundary haze problem, the regionalism of haze mitigation at the ASEAN level has served to protect the interests of the regional oil palm plantation sector, while allowing the haze to persist. By focusing on Indonesia's decade-long non-ratification, the above discussion has concentrated largely on the Indonesian position towards ASEAN cooperation, and how Indonesia managed to ensure that ASEAN outcomes catered to its national and elite interests. To further elucidate the Malaysian and Singaporean position on this issue, a particular element of the ATHP, the Adopt-A-District programmes, spearheaded by Malaysia and Singapore, are discussed below. These programmes are especially notable for focusing on haze mitigation efforts at the community level, while deliberately avoiding engagement with large-scale commercial plantation actors. While the source of the haze has been identified as coming from these commercial plantations, the programmes offer solutions that focus on small-scale slash-and-burn farming. This illustrates how, even when offering assistance, Malaysian and Singaporean initiatives continue to protect the interests of their investments in Indonesia.

Adopt-A-District: whither commercial plantations?

A common underlying issue running throughout the process of regionalism of haze mitigation in ASEAN has been the tendency to concentrate too much on the burning activities of the community and smallholdings (Balamurugan [M40], 2010; Casey [I46], 2011; Chee [M27], 2010; Interviewee M23, 2010; Moore [I5], 2010; Ramakrishna [M20], 2010; Singh [M18], 2010; Udiansyah [I15], 2010; Wibisino [I44], 2011), with very few initiatives and programmes focusing on concessionaires (*Jakarta Post*, 2006a). An interviewee lamented that in typical 'tropical government' fashion (the tendency of such governments to blame forest-dwellers for various types of forest degradation) (Wibisino [I44], 2011), member states tend to put more focus on socialization programmes for smallholder villagers who traditionally practice swidden agriculture instead of on plantation firms (Tan [S7], 2010), even though these communities have been shown to only contribute 20 per cent of fires (Casson, 2002: 234–239). Again, this shows how the ASEAN organization was limited in its capacity to shape coherent policy programmes that suitably matched the problem at hand.

For example, within the 1997 RHAP, described above, a key element that the ASEAN ministers identified as a solution to the haze was public education and incentives against open burning at the village level (Parliament of Singapore, 1998b). Also, the 2002 APMI was also designed to mainly promote sustainable management of peatlands at the community, not corporate level (Anshari [I42], 2011). Furthermore, any discussion at the ASEAN level for legal action to be taken by home or host countries against errant foreign and local companies was quickly dismissed 'in the spirit of ASEAN solidarity' (Interviewee M44, 2012). This tendency has been identified by many interviewees as a major weakness of ASEAN initiatives on haze (Balamurugan [M40], 2010; Casey [I46], 2011; Chee [M27], 2010; Interviewee M23, 2010; Moore [I5], 2010; Ramakrishna [M20], 2010; Singh [M18], 2010; Udiansyah [I15], 2010), with regional initiatives privileging the economic actors that are close allies of the political elite (Nesadurai, 2008: 237). The ATHP and its programmes also suffered from a similar fate. At an ATHP meeting for a Fire Danger Rating System, country representatives reiterated the importance of focusing on what they described as 'human factors', with community education programmes, socialization dialogue, and micro-financing for local community to clear land without burning (Global Environment Center, 2010: 30).

The Adopt-A-District programmes that were adopted as part of the ATHP further solidified this tendency of haze cooperation and assistance in the region. At a Conference of the Parties meeting in early 2006, Indonesian representatives presented its National POA on the haze to the ASEAN forum (Khalik, 2007b; Parliament of Singapore, 2006). As part of the plan, the central government proposed an education campaign to get villagers to abandon slash-and-burn cultivation, and to a lesser extent, enhance law enforcement and management of peatland areas (Khalik, 2007b; Moore [I5], 2010). Indonesia announced that it was planning to raise the budget for the POA mainly through contributions from neighbouring donor countries. The Ministerial Steering Committee (MSC) welcomed the POA under the ATHP framework, stating that it was prepared to assist Indonesia in implementing its POA (Parliament of Singapore, 2010b) and that neighbouring countries were prepared to commit resources as well (Khalik, 2007b; Moore [I5], 2010). However, when Indonesia requested up to $50 million in assistance, ASEAN and its member governments were unable to help with such a large amount (Interviewee M44, 2012).

Therefore, in November 2006, Indonesia returned to the Southern Sub-Regional MSC in Cebu, Philippines with an alternative plan (Interviewee M44,

2012), and invited the four other MSC members (Malaysia, Singapore, Thailand and Brunei) to 'adopt' some of its fire-prone districts and help build up their capacities to implement measures to prevent and suppress land and forest fires, as part of its POA against the haze (Asmarani, 2006; Interviewee M32, 2010; Interviewee S4 and Interviewee S5, 2010; Lee, 2006a, 2006b; Nagulendran [M34] and Interviewee M35, 2010). Following this, Malaysia committed to adopt and assist Riau, and Singapore committed to assist Jambi (Interviewee A4 and Interviewee A5, 2010; Khalik, 2007a; Letchumanan [A6], 2010; McIndoe, 2006; Parliament of Singapore, 2006; Peh, 2006; *The Straits Times*, 2006; Syaf [I27], 2010). Fires in the Riau province would bring smoke directly to Peninsula Malaysia, and haze from Jambi usually blows towards Singapore; this was the basis of these decisions (Channel NewsAsia, 2007b; Interviewee S14 and Interviewee S15, 2010).

These bilateral projects were inserted under the ATHP POA framework (Interviewee M2, 2010; Interviewee M4, 2010; Interviewee A4 and Interviewee A5, 2010; Letchumanan [A6], 2010; Ong [A3], 2010; Singh [M18], 2010) and were meant to 'complement ASEAN level efforts by reaching down to the community level' (Satyawan [I20], 2010) and assisting local governments in strengthening their haze prevention and monitoring capacities (Nguitragool, 2011: 376). However, as the following subsections detail, adopter countries limited their assistance to community work and fire control, and 'did not significantly engage with plantations' (Udiansyah [I15], 2010). Even when Malaysian and Singaporean companies did get involved, the obliging company only carried out 'socialization' projects with smallholders in (as part of their nucleus-plasma schemes) and around their plantation concession area, instead of any inward-looking improvement of their own plantation operations (Abdul Mutalib [M42], 2010; Interviewee I24, 2010; Interviewee M17, 2010). Essentially, this meant that Malaysian and Singaporean assistance was primarily focused on 'educating' smallholders and slash-and-burn farmers against the dangers of open burning.

As a result, interviewees pointed out that only brief, small-scale projects within the Riau and Jambi areas were carried out (Hariri [I30] and Ardiansyah [I31], 2010; Maitar [I12], 2010; Yusuf [I19], 2010), targeting a very limited area and number of village people, severely limiting the long-term effectiveness of ATHP efforts in terms of haze mitigation (Balamurugan [M40], 2010; Udiansyah [I15], 2010). The following subsections focus on the outcomes of these projects on the ground, showing that overwhelmingly outcomes have favoured the interests of plantation companies. Specifically, the Malaysian and Singaporean programmes continued to focus on the practices of smallholders and slash-and-burn farmers, and leave the operations of commercial plantations relatively uninterrupted.

The Malaysia-Riau collaboration

The Riau province is located in Central Sumatra and has a population of 5.5 million people with a land area of 7.3 million hectares. Currently 1.4 million hectares have been converted to oil palm plantation land, a substantial amount of which is reportedly controlled by Malaysian companies. For example, Malaysian GLC THP owns the development rights to 200,000 hectares of land in Riau (*The Star*, 2007), and PT API, a subsidiary of Malaysia's KLK, owns 27,760 hectares of plantation land there (WALHI *et al.*, 2009: 5–9). PT Minamas, a subsidiary of the major Malaysian GLC Sime Darby, also has landholdings in the province (Interviewee M24 and Interviewee M25, 2010).

Upon approval of the Adopt-A-District project from the Malaysian Cabinet, Malaysia sent a fact-finding mission to the Riau province in April 2007 (Bahagian Udara, 2010). With the results from the fact-finding mission, Malaysia developed a plan of assistance that was presented to the MSC in Jambi, Indonesia in June 2007 (Ghani, 2007b). Malaysia and Indonesia signed a Memorandum of Understanding (MOU) on Haze Management in the Riau Province in Sumatra in June 2008. The MOU was to remain in force for five years from the date of signing, until June 2013. The MOU reflected ASEAN values such as the non-involvement of outside parties in the settlement of disputes (Article XIII), the non-engagement of each party in political affairs (Article VIII) and the sovereign right of each party for the suspension of the MOU (Article XI) (Malaysia and Republic of Indonesia, 2008).

Under this MOU, Malaysia would provide $670,000 (Abdul Wahab, 2008) worth of community training and capacity-building projects, peatland rehabilitation assistance and install a haze early warning system in the province (Ibrahim [M39], 2010; Nagulendran [M34] and Interviewee M35, 2010). Key elements to this project included canal blocking and water storage wells for fire prevention and control, enhancing community outreach and partnership development, community training and socialization for peatland management, developing awareness material for the community and establishing community patrol teams for fire prevention and control (Global Environment Center, 2010: 8). Indonesia in return was required to facilitate Malaysia's access to these areas so that the projects could be carried out (Ibrahim [M39], 2010; Nagulendran [M34] and Interviewee M35, 2010).

Activities under the Malaysia-Riau MOU focused on two sub-areas in the small regency of Rokan Hilir in Riau, involving six specific villages (Interviewee M44, 2012). The first phase of this MOU project saw community leaders and farmers from Rokan Hilir province being invited by the Department of Agriculture to Selangor, Malaysia for a training workshop on zero-burning techniques in July 2008, and also a community fire-fighting training project in Riau in August 2008. However, as interviewees explained, these projects were not well-received by the community. For example, at the training workshop in Riau, no members of the community attended. Attendees were mostly made up of officials from both countries (Yusuf [I19], 2010). Interviewees indicated that the villagers did not support this programme because they were angry about being unfairly targeted by Malaysia for causing the haze (Maitar [I12], 2010; Syaf [I27], 2010; Yusuf [I19], 2010).

Partly because of this failure, and also because of lack of expertise, the

Malaysian Department of Environment subcontracted out the following five pilot projects to the Malaysian-based NGO GEC, under collaboration with Jikalahari, a local Indonesian NGO, during the time period of December 2008 to November 2009. GEC had expertise in peatland management and was previously involved in the ASEAN Peatland Management Initiative (Bahagian Udara, 2010). Interviewees from GEC were positive of such an approach, saying that such localized initiatives were a good way to overcome the endemic patronage and corruption culture that cannot guarantee that significant amounts of assistance would trickle down to the local level (Chee [M27], 2010; Lew [M6] and Interviewee M7, 2010).

The following year, Alam Sekitar Malaysia (ASMA), a consultant contracted by the Malaysian government, sponsored an air quality monitoring station in Bagan Siapi-Api, in the regency of Rokan Hilir in May 2009 (Anonymous, 2009; Bahagian Udara, 2010; Interviewee M5, 2010). As evidence of the endemic corruption that pervades Indonesian society, the interviewee from ASMA confessed that ASMA had to pay $1,000 in bribes in order to release the machinery for the station that was detained at Indonesian port customs for four days. He also explained how ASMA had determined an ideal site for the station based on a needs assessment study, but was abruptly informed by the Malaysian government of a last minute change of location for the site. While no official reason was given for this change, the interviewee expressed that this might have been because the original suggested location of the station was too close to influential commercial plantation companies (Interviewee I24, 2010). Despite this shift in location, the ASMA interviewee still witnessed open burning occurring just beside the installation site, and he said that this might have been on commercial land.

Throughout all this, Malaysian plantation companies operating in Riau were reluctant to be involved in these projects. The GEC manager who was interviewed explained that when GEC approached the two largest oil palm plantation investors to enhance their role and cooperation with local authorities in efforts to address peat and forest fires, the companies were reluctant to participate on the pretext that they 'do not burn'. They were afraid that participation would portray an acceptance of guilt (Chee [M27], 2010). Interviewees explained that at the end only one Malaysia company, PT Minamas (under Sime Darby), agreed to participate (Interviewee M24 and Interviewee M25, 2010). However, PT Minamas only carried out what they called 'socialization' projects among smallholders in and around their plantation area, instead of any inward-looking improvement of their own activities (Abdul Mutalib [M42], 2010; Interviewee I24, 2010; Interviewee M17, 2010). These socialization activities involved spreading awareness on fire prevention, training and demonstrations of alternative profitable techniques of clearing land among villagers. These also included training the surrounding community about what to expect during fires (Abdul Mutalib [M42], 2010; Interviewee M5, 2010). The company also provided villagers with chainsaws to facilitate land clearing, but this was perceived by local NGOs as encouraging deforestation, so this practice was discontinued (Interviewee S14 and Interviewee S15, 2010).

The projects did produce some significant achievements. These included the introduction of the concept of canal blocking for better water management to villagers in the regency, and the translation of awareness material into the Indonesian language, including the ASEAN Guidelines for Zero Burning and Controlled Burning. The projects also reported a significant change of attitudes at the community level towards adopting zero-burning practices and alternative livelihoods, especially towards pineapple farming in lieu of small-scale oil palm cultivation (Bahagian Udara, 2010; Interviewee M4, 2010; Interviewee M17, 2010; Ibrahim [M39], 2010; Lew [M6] and Interviewee M7, 2010). Also, there were no records of fire in the regency throughout the project period from January to November 2009[13] (Global Environment Center, 2010: 9).

Therefore, many Malaysian officials who were interviewed regarded the projects carried out under the MOU as a success (Interviewee M17, 2010; Interviewee M1, 2010; Interviewee M4, 2010; Interviewee M32, 2010; Nagulendran [M34] and Interviewee M35, 2010). Most optimistically, several interviewees opined that because of the progress of this MOU, it did not really matter whether the ATHP was signed or not (Interviewee M11, 2010; Law [M29], 2010). Furthermore, a senior officer from the Malaysian Ministry of Plantation Industries and Commodities who was interviewed commended the programme by stressing that focusing on community-level projects was key to solving open-burning issues. In a continuation of the defensive manner that was observed among Malaysian government officials in Chapter 3, he reiterated that there was no need to focus on plantation companies as they were 'behaving themselves' (Interviewee M41, 2010). Furthermore, a senior official at Department of Environment said that Malaysia was 'eager to continue funding for these types of projects' (Interviewee M17, 2010).

However, NGOs and academics who were interviewed did not share the optimism of Malaysian government officials on the outcomes of these projects. A major problem that was identified was the overwhelming focus on smallholders (and only in the small area of Rokan Hilir too) rather than commercial plantation companies in Riau. Official documents on the project justified this, saying that 'the involvement of the local community in fire prevention efforts was deemed the most strategic and effective as they were identified as the main actors for problem resolution' (Global Environment Center, 2010: 8), without acknowledging the even larger role of commercial plantations as a source of the fire problem. Malaysia's biased focus further contributed to the weak reception of these projects by the target community, as villagers were unhappy and alienated for being unfairly targeted by Malaysia for fires when they knew that the overwhelming source of the fires was in fact from politically important plantation companies who were left largely alone by these initiatives (Maitar [I12], 2010; Syaf [I27], 2010; Yusuf [I19], 2010). Malaysia's decision to focus on smallholders rather than commercial plantations can be explained through the patronage lens; patrons in the Malaysian government were inclined to make decisions based on what was best for their clients, and not society at large. As a result, the Malaysian government's capacity to make apt policy choices when it came to structuring such assistance was reduced. Hence, these interviewees felt that as a result of all this, the outcomes of the Malaysian projects failed to address the real source of the problem (Balamurugan [M40], 2010; Chee [M27], 2010; Interviewee M23, 2010; Ramakrishna [M20], 2010; Singh [M18], 2010).

Despite positive reviews by the Malaysian government representatives, interviewees explained that after one year, the Malaysian Department of Environment decided not to implement additional projects under the MOU, which was supposed to run for five years (Interviewee M44, 2012). Malaysian Department of Environment officials explained that this was due to budget cutbacks resulting from the recent financial crisis of 2008 (Interviewee M32, 2010; Interviewee M17, 2010; Interviewee M4, 2010; Nagulendran [M34] and Interviewee M35, 2010). However, interviewees detailed that funding for all five years of the project was already preapproved by the Ministry of Environment and Natural Resources, with additional funding from the ASEAN Haze Fund. Malaysia was allowed to utilize this fund because it had already ratified the ATHP (Nagulendran [M34] and Interviewee M35, 2010).

A GEC representative who was present at meetings on the matter explained that Malaysia's decision to discontinue funding for the project was as a result of an altercation between Malaysian and Indonesian representatives. Indonesian representatives felt that they had obtained experience and learnt sufficiently from Malaysia during the first round of projects, and thus requested for the budget and resources for following projects to be channelled directly to the central government. This was so that they could implement the projects themselves without having to rely on the Malaysian government. However, Malaysia was unwilling to change their hands-on approach (Interviewee M44, 2012), most probably for fear of Indonesian interference of Malaysian plantation interests in the area, resulting in the current impasse where subsequent projects have been suspended (Interviewee M44, 2012).

The Singapore-Jambi collaboration

Similar outcomes were observed for the Singapore-Jambi collaboration as well. Jambi province is located in Southern Sumatra and has a population of 2.7 million with a land area of 5.3 million hectares of which 92,000 hectares have already been converted to oil palm plantation land (Anonymous, 2009: 5). Singapore's GAR is a major landowner in the province, with a substantial amount of this land situated on peat (Munadar *et al.*, 2010: 1). Singapore conducted a fact-finding mission to the region and also hosted officials from the Indonesian Ministry of Environment and the Jambi Provincial Government for a bilateral workshop to put together the framework of the master plan in January 2007 (National Environment Agency, 2009: 5–6; Parliament of Singapore, 2007; Selamat, 2007: 4; Tan, 2007, 6). Based on this mission, a letter of intent for the Framework for a Master Plan to Prevent and Mitigate Land and Forest Fires in the Muaro Jambi Regency was presented to Indonesia in early 2007 (Channel NewsAsia, 2007c; Ghani, 2007a). Like the Malaysia-Riau collaboration, the collaboration was limited to only one out of the nine regencies in the province, namely Muaro Jambi. Under the master plan, Singapore would assist in funding, technical expertise and assistance to implement seven specific haze-mitigation programmes at the community level (National Environment Agency, 2009: 7–9).

Under the plan, Singapore would provide $831,000 to Jambi for the programmes over a period of two years (National Environment Agency, 2009: 7–9). This included providing technical equipment (two fire danger rating stations), training officials to interpret satellite pictures of hotspots and reviewing the regency's fire-fighting capabilities (Channel NewsAsia, 2007a; Chow, 2008; Mulchand, 2007a; Parliament of Singapore, 2006). More extensive follow-up programmes included training for villagers on alternative land-clearing methods that did not involve fire (Parliament of Singapore, 2006), aquaculture training to encourage farmers to farm fish for export instead of growing crops (to reduce the need for slash-and-burn) and water management programmes to keep water levels in the peatlands up to prevent fires (Liaw, 2008). In November 2007, Indonesia approved Singapore's letter of intent for the Jambi master plan (Channel NewsAsia, 2007b; Chow, 2008; Mulchand, 2007b,). Since then, eight action programmes have been completed (Parliament of Singapore, 2010b).

As a result of these programmes, Singapore reported that there were no fires in the Muaro Jambi area in 2009, where their bilateral programmes with the district were concentrated (Huang, 2009; Parliament of Singapore, 2009). Later in the year, it was reported that hotspots in the whole Jambi region went down by 23 per cent in the two years since Singapore's involvement (Gunasingham, 2009). The Singaporean Minister of Foreign Affairs commented that this ongoing bilateral cooperation, based on 'genuine friendship and close relationship built up over the years between officials from both countries', had helped reduce the haze problem since the bad episode in 2006 (National Environment Agency, 2009: 20, Singapore Government News, 2010). However, upon completion of the projects, the Ministry of Environment and Water Resources announced that, while it would be willing to share 'expertise' with other provinces that were willing to work with them, it would not be extending its projects to other provinces due to budget limitations (Parliament of Singapore, 2009). The real reason for this withdrawal of funding however is most probably similar to Malaysia's reason: because Indonesia had wanted funding to be channelled directly to the central government.

The outcomes of the Singapore-Jambi projects have also been criticized by interviewees. For example, one interviewee expressed that the project's effectiveness was limited due to 'the small size of the designated Muaro Jambi area' (Interviewee S21, 2010). Also, NGO representatives who were interviewed explained that one major project involved introducing dyke systems in peatland areas to collect water to use in case of fire. However, a side effect of these dykes was that it dried out the peatlands, and essentially prepared them for plantations (Surya [I9] and Akbar [I10], 2010). This may have been due to Singapore's lack of expertise in managing peatlands[14] (Chee [M27], 2010). Interviewees pointed out that 'this of course worked out to the benefit of commercial oil palm plantations' (Surya [I9] and Akbar [I10], 2010), including, ostensibly, Singaporean companies who had substantial landholdings there. Another shortcoming was the lack of participation from the public sector. An interview explained how only one subsidiary of GAR, Sinar Mas, was willing to get involved in these projects, through village socialization programmes. However, the interviewee pointed out that just like the Malaysia-Riau projects, these socialization plans 'did not involve any inward operational scrutiny' (Satyawan [I20], 2010). Indeed arguably, their involvement ensured that the project's reach was limited to educating smallholders in zero-burning techniques and creating surveillance mechanisms, instead of establishing enforcement mechanisms strong enough to take on powerful corporate interests (Hameiri and Jones, 2013: 472).

As a whole, both the Malaysia-Riau and Singapore-Jambi projects were able to boast an improved reduction in terms of number of hotspots in these respective areas (Satyawan [I20], 2010). However, as discussed previously, interviewees indicated that this could be credited to the El Niño cycle over the past few years that did not bring severe drought to the region (Joedawinata [I33] and Sartono [I34], 2010), and not specifically to these programmes.

One major issue was the myopic focus on villagers and smallholders. This again clearly underlines how commercial plantation companies use these local smallholders as a scapegoat to distract attention away from their own practices. While it cannot be denied that villagers also burn the land from time to time, this book has consistently shown how the effects of commercial burning have been more severe, especially in terms of its contribution to transboundary haze. Also, clearly commercial companies are better-placed to change their practices with regards to fire usage as compared to villagers and smallholders who may not have sufficient funds to use the more expensive land-clearing options (Hameiri and Jones, 2013: 471). Therefore, the supposedly altruistic actions of plantation companies in carrying out fire education programmes for surrounding communities and smallholders are not only patronizing but also quite misplaced. Furthermore, companies are already legally responsible for the practices of smallholders who are linked to them via nucleus-plasma schemes, which constitute about 11 per cent of all oil palm plantation land in Indonesia (see Figure 2.4) (Boer *et al.*, 2012: 67; Ministry of Agriculture, 2013), so engaging with these smallholders on fire management does not go far beyond the already standing responsibilities of these companies. Hence, a Singaporean opposition MP commented that the ATHP and its related Adopt-A-District programmes should not have just been limited to public education and putting out fires at the community level, but instead focused on training plantation owners who were the major cause of the fires (Parliament of Singapore, 2007).

Besides the misplaced focus on smallholders, interviewees further argued that these types of projects could only bring about short-term, site-specific results, not more important broader long-term policy mechanisms (Lew [M6] and Interviewee M7, 2010; Udiansyah [I15], 2010; Widodo [I11], 2010). Furthermore, several interviewees noted that it is difficult to determine if there were any long-term maintenance and follow through at the local level after the completion of these projects (Interviewee S22, 2010; Sun [S17], 2010).

Another interviewee expressed that by getting involved this way, Malaysia and Singapore were able to show that 'they were being proactive', while continuing to focus on elements that did not affect their plantation business interests in Indonesia (Interviewee I4, 2010). Therefore, these projects, along with the other ASEAN-level haze initiatives discussed above, can be seen as mere rhetoric and half-hearted efforts by all parties concerned in response to heightening civil society concerns about the haze, with little emphasis given to actual effective haze mitigation (Chang and Rajan, 2001: 666). One interviewee opined that 'it seems that they just wanted to show the public that they are doing something' (Wibisino [I44], 2011). Indeed, the short timeframes and rhetoric value of the projects became clear with representatives from both the Malaysian and Singaporean governments expressing their disinterest in the continuation of similar collaborative projects with Indonesia once the initial projects were deemed 'successful' (Interviewee M32, 2010; Interviewee M17, 2010, Interviewee M4, 2010; Nagulendran [M34] and Interviewee M35, 2010; Parliament of Singapore, 2009).

Conclusion

This chapter has shown that regional solutions have failed to effectively address the source of the haze. While member states acknowledged that they had environmental problems in common, their material interests in addressing them through ASEAN arose from the importance of domestic economic progress: to maintain the availability of, and access to natural resources, in this case, land for oil palm. Motivated by member state elites' close relationships with key plantation owners in the region as explained in Chapters 3 and 4, ASEAN member states were encouraged to ensure outcomes at the ASEAN level that ended up privileging economic actors that are close allies of the political elite. To do this, member states at the ASEAN level have chosen to closely adhere to the ASEAN Way principles, while negotiating and implementing initiatives such as HTTF, RHAP and ATHP. This has resulted in highly watered-down plans and documents that continue to protect national economic interests, preserve state sovereignty and deflect responsibility on the haze issue. Furthermore, adherence to the non-interference principle has enabled Indonesia, under the influence of powerful business interests, to withhold ratification of the ATHP for more than a decade, further contributing to the ineffectiveness of the Agreement. Member states have also ensured that haze mitigation mainly engaged with small-scale slash-and-burn community farmers, while overlooking the important contribution the commercial plantation sector makes to the regional haze, as illustrated through the Adopt-A-District programmes discussed above.

This chapter has therefore demonstrated that the regionalism of haze mitigation at the ASEAN level has enabled member states, especially Indonesia, Malaysia and Singapore, to reassert their national authority in the region in order to preserve crucial economic interests. This has allowed the oil palm plantation sector to flourish under present operating procedures. While scholars have argued that regionalism should be able to help streamline national policy positions around a joint regional position to better facilitate the implementation of useful multilateral agreements (Koh and Robinson, 2002: 1–2), regionalism of haze issues at the ASEAN level has not been able to do this. As mentioned above, the model of ASEAN regionalism that prioritizes the maintenance of national sovereignty has severely weakened the ASEAN organization's capacity to make and enforce effective initiatives and agreements. Instead, this model of regionalism enabled member states to shape haze initiatives in accordance with their national interests. As a result, initiatives were deliberately shaped in the spirit of the ASEAN Way, especially the non-interference norms guiding engagement and the priority given to the overarching goal of economic development. Therefore, instead of curbing the haze, this ASEAN regionalism complements the further economic regionalization of the oil palm plantation sector. ASEAN regionalism has prioritized economic development over environmental matters at the regional level, while providing a visible platform for rhetoric and policy pronouncements to appease civil society with little emphasis on actual effective haze mitigation. This chapter therefore argued that the failure of the regionalism strategy through ASEAN to effectively engage with the major actors of the regional oil palm plantation sector results in a free-rider situation where haze persists and the environmental costs continue to be passed on to the Indonesian and Southeast Asian societies. Hence, with member states under influence from patronage networks free to shape regional-level outcomes in ASEAN, this book demonstrates that ASEAN is not the appropriate level to address haze because the organization is not empowered with the capacity to do so effectively.

Notes

1 Parts of this chapter have appeared in Varkkey (2011, 2013), Quah and Varkkey (2012) and Muhamad Varkkey (2012).

2 The EU has its origins in the creation by six countries of the European Coal and Steel Community in 1957. The organization has undergone three successful waves of enlargement and at the time of writing comprises 27 member states (Rosamond, 2004: 62).

3 To a certain extent, this has indeed been the case. For example, the Asian Development Bank (ADB) came on board as a consultant in support of implementation of ASEAN haze initiatives (Tay, 2008: 60). A $1 million regional technical assistance grant was provided by the ADB to ASEAN to improve ASEAN's capacity to prevent and mitigate haze pollution across borders (Chang and Rajan, 2001: 665–666). ASEAN staff who were interviewed noted that the project brought in two international consultants, and the project's staff were later permanently institutionalized into the ASEAN Secretariat (Interviewee A7, 2010; Mat Akhir [A1], 2010). One of the outcomes of the ADB project is the ASEAN HazeOnline website (in collaboration with AusAID, the Australian government's overseas aid programme), which provides meteorological information in a timely manner (Chang and Rajan, 2001: 665–666). Other international bodies that have also provided funding and technical assistance to ASEAN for haze mitigation include the UNEP itself, the United States' USAID and the International Development Research Centre under the Canadian government.

4 The ASMC is located in Singapore and was originally established in 1993 as an ASEAN project to facilitate the development of weather prediction models and

related research and development programmes in the region. It has since expanded its duties and capabilities to include haze monitoring for the region (Woon, 2002: 135; Yahaya, 2000: 46). This includes processing satellite pictures depicting regional hotspots and smoke haze; producing schematic regional haze maps showing hotspots, smoke haze and wind flow; disseminating regional weather/haze status and outlooks; and providing a compiled El Niño outlook (Global Environment Center, 2010: 7).

5 Malaysia and Singapore by contrast, ratified the ATHP fairly quickly. As explained further below, Indonesia was mainly concerned about arising sovereignty issues with the ATHP. In contrast, Malaysia and Singapore, as home (and not host) countries for oil palm investment, did not feel threatened the same way Indonesia was by the ATHP, as haze mitigation initiatives would rarely involve any activity on their land.

6 The new President Joko Widodo however has recently announced his plans to revive the Agrarian Ministry (closed in 1999) to centralize policies related to spatial planning and to resolve land disputes (*Jakarta Post*, 2014). How the present ministries of agriculture, forestry and environment are affected by this new ministry would make for interesting research analysis in the future.

7 The Indonesian National Legislative Parliament is composed of three bodies: the People's Consultative Assembly (Majelis Pemusyawaratan Rakyat), House of Representatives (Dewan Perwakilan Rakyat) and the DPRD. The Indonesian Parliament one of the largest in the world, with over 500 members in its lower house, the House of Representatives alone (Skeretariat Jenderal DPR RI, 2014).

8 However, as mentioned above, Indonesia finally did ratify the treaty on 16 September 2014, after a major change in political leadership. The link (if any) between this change of leadership and ratification of the Agreement to the patron-client relationships in the sector lies beyond the scope of this book and will require new research and analysis.

9 For example, the SRFA for Kalimantan was renamed SRFA Borneo after a Ministerial Meeting on the Haze, to include Sabah and Sarawak as well (ASEAN Secretariat, 1998).

10 Again, further research is needed to examine if Indonesia's recent ratification can be traced to any fundamental change in the patron-client relationship in this sector under the new leadership.

11 No doubt, Indonesia's recent ratification of the Agreement will have some effect on the issues of fire-fighting, coordination, policy making and future directions of the Agreement as discussed in this book. These effects will become clearer over time (for example, the establishment of the ASEAN Coordination Center for Haze and its Dedicated Secretariat can finally be put into motion), and will definitely be of much interest to researchers in the future.

12 Malaysia also supported Indonesia on this, citing that Malaysia could not make concession maps publicly available due to legal limitations.

13 However again, this reduction could be credited to the mild El Niño cycle, not action on the ground (Joedawinata [I33] and Sartono [I34], 2010).

14 An interviewee explained that Singapore was close to hiring the more experienced GEC as their subcontractor for the Singapore-Jambi projects as well, but there was a last-minute switch to a Netherlands-based company (Chee [M27], 2010).

References

Abdul Mutalib [M42], N. H. 22 July 2010. *RE: Executive Secretary, Association of Plantation Investors of Malaysia in Indonesia.*

Abdul Rahim [M16], A. R. 31 March 2010. *RE: Deputy Director General of Forestry, Forestry Department of Peninsular Malaysia.*

Abdul Wahab, Z. 2008. Southeast Asian Countries Brace for Haze Pollution. *Bernama*, 23 June.

Abdullah [M43], A. M. 8 November 2011. *RE: Deputy Dean, Faculty of Environmental Studies, Universiti Putra Malaysia.*

Abdullah, A. 2002. *A Review and Analysis of Legal and Regulatory Aspects of Forest Fires in South East Asia*. Jakarta: Project Fire Fight South East Asia.

Aggarwal, V. K. and Chow, J. T. 2010. The perils of consensus: How ASEAN's meta-regime undermines economic and environmental cooperation. *Review of International Political Economy*, 17, 262–290.

Albar [I17], I. 13 July 2010. *RE: Head, Directorate of Forest Fire Control, Ministry of Forestry.*

Anonymous 2009. Transboundary Haze Pollution. Johns Hopkins University Model United Nations Conference, 2009.

Anshari [I42], G. Z. 9 November 2011. *RE: Center for Wetlands People and Biodiversity, Universitas Tanjungpura.*

ASEAN Secretariat 1967. *The ASEAN Declaration (Bangkok Declaration) Bangkok*. 8 August 1967. Bangkok: ASEAN Secretariat.

ASEAN Secretariat 1995. *ASEAN Meeting on the Management of Transboundary Pollution*. Kuala Lumpur: ASEAN.

ASEAN Secretariat 1998. Documentation: Fourth ASEAN ministerial meeting on haze: Singapore, 19 June 1998: Joint press statement. *ASEAN Economic Bulletin*, 15, 2, 223–225.

ASEAN Secretariat 2002a. *ASEAN Agreement on Transboundary Haze Pollution*. Kuala Lumpur: ASEAN.

ASEAN Secretariat 2002b. *ASEAN Agreement on Transboundary Haze Pollution*. Haze Action Online. Available: http://haze.asean.org/?page_id=185 [accessed 8 August 2014].

ASEAN Secretariat 2003a. *ASEAN Peatland Management Initiative*. Manila: ASEAN.

ASEAN Secretariat 2003b. *Guidelines for the Implementation of the ASEAN Policy on Zero Burning*. Jakarta: ASEAN.

ASEAN Secretariat 2004. 4: Transnational Issues. *ASEAN Annual Report*. ASEAN.

ASEAN Secretariat 2007. Review of existing ASEAN institutional mechanisms to deal with land and forest fires and transboundary haze pollution. *2nd Preparatory Meeting for the 2nd Meeting of the Conference of the Parties.* Bandar Seri Begawan: ASEAN.

Asmarani, D. 2006. Battling the haze, one district at a time. *The Straits Times*, 22 November 2006.

Bahagian Udara 2010. *Malaysia-Indonesia Collaboration in Preventive Measures to Deal with Land and Forest Fires and Haze in Riau Province*. Putrajaya: Department of Environment.

Balamurugan [M40], G. 30 April 2010. *RE: Managing Director, ERE Consulting Group.*

Beeson, M. 2007. *Regionalism and Globalization in East Asia: Politics, Security and Economic Development.* New York: Palgrave.

Boas, M. 2000. The trade-environment nexus and the potential of regional trade institutions. *New Political Economy*, 5, 415.

Boer, R., Nurrochmat, D. R., Ardiansyah, M., Hariyadi, Purwawangsa, H. and Ginting, G. 2012. *Indonesia: Analysis of implementation and financing gaps Project Report.* Bogor: Center for Climate Risk and Opportunity Management, Bogor Agricultural University.

Bratasida [I36], L. 29 July 2010. *RE: Assistant Minister of Global Environmental Affairs and International Cooperation, Ministry of Environment.*

Breslin, S. and Higgott, R. 2003. New regionalism(s) in the global political economy. Conceptual understanding in historical perspective. *Asia Europe Journal*, 1, 167–182.

Budianto, L. 2008. Lawmarkers refuses to endorse forest haze bill. *Jakarta Post*, 14 March 2008.

Caballero-Anthony [S3], M. 13 May 2010. *RE: Head, Centre for Non-Traditional Security Studies, NTU.*

Campbell, L. B. 2005. The political economy of environmental regionalism in Asia. *In:* Pempel, T. J. (ed.) *Remapping East Asia: The construction of a region.* Ithaca: Cornell University Press.

Casey [I46], M. 22 November 2011. *RE: Writer, Associate Press.*

Casson, A. 2002. The political economy of Indonesia's oil palm sector. *In:* Colfer, C. J. and Resosudarmo, I. A. P. (eds) *Which Way Forward? People, forests and policymaking in Indonesia.* Singapore: Institute of South East Asian Studies.

Chang, L. L. and Rajan, R. S. 2001. Regional versus multilateral solutions to transboundary environmental problems: Insights from the Southeast Asian haze. *Transboundary Environmental Problems in Asia*, 655–670.

Channel Newsasia 2006. Haze worsens in Singapore, PSI hits new high for the year. Channel NewsAsia, 7 October 2006.

Channel Newsasia 2007a. ASEAN ministers to review 12-year-old haze efforts. Channel NewsAsia, 1 March 2007.

Channel Newsasia 2007b. S'pore contributing S$1m to help tackle haze in Jambi, Indonesia. Channel NewsAsia, 7 Noember 2007.

Channel Newsasia 2007c. S'pore offers help to regency in Jambi to fight haze problem in Indonesia. Channel NewsAsia, 6 March 2007.

Chee [M27], T. Y. 14 April 2010. *RE: Manager, Global Environment Center.*

Chow, K. H. 2008. Five Asean nations step up efforts to fight haze. *The Straits Times*, 9 April 2008.

Christoph, O. M. 2005. Convergence towards a European strategic culture? A constructivist framework for explaining changing norms. *European Journal of International Relations*, 11, 523.

Cotton, J. 1999. The 'haze' over Southeast Asia: Challenging the ASEAN mode of regional engagement. *Pacific Affairs*, 72, 331–351.

Deutsch, A. and Sender, H. 2011. Boom and bust. *Financial Times*, 8 June 2011.

Eaton, P. and Radojevic, R. 2001. *Forest Fires and Regional Haze in Southeast Asia,* New York: Nova Science Publishers, Inc.

Elliott, L. 2000. ASEAN's environmental regime: pursuing sustainability in Southeast Asia. *Global Environmental Change*, 10, 237–240.

Elliott, L. 2001. Regional environmental security: Pursuing a non-traditional approach. *In:* Tan, A. T. H. and Boutin, J. D. K. (eds) *Non-Traditional Security Issues in Southeast Asia.* Singapore: Select Publishing Pte. Ltd.

Elliott, L. 2003. ASEAN and environmental cooperation: Norms, interests and identity. *The Pacific Review*, 16, 29–52.

Enderwick, P. 2005. What's bad about crony capitalism? *Asian Business and Management*, 4, 117–132.

Ferguson, R. J. 2004. ASEAN Concord II: Policy prospects for participant regional 'development'. *Contemporary Southeast Asia*, 26, 393.

Florano, E. R. 2003. Asssesment of the 'strengths' of the New ASEAN Agreement on Transboundary Haze Pollution. *International Review for Environmental Strategies*, 4, 127–147.

Florano, E. R. 2004. *Regional Environmental Cooperation without Tears or Fear: The Case of the Asean Regional Haze Action Plan.* International Environmental Governance Conference, 15 and 16 March. Paris: Institut du Developpment Durable, 1–12.

Ghani, A. 2007a. S'pore-Jakarta anti-haze project 'progressing well'. *The Straits Times*, 23 June 2007.

Ghani, A. 2007b. Singapore and Malaysia update Asean haze plans. *The Straits Times*, 20 June 2007.

Global Environment Center 2010. *Technical Workshop on the Development of the ASEAN Peatland Fire Prediction and Warning System.* Workshop Report. Kuala Lumpur: ASEAN Peatlands Forest project.

Grennfelt, P. and Hov, O. 2005. Regional air pollution at a turning point. *Ambio*, 34, 2.

Gunasingham, A. 2009. Severe haze likely to hit Singapore. *The Straits Times*, 20 June 2009.

Hameiri, S. and Jayasuria, K. 2011. Regulatory regionalism and the dynamics of territorial politics: The case of the Asia-Pacific region. *Political Studies*, 59, 20–37.

Hameiri, S. and Jones, L. 2013. The politics and governance of non-traditional security. *International Studies Quarterly*, 57, 462–473.

Hamilton-Hart, N. 2007. Government and private business: Rents, representation and collective action. *In:* McLeod, R. H. and Macintyre, A. (eds) *Indonesia: Democracy and the promise of good governance.* Singapore: Institute of Southeast Asian Studies.

Hariri [I30], D. and Ardiansyah [I31], I. 27 July 2010. *RE: WWF-Indonesia.*

Haryanto [I16], D. 13 July 2010. *RE: NOAA-MODIS Satelites Operator, Directorate of Forest Control, Ministry of Forestry.*

Hedradjat [I14], N. 8 July 2010. *RE: Director of Crop Protection, Ministry of Agriculture.*

Ho, W. F. 1997. The big haze: Indonesian plantations' denial 'incredulous'. *The Straits Times*, 2 October 1997.

Huang, H. F. 2009. S'pore not affected by haze in Sumatra. *The Straits Times*, 22 February 2009.

Hudiono, U. 2003. RI missing out on ASEAN haze agreement: Activist. *Jakarta Post*, 3 December 2003.

Hurrell, A. 1995. Explaining the resurgence of regionalism in world politics. *Review of International Studies*, 21, 331–358.

Hussain, Z. 2013. Jakarta's information law forbids sharing of maps: But exemptions are possible, says official. *The Straits Times*, 19 July 2013.

Ibrahim [M39], C. A. 2010. *RE: former Director (Air), Department of Environment.*

Interviewee A2. 7 June 2010. *RE: former ASEAN Secretariat staff.*

Interviewee A4 and Interviewee A5. 23 June 2010. *RE: Environment Division.*

Interviewee A7. 1 July 2010. *RE: formerly of ASEAN Environment Division.*

Interviewee I4. 25 June 2010. *RE: Sinarmas Forestry.*

Interviewee I7 and Interviewee I8. 28 June 2010. *RE: Ministry of Environment*

Interviewee I18. 14 July 2010. *RE: National Council on Climate Change.*

Interviewee I24. 19 July 2010. *RE: ASEAN-German Regional Forest Programme, German Technical Cooperation.*

Interviewee I25. 20 July 2010. *RE: Channel NewsAsia.*

Interviewee I48. 30 November 2011. *RE: Fauna Flora International.*

Interviewee M1. 4 March 2010. *RE: Ministry of Natural Resources and the Environment.*

Interviewee M2. 4 March 2010. *RE: National Security Council.*

Interviewee M4. 15 March 2010. *RE: Department of Environment.*

Interviewee M5. 16 March 2010. *RE: Alam Sekitar Malaysia.*

Interviewee M11. 24 March 2010. *RE: Ministry of Foreign Affairs.*

Interviewee M17. 1 April 2010. *RE: Department of Environment.*

Interviewee M23. 9 April 2010. *RE: Universiti Kebangsaan Malaysia.*

Interviewee M24 and Interviewee M25. 12 April 2010. *RE: a major Malaysian plantation corporation.*

Interviewee M32. 19 April 2010. *RE: formerly of Department of Environment.*

Interviewee M36. 28 April 2010. *RE: Lecturer, Monash University Sunday Campus.*

Interviewee M41. 11 May 2010. *RE: Ministry of Plantation Industries and Commodities.*

Interviewee M44. 5 January 2012. *RE: Global Environment Center.*

Interviewee M53 and Interviewee M54. 26 January 2012. *RE: Malaysian Palm Oil Council.*

Interviewee S1. 12 May 2010. *RE: Economy and Environment Program for South East Asia*

Interviewee S4 and Interviewee S5. 14 May 2010. *RE: National Environment Agency.*

Interviewee S14 and Interviewee S15. 19 May 2010. *RE: Ministry of Environment and Water Resources.*

Interviewee S16. 25 May 2010. *RE: Singapore Environment Council.*

Interviewee S18. 26 May 2010. *RE: Conservation International.*

Interviewee S21. 26 May 2010. *RE: former Environmental Reporter, Straits Times Press.*

Interviewee S22. 27 May 2010. *RE: Channel NewsAsia.*

Jakarta Post 2006a. A bad neighbour. *Jakarta Post*, 10 October.

Jakarta Post 2006b. Environmental law should target haze. *Jakarta Post*, 30 November.

Jakarta Post 2014. Jokowi to have new ministries, eliminate deputy ministers *Jakarta Post*, 15 September.

Jayasuria, K. 2004. Introduction: The vicissitudes of Asian regional governance. *In:* Jayasuria, K. (ed.) *Asian Regional Governance: Crisis and change.* London: RoutledgeCurzon.

Joedawinata [I33], A. and Sartono [I34]. 28 July 2010. *RE: Indonesian Palm Oil Commission.*

Johannessen, T. 2009. Clean air policy under the UNECE Convention on long-range transboundary air pollution: how are monitoring results 'translated' to policy action. *iForest*, 2, 49–50.

Jones, D. M. and Smith, M. L. R. 2002. ASEAN's immitation community. *Orbis*, 46, 1, 93–109.

Jones, D. S. 2004. ASEAN Initiatives to combat Haze pollution: An assessment of regional cooperation in public policy-making. *Asian Journal of Political Science*, 12, 59–77.

Jones, D. S. 2006. ASEAN and transboundary haze pollution in Southeast Asia. *Asia Europa Journal*, 4, 431–446.

Kamaruddin [M26], H. 13 April 2010. *RE: Lecturer, Faculty of Law, UKM.*

Karim, M. S. 2008. Future of the haze agreement: Is the glass half empty or half full? *Environmental Policy and Law*, 38, 328–334.

Katanyuu, R. 2006. Beyond non-interference in ASEAN: The Association's role in Myanmar's national reconciliation and democratization. *Asian Survey*, 46, 5825–5838.

Keraf [I35], S. 28 July 2010. *RE: former Minister of the Environment and Vice Chairman of Commission 7 (Environment, Energy and Research and Development), Parliament of Indonesia.*

Khalik, A. 2006. ASEAN ups pressure on haze as lawmakers bicker. *Jakarta Post*, 14 October.

Khalik, A. 2007a. ASEAN agrees to Indonesian haze action plan. *Jakarta Post*, 5 March.
Khalik, A. 2007b. RI plans to launch intensive anti-haze campaign. *Jakarta Post*, 23 February.
Khoo, N. 2004. Deconstructing the ASEAN security community: A review essay. *International Relations of the Asia Pacific*, 4, 35.
Kim, M. 2011. Theorizing ASEAN integration. *Asian Perspectives*, 35, 407–435.
Kivimaki, T. 2001. The long peace of ASEAN. *Journal of Peace Studies*, 38, 5–25.
Koh [S2], K. L. 13 May 2010. *RE: Director, Asia Pacific Centre for International Law, NUS.*
Koh, K. L. 2008. *Regional and State Level Environmental Governance ASEAN's Environment Governance: An Evaluation.* UNITAR/Yale Conference on Environmental Governance and Democracy, 10–11 May. New Haven.
Koh, K. L. and Robinson, N. A. 2002. Regional environmental governance: Examining the Association of South East Asian Nations (ASEAN) model. *In:* Esty, D. C. and Ivanova, M. H. (eds) *Global Environmental Governance: Options and Opportunities.* Yale: Yale Center for Environmental Law and Policy.
Kratochwil, F. V. 1984. The force of prescriptions. *International Organization*, 38, 685–708.
Kratochwil, F. V. 1989. *Rules, Norms, and Decisions: On the Conditions of Practical and Legal Reasoning in International Relations and Domestic Affairs.* Cambridge: Cambridge University Press.
Kurer, O. 1996. The political foundations of economic development policies. *Journal of Development Studies*, 32, 645–668.
Kurniawan, M. N. 2002. RI to speed up ratification of ASEAN haze accord. *Jakarta Post*, 15 November.
Larson, A. M. and Soto, F. 2008. Decentralization of natural resources governance regimes. *Annual Review of Environment and Resources*, 33, 213–239.
Law [M29], H. D. 15 April 2010. *RE: former Minister, Ministry of Natural Resources and Environment.*
Lee [S20], P. O. 26 May 2010. *RE: Fellow, Regional Economic Studies, Institute for South East Asian Studies.*
Lee, L. 2006a. Asean needs help to tackle haze: PM. *The Straits Times*, 6 November.
Lee, L. 2006b. Right to raise haze issue with UN. *The Straits Times*, 9 November.
Leonal, B. and Wulandri, F. 2014. Haze fines win Indonesia's support with caveats: Southeast Asia. *Bloomberg*, 30 July 2014.
Letchumanan [A6], R. 25 June 2010. *RE: Head, ASEAN Environment Division.*
Levy, M. A. 1992. Acid rain in Europe. *Environment*, 34, 16.
Lew [M6], S. and Interviewee M7. 18 March 2010. *RE: Peatland Programme, Global Environment Center.*
Liaw, W. C. 2008. Haze likely in next 3 months. *The Straits Times*, 24 June.
Lim [S13], M. A. 18 May 2010. *RE: Manager, Policy Research, Singapore Institute of International Affairs.*
Maitar [I12], B. 2 July 2010. *RE: Forest Campaign Team Leader, Greenpeace-Southeast Asia.*
Malaysia and Republic Of Indonesia 2008. *Memorandum of Understanding between the Government of Malaysia and the Government of the Republic of Indonesia on Collaboration in Preventive Measures to Deal with Land and Forest Fires and Haze in Riau Province.* Jakarta: Ministry of Natural Resources and Ministry of the Environment.

Mat Akhir [A1], A. 8 April 2010. *RE: former Senior Assistant to ASEAN Secretary General.*

Mathews [M33], P. 19 April 2010. *RE: former Assistant Director General, Institute for Strategic and International Studies.*

Maulidia, M. 2006. Indonesia must ratify anti-haze treaty. *Jakarta Post*, 28 January.

Mayer, J. 2006. Transboundary perspectives on managing Indonesia's fires. *The Journal of Environment and Development*, 15, 202–233.

McIndoe, A. 2006. Five Asean countries approve anti-haze plan. *The Straits Times*, 10 November.

Ministry Of Agriculture 2013. *Corporate Social Responsibility (CSR) in Indonesian Plantation. Public-Private Dialogue on Investment.* Asia Pacific Economic Cooperation (APEC), Jakarta. PowerPoint Presentation.

Moore [I5], P. F. 27 June 2010. *RE: Project Manager, IUCN-WWF Project Firefight Southeast Asia.*

Muhamad Varkkey, H. 2012. The ASEAN Way and haze mitigation at the ASEAN level. *Journal of International Studies*, 8, 77–97.

Mulchand, A. 2007a. Spike in Sumatra fires signals start of haze season. *The Straits Times*, 5 July.

Mulchand, A. 2007b. Tie-up with Indonesians to fight haze. *The Straits Times*, 5 November.

Munadar, A., Ruth, D. and Putra, A. 2010. *Rejection REDD Plus program Australia-Indonesia in Jambi.* Position Paper. Jambi: Regional Executive WALHI Jambi.

Murray, P. 2010. The European Union as an integration entrepreneur in East Asia – Yardstick or cautionary tale? *Australian Political Studies Association Conference*, 27–29 September. Melbourne.

Nagulendran [M34], K. and Interviewee M35. 20 April 2010. *RE: Deputy Under Secretary, Ministry of Natural Resources and Environment and officer.*

Narine, S. 1998a. ASEAN and the management of regional security. *Pacific Affairs*, 71, 195.

Narine, S. 1998b. Institutional theory and Southeast Asia: The case of ASEAN. *World Affairs*, 161, 33.

National Environment Agency 2009. *Indonesia-Singapore Collaboration to Deal with the Land and Forest Fires in Jambi Province.* Singapore: National Environment Agency.

Nesadurai, H. 2008. The Association of Southeast Asian Nations (ASEAN). *New Political Economy*, 13, 225.

Nesadurai, H. E. S. 2003. Attempting developmental regionalism through AFTA: The domestic sources of regional governance. *Third World Quarterly*, 24, 235.

New Straits Times 1997. EPSM wants haze constituents to be made public. *New Straits Times*, 25 September.

Nguitragool, P. 2011. Negotiating the haze treaty. *Asian Survey*, 51, 356–378.

Nischalke, T. I. 2000. Insights from ASEAN's foreign policy co-operation: The 'ASEAN way', a real spirit or phantom? *Contemporary Southeast Asia*, 22, 89.

Nurhidayah, L. 2012. *The Influence of International Law upon ASEAN Approaches in Addressing Transboundary Haze Pollution in the ASEAN Region.* 3rd NUS-Asian SIL Young Scholars Workshop. NUS Law School: Asian Society of International Law.

Nuruddin [M10], A. A. 23 March 2010. *RE: Lecturer, Department of Forestry, Universiti Putraa Malaysia.*

Ong [A3], K. Y. 8 June 2010. *RE: former ASEAN Secretary General.*

Ortuoste, M. C. C. 2008. Internal and external institutional dynamics in member-states and

ASEAN: Tracing creation, change and reciprocal influences. PhD thesis, Arizona State University.
Parliament of Singapore 1998a. ASEAN Region Haze Action Plan (Fulfillment of Obligations) (1998-01-15). Singapore.
Parliament of Singapore 1998b. Haze pollution (motion) (1998-06-30). Singapore.
Parliament of Singapore 2006. Haze situation (Update) (2006-11-14). Singapore.
Parliament of Singapore 2007. Estimates of expenditure for the financial year 1st April, 2007 to 31st March, 2008 (2007-03-06). Singapore.
Parliament of Singapore 2009. Haze situation (Action plan) (2009-09-15). Singapore.
Parliament of Singapore 2010a. Haze and forest fires (Commitment from Indonesia) (2010-11-22). Singapore.
Parliament of Singapore 2010b. Tackling transboundary haze (2010-11-22). Singapore.
Peh, S. H. 2006. Haze: No all-celear yet, but it's getting better. *The Straits Times*, 15 November.
Pempel, T. J. 2005. Introduction: Emerging webs of regional connectedness. *In:* Pempel, T. J. (ed.) *Remapping East Asia: The construction of a region.* Ithaca: Cornell University Press.
Prasiddha, R. 2009. *Update on the implementation of the ASEAN Agreement on Transboundary Haze Pollution*. 2009 Pan Asia Forest Fire Consultation, 2–7 February. Busan, Korea: ASEAN Secretariat.
Qadri, S. T. 2001. *Fire, Smoke and Haze: The ASEAN Response Strategy*. Philippines: Asian Development Bank.
Quah [S24], E. 8 June 2010. *RE: Head of Economics, NTU.*
Quah, E. and Varkkey, H. 2012. The political economy of transboundary pollution: Mitigating forest fires and haze in Southeast Asia. *In:* Sei, H. H. (ed.) *The Asian Community: Its Concepts and Prospects.* Tokyo: Soso Sha.
Ramakrishna [M20], S. 7 April 2010. *RE: Coordinator, Malaysian Environmental NGOs.*
Resosudarmo [I26], B. P. 22 July 2010. *RE: Associate Professor, Development and Environmental Economics.*
Rosamond, B. 2004. Europe. *In:* Payne, A. (ed.) *The New Regional Politics of Development.* Hampshire: Palgrave Macmillan.
Roswiniarti [I13], O. 8 July 2010. *RE: Director, Remote Sensing Data Centre, Indonesian National Institute of Aeronautics and Space.*
Rukmantara [I45], A. 14 November 2011. *RE: Former environmental journalist, Jakarta Post.*
Saravanamuttu [S23], J. 7 June 2010. *RE: Visiting Senior Research Fellow, Institute for South East Asian Studies.*
Satyawan [I20], L. S. 16 July 2010. *RE: Lecturer, Forest Fire, Department of Silviculture, Institute Pertanian Bogor.*
Selamat, F. 2007. Dousing Indonesia's hotspots: S'pore, Jambi launch master-plan to stop haze-causing fires in province. *Today*, 10 March 2007.
Severino, R. C. 2006. *Southeast Asia in Search of an ASEAN Community: Insights from the former ASEAN Secretary-General.* Singapore: ISEAS.
Severino, R. C., Hew, D., Suryadinata, L., Hsu, L. and Moeller, J. O. 2005. *Framing the ASEAN Charter*. Singapore: ISEAS.
Severino, R. F. 1999. *Fighting the Haze: A Regional and Global Responsibility.* Final Regional Workshop of the Regional Technical Assistance Project on Strengthening ASEAN's Capacity to Prevent and Mitigate Transboundary Atmospheric Pollution. Jakarta: ASEAN Secretariat.

Shelton, D. 2003. *Commitment and Compliance: The role of non-binding norms in the international legal system*, New York, Oxford University Press.

Sijabat, R. M. 2006. Environment minister warns of haze's serious effects. *Jakarta Post*, 10 October.

Sijabat, R. M. 2007. Government, House discuss bill on transboundary haze. *Jakarta Post*, 13 March.

Singapore Government News 2010. Singapore expresses concern on haze caused by Sumatra fires. *Singapore Government News*, 22 October.

Singh [M18], G. 2 April 2010. *RE: Chairman, Center for Environment, Technology and Development.*

Skeretariat Jenderal DPR RI. 2014. *Keanggotaan*. Jakarta. Available: www.dpr.go.id/id/tentang-dpr/keanggotaan [accessed 15 August 2014].

Sliggers, J. and Kakebeeke, W. 2004. *Clearing the air: 25 Years of the Convention on Long-Range Transboundary Air Pollution*. Geneva: United Nations Publications. Smith, A. L. 2000. *Strategic Centrality: Indonesia's Changing Role in ASEAN*. Singapore: Institute of South East Asian Studies.

Smith, A. L. 2004. ASEAN's ninth summit: Solidifying regional cohesion, advancing external linkages. *Contemporary Southeast Asia*, 26, 416.

Soeharto [I51], R. 16 January 2012. *RE: Executive Chairperson, Indonesian Sustainable Palm Oil Commission.*

Solingen, E. 1999. ASEAN, Quo Vadis? Domestic coalitions and regional co-operation. *Contemporary Southeast Asia*, 21, 30.

Solingen, E. 2005. East Asian regional institutions: Characteristics, sources, distinctiveness. *In:* Pempel, T. J. (ed.) *Remapping East Asia: The construction of a region*. Ithaca: Cornell University Press.

Sun [S17], D. 25 May 2010. *RE: CEO, Carbon Conservation.*

Surya [I9], M. T. and Akbar [I10], A. 30 June 2010. *RE: Deputy Directors, Wahana Lingkungan Hidup Indonesia.*

Swajaya [I37], N. 30 July 2010. *RE: Country Permanent Representative to ASEAN, Ministry of Foreign Affairs.*

Syaf [I27], R. 24 July 2010. *RE: Director of Conservation Information, Wahana Informasi.*

Syarif [I2], L. M. 24 June 2010. *RE: Chief, Cluster of Security and Justice Governance, Kemitraan Partnership.*

Syarif, L. M. 2010. The source of Indonesian environmental law. *IUCN Academy of Environmental Law*, 1, 1–18,

Syarif, L. O. M. 2007. Regional arrangements for transboundary atmospheric pollution in ASEAN countries. PhD thesis, University of Sydney.

Tan [S7], A. K. J. 17 May 2010. *RE: Vice Dean, Faculty of Law, NUS.*

Tan, A. K. 2005. The ASEAN Agreement on Transboundary Haze Pollution: Prospects for compliance and effectiveness in post-Suharto Indonesia. *N.Y.U. Environmental Law Journal*, 13, 647–722.

Tan, A. K. J. 1999. Forest fires of Indonesia: State responsibility and international liability. *International and Comparative Law Quarterly*, 48, 826–885

Tan, A. K. J. 2004. Environmental laws and institutions in Southeast Asia: A review of recent developments. *Singapore Year Book of International Law*, 177–192.

Tan, B. 2005. The norms that weren't: ASEAN's shortcomings in dealing with transboundary air pollution. *International Environmental Politics*, Spring, 1–6.

Tan, T. 2007. Haze fight: S'pore to work with slash-and-burn farmers. *The Straits Times*, 18 August.

Tarigan [I23], A. 16 July 2010. *RE: Executive Director, Sawit Watch.*
Tay [S12], S. 18 May 2010. *RE: Chairman, SIngapore Institute of International Affairs.*
Tay, S. 2008. Blowing smoke: Regional cooperation, Indonesian democracy, and the haze. *In:* Emmerson, D. K. (ed.) *Hard Choices.* Singapore: ISEAS.
Tay, S. S. C. 1998. South East Asian forest fires: Haze over ASEAN and international environmental law. *Reciel*, 7, 202–208.
Tay, S. S. C. 2002. Fires and haze in Southeast Asia. *In:* Noda, P. J. (ed.) *Cross-Sectoral Partnerships in Enhancing Human Security.* Tokyo: Japan Center for International Exchange.
The Star 2007. Environmental hazard. *The Star*, 11 December.
The Straits Times 2006. Yudhoyono serious about war on haze. *The Straits Times*, 4 December.
The Straits Times 2009. Indonesia 'should ratify haze pact'. *The Straits Times*, 15 October.
Tuinstra, W. 2008. European air pollution assessments: Co-production of science and policy. *International Environmental Agreements: Politics, Law and Economics*, 8, 35–49.
Udiansyah [I15]. 28 July 2010. *RE: Faculty of Forestry, Lambung Mangkurat University.*
Varkkey, H. 2011. ASEAN as a 'thin' community: The case against adopting the EU Acid Rain Framework for Transboundary Haze management in Southeast Asia. *Jebat: Malaysian Journal of History, Politics and Strategic Studies* 38, 1–26.
Varkkey, H. 2013. Regional cooperation, patronage, and the ASEAN Agreement on Transboundary Haze Pollution. *International Environmental Agreements: Politics, Law and Economics*, 14, 65–81.
WALHI, Sawit Watch and CELCOR 2009. *Malaysian Palm Oil and Logging Investments and Operations*. Factsheet. WALHI, Sawit Watch and CELCOR.
Wettestad, J. 2002. Clearing the air: Europe tackles transboundary pollution. *Environment*, 44, 32.
Wibisino [I44], I. T. C. 10 November 2011. *RE: Wetlands International.*
Widodo [I11], E. 1 July 2010. *RE: Deputy Director, Sumatra Initiative, WWF Indonesia.*
Woo, S. B. 2013. Haze meeting: Govts agree to share concession maps. *Today*, 18 July.
Woon, S. L. 2002. *Monitoring and Remote Sensing in ASEAN: ASMC's Role, Capacities and Activities in Relation to ASEAN's Regional Haze Action Plan*. World Land and Forest Fire Hazards: Kuala Lumpur.
Yahaya [M13], N. 26 March 2010. *RE: former Deputy Secretary General, Ministry of Natural Resources and Environment.*
Yahaya, N. 2000. Transboundary air pollution: Haze pollution in Southeast Asia and its significance. *Journal of Diplomacy and Foreign Relations*, 2, 41–50.
Yoshimatsu, H. 2006. Collective action problems and regional integration in ASEAN. *Contemporary Southeast Asia*, 28, 115.
Yusuf [I19], A. A. 14 July 2010. *RE: Center for Economics and Development Studies, Universitas Padjadjaran.*
Zainal Abidin [M38], A. 29 April 2010. *RE: Deputy Director, Pusat Tenaga Malaysia.*

6 Conclusion

This study set out to provide an original political economy argument to explain the persistence of transboundary haze in Southeast Asia by simultaneously analyzing the source of the haze and the attempted solutions undertaken to address the issue. Previous studies have attempted to explain the persistence of the haze from a singular perspective, either discussing the source or the solution individually. According to these earlier studies, the persistence of the haze was caused either by poverty and underdevelopment, external debt pressure or flawed public policy. And the ASEAN Way was identified as the reason why ASEAN solutions have failed. These explanations isolated different agents and underlying factors that result in transboundary haze, but they do not provide a broader context in which to understand the persistence of the problem. An alternative explanation to the persistence of haze in the region was thus offered, while addressing the limitations of these earlier explanations. By simultaneously engaging with the source and the (failing) solution, this book has been able to more effectively analyze the underlying reasons for the persistence of haze.

While previous scholars have identified poverty and developmental issues as driving haze (arguing that slash-and-burn agriculture by lesser-educated swidden farmers is a major cause of uncontrolled fires), more recent research has established a clear link between haze-producing fires and commercial oil palm plantations in Indonesia. These commercial plantations have been found to contribute up to 80 per cent of the haze in the region. As a result, haze continues to plague Southeast Asia on an almost annual basis, with Indonesia, Malaysia and Singapore suffering the worst of its effects, both in terms of socioeconomic well-being and public health. This is the puzzle that this book engaged with. It asked: Why have the governments of Indonesia, Malaysia and Singapore thus far failed to effectively address the regional haze problem despite clear evidence of the culpability of the oil palm plantation sector in Indonesia? This book has used the concept of the varieties of regional integration as a framework to analyze this question. Arguably, the persistence of haze can be explained by a combination of intense economic regionalization in Southeast Asia's oil palm plantation sector (the source) and the failure of environmental regionalism at the ASEAN level (the solution), with vested interests and patronage politics playing important roles in both instances.

Useful answers were found through a close analysis of Indonesia's oil palm plantation sector. Previous scholars have blamed national-level governance factors such as external debt pressure and flawed public policies for the increased focus on oil palm as a plantation crop in Indonesia. This book showed instead that regional-level corporate economic motivations have driven plantation investments in Indonesia, which in turn have encouraged commercial open burning there. As a result, the Indonesian oil palm plantation sector is populated not only by local commercial plantation companies, but also by foreign plantation firms, especially Malaysian and Singaporean ones. Indeed, companies from these countries currently control about half of all oil palm plantations in Indonesia. When compared to the culpability of the sector for haze, which based on some sources is as high as 80 per cent, it becomes clear that these unscrupulous practices are not limited to local plantation firms but are often carried out by Malaysian and Singaporean firms operating in Indonesia as well. Therefore, the explanation for the persistence of haze cannot be limited to analyses of issues of Indonesian-level governance, such as debt pressures and public policy. This point was the first step on the way to addressing the research question.

Thus, a closer examination of the regional integration of the oil palm plantation sector was required. The concentration of Malaysian and Singaporean plantation interests in Indonesia was indicative of high levels of economic regionalization of the Southeast Asian plantation sector. This study recognized that regionalization in Southeast Asia often displays several characteristics unique to the region. First, regionalization in Southeast Asia, while market-driven, is often heavily facilitated by home governments. Second, similar patronage cultures that exist among Southeast Asian societies are an important motivator for regionalization to other similar countries in the region. These two factors were important drivers of the regionalization of Malaysian and Singaporean commercial oil palm companies to Indonesia. The governments of Malaysia and Singapore were highly encouraging of their companies to invest in the vast lands of Indonesia due to the limited space available for plantations in their home countries. At the same time, these companies were eager to enter Indonesia due to its close psychic distance, especially in terms of similar patronage cultures.

These characteristics encouraged the regionalization of the Southeast Asian plantation sector. This book extended this analysis by arguing that these same characteristics are also important drivers of transboundary haze. First, a closer analysis of state facilitation revealed motivations behind heavy involvement by Malaysian and Singaporean governments in the regionalization process. Most of the companies that entered the Indonesian oil palm plantation sector were either government-linked companies (GLCs) or privately owned companies well-connected to the respective governments. Many senior positions in these companies were held by present and retired government staff, and the respective governments often held substantial ownership of these companies. Therefore, Malaysian and Singaporean governments had significant vested interests in the well-being and continued profitability of these companies in Indonesia. Hence, state facilitation has been an important driver of haze. Because of these vested interests, state facilitation of these investments extended well beyond mere facilitation of entry for these companies into Indonesia. Home governments often acted to protect the interests of these companies in Indonesia throughout the life of their operations. This came in handy for the companies when faced with accusations of open burning that caused haze in the region. The companies may not intend to cause haze directly, but haze is a result of corporate decisions made to ensure cost effectiveness and competitiveness within the sector. As a result, Malaysian and Singaporean governments have been observed to ardently use their influence and resources to appease regional and global environmental concerns by downplaying the severity of haze, while at the same time denying the complicity of their firms in the Indonesian fires. The Malaysian government, through a specially formed industry lobby group, APIMI (Association of Plantation Investors of Malaysia in Indonesia), even brokered special treatment for Malaysian plantation companies that would avoid any legal recourse when suspected of open burning. In these ways, home-state facilitation can be identified as an important driver for haze, as it protects plantation companies from suffering the worst consequences of their haze-producing actions.

Second, the patronage culture that is common across Indonesia, Malaysia and Singapore, which is another important driver for the regionalization of the plantation sector, can also be identified as a driver for haze. Patronage politics is an important part of doing business in Indonesia. This close psychic distance in terms of business culture has been a motivator for the regionalization of Malaysian and Singaporean firms to Indonesia. Patronage politics is especially important for the oil palm plantation sector because of its long timeframes (with a crop rotation of about 20 to 30 years) and high level of illegal activity involved, for example in illegal licensing and land clearing. Therefore, firms often need to cultivate long-term patronage relationships throughout their operations. Malaysian and Singaporean firms, which are already well-versed with patronage practices back home, were able to insert themselves easily into local patronage networks alongside local commercial plantation companies. Indeed, Malaysian and Singaporean companies in Indonesia are more likely than other foreign companies to engage in patronage practices in Indonesia. Indonesian, Malaysia and Singaporean companies can be observed to have 'functional directors' appointed to perform 'extra-economic functions' and 'advisors' who are elected on a retainer basis. These individuals are often retired local- or central-level politicians or bureaucrats and are elected to these posts by virtue of their connections with key government elites, and on their ability to use these connections to facilitate the operations of these companies. These relationships have been especially useful for obtaining attractive but fire-prone peatlands for the establishment of plantations, and avoiding investigation and prosecution when faced with accusations of open burning. This specific use of bureaucratic instruments by the elites in favour of their clients has weakened the capacity of the state to effectively manage Indonesia's forests, resulting in policy paralysis. As a result, while many local and foreign companies have been found to be involved in burning practices, only one commercial oil palm company (pending final decision on PT Kallista

Alam's case as mentioned above) has ever been successfully charged in court for burning misconduct, and even then, with a reduced sentence. Hence, the culture of patronage politics is another driver for transboundary haze, where major local and foreign plantation companies are again able to escape the consequences of their actions due to these connections.

Therefore, the same factors that have driven economic regionalization of the Southeast Asian oil palm sector have also driven transboundary haze. In other words, transboundary haze is a consequence of the regionalization of this sector. This explains why the problem of transboundary haze has risen in severity around the same time as the shift of economic focus of the region from logging to palm oil, which was during the late 1990s. The vested interests of both home and host governments in the continued well-being of these commercial plantation companies, coupled with the flawed decentralization process in Indonesia, provide layers of protection to these companies and allow them to elude legal action and burn with impunity.

However, an explanation was also required to shed light on the persistence of transboundary haze over the years. With the added severity of the haze, civil society outcry placed pressure on regional governments to take action against the haze. As a result, Indonesia, Malaysia and Singapore decided to engage in haze mitigation activities at the ASEAN level. However, these ASEAN efforts have been largely unsuccessful in bringing about any permanent solutions to haze.

This book thus offered further arguments on why these ASEAN initiatives failed in their purpose to curb transboundary haze, again using the varieties of regional integration explanation. Political regionalism in Southeast Asia has taken the form of ASEAN. The literature predicts that political regionalism should be a useful strategy in solving common regional problems, especially those problems arising from increased levels of regional interdependence. Indeed, the haze is an issue arising from increased levels of regional interdependence within the oil palm plantation sector. However, the particular *model* of political regionalism is an important determinant of whether the regionalism process is effective in solving regional problems or not. The ASEAN model of regionalism, which prioritizes the maintenance of national sovereignty and self-determination, results in only weak organizational capacity for ASEAN to shape and enforce agreements and initiatives for the collective regional good. This model of regionalism instead has enabled member states to shape haze initiatives in accordance with their national interests. As a result, initiatives were *deliberately* shaped in the spirit of the ASEAN Way, especially the non-interference norms guiding engagement and the priority given to the overarching goal of economic development. This is in contrast with the arguments of previous scholars that proposed that states *had no choice* but to observe the ASEAN Way of regional engagement, which became a limiting effect on effective state action over the haze.

Complemented by the political elites' close relationships with key plantation owners in the region, this has resulted in ASEAN haze initiatives that often privilege economic actors that are close allies of these elites, with little concern for the regional environment. The influence of patronage politics was especially visible where decisions at the ASEAN level were swayed by influential private actors and lobby groups. As a result, ASEAN initiatives by and large did not bring about any constructive engagement with commercial plantation companies (which have been identified as the major culprit of these fires and haze) but instead targeted small-scale slash-and-burn farmers. This was especially obvious in the Adopt-A-District programmes spearheaded by Malaysia and Singapore, and based in Indonesia. With the wrong actors being targeted, it is not surprising that transboundary haze continues to persist to this day. Therefore, instead of curbing the haze, this regionalism of haze issues (under the ASEAN model) complements the further regionalization of the oil palm plantation sector by prioritizing economic development over environmental matters at the regional level, while providing a useful platform for rhetoric and policy pronouncements to appease civil society, with little emphasis on actual effective haze mitigation.

In summary, this book offered two related explanations for the persistence of transboundary haze in Southeast Asia. The haze developed into a regional annual problem as a result of the regionalization of the oil palm plantation sector, which concentrated Malaysian and Singaporean commercial plantation companies in the vast lands of Indonesia, alongside local plantation companies. Bolstered by home-state facilitation and local patronage networks, these companies were able to act with impunity, using the most cost-effective ways to establish their plantations, including setting up plantations on fire-prone peatlands and using fire as a cost-effective way to clear land in preparation for planting. The resulting smoke haze travelled across boundaries and became an annual problem in the region during each dry season. When haze became so severe as to garner serious outcry from civil society, Indonesia, Malaysia and Singapore pledged to take action, by focusing mitigation efforts at the regional level. However, the regionalism of haze issues at the ASEAN level proved ineffective because ASEAN-level outcomes were also being influenced by commercial interests.

Therefore, transboundary haze continues to persist despite clear evidence of the culpability of commercial oil palm companies in Indonesia. Indonesian, Malaysian and Singaporean vested interests in this sector continued to ensure that commercial plantation companies were able to carry out burning unscrupulously. This is a manifestation of the free-rider problem. The importance of the oil palm industry to the Indonesian, Malaysian and Singaporean economies, coupled with the vested interests that have been cultivated among elites in the sector takes priority over the well-being of the Indonesian, Malaysian and Singaporean societies, which continue to suffer annually as a result of haze. As explained by the literature, in cases such as this, the government would not necessarily make decisions based on what is rational at the society level, but instead would make decisions that benefit the well-connected minority. Thus, transboundary haze persists and the environmental costs continue to be passed on to the general public. Hence, this book as a whole argues that economic regionalization of the Southeast Asian oil palm sector is a major driver of transboundary haze. Furthermore, state vested interests within the sector are the main cause of the continued failure of regional-level ASEAN haze mitigation efforts, resulting in the persistence of the haze.

Future research extending the arguments of this book should focus on explaining Indonesia's sudden ratification of the ASEAN Agreement on Transboundary Haze Pollution (ATHP) on 16 September 2014, after more than a decade. What changed at the ministerial, and especially at the parliamentary level, that allowed this bill to finally be passed? Did this drastic change of heart come from the top, as a result of the new leadership, or from the bottom, reflecting a possible change in the nature of the patron-client relationships in the sector? Was there any change in terms of pressure from the ASEAN level? Furthermore, research will be needed into how (if at all) Indonesia's ratification affects the prospects of cooperation over haze issues at the regional level, specifically in the context of the implementation of the ASEAN ATHP. In these and other respects, study into the political economy of the persistence of haze in the Southeast Asian region should continue to offer intriguing theoretical and empirical challenges to researchers for some time to come.

Index

Abdul Ghani bin Abdullah 82
Abdul Jamil bin Haji Ahmad 82
Aceh 135, 141–2
acid rain 162–4, 178
Adopt-A-District 10, 20, 195–203, 218
Advertising Standards Authority 84
advisors 120, 216
Aggarwal, V.K. 14, 19, 166
Agreement on the Conservation of Nature and Natural Resources 171
Agreement on Transboundary Haze Pollution (ATHP) 10, 20, 176–81, 201–2, 219; Adopt-A-District 194–5, 198–9; Indonesia's non-ratification 181–2; limited effectiveness 189–93; ministerial resistance 183–4; parliamentary resistance 184–9
agribusiness 39–41, 88, *see also* oil palm plantation sector
agriculture 38–42, 53–5
Aidenvironment 94
Aiken, S.R. 13, 17, 148
Air Pollution Index (API) 93
air transport 3–5
Alam Sekitar Malaysia (ASMA) 197
Ali-Baba arrangements 81–2
Amanah Saham Trustee Berhad 81
AMDAL 128–30
Amin bin Osman 82
Anti-Plantation Mafia 125
Apkindo 126
Apriyantono, A. 121
archival research 23–4
Argentina 37
ASEAN 1, 10–12, 14–15, 202–3, 214, 217–19; 1985-2003 initiatives 171–6; 2003 Agreement 176–81; Adopt-A-District 196–202; blame-shifting 193–4; economic regionalization 76, 149–50; Indonesia's non-ratification of ATHP 181–9; limited effectiveness 189–93; political regionalism 160–9; research methods 20, 23
ASEAN Haze Fund 177, 188, 199
ASEAN Ministerial Meeting on Haze 172
ASEAN minus X 181–2
ASEAN Peatland Management Initiative (APMI) 174, 194
ASEAN Policy on Zero Burning 143, 174
ASEAN Specialized Meteorological Centre (ASMC) 164, 174–6
ASEAN Way 14, 19, 165–72, 175–6, 179–81, 192
Asian Development Bank (ADB) 2
Asian financial crisis (AFC) 13, 42–3, 72, 74–5, 89, 98
Aspinall, E. 120, 125
Association of Oil Palm Plantation Investors of Malaysia in Indonesia (APIMI) 84–5, 95–6, 216
Association of Southeast Asian Nations *see* ASEAN
Astra Agro 77, 131–2, 134–5, 141–2, 186
Australia 83–4, 92, 167

backlash 90–8
Badan Pengendalian Dampak Lingkungan 136, 140
Bagan Siapi-Api 197
Bakrie, A. 121
Bakrie and Brothers Group 121
Bakrie Sumatra Plantations (BSP) 77, 120–1, 131
Balikpapan 172
Bank Islam 81
Barr, C.M. 125
Basic Agrarian Law 73–4, 136
Basiron, Y. 83–4

Beeson, M. 17
biodiversity 49
Biodiversity Conservation Acts 126
biofuels 37, 47–8, 84
Borneo 3, 53, 131, 174, 187
Borneo People's Contact 130
boycott 97
Brazil 37, 80
Breslin, S. 7
Brunei 2, 165, 177
BSP 77, 120–1, 131
Bupatis 123–4, 140
burden of proof 137–8
bureaucracy 113–17, 119–20, 129–30
Burger King 97
burning *see* fires

Campbell, L.B. 162
capital 88–9
carbon emissions 2, 57–8
carbon sinks 53, 57
Cargill 121
censorship 93–4, 96
Central Forestry Law 128
Chang, L.L. 14, 166
Chin, P. 95
China 37, 46
Chinese Malaysians 80–2
Chow, J.T. 14, 19, 166
Chua Phuay Hee 90
Clean Air for Europe (CAFE) 163–4
climate 41
climate change 2, 57
CNN 94
Colfer, C.J. 12, 51
collective action *see* free-rider problem
colonial era 38–9, 42, 115
commercial plantations *see* oil palm plantation sector
commissioners 120–1
Commonwealth Heads of Government Meeting 79
comparative advantage 86
concessionaires 54–6, 139, 148, *see also* oil palm plantation sector
concessions 13, 43, 49, 128, 130–2
Conference of the Parties 177, 192, 194
Constitution 126
Convention on Long-Range Transboundary Air Pollution (CLRTAP) 163–5, 178–9
Cooperation Plan on Transboundary Pollution 172, 175
Coordination Centre for Haze 191

Copenhagen Climate Conference 57, 79
corruption 123–4, 197, *see also* patronage
Cotton, J. 17–18, 148
crony capitalism 17, 116
crop rotation 120, 136
Crouch, M. 120
crude palm oil (CPO) 13, 36–7, 40, 42–6, 84–5, 91–2, 97
cultural familiarity 8, 118–19

data collection 21
Datuk Hj Mohd Khalil B Dato' Hj Mohd Noor 82
Dauvergne, P. 12, 17–18, 115–16, 119
debt 13, 15–16, 98
decentralization 16, 122–3, 139–41; land licensing 127–9, 132
deforestation 17–18, 49
demand 35–8, 47
Department of Environment Library 23
Department of Environment (Malaysian) 197–9
development 41–2, 46, 48, 69; false explanation of haze 12–13, 15, 51
Dewan Perwakilan Rakyat 184–5
Dewan Perwakilan Rakyat Daerah (DPRD) 121, 124
directors 120
Directorship and Consultancy Appointments Committee 86
Dow Jones Factiva 23
drainage 53–4
drought 49–50
Duta Palma 77, 121; haze-producing fires 139, 141–2, 147; land licensing 130–1, 134
Dutch 37, 42, 91, 121

Eaton, P. 13, 17, 148
Economic Development Board (EDB) 87
Economic and Financial Resilience Council 121–2
economy 3–7, 13, 19; ASEAN regionalism 168–9, 171; Malaysia 93; oil palm sector 35, 38–48; patronage politics 119, 149; regionalization 68–72, 76–7, 97–8
ecosystems 53–5, 163
Education Ministry (Malaysia) 93
El Niño 49–50, 188, 201
elites 40, 114–17, 148–9; ASEAN regionalism 160–1, 168; economic regionalization 80–2, 90, *see also* patronage

Elliott, L. 14
Employees Provident Fund (EPF) 81–2
Enderwick, P. 113
energy 37, 47–8, 84
environment 9, 48–9, 136–8; ineffective revisions to burning laws 147–8; regionalisms 162–9
Environment Impact Management Agency 136, 140
Environment Ministry *see* Ministry of Environment
Environment Protection Agency 91, 96
Environmental Management Act (EMA) 137–8, 146; 2009 Act 147
Estate Crops 46
Estate Transmigration Programme 43
European Economic Community 163
European Union (EU) 37, 162–5, 167
European Union Renewable Energy Directive 84
Export-Import Bank of Malaysia Berhad (EXIM Bank) 78
exports 41, 45–6, 69

Fire Danger Rating System 194
fires 1–3, 5–6, 20; 1985-2003 initiatives 172–6; Adopt-A-District 195–202; blame-shifting 193–4; ineffective revisions to burning laws 147–8; land clearing policy 136–8; literature review 12–18; non-enforcement of burning laws 139–47; non-ratification of ATHP 188, 190–2; oil palm plantations 49–52; patronage politics 148–9; peatlands 56–8; responses to haze backlash 90–2, 94–8
fiscal incentives 70–1, 73–4, 78
Florano, E.R. 164–5
Food Standards Amendment 83
foreign debt 13, 15–16, 98
foreign direct investment (FDI) *see* investment
Foreign Investment Committee of Malaysia 82
Foreign Investment Law (FIL) 72–3, 76
forests 79, 126–9, 183; degraded 51–2; oil palm sector 38–43, 48, 54; patronage networks 126–9, *see also* fires
Framework Agreement 76
free-rider problem 114, 149, 182, 203, 218
Freedom of Information Law 192
Friends of the Earth 49
Fujiwara, K. 10
functional directors 120, 216

GAPKI 134, 138, 186
GAR 89–90, 97, 122, 124; Adopt-A-District 199–201; haze-producing fires 139, 143; land licensing 130–4
Garuda Indonesia 4
GDP 42, 46, 149
Gellert, P.K. 13, 97–8
Genting Plantations 80, 82
Giluk Dompok, B. 95
Global Environment Centre (GEC) 142, 174, 189, 197
Gobel, R. 122
Gobi, C. 146
Golden Hope Plantations 80
Golden-Agri Resources *see* GAR
Golkar 121
government *see* policy; state
government-linked companies (GLCs) 8, 68; Adopt-A-District 196, 199; Malaysian 78, 80–1, 83; Singaporean 86
greenhouse gas 2, 49, 57–8, 91
Greenpeace 141–3, 145, 148
growth 38, 41–2, 45–7; ASEAN regionalism 168–9; patronage politics 119
Guam 2
Guthrie Corporation 80

Hadiz, V.R. 117, 123
Hak Guna Usaha (HGU) 74, 76
Hameiri, S. 169
Hanafiah, H. 146
Hanoi Declaration 76, 174
Hasan, B. 126
Hasan, Z. 77
haze 1–5, 48, 202–3, 214–19; 1985-2003 initiatives 172–6; 2003 Agreement 176–81; Adopt-A-District 195–202; blame-shifting 193–4; book outline 24–6; first serious events 43; Indonesian land clearing/fire policy 137, 141; Indonesia's non-ratification of ATHP 181–2; limited effectiveness 189–93; literature review 12–20; ministerial resistance 183–4; oil palm plantations & fires 50, 52; parliamentary resistance 184–9; patronage politics 143, 145, 148–9; peatlands 56–8, 135; political regionalism 161–9; research methods 20, 23; research question 6–12; responses to backlash 90–8
Haze Monitoring System (HMS) 177, 192
Haze Technical Task Force (HTTF) 172, 175

health 2–5, 93, 96
Henderson, V. 68
Higgott, R. 7
Hijau, R. 125
Hiratsuka, D. 22
Hirwan, S.B. 122
House of Representatives 184–5; Regional 121, 124
Hume, C. 122, 143
Hurrell, A. 7, 9, 69, 162, 165
hutan produksi konversi (HPK) 127–9

Ibrahim, Y. 96
incentives 70–1, 73, 78, 86–7
India 37, 46
Indo Agri 89–90, 122, 131, 144
Indonesia 1–4, 13, 15–16, 18–19, 214–19; Adopt-A-District 194–202; ASEAN regionalism 167, 169–74, 176, 180; conversion of degraded lands 51–2; future projections 47–8; haze backlash 94–8; importance of oil palm sector 39–46; ineffective revisions to burning laws 147–8; land clearing & fire policy 136–8; land licensing 125–35; Malaysian investments/firms 77–85; non-enforcement of burning laws 139–47; non-ratification of ATHP 181–4; oil palm plantations & fires 48–51; parliamentary resistance to mitigation 184–93; patronage 116–25, 148–9; peatlands 53–8; regionalization 68, 71–7; research methods 20, 22–3; research question 6–8, 11; Singaporean investments/firms 86–90
Indonesia-Malaysia Palm Oil Group 85
Indonesian Democratic Party 124
Indonesian Palm Oil Association (GAPKI) 134, 138, 186
Indonesian Sustainable Palm Oil Commission 186
Indonesian Wood Panel Association 126
Institute of Strategic and International Studies 23
insurance 138
International Finance Corporation 97
International Monetary Fund (IMF) 13, 16, 74, 98
interviews 21–3
investment 8, 13, 16, 22, 43–4; Malaysia to Indonesia 78–80, 82–3; patronage 119; Singapore to Indonesia 87–9; state facilitation 70–8, 98
investment development path 69
investment guarantees 78
IOI Corporation Berhad 80, 82, 130, 132, 142–3
Irian Jaya 53
Italy 37
IUP 129–30, 144

Jakarta 84, 87, 123
Jakarta Resolution 169
Jambi 3, 5, 124, 131, 147; Adopt-A-District 195, 199–202
Japan 17–18
Java 41
Jikalahari 197
Johnston, M. 12, 51
joint ventures 74, 77
Jones, D.S. 177
Jones, L. 169

Kakebeeke, W. 162
Kalimantan 3, 49, 80, 124; ASEAN regionalism 180, 187–8; 'green gold' 42–3, 47; haze-producing fires 139, 141–5; land licensing 128, 130–2, 134
Kambuaya, B. 185
Karim, M.S. 164–5
Kartasasmita, G. 121
Katzenstein, P.J. 7, 10
Kee Kwong Foo, E. 90
Keraf, A.S. 184–5
Kim, M. 165
KLK *see* Kuala Lumpur Kepong
Koh, K.L. 162, 170
Kuala Lumpur 171, 177, 185
Kuala Lumpur Kepong (KLK) 94, 131, 146; Adopt-A-District 196–7; regionalization 74–5, 80, 82–3
Kuching 4
Kuok Khoon Ean 90
Kurer, O. 113

labelling 83–4, 91
labour costs 71–2
land 115
land banks 73–4, 77, 80, 94
land clearing 6, 136–8; non-enforcement of burning laws 138–47
land degradation 51–6, 71
land licensing 125–7; decentralization 127–9; peatlands patronage 130–5
land rights 39–41, 126; fires 52, 55; state facilitation 73–4, 76, 85
land swaps 135
Laos 182

Latin America 37
laws 136–41, 147–8
Lee Oi Hian 83
Lee Yeow Chor 83
Lembaga Penerbangan dan Antariksa Nasional 176
Lembaga Tabung Haji 81
Leong Horn Kee 90
Leuser Ecosystem area 142
Lew Syn Pau 90
liability 137–8
Lim Hock San 90
lobby groups 82–5, 138, 185–6, 216
local level 16, 139–41; patronage networks 119–25
logging 18, 38, 51, 54
loyalties 113–17

McCarthy, J.F. 16, 122, 125
Mahathir Mohamed 94
Makin Group 77, 131, 147
Malaysia 4, 98, 187, 214–18; Adopt-A-District 195–9, 202; ASEAN initiatives 174–6, 190; economic regionalization 68, 71–2; 'green gold' 39–41; literature review 13, 15, 18; oil palm sector 42–4, 46, 49; outward investments to Indonesia 77–9; patronage 116, 118–19, 121–2, 124–5, 131–2; patronage/fires 142, 144, 146; plantation companies in Indonesia 79–82; regionalization 74–7; research methods 20, 23; research question 6–8, 11; responses to haze backlash 91–6; state support for firms in Indonesia 82–5
Malaysian External Trade Development Corporation (MATRADE) 78
Malaysian Industrial Development Authority (MIDA) 78
Malaysian Ministry of Plantation Industries and Commodities 83
Malaysian Palm Oil Council (MPOC) 82–5, 95
management structure 120
mapping 50, 175–7, 192
Marbun, S. 121
Marinova, N. 13, 98
Mayer, J. 16–17, 122, 125, 127
media 93–4; research 23–4
Memorandum of Understanding (MOU) 196, 198–9
Merrill Lynch 89
Middle East 37
Milieudefensie 142–3, 145
military 121, 142
Ministerial Steering Committees (MSCs) 178, 194–5
Ministry of Agriculture 55, 122, 138, 183
Ministry of Environment: ASEAN 183–5, 187, 189, 191; patronage politics 137, 140, 143–5, 147–8
Ministry of Finance (Singapore) 90
Ministry of Forestry 48, 129–30, 134, 140, 144; non-ratification of ATHP 183–5
Ministry of Science, Technology and Environment (MSTE) 93
Monetary Authority of Singapore 90
moratoria 133–5
MPOABC 82–3
Muaro Jambi 199–200
Murray, P. 165
Musim Mas 77, 131–2, 141
mutual hostage relations 113, 124, 131
Myanmar 161

National Biofuel Development Team 47
National Deregulation Policy Package 128
national focal points (NFPs) 172, 175
National Institute of Aeronautics and Space 176
native customary rights (NCR) 39–41, 52, 55, 85
Natural Disaster Management and Relief Committee 94
Nesadurai, H.E. 160
Nestlé 97
Netherlands 37, 42, 91, 121
New Investment Law 76
New Order Era 116, 118, 120
New Zealand 91
newspapers 23
NGOs 141–5, 197–8
Nguitragool, P. 14, 166
Nischalke, T.I. 166
non-interference 165–8, 202; ASEAN Way 171, 179–81, 189, 193
Noordin bin Md Noor 81
Northern Mariana Islands 2
Norway 133
nucleus-plasma schemes 44, 201

office-holders 113
Official Secrets Act 93
offshore 89
oil palm 36–7, 39, *see also* palm oil

oil palm plantation sector 1, 6–11, 214–18; Adopt-A-District 195–8, 200–2; ASEAN regionalism 170–1, 202–3; fires 48–52; future projections 47–8; importance 41–6; ineffective revisions to burning laws 147–8; land clearing/fire policy 136–8; land licensing 126–35; literature review 13, 15–17; Malaysian-owned 79–85; non-enforcement of burning laws 138–47; non-ratification of ATHP 180–4, 186–90, 193; patronage 120–5, 148–9; peatlands 52–8; regionalization 72–7; research methods 20, 22; responses to haze backlash 90–1, 94–8; Singapore-owned 88–90
olein 36
open burning *see* fires
Overseas Enterprise Incentive 87
ownership figures 44–5

Pakistan 37
palm kernel oil (PKO) 36, 91–2, 97
palm oil 6–11; global demand 35–8; Malaysian state support 82–4; Southeast Asia's 'green gold' 39–41, *see also* oil palm plantation sector
Panel of Experts (POE) 23, 178, 180, 190
Papua 42, 47, 124–5, 143
Papua New Guinea 80
parliamentary level 184–9
Partai Demokrasi Indonesia 124
Partai Keadilan Sejahtera 124
Party of the Functional Groups 121
patronage 8–9, 11, 43, 112–19, 215–18; ASEAN regionalism 160–1, 168; ineffective revisions to burning laws 148; land licensing 125–35; literature review 15–19; local networks 119–25; non-enforcement of burning laws 138–47; non-ratification of ATHP 182–7, 192
peatlands 52–8, 141; Adopt-A-District 199–200; ASEAN initiatives 174; licensing 126–35
People's Action Party 90
Permodalan Nasional Berhad (PNB) 80
Perry, M. 22
Philippines 2, 194
Plan of Action (POA) 178, 194–5
plantation approach 39–40, *see also* oil palm plantation sector
Plantation Production and Development Indonesia 47
Plantation Revitalization Programme 43
police 138–41, 145
policy (paralysis) 9, 11; literature review 13–14, 16–19; patronage politics 124–6, 131, 136–8, 147–8; regionalisms 162–9
political economy 14–15, 19–20
political regionalism *see* regionalism
Pollutant Standards Index (PSI) 3, 5
pollution 57, 96, 137, 163–4, 171–2, 187
Pollution Control Department (PCD) 96
population 37
poverty 12, 46
preferred memory 23
Presidential Decrees 55, 136–7
Presidential Directives 47
prices 37–8
Prime Minister's Department (PMD) 85, 96
privatization 43
product cycle theory 69
property rights *see* land rights
Prosperous Justice Party 124
psychic distance 8, 118
PT Adei Plantation and Industry (PT API) 75, 94, 131, 146, 196
PT Asiatic Persada 121
PT Kallista Alam 146, 216–17
PT Minimas 196–7
PT Purimas Sasmita 42–3
Purnomo, A. 122, 134

Quah, E. 12, 51

Radojevic, R. 13, 17, 148
Rahman, A. 124
Rainforest Action Network (RAN) 142
Rajan, R.S. 14, 166
Rajenthran, A. 125
REDD 133–5
Regional Autonomy Law 128
Regional Haze Action Plan (RHAP) 172–5, 177, 179, 182, 194
Regional House of Representatives 121, 124
regional integration 7–11, 19, 69
regionalism 7, 9–12, 15, 19, 160–2, 202–3, 217; 1985-2003 initiatives 172, 175; ASEAN model 165–71; ATHP 178–81; transboundary environmental issues 162–5
regionalization 7–8, 44, 98, 161, 215, 218; economic 68–72; literature review 14–15, 18–19; oil palm sector 72–7;

patronage 112, 118–19, 149; responses to haze backlash 90–2; Singaporean firms 86–9
revenues 45–6
Riau 3, 5, 42, 174, 191; Adopt-A-District 195–9; patronage 124, 130–1; patronage/fires 140–1, 143–4; regionalization 75, 87
Riau Provincial Justice Team 146
Richardson, C.L. 125
Right to Cultivation 74, 76
RIO+20 79
Rio Earth Summit 79
Riyanto, S. 124
Robinson, N.A. 162, 170
Robison, R. 120
Rokan Hilir 196
Ross, M.L. 115–16, 120
round-tripping 88–9

Salim, A. 122
Salim, E. 122
Salim Group 89, 122
Saragih, B. 120
Sarawak 4, 93, 172
Sarawak Land Development Board (SLDB) 81, 116
Sarawak Plantation Services 81
Sarwono K. 148
satellite data 50–1, 137, 174–6
Secretariat for Forest Protection 49
Seruyan 128
Severino, R. 182
Sharom, A. 192
Sihotang, M. 124
Sim, A.B. 7–8, 68–70
Sime Darby 80–1, 83–5; Adopt-A-District 196–7; dealing with backlash 94–5; patronage politics 116, 122, 131–3, 141
Sinar Mas 89, 201
Singapore 5, 167, 214–18; Adopt-A-District 195, 199–202; ASEAN initiatives 174, 190; dealing with backlash 91–2, 96–8; 'green gold' 39, 43–4, 46; literature review 13, 15, 18–19; patronage 118–19, 121–2, 131–2, 142–3; regionalization 68, 71–2, 74–7, 86–90; research methods 20, 22–3; research question 6–8, 11
Singapore Resolution 172
Single European Act 163
Siregar, A. 122
Sliggers, J. 162
smallholders 44–5, 51, 193–8, 201
smoke 57–8
snowball method 21
socialization 194–7, 201
soil quality 51, 53–4
Solingen, E. 170
Southeast Asia 38–9, 91–2; economic regionalization 70–2; models of regionalism 165–9; patronage politics 115–18, *see also* ASEAN
sovereignty 10, 14, 160; ASEAN Way 175–6, 187, 193; regionalism 165, 167
soy 36–7
Spain 37
Standard Operating Procedures 192
state 6–11, 14, 18, 35, 129; facilitator of regionalization 70–1, 77, 98, 149, 215–16; Malaysian 77–85, 92–6; patronage politics 115–16, 124–5, 134; Singaporean 86–7, 89–90, 96–8
State Secretariat 185
stearin 36
Strategic Economic Plan (SEP) 86
Sub-Regional Fire-Fighting Arrangements (SRFA) 174, 176
Suharto 116, 118, 120, 124, 126
Sulawesi 42, 47
Sumatra 3–5, 80; Adopt-A-District 195–6, 199; ASEAN Way 174, 188; oil palm sector 42–3, 47, 49, 51, 53; patronage 124, 131, 139, 142–4
Supreme Court 124, 146
Supriyono, J. 134–5, 186
sustainability 84, 91
swidden agriculture 12, 15, 51, 194
Switzerland 91
Syarif, L.M. 164–5

Tabung Haji Plantations *see* THP
Tan, A.K. 179
Tan, B. 14, 166
Tanjung Jabung Barat 124
tax 85; exemptions 70–1, 73–4, 78
Tax Law 73
Tay, S.S.C. 14, 166
Technical Working Groups 178
Teng, T.S. 22
Thailand 2, 49
Thompson, H. 13, 17, 148
Thong Yaw Hong 82
THP 80–1, 83–4; Adopt-A-District 196–7; patronage networks 131, 142, 144
timber 17–18, 54, 125–6
Timnas Bahan Bakar Nabati 47
tourism 4–5, 93

trade barriers 83–4
transport 3–4
Treaty of Amity and Cooperation 14
triangulation 21, 23

Unilever 97
United Kingdom 80, 84
United Malay National Organization 81
United Nations Environment Programme (UNEP) 170
United Nations (UN) 79, 190; REDD 133–5
United States 37, 91, 121–2, 167
Universiti Putra Malaysia 93
Uppsala model 69

Van Klinken, G. 120
Varma, A. 12, 51
vested interests 8, 10, 19, 215–16, 218; ASEAN Way 186–7, 190; regionalization 81–2, 85, 98

wages 71, 87
Wahana Lingkungan Hidup Indonesia 141
Wettestad, J. 162
Widodo, J. 185
Wilmar International 121, 145; land licensing 130–2, 134; state facilitation 74, 88, 90, 97
Working Group on Haze 177
Workshop on Transboundary Pollution and Haze 172
World Bank 13, 42, 49, 91, 97
World Growth 84
World Health Organization 96
World Resources Institute 51
World Trade Organization 84, 98
World Wildlife Fund for Nature 49

Yahaya, N. 14, 166
Yeo Cheow Tong 96
Yeo, G. 97
Yeo Teng Yang 90
Yoshimatsu, H. 165
Yudhoyono, S.B. 147, 185
Yusof, I. 135

Zahidi bin Hj Zainuddin 82
Zakaria, A. 128
ZOPFAN 167